England's First Family of Writers

England's First Family of Writers

Mary Wollstonecraft, William Godwin, Mary Shelley

JULIE A. CARLSON

The Johns Hopkins University Press
Baltimore

© 2007 The Johns Hopkins University Press
All rights reserved. Published 2007
Printed in the United States of America on acid-free paper

2   4   6   8   9   7   5   3   1

The Johns Hopkins University Press
2715 North Charles Street
Baltimore, Maryland 21218-4363
www.press.jhu.edu

Library of Congress Cataloging-in-Publication Data
Carlson, Julie Ann, 1955–
England's first family of writers : Mary Wollstonecraft, William Godwin,
Mary Shelley / Julie A. Carlson.
p. cm.
Includes bibliographical references (p.   ) and index.
ISBN-13: 978-0-8018-8618-8 (hardcover : alk. paper)
ISBN-10: 0-8018-8618-X (hardcover : alk. paper)
1. Shelley, Mary Wollstonecraft, 1797–1851—Criticism and interpretation.
2. Godwin, William, 1756–1836—Criticism and interpretation.
3. Wollstonecraft, Mary, 1759–1797—Criticism and interpretation.
4. Authors, English—18th century—Family relationships. 5. Authors,
English—19th century—Family relationships. 6. England—Social life and
customs—18th century. 7. England—Social life and customs—19th century.
8. Influence (Literary, artistic, etc.) I. Title.
PR5398.C37 2007
823'.7—dc22   2006034763

A catalog record for this book is available from the British Library.

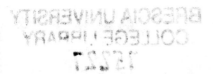

For
Ron Paris
Laurie Carlson
and the Fun Club:
Aranye Fradenburg, Elisabeth Weber
Gisela Kommerell, and Susan Derwin

CONTENTS

ACKNOWLEDGMENTS

This book was begun under the financial support of an American Council of Learned Society's Fellowship (2001–2002) and a grant from the UC Santa Barbara Interdisciplinary Humanities Center (2002), for which I am very grateful. A small portion of chapter 5 appeared in *Texas Studies in Literature and Language* 41.4 (1999) and a larger portion of chapter 4 in *European Romantic Review* 14.2 (2003). I am especially grateful to those writers who have facilitated my thinking about this family of writers: James Chandler, L. O. Aranye Fradenburg, Sonia Hofkosh, Mary Jacobus, Theresa Kelley, Anne Mellor, and Tilottama Rajan; thanks also to Elisabeth Weber for her work and our class on trauma. I also thank several research assistants, especially J. Jennifer Jones and Margaret Sloan, helpful staff at the Bodleian Library and UCLA Special Collections, and my copy editor, Barbara Lamb. Many others have sharpened my sense of the power of writing to bring "sometimes consolation, sometimes aggravation of grief"; they include Deborah Feilberg, Janel Mueller, Walt Carlson, Jacee Carlson, Vicki Weeks, Rhonda Dines, Cynthia Brown, Claudine Michel, Douglas Daniels, Mary Favret, Kay Young, Joel Faflak, Diane Boggess, Babatunde Folayemi, Cheri Swank, and the persons to whom this book is dedicated.

England's First Family of Writers

Family, Writing, Public

Why is it that the life stories of the Wollstonecraft-Godwin-Shelley family tend to fascinate readers even more than their written works? The history of the critical reception of Mary Wollstonecraft, William Godwin, and Mary Wollstonecraft Shelley as writers as well as the pop-cultural images of this family suggest that their biographies are more compelling than their writings and their life as a family more interesting than their individual lives.[1] This is unusual for authors of a former age, some of whose works were major literary-political sensations in their day (*A Vindication of the Rights of Woman*, *Enquiry concerning Political Justice*, and *Caleb Williams*), with one that has become truly mythic in scope and reception (*Frankenstein; or, The Modern Prometheus*). There is no denying the extraordinary nature of their lives and the formative events that compose them, especially in the case of Mary Wollstonecraft Shelley. Legend has it that young Mary's favorite reading spot was on the grave of her mother, the same spot where she and a twenty-one-year-old Percy Shelley, the young poet then married to Harriet Westbrook and father to Ianthe, consummated their love and hatched their plan to elope to the Continent. Other stories rehearse the tragic outcomes of that passion, encompassing the deaths of three of their four children before the age of three, the waning and wanderings of Percy's passions, and then his death by drowning at the age of twenty-nine.

The parents' lives had similar moments of high drama, especially Mary Wollstonecraft's. These involved her unrequited passions for Fanny Blood, Henry Fuseli, and Gilbert Imlay and the psychic as well as geographical and literary extremes to which they took her. They included her famous jump off Putney Bridge into the Thames, a prior suicide attempt, and her protracted death from complications of giving birth to daughter Mary. The events of Godwin's life were tamer but no less controversial, including his marital embrace of "fallen" women, his rejection of Mary and Percy until they married, his relentless harassment of them for financial and emotional support, and his eventual bankruptcy. Such stories speak to the imaginations of readers both then and now, in part for what they bespeak about modern family life.

At the same time, these life stories would not fascinate us so much, nor would we even know them in such intimate detail, were they not about a family of writers whose lives, fortunes, afterlives, and fates were completely bound up with reading and writing. The lives of this family embody some of our best information on the psychosocial dynamics of being a writer and the attractions, even sexiness, of a life devoted to mental pursuits. Indeed, much of the fascination of these life stories for literary persons is how the events in them are tied to the reading and writing of books, a connection that this family promoted as an interpersonal and an international imperative, since, in their view, books teach people how to love, to love reading, and to love one another through reading. Perception of this linkage between living and writing arises in part because these life stories pertain to England's first family of writers, who recorded their own lives so insistently, edited and revised each other's lives, and, in the process of doing both, uncovered and discovered the literally constitutive role of writing in their lives. It is also because their fictional productions so often drew from events and personages in their own lives that their novels are viewed as autobiographical or as biographical commentaries on family members and friends. Even their own self-analyses ascribe life-changing moments to books. Godwin claims that Wollstonecraft's *A Short Residence in Sweden, Norway, and Denmark* caused him to fall in love with its author, and he attempted to return the favor by commemorating her life in a book, but to disastrous ends. His loving tribute to Wollstonecraft's life/writings, *Memoirs of the Author of "A Vindication of the Rights of Woman"*—a title that itself highlights the intimacy between book and person—has long been viewed as having destroyed her reputation for generations. Shelley not only relied solely on books and stories for access to her mother's life but she consummated various collaborations with Percy by reading her parents' books—collaborations that are both sexual and textual.[2] True to this spirit, after he died Shelley housed Percy's heart, wrapped in the leaves of *Adonais*, in her portable writing desk for the rest of her life.[3] Similarly, her "excessive & romantic attachment" to her father was expressed, mediated, and reciprocated most successfully through books.[4]

One major claim, then, of *England's First Family of Writers* is that this family's interest and fame reside in the inextricability of their lives and writings. The book views cultural fascination with their life stories not as dismissive of their writings but as comprehending one of their chief aims and contributions: blurring the boundaries between person and text, private and public, living and writing, works of literature and works of mourning. It means to interrogate what is involved in having a literary life, being bookish people, or living by writing. The fluidity between these domains in their writing is indicated in mine by referring to the objects of textual analysis by the terms *life/writings* and *im/personalities*, by which the constitution of "life" for them is an issue of writing and personalities are construed as transpersonal, intertextual, and deeply literary.[5] *England's First Family of Writers* posits their lives and writings as inextricably connected, seeing each as not only facilitating but also undermining the other, which does not mean that it conceives the two arenas as identical or indistinguishable.

Affirming this fluidity re-evaluates what has frequently been viewed as a downside or an embarrassment in the critical reception of these writers, especially Mary Shelley, namely, the sexism that, up until the 1980s, has valued Shelley's life over her writings and has valued both her life and her writings primarily for what they reveal about her more famous husband and father.[6] But it also welcomes the con/fusions of fact and fiction in the oeuvres of all three writers because of the slippages they solicit between their novels and biographies as well as the interconnections they forge between history and romance. Such slippage has occasioned further difficulties in discerning the validity and objectivity of their so-called nonfictional writings, objections that have plagued assessments of Wollstonecraft's feminism and Godwin's political theory and historiography. It also complicates evaluations of the originality or autonomy of any of their ideas, visible in every critical biography of any of these individuals, and has led to another customary devaluation of Shelley, whose works are viewed not only as secondary to her parents' and husband's writings but also as a retreat from their radicalism. Reading these writers as a family shifts the valence of the authority, autonomy, and authenticity often ascribed to authorship.

One controversial implication of this study concerns the derivative status of many of Percy's ideas, especially pertaining to the triumph of life. Put less negatively, it views his claim to fame *as* his status as poet, the one domain of writing in which none of these other writers excels or even competes—a status, moreover, invested in transcending the cult of personality, personhood, and ties to family. Even here, Percy Shelley's most famous assertion of the influence of the poet on public life is a direct borrowing from Godwin, who wrote in *Life of Chaucer* that "the poet" is the "legislator of generations and the moral instructor of the world" (1:370).[7]

A second major claim of this book is that the life/writings of this family are best explicated and evaluated in terms of the interconnections that they forge among family, writing, and public life. For each of these writers was a public intellectual, whose commitment to social reform in their views necessitated sustained critique of the family, a topic that they pursued in a vast number and array of texts. Moreover, each of these social commentators experienced the greatest difficulties in gaining a positive public reception of their ideas because of their critiques and enactments of family. *England's First Family of Writers* seeks to keep these two facts of their life/writings interconnected for what the connection reveals about the relation among family, writing, and public life. It explores how their status as a *family* of writers affected their notions of authorship, personhood, and publicity and how their status as a family of *writers* influenced their conceptions of family and their lives and afterlife as a family. It also asks how the public reception of their writings on family affected their conviction that writing changes the world.

England's First Family of Writers finds striking the degree to which this family's writings address the topic of family. Reform of the family is central to Wollstonecraft's and Godwin's political theories, their notions of perfectibility, and their proposals for more equitable social conditions.[8] Wollstonecraft's most famous text, *A Vindication of the Rights of Woman* (1792), and the most (in)famous passage of Godwin's most famous text, *Enquiry concerning Political Justice* (1793), identify existing marital relations and domestic affections as the chief impediment to social justice. The novels of all three writers are preoccupied with family relations—indeed, Shelley's nonhistorical novels (*Frankenstein* [1818], *Matilda* [1819], *Lodore* [1835], and *Falkner* [1837]) basically address no other topic. Other of Godwin's and Shelley's most famous texts edit the writings and recompose the *Lives* of various family members. All three wrote extensively for and about children and were major innovators in the field of children's literature. Equally striking is the degree to which the reputations of all three suffered from glaring contradictions between their textual pronouncements on family and their practice as family members: for starters, the marriage between England's two most outspoken opponents of marriage as well as the passion that undermined at least one partner's rationalist credentials; or, that nonstarter, the death dealt to Wollstonecraft's afterlife through Godwin's textual memorial to her life as a writer. Only in the last two decades has an "other Mary Shelley" begun to emerge as the author not just of works other than *Frankenstein* but also of characters and concerns unrelated to her family.[9] But there are also productive dimensions to the critical practice that reads for family resemblances. One establishes a Godwinian school of fiction identified by a philosophical and thus transpersonal approach to character.[10] A second identifies the legitimate progeny of the proclaimed mother of liberal feminism.[11] A third perceives their anticipation of trauma studies.[12]

Exploring how this family's notions and enactments of "family" and "writing" are inseparable from the "public" that they at once addressed, sought to reform, and themselves become is important for comprehending not only the nature of their writings and the contribution of their writings to social reform but also the effects of those projects on their reassessments of writing. Each of their efforts at revision were extensive, encompassing revisions of the Western canon of writing, of various disciplines and genres of writing, of each other's writings, and of their own prior writings. This dynamic is especially prominent in the political theories of Godwin and Wollstonecraft, both of which began by making thoroughgoing critiques of family. Put simply, Godwin objects to domestic affections because their privacy and partiality impede justice, and he spent his entire career seeking to disentangle family from feelings for and about it. More partial to some aspects of family, Wollstonecraft works to disarticulate women from the sentiments that have assigned them throughout history to the private sphere. For each of them, these processes could not be accomplished apart from investment in writing, not just in the obvious senses that both publicized their reforms through writing and popularized their major theoretical work by pairing it with a novel. Godwin aimed at public/ izing a new family, which included redefining family as a form of attachment grounded in similarity of thought and thus as an emergent public sphere constituted by shared reading and writing. Wollstonecraft altered women's position within family by vindicating the rights of women within and outside of marriage and asserting women's right to write about women, both of which projects associated women with rationality, public service, and inquiring minds. So did Shelley, concerned to rewrite classic legends of girlhood sexuality.

Such social reforms necessitated making extensive textual and literary reforms, for the Western literary tradition, as all three recognized, has a long history of repressing certain people's voices and opportunities. From the start of their writing careers, Wollstonecraft and Shelley wrote in explicit opposition to the dominant plotlines, prototypes, and sentiments of women. Woll-

stonecraft generally sought to create afresh, whereas Shelley revised and up-
dated cultural myths.[13] Godwin too, questioned the adequacy of traditional
disciplines of writing, especially history and biography, to his notions of truth
and character.[14] This makes all three acknowledged innovators in fiction as
well as in social-familial practice and shows how the revision of prior forms of
writing works to complement their rescripting of reality. Here Shelley led the
way in both the popular and literary imagination as the creator of *Frankenstein* and the critic of various social science fictions.[15] But Wollstonecraft and
Godwin, too, produced works of a new species, starting with Wollstonecraft's
embodiment of that "new genus," the woman writer, and her novel portrayal
of a "woman with thinking powers" (Advertisement to *Mary, a Fiction*) and
extending to Godwin's and Shelley's hybridizing of several genres: philosophical fiction, history as romance, necromantic history, illustrious *Lives*. Their
books for children seek to remake a child's mind as part of that new reality.
This family's status as generic innovators also distinguishes the radicalism of
parents from child. Whereas Wollstonecraft and Godwin are known equally as
social and generic reformers, Shelley contributes to social reform primarily
through her literary reforms. Put another way, as a product of these parents
and a "new" woman, she *was* a social reform who tried to rework that status
and the responsibilities owed to it.

Such efforts to reform the family through writing and through reforming
various traditions of writing are key to making this family highly public as
writers and family members. Indeed, the publicity of their writings against
family vies with the publicity of their family life in at once perpetuating
their fame and undermining their validity as social reformers. Members of
this family remain famous as sexual innovators, many of whose domestic
rearrangements, especially the location of each partner's work space in separate domiciles, still facilitate the life/works of women as well as men today.
Their infamy provides a valuable early negative example of the dependence of
public service on the affirmation of family values.[16] This is the point of
designating them England's "first family" of writers, the publicity of whose
life/writings on the dys/functions of family undermined their credibility as
leading shapers of public opinion. Wollstonecraft was vilified by the press and
snubbed in polite society for her sexual experimentation. Godwin had to resort
to pseudonyms in order to write and publish literature for children, and
prefatory remarks to his post-Wollstonecraft fiction were compelled to voice
an appreciation of marriage and family life. Shelley was never fully accepted
into respectable British society owing to her sexual exploits as a teenager, even

as she was also repeatedly criticized for not staying true to their spirit in her subsequent conformity. Indeed, ascertaining the desirability of the interconnections among family, public, and writing was especially fraught for Shelley, because she inherited the project at its second stage. The publicity of her parents' writing and family life, and especially her own sex life with Percy, intensified the search in her life/writings for some sphere of privacy away from her highly public family life and writings.[17] For all three, reactions to this negative publicity profoundly shaped their views on history and the advisability of having a place in it.

The broadest aim of *England's First Family of Writers* explores how this family's attempts to affirm the interconnections among family, writing, and public life altered their initial convictions regarding the power of writing to affect reality. For the difficulties that they encountered in attempting to alter public opinion on the family caused them to qualify, without invalidating, their optimism as social-literary reformers. All three felt personally abused by contemporary reading practices, which refused to look beyond the personhood or personality of writers and thus discredited their writings because of their putative failures or contradictory behaviors as family members.[18] As a consequence, their notions of writing asked not only what writing does to reality but also what the reality of being a public person does to one's writing, personhood, or membership in a family. Reflections on this topic intensified when they wrote in the wake of the death of a family-writing member.

Godwin sets the terms for this discussion, both because he is the first of the three to mourn publicly and because only he ever began from an uncomplicated notion of the relation of writing to truth. Sustained outcry over Godwin's *Memoirs of the Author of "A Vindication of the Rights of Woman"* (1798), especially the accusation that in it he "stripped his dead wife naked" before the public, alerted him to the public's resistance to being enlightened on certain topics, especially pertaining to one's so-called personal life, and it shaped his subsequent theories of publication and (self) revision.[19] From the start, Wollstonecraft recognized the shortfalls of writing, especially in depicting women, but her efforts to change women's reality were also hampered by public misperceptions of her passions—that is, her articulated views on passion as well as her own unruly passions. In either case, that passion was said to invalidate both rationality and the value that she ascribes to women's reason rather than being perceived as propelling the drive toward thinking that, according to her, eventuates in more satisfying life choices. Besides the general charge that Shelley's writings do not live up to her parents' radicalism, two other alleged personal inadequacies profoundly influenced her conceptions of writing: coldness toward Percy, and a preference for the dead over the living. Coldness gets linked to her realism, both as a narrative mode and an affront to her parents' and Percy's idealism. Preference for the dead challenges the animation associated with writing. Does writing kill, mourn, or vivify?[20] Compose or decompose? What of the literary remains?

This account of the interweavings within their life/writings of the topics of family, writing, and public life is also meant to specify this family's position in several major social and literary debates of their age. *England's First Family of Writers* draws on many critical studies attentive to these writers' views on each of these topics, but it also contends that to treat any of the three in isolation misses their distinctive contribution to discourse in and about the public sphere.[21] Discussions of the publicity and publics-making associated with writing have grown voluminous since the English translation in 1989 of Jürgen Habermas's *Structural Transformation of the Public Sphere*. This family's views intersect with two aspects of Habermasian theory that have animated literary-cultural critics of late-eighteenth-century English culture: the political ramifications of the extraordinary expansion of print culture during this century and the consequences of those ramifications for reconfiguring private and public spheres.[22] Their writings are famous for underscoring the influence of writing on public opinion, the impact of public opinion on governmental reform, and the possibility of making existing social reality coincide with the normative ideal of public rational-critical debate.[23] In their approach to these goals, moreover, they avert in advance what have become two major branches of Habermasian critique. Feminists have often asserted that Habermas's formulations downplay the public contributions of women to a greater extent than historical evidence warrants, both in their theoretical underpinnings and their analyses of social practice.[24] Poststructuralists question the adequacy both of Habermas's characterizations of the bourgeois public sphere as rationalist and his endorsement of rational social converse.[25]

In *Mothers of the Nation: Women's Political Writing in England, 1780–1830*, Anne Mellor offers the boldest attack to date on the inaccuracy of Habermas's formulations as they relate to the situation of women at the end of the eighteenth century. According to her, Habermas's limitation of the public sphere to "men of property" is simply "historically incorrect." During the Romantic era, women participated so fully in the "public sphere as Habermas defined it," both as social commentators and agents of publicity, that their accomplishments cannot be relegated to a "counter" public sphere.[26] Concentrating on the situation of women in England at mid-century, Harriet Guest, in *Small Change: Women, Learning, Patriotism, 1750–1810*, specifies in what ways women writers and discourse on femininity began to alter public political consciousness regarding the status of women. Seeing no reason to "throw out infant political possibilities with the bathwater" of women's legal exclusion from categories of citizenship, she foregrounds "small changes" that resulted from the "extraordinary expansion" of women's access to the "public world of print" in their ability to "claim or imagine a status as citizens despite oligarchy and ethnic, class, and gender inequalities."[27] The "cumulative effect" of these changes, she argues, resulted in writers like Wollstonecraft (and "to some extent Mary Hays, Catharine Macaulay, and Anna Laetitia Barbauld"), who, for the first time, "define their gendered identities through the nature and degree of their approximation to the public identities of political citizens."[28] Saba Bahar fleshes out this claim in *Mary Wollstonecraft's Social and Aesthetic Philosophy* by establishing the novelty and legitimacy of Wollstonecraft's claim to the status of "public woman," thus reversing the connotations instituted by the *Anti-Jacobin Review of 1798* in its indexing of Wollstonecraft under "Prostitute."[29]

My interest in the "infant political possibilities" found in this family's reformulations of publicity runs initially in the other direction, toward its effects on the "intimate sphere of the conjugal family" and their sense of the interconnections among progeny and books.[30] No other writers of the period worked so hard to nullify two sets of opposition that demarcate the intimate from the public sphere: private and public, feeling and reason—even granting that these oppositions are far more nuanced and triangulated in Habermas's formulations than is often recognized.[31] For it is precisely the intimate portions of the private sphere that they sought to rewrite *by* publicizing them, in the senses that their writings (1) foreground the psychosexual dys/functions of family life, (2) establish a concept of family that is wary of privacy and sentimental feelings, (3) value sex to the degree that it is a literary and an imaginative act, and (4) portray as the chief function of family the cultivation of reading and writing—even, in their own case, making a family business out of composing, publishing, and selling books. Their efforts to deny, externalize, or textualize the interiority associated with intimacy alter the connotations of the "humanity" that, according to Habermas, has as its "genuine site" the bourgeois family, the theatricality of which he admits by defining the intimate sphere as an "audience-oriented" domain.[32] For these writers, because the human is a literary construction, one that is both defined in books and whose deepest feelings often come from books, their writings stress the impersonal, transpersonal, and extrapersonal dimensions of being a "person," accentuate the geographic and temporal transport provided by reading, and redraw the boundaries between being dead or alive.

This third opposition suggests the most radical component of what their life/writings, in challenging the deadness of the dead, contribute to the public sphere as constituted by writing. Edmund Burke famously levels this challenge, too, in underscoring the social contract as occurring between the dead, the living, and the unborn, but as a means toward squelching revolution and slowing the pace of change. This family's writings address all three audiences toward more liberatory ends by viewing the discipline of history as a revival of the dead (Godwin), training very young children, even beings in utero, to perceive reading as an interactive and interpersonal project (Wollstonecraft), and showcasing the effect of the dead in and on the living in their fictions, historical romances, and life/writing (Shelley). The public ends of underscoring this commerce with the un/dead are clearest in their deep preoccupation with mourning. Godwin characterizes mourning as a public duty that is in the interests of Parliament to inculcate and enjoins survivors to acquire the "craft" of making the "earth and ocean" give up their dead alive *(Sepulchres,* 6). In her "personal" struggles with the dead *and* this injunction of Godwin's to mourn them, Shelley eventually came to accept writing as a consolation through being occupied with remains. She then turned to biography as a means of making peace with the illustrious dead by contributing to Dionysius Lardner's encyclopedic *Lives of Eminent Literary and Scientific Men of Spain, Portugal, Italy, and France.* This intimacy with the powers and limits of writing to represent death characterizes the special liminality of their writing's public and private dimensions. That is, because so much of their writing is addressed to the dead, seeks to reanimate the illustrious dead as a means of perfecting the future, and attempts to craft works of a new species out of the un/dead, they emphasize not only the insentience of signification but also the quite striking degree to which bookish people find their life in nonfeeling things.

This is not to say that all three of them agreed on the methods, rationale, or desirability of this publicizing of family—not to mention the next generation's massive efforts to alter and destroy all evidence of this family's, especially Percy Shelley's, less than ideal features.[33] It is to say that, in writing about it, they provide a public record not only of family life and the difficulties of reforming, challenging, or questioning its values but also of how being this kind of person means that one is aware of being at once more isolated than others and never capable of being fully alone (or ever let alone, whether by society or textuality). Their writings characterize this experience of being occupied by writing through the kinds of person that they foreground. Their protagonist is often portrayed as a genre ("a woman with thinking powers," a man of the sixteenth century), a case (whether pathological [Fleetwood, Mandeville], or legal [Caleb Williams, Maria]), or a legend (Proserpine, Beatrice, Frankenstein). The Godwinian school of fiction has as its hallmark a confessional voice that speaks for a genre and defines its particularity by delineating its historical and political contexts.[34] Godwin's and Shelley's biographies privilege the individual but as a magnet for organizing the otherwise scattered fragments that make up a period or culture.[35] Wollstonecraft's fiction is arguably part of the Godwinian school (and Juvenile Library). The Mary of *Mary, a Fiction* comes to her character primarily through penning effusions on sensibility, and three individuals' personal narratives on love constitute the third-person narration of *Wrongs of Woman*. The confessions of *Letters Written during a Short Residence in Sweden, Norway, and Denmark* are cultural anthropology.

The so-called private writings are equally con/fused regarding the nature of their publicity, especially when, as in many of Shelley's, they assert their aversion to it. Not that these expressions are wholly disingenuous, but they stand in a curious relation to her many published statements regarding the self-constitutive aspects of literature and the deeply scripted and literary components of her self. Wollstonecraft's love letters to Imlay, as is well known, became the cultural anthropology of *A Short Residence*. Less sensationally, as Janet Todd notes, "no letter writer of the time assumed complete one-to-one privacy" but at the least envisioned a collective or coterie readership.[36] Compared to the letters of other women writers of the period, the "I" of Wollstonecraft's letters is never domesticated; she rarely appears inside any domestic space other than her mind, which is hardly that. Comparison with Wollstonecraft's letters exposes a different paradox in evaluations of Godwin's and Shelley's journals. Readers find them disappointing in their lack of self-disclosure, composed as they largely are of lists of books read, written, or translated and persons seen. But for authors and serious readers, registers of what one is reading are highly revelatory of what is going on inside.

These complexities make highly tenuous conventional divisions between reason and sentiment, at the same time that they underscore important distinctions between sentiment and passion, the latter being far closer to what we now call desire. Understood correctly, the merger of reason and passion—and passion's disassociation from sentiment—is central to the feminism of this family and to their relevance as (post) Enlightenment thinkers. For them, combining reason and passion was crucial to facilitating both the love of truth that drove their knowledge systems and the greater access to publicity that they sought through their reformulations of family. Cultivating that type of love occasions sustained critiques of sentiment, sustained pursuit of scholarship, and sustained rewritings of each other's lives. It invalidates the gendered associations of home and the tendency to perceive the "privatization" of civic virtue, with its emphasis on civility, manners, and sociability, as indicating an advance for women (either in terms of increased respect or opportunities for them).[37] For both Wollstonecraft and Godwin aimed to make the domestic sphere more "manly" by promoting disinterested conduct for women and men, an aim that frustrates feminists seeking to affirm the difference of Wollstonecraft. Despite the "bugbear" of "masculine women," enlightened masculinity *is* the kind of femininity that Wollstonecraft desires for women.[38] Shelley works to include women in the ranks of the eminent scientific and literary men of Europe. In contrast (and perhaps to keep a contrast), the Godwinian fictional male is characteristically prebourgeois, for, despite all the illusions of chivalric honor that Godwin castigates, at least men in the feudal period looked and acted like men.[39] In each, the aim is to reject feeling as the chief characteristic of women or of a newly humanized man. This aim also characterizes their fiction, often defined as a "history of man" or a work of philosophy.

Redefining what constitutes the rationality of this family leads to a bolder claim, that their writings enact a dialectic of Enlightenment. Both their concepts of reason and their efforts to resolve the difficulties that their reliance on reason occasions underscored *to them* (not just to later readers) the insufficiency of rationality to the aims of truth as they conceived the latter. This is not the usual romantic claim that rationalism succumbs to imagination, for their imagination retained a backward-looking connection to fancy that links transcendence to de-animation. The truth that their reason serves is at once skeptical and desirous, geared toward fulfilling the requirements of conscious change and the unconscious propulsions of desire as (and for) change.[40] For different reasons, all three affirmed writing over reason as the means to truth, Godwin as the result of a conscious shift in his thinking, Wollstonecraft and Shelley from the start. But even the early stages of Godwin's rationalism link enlightenment to magic, necromancy, and fancy, and they measure progress in its hospitality to the latter activities. Shelley's writings erupt with desire, especially when they reflect on the forms of life that writing at once animates and terminates. The family's awareness of the dialectic was heightened by public reactions to their enactments of family, causing them to question the epochs and mobility associated with progress and to formulate what about life, writing, family, or desire for change never changes.[41]

~

Showcasing these dynamics in their writing influences my methodology, which seeks in several ways to reflect this family's vision of the im/personal dimensions of living. *England's First Family of Writers* is neither a biography of a family nor a comprehensive literary-critical analysis of all their writings. William St. Clair accomplished the former in his *The Godwins and the Shelleys: The Biography of a Family* (1989). No one to date has ventured the latter, even before the major surge in scholarship on all three authors in the past decades.[42] Instead, mine is a reading of a family of writers whose writings seek to defamiliarize what has counted as family in order to clear space for new species and manners of being. It employs critical strategies that affirm in these writers the inseparability of biography and fiction, living and writing, as articulated for these writers especially by Tilottama Rajan and Graham Allen. Rajan terms the practice *autonarration,* which she claims is employed by Mary Hays but largely "invented" by Godwin and especially relevant to Wollstonecraft, who "lived fiction and ideas as life, while rethinking life through fiction."[43] In his focus on the works of Mary Shelley, Allen asserts the necessity to go "beyond biographism" and resist converting "figurative language into historical or psychological referents."[44] These accentuated slippages between person and text, these writers' focus on how fiction informs a person's lived practice and psychic reality, and thus affects one's notion of truth, underscore the relevance of psychoanalytic concepts to interpretation of their life/writings. Indeed, Laura Mandell proposes that we read Wollstonecraft (and Mary Hays) as early psychoanalysts, and Gary Handwerk, Mary Jacobus, and Rajan demonstrate the efficacy of each of their various psychoanalyses of historical periods, historical and interpersonal romance, and cultural and individual traumas.[45]

England's First Family of Writers is indebted to these approaches and the highly nuanced readings to which they have given rise. It offers a further claim. These writers not only are proto-psychoanalytic in their representations of subjectivity—psychoanalysis being the hermeneutic system most attuned to the impossibility of distinguishing rigorously interior from exterior, self from other/Other, private from public—but at times they also portray, *avant la lettre,* humanity's trouble with the signifier and the Lacanian understanding of our being-as-signifier.[46] This is the case especially with Mary Shelley, whose early *Frankenstein* and incomplete mourning of Percy Shelley instance from opposite ends how human the signifier appears in its indifference to life and humanity.

The book's concentration on a family of writers means that authorship is envisioned neither as individual nor collaborative but instead as collective, as something incorporated. As such, authorship is conceived as transpersonal and transferential, by which I mean that it comprises more than one person and not simply persons but also books, that its modes of exchange are intertextual as well as interpersonal, and that the study of authorship is concerned less with influence than transference understood in Freud's sense: as "new editions (*Neuauflagen*)" of the "impulses and phantasies" that both constitute change and complicate forward motion.[47] This interest in a collective also means to specify the distinctiveness of this family of writers within romantic categories of authorship. The obvious contrast is with notions of author as "individual," "original," "genius," and "male," qualities that have all been challenged recently but have long been linked to romanticism as a historical-aesthetic development and as an ideology based on the primacy of poetry. But it also includes other alternatives in this period, ranging from other families of authors or partnerships to circles composed of family members, lovers, or friends. Indeed, the number of collective projects in the period makes one wonder how the cult of the isolated genius ever became associated with this age.[48]

Still, two things distinguish the Wollstonecraft-Godwin-Shelley family from, for example, the Edgeworth family and the Wordsworth-Coleridge circle, in other respects their closest analogues.[49] Only this unit is entirely nuclear, in the sense of being composed of both parents and child, rather than the more common (though still unusual) configurations of father-child or siblings.[50] Only this unit takes as one of its most important projects making family indistinguishable from broader community. Because of this extendability of their family, I differ from one component of Mitzi Myers' astute analysis of how the public/private opposition obstructs comprehension of Shelley's writings and stature. Considering Shelley in the context of Godwin's *notion* of family does not automatically reduce her to "Percy's-wife" or "daddy's-girl" but shows her to be fully "imbricated" within what Myers proposes as the opposite of family but what this family sees as a major constituent of it, namely, the "sociopolitical and literary cultures of [her] times."[51] The combination of these two traits separates this family as well from other models of group life said to constitute the bourgeois literary public sphere. Unlike the clubs, coffeehouses, or coteries of eighteenth-century public life, this group embraces both sexes and spans generations. It is itself part of a coterie, as Gary Kelly has shown, but is also separable as a family unit.[52] Nor is it particularly bourgeois.

England's First Family of Writers is divided into two parts according to its major structuring claim: this family conceived of writing as performing essential family functions, regarding making love, mourning the dead, and educing the next generation. Part One, "Revising Family," comprises three chapters, each of which explores this family's efforts to rewrite the sentiments and literary conventions associated with family life. "Making Public Love" focuses primarily on the political theories and novels of Wollstonecraft and Godwin as they reformed love to make it more conducive to the autonomy of women and men. "Forms of Attachment" articulates the linkage that Godwin established between persons and books as part of his campaign against sentiment and corresponding embrace of detachment. "Family Relations" explores the interconnections between writing about family and writing about reading and writing in the novels of Shelley and underscores the perversity that she associated with family life. Part One also engages the centrality of fancy/imagination to a couple's sexual and textual lives, a discussion initiated in Wollstonecraft's *The Wrongs of Woman; or, Maria,* and the extent to which reading not only propagates life but also humanizes and dehumanizes beings, brought to its fullest examination in *Frankenstein.*

Part Two, "Life Works," is composed of three chapters that address how this family's approaches to life and death affect their writings, conception of writing, and generic experimentation. "Fancy's History" considers each writer's embrace of fancy *for* its alleged deadness and antiquation and delineates the differing regions and genres to which each of their fancies led. "Living Off and On: The Literary Work of Mourning" engages this family's history of depression, tragedy, and trauma by exploring how writing allowed them to mourn, memorialize, and reanimate the dead. It highlights the public functions of their mourning practices, as articulated in Godwin's *Essay on Sepulchres* and explores their ramifications on Shelley's novels and subsequent turn to writing biography. "The Juvenile Library, or Works of a New Species" considers the many texts that this family wrote for and about children as efforts to ensure a different future through reforming the materials out of which it would be made. It stresses an enabling ambiguity in their understandings of progeny (child, book, creature-in-the-making, creature-of-bookmaking) and what progenitors owe their progeny as conceived in any of these domains. An epilogue,

"On Percy's Case," explores how Percy Shelley's priority has depended on a long history of considering his life/writings apart from this family and his views on, and enactments of, family life.[53]

～

England's First Family of Writers stands or falls on the degree to which focus on the interconnections among concepts of family, public, and writing illuminates the life/writings of this extraordinary family of writers. But it also seeks to affirm the truth of several of their political claims, especially as they facilitate the errant method and split subject inherent in their notions of truth. On a basic level, this book endorses the rationality of the now-notorious question that Godwin poses to domestic affection when he asks in *An Enquiry concerning Political Justice*, "What magic is there in the pronoun 'my,' to overturn the decisions of everlasting truth?" (50). It finds troubling the extent to which reasoned discussion of social policy is still aborted when any particular policy is seen to affect one's own children or property, and it affirms the justice of inquiring what about family is antipathetic to justice and difference. Why do debates over the morality of war shift when someone from "my family" has been killed by the enemy? Why do persons voice support of social services until they are built in "my backyard"? What is moral about impeaching a president for sexual improprieties and electing another who declares open war on dark people, gays and lesbians, the poor? In posing the question, Godwin's point is not to (further) neglect children or adult family members but to ensure that a society's fundamental mode of attachment is openness to others. Looking to one's own *does have* a tendency to blind one to the needs, even existence, of others. This can be defended on pragmatic grounds, but it is usually touted as a moral accomplishment. Nor has the situation of children in the United States improved, for all the pieties regarding "our children."[54]

England's First Family of Writers, then, promotes the elements in this family's writings that extend the sphere of family beyond relations in blood. It affirms with them the deep kinship provided by friends and books and believes that a commitment to viewing others as "family" can be an important step toward breaking cycles of violence and revenge (or of understanding why those cycles are so difficult to break). On similar grounds, it supports their assessment that family values privilege sameness, identity, and familiarity in part because family conceives the connection between itself and sentiment as self-evident, in the sense of being assumed and necessary to the constitution of a self. As recent scholarship on abolition has shown, the cult of sentiment, like the cult of romantic imagination, primarily aims to turn difference into sameness.[55] The "I" of sentiment loves, identifies, and sympathizes with the other to the extent that the other can appear like one of us. But this family objects to conformity on several levels, not all of which cohere or even wish to come together.[56] Moreover, they maintain an allegiance to fancy in their wildest imaginings because of the ways that fancy amalgamates, associates, or hooks up unlike things.[57] Plus, fancy loves to fabricate, especially its history. And it animates creatures that continue to replicate and fascinate popular and academic cultures.

A second value of Godwin's question lies in its linkage of justice to inquiry into magic, where "magic" is not invoked rhetorically as a sign that the domain should be, or is, discredited on enlightened grounds.[58] More relevant is Derrida's concept of hauntology, by which justice requires a "principle of some responsibility, beyond all living present, within that which disjoins the living present, before the ghosts of those who are not yet born or who are already dead."[59] Put the other way, these writers query why "my" exercises a pull that is so hard to withstand, even in a disseminated "self," one that has hardly ever been withstood on the grounds of "your" or "ours." More to the point, the linkage recognizes that rhetoric *is* a magical art that attends to the transformational property of words. Dead serious about words, each of these writers was at once animated and terrified by the performative qualities of writing.[60] For all three, words awaken and terminate love, alter and prognosticate events, plant seeds for the future, vivify and stupefy minds. At the same time, they witness (to) the black-magical aspects of writing, its capacity to spellbind, intoxicate, turn persons to stone. Reader, beware! This writing will make you other—form an epoch in your mind, turn you out as hero, lover, or monster. Writer, beware! The public can declare you dead, accuse your words of murder, take you up on actions you never foresaw. This receptivity to the magical properties of writing helped to facilitate their openness to alterity. They recognized human attraction to things, to being thing-like, and they characterized attraction to persons as electric and magnetic.[61] This kept them sensitive to the otherness of print, even as they deemed the book artifact inherent to the human.

Emphasizing magic and my-ness, or the lure of the personal, is usually viewed as Shelley's domain, visible in her critiques of science, masculine ambition, and her parents. But magic is a major component of Godwin's enquiries—not as something to discredit but to historicize *and* revive as crucial to history, historical method, and reality. His interest in the occult, the paranormal, the invisible spanned his entire writing life and was bequeathed to his novel-writing children, not only daughter Mary but son William Jr., whose one novel is entitled *Transfusion.* Godwin cut his authorial teeth on magic, publishing his translation of the 1784 proceedings in Paris against Franz Mesmer in 1785, and ended his publishing life with *The Lives of the Necromancers* (1834). That book is the last in a series of *Lives* of illustrious men, the goal and method of which research was to repopulate the world with trusted friends. His last written, but unpublished, work is in a similarly pro-magic and irreligious spirit, *Christianity Unveiled.*

A third truth of the political writings of these three pertains to their desirous subject and the ends that it is after. From different angles, all three challenge constituents of the "possessive individual" for the impediments that such a concept of selfhood poses to the radical pursuit of truth, justice, and life. Wollstonecraft and Shelley accentuate its gender one-sidedness and its efforts to restrict, silence, and disempower marginalized persons. At times, their life/ writings seem to posit a "self" for such persons, but the autonomy that they seek, especially for women, does not deny a person's occupation by the dead or her freedom to wander, err, stray. Moreover, their "I" is inhabited by voices, fictional characters and conventions, melancholy. Godwin objects to the possessive individual's presumed opposition to "thing" and the things that possess him, portraying existence as being linked in a chain that acknowledges the impact of the dead on the living not as restriction, conformity, or anxiety producing but as a mandatory building on. Despite the boldness and at times baldness of their pronouncements, they are rarely confident about the outcome that their methods and revisions struggle to effect. Indeed, increasingly that outcome is envisioned as change, forward motion, or simply movement, the destination impossible to predict in advance. Trial and error constituted the optimism of their skepticism, a method essential to a feminism defined by granting women wider margins for success or error.[62] They applied this method to the literary tradition, revising their own prior writings and the entire literary canon. As *Wrongs of Woman* displays, marginalia is the thinking woman's language of passion, and that language needs serious reworking.

In this regard, their personal is political in being im/personal, split, inhabited by others but still response/able, still working toward justice. Godwin's warning in *Political Justice* that government "insinuates itself" into our "private dispositions" becomes Shelley's (and arguably the latter Godwin's) conviction that writing inhabits our person, for good and for ill (*Political Justice Var.,* 12). Insinuation is one of literature's chief modes, the source of its richness, beauty, and self-dissemination. Neither characters nor readers can be sure where their ideas or sensations are coming from. Recognizing this, as Shelley's writings show, slows the impulse to tout the political efficacy of one's writing. Because the literary depends on conventionality for its legibility, radical ideas have to bide their time awaiting the audience they have sought to create. Meanwhile, innovators go under, lose heart, jump ship. Or, as Godwin recognized, because knowledge-making is a group project, intellectual culture encourages taking a "sullen" approach to innovative ideas (*Political Justice*, 121).

In intentional and unintended ways, the life/writings of this family express the damage wrought on a writing subject who discovers that his or her best ideas fall on deaf ears. Their writings address the intransigence of reading publics and the media of print—the former so often remaining entrenched in their initial, crude, or dismissive impressions, the latter materially impeding revisions of their truth. Godwin was most shocked by this experience and therefore most explicit about developing strategies to lessen the frustration, which involved distinguishing between writing and publishing (especially radical ideas of youth) and applying his gradualism to literary reception, including efforts to enlist his daughter in cultivating his posthumous fame. The early Shelley wards off disappointment by thematizing the insecurities of reception and, in latter years, writing less apparently objectionable books. The life/writings of all three, moreover, indicate that public resistance to innovation grows in proportion to its intrusion into so-called private spheres. Here they do not forsake the project but instead challenge the demarcation of spheres and investments in maintaining them. Far more than illiteracy, they imply, impedes a person's or a people's ability to read. Responsible writing should begin from this resistance, not argue against it. Only then does it stand a chance of initially engaging the mind that it hopes to alter.

Godwin defines responsible reading in his most Wollstonecraft-inspired writing, the essays that make up *The Enquirer*, which St. Clair claims the two discussed jointly before Wollstonecraft's death.[63] By way of discrediting several customary arguments against allowing children to choose the books that they wish to read, Godwin distinguishes between the "moral" of any work ("that ethical sentence to the illustration of which the work may most aptly be applied") and its "tendency," which is the "actual effect it is calculated to produce upon the reader and [that] cannot be completely ascertained but by the experiment" (139).[64] A work's tendency, that is, has less to do with the intentionality of an author than the psycho-historical situation of any particular reader. It diffuses author *and* reader by viewing those effects as ongoing and ever-changing. Tilottama Rajan highlights this reading practice as underlying Godwin's memorializing of Wollstonecraft, showing how *Memoirs of the Author of "A Vindication of the Rights of Woman"* and his editorial decisions in publishing her *Posthumous Works* apprehend and promote the open-endedness of her life/writings.[65] This refusal to monumentalize Wollstonecraft is true to his subject and part of his "attempt to write the revolutionary subject into history so as to initiate the uncertain process of her future reading," an attempt that also characterizes the mourning strategies of daughter Mary.[66] Indeed, the uncertainty of this process of reading is key to how the illustrious dead live on and grow to become more inclusive of others. Reading for tendency, then, not only characterized the reading and pedagogical practices of all three but also ensured an afterlife for their life/writings that is dynamic, interactive, and changes with the times. Ironically, this precise mode of living on through situated reading is ascribed to the life/writings of Percy Shelley, which have a long history of occluding, through the alleged transcendence of the Poet, many of the situations that informed him.[67]

This reading for tendency is the most promising aspect of their life/writings for literary-cultural study. By identifying text and author in their effects, not as each other's cause, it decouples the two and propels both into uncertain histories of reading. It produces analyses that are deeply contextualized but not historically specific; the intertextual and transferential dimensions of texts not only call and respond to each other across time but also locate their hope in measuring the space between them.[68] Godwin and Shelley variously characterize an author as disseminated across time and around the globe. Godwin's "lives on" in the "consequences that do not cease to flow from" his or her words, even in places where they have never heard of that author (*Sepulchres*, 23).[69] Shelley's bypasses the human (*Frankenstein*), terminates it (*The Last Man*), and occupies herself with collecting and disseminating remains. Important for syncopating the subject and march of history, reading for tendency has the potential to alter the tenor of engaged critique. It is less self-congratulatory in exposing the errors and shortsightedness of authors that become visible in large part because their works are read from a later perspective. Stressing the mutual and ongoing interaction between text and critique connects truth to its provisionality—the most visionary aspect of the life/writings of Wollstonecraft, Godwin, and Shelley. Their commitment to undermining boundaries, pieties, family secrets; recording the consolation and aggravation brought by their wandering fancies; dispelling the magic of "my"; and challenging writing by reading for tendency keeps writing dynamic and helps keep the humanities unsentimental about its humanity.

PART ONE

REVISING FAMILY

What magic is there in the pronoun "my," to overturn the decisions of everlasting truth? My wife or my mother may be a fool or a prostitute, malicious, lying or dishonest. If they be, of what consequence is it that they are mine?

Enquiry concerning Political Justice

[T]he regulation of passions is not, always, wisdom.—On the contrary, it should seem, that one reason why men have superiour judgment, and more fortitude than women, is undoubtedly this, that they give a freer scope to the grand passions, and by more frequently going astray enlarge their minds.

A Vindication of the Rights of Woman

And now, once again, I bid my hideous progeny go forth and prosper. I have affection for it, for it was the offspring of happy days, when death and grief were but words, which found no true echo in my heart.

Author's Introduction to *Frankenstein*

CHAPTER ONE

Making Public Love

We must then woo philosophy *chez vous ce soir, n'est-ce pas;* for I
do not like to lose my Philosopher even in the lover.
Mary Wollstonecraft to William Godwin, 15 September 1796

Mary Wollstonecraft and William Godwin are famous for their problems
making love. Different kinds of things troubled each of them, but both of their
lives and careers were shaped by fallout over the ways that they made love as a
textual and sexual activity. Wollstonecraft's problems were more conventional,
in part because she loved more readily. From start to finish, her writing life
was dictated by the imperative to reformulate love so that experiences of it no
longer defeat women. *A Vindication of the Rights of Woman* (1792) goes the
farthest in denouncing love and its enthusiasts, but her first novella, *Mary, a
Fiction* (1788), joins her posthumous novel, *The Wrongs of Woman; or, Maria*
(1798), in delineating the difficulties for women that attend loving the wrong
man. Her so-called personal life tells the same story at least twice, with Henry
Fuseli and Gilbert Imlay, before promising a happier outcome with William
Godwin. Even then, the promise was short-lived; indeed, the consequences of
making love to a more plausible man were no less lethal. The critical reception of Wollstonecraft still identifies love as a major stumbling block in her
life/writing, highlighting discrepancies between head and heart, theory and
practice, saying and doing, dying and generating. Ever since her death, Wollstonecraft's feminist credentials have been seen as severely compromised by
the passion—and the variety of passions—with which she lived her life.[1]

Godwin raises less conventional problems because he approached love with
such declared ambivalence. Until Wollstonecraft, his treatment of the topic
was either so vague or superficial that it occasioned little comment. His love
for and marriage to Wollstonecraft caused some initial troubles, owing espe-

cially to his clear condemnation of marriage as an unjust, degrading, and monopolistic institution in the *Enquiry concerning Political Justice* (1793), but, after some negative comment, the public was willing enough to let him get on with his life and work.[2] Where the public drew the line was at his most explicit composition as a married man, his *Memoirs of the Author of "A Vindication of the Rights of Woman"* (1798), written as a loving commemoration of Wollstonecraft just months after her death from childbirth. The major outrage here was that, in recounting her life, he published all the illicit details of Wollstonecraft's personal history, including her love for Fanny Blood, fantasized ménage à trois with the Fuselis, her bastard daughter, Fanny Imlay, two attempts at suicide out of despair over Gilbert Imlay, the intimate gynecological details surrounding her death, and, in so doing, ruined her reputation for generations.[3] His credibility as lover suffers to this day. My concern is not to restore his reputation as lover but rather to examine its formative impact on his life and career. Observing this draws attention to two of his favorite conceptual maneuvers: redrawing the boundaries between private and public in a way that essentially dissolves the former realm, and approaching attachment as an outcome of reading. In the latter domain, especially, he expressed fidelity to Wollstonecraft.

Even before they knew or loved each other, Wollstonecraft and Godwin each identified heterosexual love as a major impediment to their visions of social perfectibility. For both, perfectibility required achieving a society that is committed to truth and that serves and preserves the independence of the individual. For both, attaining this entailed re-educating society about the importance of freedom of thought, and therefore of education, to the strength and security of any society. For reasons that stemmed from the gender inequities of then-current social relations, Wollstonecraft viewed love as the primary impediment to autonomy, especially in the case of women, whereas Godwin considered love as one of several obstacles. At the same time, the aspects of love that Wollstonecraft censured are more restricted than those that Godwin identified, her target being passionate heterosexual love, especially as it deforms the minds and prospects of women. Otherwise, Wollstonecraft usually construes love for family and children as rational feelings, as women's chief contribution to society because one of their only means of enhancing perfectibility.[4] Women's amorous preoccupations, in contrast, render them superficial, fanciful, mindless, and dependent creatures, in large part because their entire training is devoted to captivating a man.

A Vindication of the Rights of Woman delineates the extent of this training, claiming that it underlies the literary, religious, and pedagogical traditions of the West. It also affects an entire array of female activity, from women's lack of method or application in anything other than dress to their notions of what is desirable in body, behavior, or men. Because of the crushing weight of this tradition and of most then-current women's investment in supporting it, Wollstonecraft can sound hostile to, even phobic about, any woman's desire to love a man passionately.[5] But this impression is unfair. Her target is precisely women's conviction that they must, first, win a man, and second, *captivate* in order to win him—that is, that their success in love and, therefore, life depends on their cultivation of irrational traits. This conviction retards women and their progress. Therefore, women must be raised to see that winning a man's love is compatible with developing their mental powers. A husband's enhancement of that aim is the chief criterion by which to judge a desirable attachment.

Godwin's objections to love are wider-ranging, extending to the entire set of domestic affections that he so famously indicts as impediments to justice in his *Essay concerning Political Justice.* "Justice would have taught me to save the life of Fenelon at the expense of [a family member]. What magic is there in the pronoun 'my,' to overturn the decisions of everlasting truth? My wife or my mother may be a fool or a prostitute, malicious, lying or dishonest. If they be, of what consequence is it that they are mine?" (50). Not just heterosexual but also parental and familial love intensify the feelings of partiality, obligation, gratitude, and guilt that he also identifies as independent hindrances to justice and that, in situations of extremity, impel one to look to one's own rather than seeing that one's own encompasses humanity and thus that justice resides in saving the benefactors of humanity, regardless of their personal relation to one. Those feelings (of partiality, obligation, guilt) also support a false concept of individual agency and personal responsibility, which Godwin's doctrine of necessity seeks to counter by instead defining a "person" as a "vehicle through which certain causes operate" and a "friend" as an impartial, replaceable, and extendable relation (168).

Though more extensive in scope, Godwin's objections to love are less impassioned than Wollstonecraft's, both because they apply to feelings other than love and because they are directed more at the institutions that solidify and legitimate love (such as marriage, property, and inheritance laws) than at the experience of love itself—an experience, moreover, with which Godwin the man is not overly identified, even granting men's lesser investment in the topic during this period. In fact, the word *love* does not ever occur in *Political Justice.*[6] Certainly, changes in Godwin's attachments, especially to Wollstone-

craft and Coleridge, altered his assessments of these institutions and the desirability of the love that they codify.[7] But how essentially they altered his
feelings about feeling remains a question that we need to investigate. Much of
the animus directed against Godwin presumes that he had feelings and that he
valued those that are deemed personal.

Where these two writers agree is in construing heterosexual lovemaking as
a textual, at times bookish, activity. According to Godwin, one book brought
him and Wollstonecraft together as lovers—"If ever there was a book calculated to make a man in love with its author, this appears to me to be the
book"—and another was intended to keep that author alive not only to him
after her death (*Memoirs*, 122).[8] According to both partners, reading and
writing books is fundamental to experiencing, legitimating, and reformulat-
ing love.[9] On the most basic level, both writers contend that states of falling
and being in love are informed by a history of classic love stories. This point is
central to chapter 5 of *A Vindication of the Rights of Woman* and underlies the
characterization of several of their fictional protagonists (Mary, Maria, Marguerite de Damville, Deloraine). More importantly, each claims that making a
love that is conducive to perfectibility requires devising new forms of writing,
especially new fictions of romance. For Wollstonecraft, this entails composing
romances that are reasonable in their depictions of heroines who exercise their
"thinking powers" (advertisement to *Mary*). As Claudia Johnson notes, the
unprecedented nature of these heroines is registered in the generic designation "a Fiction," which "disaffiliates" Wollstonecraft from the more conventional "novel," "romance," or "history," which portrays and thereby perpetuates female mindlessness.[10] For Godwin, it means viewing the "new romance"
as a truer form of history in showcasing how the circumstances that shape the
male protagonist impede his union with a woman.[11]

The most striking and consistent feature of their depictions of fictional
heterosexual couples is their portrayal of a couple's reading life as the most
sensitive barometer of their marital accord. Reading together often prepares a
couple for their eventual sexual coming together (*Wrongs of Woman, St. Leon*)
and is often portrayed as indistinguishable from sex or—in *Fleetwood*—as
preferable to it. This depiction of coupled reading within their novels dates
from their mutual love. Godwin's preconjugal novel, *Things as They Are; or,
The Adventures of Caleb Williams* (1794), explores the fruits of solitary reading and is remarkably silent on the topic of heterosexual love.[12] While *Mary*
(1788) is preoccupied with love and joins many other contemporary novels in
depicting novel reading as informing the female protagonist's conduct in love,

it does not portray reading as a shared activity that epitomizes a couple's accord.[13] (A first try, Wollstonecraft's uncompleted "The Cave of Fancy," makes the male partner's false expectations resulting from joint reading the cause of the female spirit's decision to enter into a bad marriage). It remains for Maria in *Wrongs of Woman* to fall in love with Henry *through* books, more precisely through reading the marginal notations that Darnford has made to Rousseau and thereby also to her.[14] Such a portrayal of the origins of love could only be envisaged by a person for whom the world of books is vibrantly alive.

Subsequent novels by Godwin follow this lead in making shared reading the measure of a couple's accord. *St. Leon* establishes the intimacy between St. Leon and Marguerite de Damville by detailing their habit of reading together. The process of reading their favorite works—"admirable sonnets of Petrarch," "sublime effusions of Dante," "letters of Eloisa to Abelard," and "effusions of the Troubadours"—achieves the state that these effusions depict, for reading them is said to fuse two individuals while augmenting each of them. "We were both of us well acquainted with the most eminent poets and fine writers of modern times. But when we came to read them together, they presented themselves in a point of view in which they had never been seen by us before" (44). Descriptions of the sensations elicited by shared reading sound pre- or postcoital, "when, in the presence of each other, the emotion is kindled in either bosom at the same instant, the eye-beams, pregnant with sentiment and meaning, involuntarily meet and mingle; the voice of the reader becomes modulated by the ideas of his author, and that of the hearer, by an accidental interjection of momentary comment or applause, confesses its accord" (44). More frequently, sharing the same taste in reading is presented as solidifying love. Accord in taste intensifies the "accord of our feelings" while simultaneously diminishing "what struck either as a blemish in the other." It causes a "reciprocation of benefits" in which "each gave or received something that added to the value of mind and worth of character," and thereby keeps "alive" that "mutual esteem" that is the "only substantial basis of love" (45).

Despite its more skeptical treatment of the capacity to sustain marital love, Godwin's next novel, *Fleetwood; or, The New Man of Feeling* (1805), also presents joint reading by a couple as the epitome of love. "How exquisite a pleasure may thus be derived from reading with a woman of refined understanding so noble a composition as that which engaged us!" At the same time that it acquaints the man with "the acuteness of her taste and her aptness to conceive and participate the most virtuous sentiments," it eschews words in the immediacy of their accord. "We are like instruments tuned to a correspondent pitch, . . . we communicate with instantaneous flashes, in one glance of the eye, and have no need of words" (199). Such accord is deemed indispensable to the "raptures" of sex and, more importantly, to the kind of rapture that Godwin deems suitable to it. *Fleetwood* (book and man) specifies as the "true ingredients" of "rapture" "a heart-felt esteem of each other's character; a perception that, while the eye we see sparkles, and the cheek glows, with affection, the glow is guiltless of any unhallowed and licentious propensity" (190). It also underscores the role that sexual difference should play in literary culture in affirming that "no decision upon a work of art can be consummate, till it has been pronounced on by both" genders (199).

There is something distinctly unappealing about the rapture that Godwin awards his lover/readers. Its sobriety brings into focus both Godwin's characteristic preference for reading over sex even in the nature of the sensations it arouses and Wollstonecraft's greater enthusiasm for both activities.[15] Exploring this asymmetry helps to mitigate concerns that Wollstonecraft is hostile to sexual pleasure. A look at their varying references to "voluptuousness" speaks volumes about differences in their embrace of wanton reading. After reading *La Nouvelle Heloïse*, Maria experiences the air sweeping across her face as "voluptuous" and more than once describes ideas in the same vein (*Wrongs of Woman*, 89, 98).[16] This conjunction echoes Wollstonecraft's own epistolary raptures, which anticipate her definition of voluptuousness in *A Short Residence* as involving a "mixture of sentiment and imagination" (258). "You know not how much tenderness for you may escape in a voluptuous sigh, should the air, as is often the case, give a pleasurable movement to sensations, that have been clustering round my heart, as I read this morning—reminding myself . . . that the writer loved me."[17] Godwin then repeats the term in characterizing the love between St. Leon and Marguerite, a love usually read as expressing his feelings for Wollstonecraft and registering a change in his attitude toward domestic affection: "A judicious and limited voluptuousness is necessary to the cultivation of the mind, to the polishing of the manners, to the refining of sentiment and the development of the understanding" (*St. Leon*, 36). "Ours [Marguerite and St. Leon's] was a sober and dignified happiness, and its very sobriety served to give it additional voluptuousness" (43). Such redefinitions suggest that the prudishness often ascribed to Wollstonecraft applies more justly to Godwin, but that he even ventures the term suggests the depth of her influence on him and his views of reading. Indeed, as we will see, the domain of reading is the one sphere in which he consistently affirms women's rights to equality. This is also because reading, and the unions attained through it, do not necessarily support the my-ness, or ego-boundedness, characteristic of the possessive individual. It makes two one and one two through the medium of a third party, whether that party be conceived as the author or the entire literary world. "The voice of the reader becomes modulated by the ideas of his author," to which "that of the hearer . . . confesses its accord" (44).

Emphasis, then, on the textual and literary dimensions of heterosexual love is what this couple shares in their life/writings and what they transmit to their daughter—the view both that a person's conceptions and experiences of love are informed by the literary tradition and that a couple's shared literary tastes and activities are the best indicator of the quality and duration of their love. Distinctive about their novelistic depiction of reading is the emphasis it places on adult eroticism. Their scenes of reading feature adult heterosexual couples or adult pairs rather than assembled family members or parent and young child. Nor is there any suggestion of the autoeroticism linked to solitary reading, or any endorsement of the fantasies, invariably heterosexual, linked to the solitary, but usually married, woman's reading.[18] For them, reading expands and extends couple life, spices up a marriage of minds, and, by returning to a book the couple once read together, gives each partner the capacity to re-evoke the other, even when one is permanently gone.

Equally telling is that each of them comes to this emphasis in their novels only after they begin living together and experiencing the problems of co-habitation firsthand. Up until he falls in love with Wollstonecraft, Godwin's stated problems with love are largely theoretical. Nonfictional texts portray domestic affection as impeding justice, fictional texts are indifferent to the subject, and his letters and journals are silent on it. In contrast, Wollstone-craft's experiential problems in love predate Godwin, even in assuming their highly public form. For Wollstonecraft, in *Letters Written during a Short Residence in Sweden, Norway, and Denmark* (1796), famously depicts herself as a melancholy wanderer, spurned in love, and hopeless about her future and the future of women. Because of these differences, their novels address different obstacles to the successful experience of love, but both showcase the importance of recourse to writing in redressing these concerns. Actually, both writers agree that the chief obstacle is men, but they ascribe the difficulty to different aspects of male psychology. This showcasing of writing as remedy is both representational and metadiscursive, in that each author not only employs writing to publicize how reading affects a fictional character's attitudes and approaches to love but also foregrounds the act of narration or composition and the necessary interaction between reforming love and revising stories in novels and nonfictional texts. At the same time, within these texts each writer interweaves two arguments that accentuate love's publicity: love is a nonpersonal or transpersonal feeling, and writing influences the experience of being in love. For both, making love a less private, secret, and personal activity is a major step toward liberating women and men.

Unfolding Female Minds

> From my narrative, my dear girl, you may gather . . . the counsel,
> which is meant rather to exercise than influence your mind.
>
> *The Wrongs of Woman; or, Maria*

There are good reasons for reading *A Short Residence* as the most melancholy and defeatist of Wollstonecraft's texts.[19] Its initial context, as impassioned letters to Gilbert Imlay, and their lack of success in winning him back occasion a melancholy that is voiced by the "I" as anxiety for her daughter and despair over the future of women. "I dread to unfold [my daughter's] mind, lest it should render her unfit for the world she is to inhabit—Hapless woman! what a fate is thine!" (269). A decade before Germaine de Staël's *Corinne* makes a sensation out of the connection, Wollstonecraft's text delineates the antagonism between female intellect and feeling, suggesting a direct correlation between the strength of a woman's efforts to "unfold her mind" and the depth of the unhappiness that she will experience as a consequence.[20] The voice of this text is read as equally telling. Its power lies in a new softness and sensibility, which mitigate the "amazonian temper" of the *Rights of Woman* and which ostensibly retract prior assertions of the advantages for women in cultivating their reason.[21] Saba Bahar has recently countered the claim of retraction by stressing the solidarity with women that Wollstonecraft's solitary narrator both facilitates and enables, especially through her refusal to treat women in distress, including herself, as objects of pity.[22] Bahar's point is strengthened through the text's suggestion of the power of writing to alter the narrative of female unhappiness.

Following the lead of Godwin, who fell in love with the melancholy voice of *A Short Residence*, we might evaluate the attractiveness for thinking women of adopting a melancholy sensibility. After all, *this* self-fashioning won Wollstonecraft a man—just not the one that she had originally intended. Moreover, as Mary Jacobus notes in her analysis of Godwin's phrase, it was "calculated" to do so—a calculation informed by her experience of reviewing recent novels by women for the *Analytical Review*. Mitzi Myers details Wollstonecraft's expressed hostility in these reviews to the "sentimental effusions" voiced by "insipid" and "puerile" female characters that somehow still win them notice and affection.[23] What might such effusions accomplish when uttered in the voice of a thinking woman who knows the literary power of feigning surrender to men? Even in the depths of despair, this woman did not voice surrender on any level.[24] "Still harping on the same subject, you will exclaim." "Cassandra was not the only prophetess whose warning voice has been disregarded" (*Short Residence,* 325, 342). Moreover, even in despair, she took up the pen for reasons that are unclear because they are so multiple. To whom was she writing? Imlay? herself? Fanny? the British public? future women? What was she writing? love letters? travel narrative? cultural analysis of national differences? feminist analysis of sexual difference? To what end? regaining Imlay's heart? unveiling or reanimating her own? killing time? penning her last words? redressing future women's desires?

Raising these questions does not minimize or discredit the reality of suffering but places it on another level. Not only does writing about suffering open out, or publicize, feeling but it also modifies the singularity and self-absorption of her melancholy.[25] For this writing is self-consciously performative, not simply representational, with designs on the future and a future beyond this individual author. Here, too, the strategies of this text have proven successful. Even present-day publics are more apt to sympathize with female complaint if it adopts a sentimental rather than a strident tone.[26] More importantly, this recognition by female Enlightenment writers became the next step toward female enlightenment. Julia Kristeva's characterization of de Staël is equally germane to the Wollstonecraft of *A Short Residence:* "Through Germaine de Staël, the *Goddess of Reason* was replaced by the *glory of writing,* via a celebration of adversity."[27] As we will see, this shift does not entail a retraction of reason as much as an endorsement of trial and error.

Such insights regarding the interactivity of melancholy and writing are scripted into *The Wrongs of Woman; or, Maria* from the start. That book is devoted to delineating the wrongs suffered by women who love and is composed almost entirely of scenes of reading, writing, or storytelling. It would be hard to miss the text's emphasis on the first dimension, already highlighted in the title. The first page depicts Maria both lamenting that her baby is a daughter and anticipating the "aggravated ills of life that her sex rendered almost inevitable," anticipations that are actualized in all subsequent female stories in the text (by Jemima, the "lovely maniac," the landlady, Maria) (85). On these grounds, too, *Wrongs of Woman* equates marriage with slavery and imprisonment, implying that major social institutions are invested in female confinement. But the text is similarly relentless in its focus on narration and the interrelation it establishes between loving and narrating one's story. Chapter 1 ends with Jemima procuring for Maria "some books and implements for writing," which are instrumental in the attainment and redirection of her love (89). The only bright spots in any of the women's personal stories involve moments of reading or literary converse. This is especially true for the working-class Jemima, whose status as mistress to a literary libertine provides the only respite in her tale of misery and her only means of rising above it.[28] The "answer" to "your often-repeated question, 'Why my sentiments and language were superior to my station?'" is that "I now began to read" (113). This linkage—emphasized in the libertine profiting from "the criticism of unsophisticated feeling" by reading to Jemima his "productions, previous to their publication"—suggests that women's fates are tied to their ability to shape stories, especially regarding the misery that their reduction to objects of love consigns them (114). But the connection works both ways: articulating this misery is key to changing it through publicizing new stories by women. Without this emphasis, the text sounds defeatist about the prospects for women who love. Instead, *Wrongs* presents reading and writing as highly erotic activities and the best hopes for social reform.

This assertion, that *Wrongs of Woman* finds anything positive or worth maintaining about heterosexual love, goes against the grain of several powerful feminist readings that interpret the ending as expressing either Wollstonecraft's hopelessness about heterosexual love or her only hope as residing in a female-only household and a proto-lesbian sensibility.[29] Moreover, the most convincing evidence cited for the cynicism or defeatism regarding heterosexual relations turns on Maria's investment in Rousseau. Maria's admission that she models her image of Henry on St. Preux is interpreted as a rejection by *Wrongs* of Rousseau and by extension of the sentimental tradition.[30] Though accurate about the novel's depiction and analysis of the chief cause of marital despotism, such accounts underestimate its emphasis on the power inherent in narration, for good as well as ill. Construing as defeatist the negative critiques in *Wrongs* of heterosexual love and marriage, whether that critique is directed within the novel at books or life, implies that nothing positive is being envisioned through making this critique. *Rights of Woman* offers a more dynamic model, by which the literary tradition is depicted as causing female oppression but also providing a means to counter it. The elaborate frame devices of *Wrongs*, especially the presentation of Maria's story as *written* to her absent infant daughter, directs attention to the fact that Maria is writing to the future. And part of the future that this writing anticipates is women claiming their rights to heterosexual pleasure once current readers have learned to distinguish passive sentiment from active sensibility.

In this regard, *Wrongs of Woman* is profitably read as a treatise on sex education that treats each term as important to educing the other.[31] Its basic message is that society needs to be re-educated about the practices and meanings of sex so that sexual activity does not dehumanize individuals, especially women. The text does not argue against sex or its pleasures but against sexual practices that rigorously oppose body to mind or male to female in the degree of pleasure to which either body is entitled. "[Women] cannot, without depraving our minds, endeavour to please a lover or husband, but in proportion as he pleases us" (145). Passion and intellect must be equally satisfied in physical acts of love, for "the culture of the heart ever, I believe, keeps pace with that of the mind" (116). These are strikingly emancipated claims, which, by linking equality to women's share in sexual pleasure, should qualify assertions of the chasteness, even prudishness, that characterizes the Wollstonecraftian heroine. Equally forward-looking is this text's efforts to promote the pleasures of mental arousal and to instruct persons about the benefits *and* dangers of loving "by the book." As we will see, even if the genre of book (the novel of sentiment) is ultimately censured for mischaracterizing love, the notion that books play a stimulating role in love is never retracted. Nor does that stimulation remain on a cerebral plane. Maria and Henry not only fall in love through marginal textual exchanges but the passion of those exchanges anticipates, by at once postponing and preparing for, their sexual union. When the two finally meet in person, the "reserve" that makes their conversation appropriate for "all the world" to "have listened in" on is only broken when, in "discussing some literary subject, flashes of sentiment, inforced by each relaxing feature, seemed to remind them that their minds were already acquainted" (100). This activation of a former meeting of the minds, an accord strengthened by Darnford's intervening acquaintance with the written narrative of Maria's life, triggers the physical union to which both parties consent. In fact, it is the grounds of consent.

It is true that, once triggered, *Wrongs of Woman* then falls silent on the physical pleasures of sex. Comments on the scene instead focus on the effects on Maria's imagination, perhaps to suggest that the pleasures of sex are never simply physical, as suggested in the definition of voluptuous. By way of contrast, *Wrongs* is graphic in its portrayal of the prospect of unsatisfactory sex, treating the reader to disgusting visions of Maria's libertine husband. "I now see him"—the same "him" whose "tainted breath, pimpled face, and blood-shot eyes" formerly nauseated Maria—"lolling in an arm-chair, in a dirty powdering gown, soiled linen, ungartered stockings, and tangled hair, yawning and stretching himself" (139–40). It is as if Maria forces her readers to feel—and thus share—her revulsion as part of a visceral campaign to support the moral necessity of divorce. The moral case rests on exposing the violence done to a woman's *sensibilities* in forcing her to continue to have sex with such a man. The more sensitive the woman, the more damaging is the mandate that she fulfill her wifely duty. "When I recollected that I was bound to live with such a being for ever—my heart died within me; my desire of improvement became languid, and baleful, corroding melancholy took possession of my soul" (145–46). No wonder those who deny women recourse to divorce are termed "cold-blooded moralists." Not content to "bastille" women "for life," they entomb women by forcing them to turn their hearts "to stone," and in so doing extinguish "that fire of the imagination, which produces *active* sensibility, and *positive* virtue" (144, original emphasis).

Whether depicted through positive or negative means, then, *Wrongs of Woman* wants sex to retain (actually, find or regain) its mental and imaginative features. Sex without mind, her definition of libertinism, is brutish precisely in robbing persons of their recourse to fantasy. Indeed, the prospect of being enchained to a brute turns a woman to stone. On the other hand, good sex, according to this text, both fosters and *necessitates* imaginative activity. "There was one peculiarity in Maria's mind: she . . . had rather trust without sufficient reason, than be for ever the prey of doubt" (173). But affirming such visions of sex confronts several obstacles, one of the most basic being novelistic portrayals of women as "mindless," though this with an added twist. The mindlessness that this text confronts concerns mindless reading, the passive absorption of sentimental fiction. In Wollstonecraft's eyes, such passivity not only keeps women stupefied and therefore acquiescent in their unhappiness as wives but also focuses their erotic desires on romance heroes whose unrealistic features are the product of limited male fantasy. *Wrongs* aims to redress both situations. In the details of its plot and the interlocking structure of its narration, it transforms the reading of fiction into an *activity* that forces women both to think and to reconsider their options.

The text's seriousness about the need to alter practices and notions of sex is underscored by its series of framing devices—especially that of Maria writing her life story to her infant daughter in the event that she might be unable to parent her in person. That the instruction concerns the susceptibility of erotic attraction to redirection is clear from the amatory education that her memoir plots. Maria aims to teach her daughter how to make more satisfying choices in love by relating not only how a different partner (first George, then Henry) affects the daily features of her existence but also what caused her to be attracted to George in the first place: an overactive fancy, which, schooled on books and her uncle's unworldly conversations, "ma[d]e me form an ideal picture of life" (126; see 131, 137). Maria writes against this idealizing of reality, even if what she narrates is caused by repeated errors of the sort. By admitting and learning from her mistakes and then relating them to her daughter, Maria seeks to improve the next generation's happiness in love. Such improvement requires that women first break through the secrecy surrounding sex, a secrecy that is fundamental to making sex appear sacred and too intimate for public discourse.[32] For this habit of viewing sex as the most private or "personal" aspect of a couple's relationship strengthens the "marital despotism" from which the wrongs of woman stem. It keeps women from admitting to themselves, let alone to others, that their sex lives are less than ideal and thus prevents them from banding together to change things—including pursuing their erotic desires for each other. As the scene with her landlady shows, the sexual tie, precisely when it is the only palpable demonstration of a husband's connection to his wife, is the primary threat to female solidarity. It impedes women's desires to view themselves as thinking individuals because it is not in their interest to do so.

At the same time, *Wrongs of Woman* retracts the contention advanced in *Rights of Woman* that those wives who are unhappy as lovers make the best mothers.[33] This mother writes to her daughter to vindicate and broadcast her status as adulterous lover in order to safeguard her daughter's right to a sexually satisfying marriage. In the domain of marriage at least, her message is basically never to forego desire. "Acquire sufficient fortitude to pursue your own happiness." Do not "waste years in deliberating," after you "cease to doubt." "To fly from pleasure is not to avoid pain" (123). The protestant vocabulary should not overshadow the underlying message regarding a wife's right to sexual happiness. Truly immoral because it is weak-minded and therefore demeaning is retaining the "cloke" of matrimony on a body that has gone elsewhere (157).

We do not have to wait for the conclusion to this text, or its lack of a conclusion, to worry about the rationality or plausibility of these reformulations of love. The fragments of possible endings that Godwin appends to his edition of this text suggest that Henry will prove disappointing in any number of ways.[34] They also suggest that lessons, like lives, have no assured or predictable ends. But here, too, the novel anticipates our skepticism, by situating these scenes of instruction in a madhouse. This admission, I contend, rather than any lessening of Wollstonecraft's feminist convictions, constitutes the major difference between *Rights of Woman* and *Wrongs of Woman*, a difference that is consistent with the implications of the shift in titles from "rights" to "wrongs" and the latter text's narrowing of focus to "marital despotism" as the chief problem obstructing women's attainment of rights. Not that *Rights of Woman* is ever sanguine about the ease with which cultures alter their foundations, but it is "enlightened" in assuming the efficacy of demonstrating the necessity and benefits of change. This aspect of Enlightenment dogma is what *Wrongs of Woman* recants. By losing what is presented as an irrefutable case for the rational, moral, and sensible benefits of divorce to both parties, *Wrongs* exposes society's investment in the repression of women. More than ignorance or indifference perpetuates female retardation; the most cherished social institutions of the West are established to ensure that women do not advance. But even this degree of pessimism (i.e., realism) is tempered by the text's understanding of the power of truth, a power that depends on redefining the nature of truth. The best hope for positive change lies in telling less idealized or saccharine stories about love.

Stressing the narrative dimensions of love aids its reform in several respects. It includes intellect and taste in notions of attraction and standards of desirability, additions that are crucial to strengthening female independence, even in love. Cultivating those dimensions of mind heightens the experience, even the physical sensations, of being in love but without blinding women to other options. Even more fundamentally, it posits an interactive relation between fiction and reality in the constitution not only of love but also of personhood. Readers depicted in her text (as well as then and future readers of these texts) have their characters shaped in relation to the fictional characters they take in. Writers of the time often warned against this internalization of fiction, but Wollstonecraft promoted it as long as the texts internalized are not confined to sentimental and romantic novels and are deemed capable of revision. One classic fiction that she aimed to modify concerns the singularity, the uniqueness, of heterosexual love. *Wrongs* highlights instead the repetitive nature of love in the series of life stories told by Jemima, Henry, and Maria and the redundancies they share. Despite articulated distinctions in class and gender, these characters perceive their kinship (Jemima even recovers her humanity) by recounting their similar experiences of love. That the similarity concerns heartbreak and betrayal points up a second fiction that *Wrongs* revises: that marriage is a woman's chief aim because her only path to happiness. Wrong. Stressing the misery occasioned by love is the first step toward disputing the equation between marriage and female happiness and changing the grounds, or expectations, of happiness both within marriage and outside of it.

Success in this aim entails employing two literary devices, both of which stem from the text's emphasis on narration. One addresses the future associated with women's writing, and the other analyzes and revises women's fantasy lives. The two are brought together in the curious redirection of Maria's life story from her baby daughter to Henry—a shift made without comment, revision, or delay once Maria learns that her baby is dead. One could say that daughter and Henry are allied in the hope that each represents, with Henry having to assume double responsibility once the baby is discovered dead—for he becomes at once Maria's only hope for a happy future and women's hope that their daughters will have happier futures with more emancipated or literate men. One could also say that, after listening to his story, Maria deems Henry a baby who must be schooled in the new reality of thinking women who love.[35] Perhaps this explains the otherwise undermotivated nature of his confinement. He requires liberation from the confines of masculinity.

This implication is strengthened by two features of Maria's assessment of her "progress" in love. As Johnson and others contend, Henry's inability to realize his potential is not simply foreshadowed but predicted in Maria's account of what draws her to him. As in the case of George, the attraction is fueled by a fancy trained on fiction to apprehend as reality traits that are not yet or never will be substantiated in him. "His steady, bold step, and the whole air of his person . . . gave an outline to the imagination to sketch the individual form she wished to recognize" (*Wrongs*, 96). Critics construe this admission as evidence of a failure in Maria's character: in the case of love, she is unable to distinguish sufficiently between fiction and reality. They also posit this as implying a wholesale critique of men for being invested in sentimental love plots that, by rendering women passive victims, give men something to do. "Desire was lost in more ineffable emotions, and to protect her from insult and sorrow—to make her happy, seemed not only the first wish of his heart, but the most noble duty of his life" (105). Though accurate in the main, such judgments miss two crucial points. First, fancy's effect on love in itself is not the problem and indeed is necessary to the unfolding of love in its initial stages (a point explored in more detail in chapter 4). This point is affirmed in the alliance the text makes between the "stranger," Henry, on whose vanishing form Maria projects her hopes of love from her madhouse window, and the unborn "stranger," her baby daughter, whom the pregnant mother "had so long wished to view" (97, 166). In other words, *Wrongs of Woman* characterizes fancy as the faculty that *initiates* a relation, even before the beloved makes an appearance in reality. Moreover, fancy understands any relation as beginning in estrangement. Successful actualization of a relation, then, depends on one's reaction to fantasy and to current realities regarding the realization of it: that is, whether one's reality is submerged in fantasy, opposed to it, or the two are mutually informed; whether, in preferring image to reality, one never ventures beyond the idealizing stage of love, or whether current realities of men necessitate maintaining an idealizing approach.

The second tactic involves reforming the passivity associated with female reading and follows from the point in relation to fancy at which George and Henry diverge. Whereas the fictional hero in relation to whom Maria initially idealizes George is left unspecified ("In short, I fancied myself in love . . . with the disinterestedness, fortitude, generosity, dignity, and humanity, with which I had invested the hero I dubbed" [127]), the model for Henry is spelled out, and significantly fleshed out, as Rousseau's St. Preux. The identification of this hero and novel marks a partial advance for women. As Henry's marginal notation, which wins Maria's accord, rhapsodizes, "Rousseau alone, the true Prometheus of sentiment, possessed the fire of genius necessary to pourtray the passion, the truth of which goes so directly to the heart" (96).[36] Moreover, "Rousseau alone" grants passion to the "new Heloïse," Julie, for the first time in literary history extending to "heroines" the rights of "the hero . . . to be mortal," rather than "immaculate" (Author's Preface, 83). *Wrongs of Woman*, then, sanctions Maria's expression of sexual passion for Henry by suggesting that she loves "by the book" that, for once, affirms female desire. But it also criticizes that book, and the genre it exemplifies, for failing to liberate Julie from a stultifying marriage and failing to devise a new Abelard who will foster woman's autonomy even in marriage. While Rousseau and Henry admit the reality and perceive the desirability of passionate women, they remain infantile and self-absorbed in their embrace of it. It is left to Maria to address the legal and cultural impediments to a woman's sexual freedom—precisely the person whose voice in these matters is legally proscribed.

Except in the domain of fiction. Unlike its depiction of legal and governmental institutions, *Wrongs of Woman* portrays women as agents in the literary institutionalizing of their victimization and thus as capable of acting to change it. They can start telling or writing more truthful stories about the realities of love, and they can begin reading with a more critical eye on the images in relation to which women are perceived, evaluated, and confined. For, as Johnson notes, *Wrongs of Woman* is a "densely literary novel" that, by alluding to the many texts that entrap women in images of passive femininity, also suggests another reason why women have trouble breaking out of their cages: they have no plausible alternate fantasies.[37] *Wrongs of Woman* takes a first step by drawing attention to the sustained impoverishment of female fantasy and its ability to turn women to stone. This is fiction that is truer to the sentiments of women as Maria defines them—that is, as involving the fire of the imagination, which produces *active* sensibility and *positive* virtue—and, in its interlocking structure of narration, forces readers to gain distance on the stories and characters that they imbibe.

Saba Bahar shows how *Wrongs of Woman* extends this "more active science of reading to the fictional novel" through the text's rewriting of the sentimental heroine. In her account, the novel blocks elicitation of pity by both depicting women whose reactions to suffering are dignified and thus worthy of respect and introducing a narrative voice that "helps to forestall an immediate, naïve, and purely sentimental identification with the fictive universe" in order ultimately to foster on the part of readers "further interaction with the world."[38] *Wrongs* also makes clear that the world that fiction helps to realize must become legible, apprehensible, and tangible before it is safe to be inhabited. This new writing is directed at infant eyes whose maturation awaits the future.[39] At the heart of Wollstonecraft's novel writing, and of those multiple-staged scenes of writing in her novels, is the belief that eyes will eventually emerge that are capable of apprehending words written before their time. The authorial isolation that we tend to view as a normal condition of writing is for the Wollstonecraftian character a consequence of having no timely interlocutors, even sometimes in herself. *Mary* introduces this trend, whereby Mary resorts to "the little book that was now her only confid[a]nt"—now, that is, that Ann is dead and Henry elsewhere, though their worthiness as confidantes is never borne out by the text—literally to define and outline the vague sensations she is feeling (51). These scenes portray the main character's coming-to-a-character that does not exist prior to its delineation by her writing, the virtual reality of which character is accentuated in *Wrongs of Woman* by having such lines penned to an absent—and, as it turns out, dead—infant daughter. In their scripted dimensions, they also help to portray the truth of character as impersonal, transferable, and subject to change—indeed, these traits literally constitute the "mind of a woman, who has thinking powers." This process of self-creation needs time for its reality to emerge, time cut short in and by the narrative. Wollstonecraft's untimely death makes more urgent, but no less anticipated, the future readers that such words are devising for their own legibility and thus survival.

Maria's writing helps to compose this future by conveying to the next generation her indifference toward being read as a conventional mother: "It is, my child, my dearest daughter, only such a mother, who will dare to break through all restraint to provide for your happiness—who will voluntarily brave censure herself, to ward off sorrow from your bosom" (*Wrongs of Woman*, 123). It is indeed a new species of fiction that would portray a mother who is eager to foster her daughter's sexual pleasure, whether sought with men or women, rather than school her in modes of repression and denial. It is an older, but still valid, species that does this by not presenting such mothers as ones with whom current readers are in danger of overidentifying. Indeed, readers still cannot get "into" Maria's character, because her deepest feelings are presented as predictable, formulaic, and dull. Thwarting identification constitutes an ethics of Wollstonecraftian character, by which female characters prove exemplary in their resistance to being idealized. This is part of the truth that *Wrongs of Woman* stages, whereby characters offer their life stories as "counsel which is meant rather to exercise than influence your mind." Only this notion of truth strengthens the "active virtue" that estimable mothers aim to cultivate in their daughters, based as it is on stimulating, not regulating or informing, young minds. Such counsel enjoins reading without recourse to idealization or snap judgments. It explores rather than closes off options. Exemplary about Maria's character is its openness to the hazards, including the tedium, of living.[40]

Open and Shut Out

> Sketches of what . . . would perhaps have given a new impulse to
> the manners of the world.
>
>   Godwin's Preface to *The Wrongs of Woman; or, Maria*

It is a cruel irony of literary history that, in his endorsement of this approach to truth, Godwin is Wollstonecraft's ideal and most damaging reader. It is also an instructive lesson about the vagaries of literary reception that his attempts to further her vision undermined its effectiveness for years. Godwin's first public acts of mourning some four months after Wollstonecraft's death were faithful to her writings by both shepherding them into print and telling her life story in an unidealized and antisentimental fashion. Because aspects of both activities have often been construed as betraying her spirit, in specific by characterizing her *as* a sentimental heroine, we need to reconsider who and what Godwin is after in composing her life story and editing her posthumous works. The brief Editor's Preface to *Wrongs of Woman* provides a striking counter to assessments that his editing and "conclusions" dilute the revolutionary and woman-identified force of her narrative: "[Here I transcribe] sketches of what, if they had been filled up in a manner adequate to the writer's conception, would perhaps have given a new impulse to the manners of the world" (81). At the very least, this statement sees *Wrongs* as working against sentimental assumptions about female behavior and pays tribute to the transformational power and design of Wollstonecraft's novel. His characterizations in *The Memoirs of the Author of "A Vindication of the Rights of Woman"* accords, by and large, with the depictions of female character that those "sketches" provide, for Godwin presents Wollstonecraft as a woman whose thinking powers make and keep her open to loving, living, writing, and suffering. More to the point, he presents her as a writer whose suffering has literary antecedents and resolutions.

The uniformly harsh reactions to the *Memoirs* when initially published prompt reflection on what forms of respect writers owe the dead, especially in treating their personal lives. Even writers sympathetic to Godwin, like Robert Southey, faulted him for naivety, if not for "lack[ing] all feeling," by "stripping his dead wife naked" before the public, while less charitable critics questioned his humanity as well as sanity in portraying his wife as a whore.[41] In refusing these norms and these categories (private, person, honor, owe), Godwin appears unsympathetic, both to his wife and as a person. But precisely this refusal expresses his respect for Wollstonecraft, the public articulation of that respect being essential to his and her love. Moreover, by depicting her as an author, instead of a person, he portrays her as a public intellectual whose writings on love give a new impulse to the world. In so doing, he means to help alter the equation not only of woman but also of grief with expression of feeling.

The major irony in the reception of *Memoirs* is that Godwin clearly views Wollstonecraft in the category of Fénelon, not a family member. The very first line specifies as "a duty incumbent on survivors" giving "the public some account of the life of a person of eminent merit deceased," an eminence substantiated several lines later in the remarkable assertion that "there are not many individuals with whose character the public welfare and improvement are more intimately connected, than the author of A Vindication of the Rights of Woman" *(Memoirs,* 87). The public, in contrast, read the *Memoirs* as a biography of Godwin's wife that proved her to be both "a fool and a prostitute" and him a decided fool. One can say that the burden of the *Memoirs* (in both senses) rests on the lengths to which Godwin goes to demonstrate that Wollstonecraft was not "his," was not merely a "personal" relation of his, affection for whom would then be construable as succumbing to the "magic" of "my." On the obvious level, this meant giving an account of her life in which he figures only in the final two (of ten) chapters and chronicling the extent to which she had "belonged" sexually to other men. It also entailed portraying her as an author, as the full title of the *Memoirs* and the principles underlying his selection of materials make clear, and as a character shaped in part by the reality that fiction makes available. This is the kind of character—fictional human character—that it is essential to the public's welfare and improvement to understand. "Mary was in this respect a female Werter" (117).

The "not mine" that characterizes Godwin's portrayal of his relation to Wollstonecraft was part of the truth of character generally that Godwin was working to promote during this period, aspects of which predated his intercourse with Wollstonecraft and were distinct from the emphases, though not the ends, of her treatments of character. For characterizing a person as the vehicle through which a series of causes pass, as Godwin does in the *Enquiry concerning Political Justice* and throughout his subsequent works, radically destabilizes what can be said to be "mine" in the constitution of "me," let alone "you," especially when political institutions are said to "insinuate [themselves] into our personal dispositions" and "private transactions" *(Political Justice Var.,* 12; also 80). This notion, that the comprehension of national or world history is necessary for understanding the life of an (eminent) individual, culminates in 1803 in the *Life of Chaucer,* whose full title (and ambition) extends the depersonalizing implications of the *Memoirs of the Author of "A Vindication of the Rights of Woman."* The title specifies as a constituent part of the *Life of Geoffrey Chaucer* the *Memoirs of His Near Friend and Kinsman, John of Gaunt, Duke of Lancaster* and *Sketches of the Manners, Opinions, Arts, and Literature of England in the Fourteenth Century.*[42]

A second aspect of Godwin's notion of character dovetails with Wollstonecraft's writings and Godwin's editions of her. For delineating character also means making public the most intimate details of a life as relevant to understanding the formation—that is, causation—of any character, as well as apprehending those details apart from evaluative standards either of consistency or guilt. As Tilottama Rajan has demonstrated, identifying the truth of character involves ascertaining its "tendency" rather than coherence or historical specificity and, in the case of Wollstonecraft, "locates her legacy not in the moral of specific texts and acts, but in a tendency often hidden from the author herself," "unconsolidated within existing discourses," "inseparable from a work's 'effects'" but also "subjecting [those effects] to the accidents" of their own "disfiguration."[43] In other words, such a notion and reading of character apprehends an anti-idealist "spirit" within the lifeworks of an author that carries on long after the person has died. That spirit occasions a reading practice that keeps the author alive, mobile, and ever-changing. It gives rise to a character that is neither wholly dissipated over the course of time nor ever fully coherent or characterizable at any moment of time. This allows it to speak to multiple times, because it is altered in relation to the new perspectives of the various readers it has helped to form over time. To apprehend such a character means to confront the presence of a future that the author's own words shadow forth—continue to shadow forth—and on which they rely. Godwin articulates this view of tendency in *The Enquirer*, but he first activates it in his attempt to memorialize Wollstonecraft by means of it.

The degree of impersonality depicted in the *Memoirs*, both as a characteristic of Wollstonecraft's character and of Godwin's connection to her, does not mean that Godwin denies or even underplays the strength of his attachment to her once he enters the story. The concluding pages specify precisely what "I have for ever lost" in losing Wollstonecraft: the solidification into habit of the intellectual tact that characterized Wollstonecraft's mind and that Godwin was only in the initial stages of acquiring through "the daily recurrence" of her exemplification of it. "This light was lent to me for a very short period, and is now extinguished for ever" (141). This light is irreplaceable but hardly personal or, at this stage, located in any particular text or work. Indeed, precisely what he has gained and then lost in Wollstonecraft is the physical benefit of the collision of minds that characterized their lives together and that altered his "personal" habits of mind, here described as deliberateness or belatedness ("This species of intellect [hers] probably differs from the other [his], chiefly in the relation of earlier and later" [141]). In this regard, Godwin is diminished and feels his mind to be set back by the loss of her person. Nor does he appear wholly sanguine about the dissolution of self resulting from a tendential approach to character, especially when the person is now newly "for ever lost." The final pages of the *Memoir* are deeply anxious attempts to re/collect, even locate, her remains now that he has diffused her character in anatomizing it (anticipating the "I" at the Sybil's Cave in the introduction to *The Last Man*). Perhaps he is worried, too, about soliciting the charge that she *is* dissipated in light of the details he gives that he deems essential to the truth of her character. As expressions of grief, Godwin's words *are* unfamiliar, in their absence of sentiment and almost clinical interest in dissecting Wollstonecraft's character. This approach to her character should alter charges that Godwin betrays her intellect in casting her as a sentimental heroine. It is not precisely true of the voice that he deems "calculated" to win him, nor does he, by characterizing her as a "female Werter," damn with faint praise. At the least, the self-absorption often attributed to Godwin is belied by his precise accounting of his receptivity to, and intellectual dependence on, her modes of thinking.

The novels that Godwin composed in the wake of losing Wollstonecraft are often read as retracting his highly publicized denunciations of marriage and family. If one accepts A. E. Rodway's account of the "three periods of Godwin's influence in his lifetime," where 1793–97 is the period of "Fame," 1797–1805 is "Attack," and from 1805 on is "Oblivion," then *Travels of St. Leon: A Tale of the Sixteenth Century* (1799) and *Fleetwood; or, The New Man of Feeling* (1805) can be viewed as bookend texts that flank the period during which Godwin struggled to salvage his career and reputation.[44] More precisely, they can be seen as addressing two repeated public charges against Godwin's approach to love: inconsistency, especially in his views on domestic affection, and lack of feeling, whether in initially castigating marriage and love or in his subsequent performance as husband and family man. Moreover, appearing at the beginning and end of the second stage of Godwin's career, they allow us to evaluate the extent to which Godwin altered his strategies in addressing these charges.

Critics generally read both novels as furthering the project of revision already under way in the second (1796) and third (1798) editions of the *Enquiry concerning Political Justice*, in which Godwin softens his rationalist objections to marriage and domestic affection and gives more attention to motive as influencing moral behavior.[45] *St. Leon* especially, but also *Fleetwood*, feature as one of their primary plotlines the male protagonist's acquisition of, love for, and life with a worthy wife. Marguerite de Damville (*St. Leon*) and Mary MacNeill (*Fleetwood*), in their sensibility, generosity, and tact, are seen as modeled on Wollstonecraft, and St. Leon's and Fleetwood's feelings for these women are construed as new testimonies to the power of familial and heterosexual love. But while they represent new novelistic topics for Godwin that, in my assessment, too, are influenced by his intercourse with Wollstonecraft, they are neither full-scale reversals of his objections to domestic affection nor indebted to commerce with her in the ways that are usually claimed. For one thing, the marriages in both novels end tragically, and not because the wife dies before her time. Dying before her is the intimate accord between husband and wife, the sustainability of which both novels raise as a serious question. For another, each text takes great pains to narrow, if not nullify, the distance between domestic affection and universal benevolence. Rather than adopt the concentric circle model of affection famously articulated by Edmund Burke, by which love of the "little platoon" of the family is said to lead to love of the whole (a whole, however, that stops at the nation), these texts characterize family feeling as a public type of relation and present the assertion of one's feelings for family as fundamental to a person's maintaining good relations with the public.

The preface to *St. Leon* spells out the latter interconnection:

> True wisdom will recommend to us individual attachments; for with them our minds are more thoroughly maintained in activity and life than they can be under the privation of them; and it is better that man should be a living being, than a stock or a stone. True virtue will sanction this recommendation; since it is the object of virtue to produce happiness, and since the man who lives in the midst of domestic relations will have many opportunities of conferring pleasure, minute in the detail, yet not trivial in the amount, without interfering with the purposes of general benevolence. Nay, by kindling his sensibility, and harmonising his soul, they may be expected, if he is endowed with a liberal and manly spirit, to render him more prompt in the service of strangers and the public. (11)

It situates this explanation in the context of allegations regarding Godwin's inconsistencies. "In answer to" those readers who will "accuse me of inconsistency," the "affections and charities of private life being every where in this publication a topic of the warmest eulogium, while in the Enquiry concerning Political Justice they seemed to be treated with no great degree of indulgence and favour," "all I think it necessary to say on the present occasion is, that, for more than four years, I have been anxious for opportunity and leisure to modify some of the earlier chapters of that work in conformity to the sentiments inculcated in this. Not that I see cause to make any change respecting the principle of justice, or any thing else fundamental to the system there delivered" (11). Quite amazingly, Godwin then presents as evidence of the lack of contradiction precisely what prompted the allegations in the first place, his relations with Wollstonecraft. The assertion that "apprehend[s] domestic and private affections" as "not incompatible with" an "active sense of justice" borrows her phrase from *Wrongs of Woman* in defining them as "inseparable" from "what may be styled the culture of the heart" (*St. Leon*, 11; *Wrongs*, 116). And the text he references as "reconcil[ing]" these "seemingly jarring principles" of affection and justice is "a little book which I gave to the public in the year 1798," his *Memoirs of the Author of "A Vindication of the Rights of Woman."* For there, as we have seen, he asserts that the public's insight into Wollstonecraft's character is indissociable from that public's welfare and amelioration, and that the affirmation of his attachment is an act of justice to her in the service of justice for all.[46]

The content of *St. Leon* in several ways also raises doubts about whether its treatment of domestic affection represents a new departure for Godwin. On the one hand, *St. Leon* does contain the most positive statements of any Godwinian text about the value of marital accord (43–45, 63, 109, 114), the pleasures of sex (44), the desirability of feeling attached to one's child (a sentiment otherwise described as "comparatively cold, selfish, solitary, and inane" [47]), and the sufficiency of domesticity to happiness. On the other hand, it usually qualifies those passages and that happiness either by admitting that "no such thing was the effect of our intercourse" or by presenting them as an imperative: "to value my domestic blessings as I ought" (45, 84). Such qualifications are in line with the more general skepticism discernible in the text's plot—which, after all, tells the story of how a promising and affectionate young nobleman becomes the most radically isolated being in the world. The logic of the various plotlines, moreover, complicates the concentric model of attachment. On one level, the fact that St. Leon's plans of benevolence—his efforts to reform Turkey and Hungary—are rendered ineffectual once the harmony of his domestic life is dispelled could suggest that he cannot be useful to others because he has not been kind to his own. But the text also implies a collapsing of the two domains, since what impedes St. Leon's effectiveness in either sphere is recourse to secrecy, which by definition destroys the transparency and sincerity of character that are crucial to preserving intimacy at home and trust in his projects abroad. Moreover, what occasions St. Leon's secrecy is his succumbing to magic, whose particular forms—acquisition of the elixir of life and the philosopher's stone—intensify the my-ness that was formerly ascribed to the domestic affections and scorned for impeding justice. By giving unlimited time and resources to the self, the magic that transforms St. Leon's existence at once impedes his search for justice and human attachment.

St. Leon pursues to its logical end the attempt to extend indefinitely the reach of "my": total isolation. St. Leon's acquisition of immortality and unlimited wealth places him beyond the human, thus rendering impossible any meaningful form of human interaction. But this critique of St. Leon's magic does not imply a reformed embrace of the magic associated with the my-ness cultivated by domestic affection. St. Leon's assertions of love for wife and family are careful to define those affections as fostering benevolence, not individuality or domestic seclusion, the loss of which feelings is then presented as blocking his efforts to serve the public. For example, the "passions" of a "husband and a father" are characterized as "the true school of humanity: the man, whose situation continually exercises in him the softest and most amiable charities of our nature, will almost infallibly surpass his brethren in kindness to sympathise with, and promptness to relieve, the distresses of others" (51). Or again, a parent's love for his child is portrayed as disinterested, rather than selfish, for that "partiality" is in fact impartial, occasioned by "qualities visible to an impartial bystander as really to ourselves" (114). Plus, the "generosity" that parental love "breathes is its greatest charm" (351). Similarly, a child's love for his parent is the result of a "negotiation," not an obligation, something to be "courted, not compelled," and exists "in proportion as I shall have done something to deserve it" (115). In other words, love of family is valuable because it exercises a member's affections, but that affection should not be reserved exclusively for one's family.

Descriptions in *Fleetwood* of family and parental feeling are intensified because of the thematic focus on surrogate families, but they too define a person's feeling for family as establishing a relation to the public. The Rousseauistic Ruffigny instructs Fleetwood about the legitimate objects of family feeling by recounting to him Fleetwood's father's rationale for treating Ruffigny as his son: "Are all the kindnesses of the human heart to be shut up within the paltry limits of consanguinity? . . . You are my son, a son whom the concourse of sublunary events has given me, no less dear to me than the heir of my body" (122). A second passage extends the reach of family feeling around the globe, construing the "lively and ardent affection of an Englishman to his son" not only as disinterested but "as if it were directed toward the child of a Japanese" (163). Such passages acquire special significance in light of this text's quite skeptical treatment of heterosexual love as embodied in the relation between Fleetwood and Mary. While Fleetwood is similar to St. Leon in being unable to sustain marital happiness, the truly bizarre characterizations of Fleetwood's relation to Mary render all the more curious the penchant to view this phase of Godwin's writing as retracting his strictures against marriage.

Because St. Leon, with his unlimited resources and time, is literally extraordinary, his resistance to marriage can be construed as peculiar, and aberrant, on two grounds. His adventures are outside the ordinary, even the human, suggesting that his history is singular, not representative. To the extent that his adventures are portrayed as class-specific, they pertain to the nobility, the honor of which Godwin (here and elsewhere) usually portrays as divisive and delusive. In *St. Leon* male honor is explicitly pitted against female sentiment, a contest that the mysterious stranger uses to his advantage in persuading St. Leon to become party to his secret. According to this logic, which opposes feudal to bourgeois conceptions of marriage, by "confiding" in his wife, St. Leon foregoes his claims to the titles of "knight" and "Frenchman" and becomes instead the "basest of all sublunary things—the puppet of a woman."[47] Since St. Leon's captivation both by honor and magic are judged as moral failings in the text, his failure in marriage is an indictment of him, not necessarily of marriage or the possibility or desirability of heterosexual love. It is left for *Fleetwood; or, The New Man of Feeling* to associate the failure with marriage itself. Set in the age of sensibility and introducing a hero whose "adventures have occurred to at least one half of the Englishmen now existing, who are of the same rank of life," *Fleetwood* depicts bourgeois companionate marriages as even less likely than feudal alliances to result in marital harmony (13).

Fleetwood has been read as testifying for the defense in *Wrongs of Woman*, especially the necessity for divorce, by making the case through the perspective of the offending party.[48] In this, it joins the Jacobin novel, characterized by its varying critiques of despotism and, like *Wrongs*, positions the critique in relation to sentiment and feeling.[49] But whereas most Jacobin novels, including *Wrongs*, justify their support of adultery or divorce on the grounds of preserving and fostering a woman's sensibility, *Fleetwood* uses Fleetwood's paranoid suspicions regarding Mary's infidelity to suggest that sensibility itself is what undermines marriage. Or at least sensibility as it plays out in men. Recall that Mary is neither physically nor mentally unfaithful to Fleetwood—indeed, she is presented as a model wife. Yet something about her drives Fleetwood not only to denounce her and disinherit their child but, in a truly grotesque scene, to assemble on the anniversary of their marriage life-sized wax effigies of Mary and her presumed lover, Kenrick, dining together with a cradle in the background and a barrel organ playing the songs that they had once sung together, in the early days of their love.[50] The something about her that is said to "corrod[e]" Fleetwood's "vitals" is the sheer separateness of Mary's mind and being.[51] This independence is not portrayed as a feminist-style assertion of rights but merely as the expression of whims—to inhabit a certain room, meet a friend, attend a dance—that are experienced as an affront not so much to her husband's commands as to his habits of mind and daily routines (292–95, 212).[52] And this corrodibility is ascribed to Fleetwood's extreme sensitivity, fostered by his Rousseauistic upbringing in nature and reverie, which is said to "inspire a certain propensity to despotism" (19). What a man of feeling cannot bear, according to this text, is the insurmountable alterity of an other, not an other who confronts him with radical difference but who is at once most *like* him but yet still separate from him—literally, his other self—and whose daily actions, habits, and modes of thinking continually remind him of this fact of separation. For, left to its own devices—that is, unchecked by reason or justice—sensibility blocks, rather than facilitates, the "going out of the heart" that expands sympathy and thus the sphere of one's relations. When sensibility moves outward, it moves in the groove established by the reciprocal influence of reflection and feeling, which necessarily always leads back to the self. Such tracking makes any marriage a "bastille" that keeps individuals from pursuing their inner promptings.

Modifying this propensity, oddly, is the value that *Fleetwood* accords the family, here portrayed as the mechanism that ensures that individuals learn to bear the proximity of others. Still, this value of family works best if family members are related not by blood but instead by the "concourse of sublunary events," which is more likely to "cast" hearts "in the same mould" (122, 135). Daily interaction with others weakens the irritability that characterizes persons of sensibility, raised in isolation and experiencing every "cross accident" as a "usurpation" of their rights because "the sensitiveness of my temper will never allow me to bear to be thwarted, crossed, the chain of my sensations snapped and crumbled to pieces at every moment, with impunity" (201). Theoretically, "accommodation" happens over the course of a long marriage, but the longevity of a marriage is in inverse proportion to the degree of sensitivity that each partner exhibits upon entering the marriage (202). *Fleet-wood* specifies why: "No man can completely put himself in the place of another, and conceive how he would feel, were the circumstances of that other his own: few can do it even in a superficial degree. We are so familiar with our own trains of thinking: we revolve them with such complacency: it appears to us, that there is so astonishing a perverseness in not seeing things as we see them! The step is short and inevitable from complacency in our own views, to disapprobation and distaste toward the views of him by whom we are thwarted" (196). The best counter to this perversity is familiarity, seeing things in common from the start. It just so happens that gaining this familiarity usually occurs in a family, but it can happen within any set of individuals if the process begins early enough.

Reading together, then, stands in a complicated relation to this project. Undertaken with the young, who provide a "ductile and yielding substance," it helps to develop mutual trains of thinking that keep minds on the same page.[53] With adult partners, the process is more difficult, unless at least one partner has the mind of a child. Otherwise, each remains attached to his or her private associations triggered by the rereading of books. In "An Early Taste for Reading," Godwin specifies that if a taste for reading develops too late, the reader will "never [be] admitted into the familiarity of a friend" with an author, owing to the "previous obstinacy and untractableness" of the mind (*Enquirer*, 96). *Fleetwood* explores the trouble that ensues when two now-adult early readers try to get on the same page through reading. For success depends on each partner being able to maintain his or her autonomy in the reading relation, which also means not having his or her particular friendship with a given author thwarted by the partner's equally strong associations to him. Strikingly, *Fleetwood* attributes each fissure in Fleetwood's and Mary's marital harmony to scenarios associated with reading. The first disruption occurs when Mary desires to take as her own room Fleetwood's boyhood reading closet, his "favourite retreat," where he had conned his first lessons and ever since "retire[d] with some favourite author, when I wished to feel my mind in its most happy state" (194). This breach occurs on the very day that they first enter Fleetwood's "paternal mansion" at Merionethshire, a day characterized by Fleetwood as "in some sense," the "first of our marriage" and the place described as the setting for "habits, of which it would be difficult for me to divest myself," in part because they had never had to be negotiated with other living beings before now (194). This breach is widened beyond repair on the second day, when, after dinner, "I proposed reading with Mary a play of my favourite Fletcher," his "admirable" *Wife for a Month* (198).

The "experiment" begins happily enough, with Mary "seem[ing] to enter strongly into the feelings of the poet," and "agree[ing] with me" about the excellence of Fletcher's characterizations and use of the English language (198). The "pleasure" intensifies in the second act, as Mary is "roused to an extraordinary degree" by various "exhortations" such that she could "scarcely help starting from her chair" (199), when all at once the climax of plot and sensation is interrupted by the arrival of a neighboring peasant boy whom Mary had engaged on the previous day to serve as her guide on a botanical walk and "away" with whom "she tripped" (199). This interruption, which is presented as a type of coitus interruptus, has a devastating effect on Fleetwood and his esteem for Mary: "Is this the woman," he ruminates, "whom I have taken as the partner of my life, who is more interested in two or three blades of grass, or a wretched specimen of mosses, than in the most pathetic tale or the noblest sentiments? If she has no respect for the illustrious dead, who cannot feel her contempt, methinks she might have had some for me, whose heart still beats, and whose blood continues to flow. Oh, it is plain she cares only for herself" (201). He relents for a moment when he considers what Mary's love for nature indicates about her character, even vowing to "turn botanist my-self," but cannot sustain this new resolution because it entails such a violation of himself. "No, I will not go to her! . . . She has wounded me in a point, where I am most alive. . . . I could be content to yield much to her.—Ay, again I say, God bless her in her caprices!—But I cannot be content to be reduced to nothing. I must have an existence, a pursuit, a system of my own; and not be a mere puppy, dangling at her heels, and taught to fetch and carry, as she gives the word" (201–2).

On one level, of course, this treatment of Fleetwood's reaction, like the text's treatment of Fleetwood generally, is not endorsed. His overreaction is one of the clearest signs of Fleetwood's self-absorption, his inability to bear the proximity and therefore also the distance of others, an inability that extends to his con/fusion of a dead author with a live reader (201). Nor does Fleetwood himself justify his reaction: "The reader must recollect my character, as an old bachelor, as a man endowed with the most irritable structure of nerves, and who from infancy had always felt contradiction with inexpressible bitterness, to conceive how much I was disturbed with this pelting and pitiful incident" (200). Yet the text not only carefully analyzes the feeling but also presents Fleetwood's reaction as generic in two senses. It is portrayed as familiar to any "reader who has had experience of the married life" and can "easily feel how many vexations a man stored up for himself, who felt so acutely these trivial thwartings and disappointments" (202). Or, as the preface has already an-nounced, "there are few of the married tribe who have not at some time or other had certain small misunderstandings with their wives:—to be sure, they have not all of them felt and acted under these trite adventures as my hero does" (13–14). Second, it is shown to be characteristic of sensibility generally and, more importantly, of *men* who are schooled by sentiment to consider their feelings the relevant grounds of reality and of literary interpretation.

Godwin's suggestion in *Fleetwood*, that sensibility fosters, rather than counters, marital despotism, expresses his disagreement with how *The Wrongs of Woman; or, Maria* proposes to ameliorate woman's fate: by defending divorce on the grounds of preserving a woman's sensibility and by advocating reform of the literary canon to include the voices and experiences of women. *Fleetwood* carries Wollstonecraft's gendered critique of Rousseau to a new level by implying that those who conduct marriage according to the dictates of sensibility will feel themselves "bastilled" by any marriage, whether they are women or men. Emphasizing the literature of sensibility is one function of the second half of the title, whose claim to update Henry Mackenzie's reworking of Rousseau in *The Man of Feeling* (1771) sheds little light on the narrative proper except to accentuate its lineage in sensibility. Moreover, its focus on "man" when the plot borrowings that stem from Mackenzie come from *Julia de Roubigné* (1777) suggests that Godwin is concerned with the gender more than the species. For Fleetwood as a character does not merely dramatize what the fragmented endings of *Wrongs* suggest—that Darnford cannot live up to the areality of St. Preux. As book, *Fleetwood; or The New Man of Feeling* positions the novel of sensibility at the end of a literary line whose take on marriage, especially the correlation between self-actualization and companionate marriage, has rendered men and women unhappier than they were in the unsentimental arrangements of former times. Making this point seems to motivate the particular endpoint given to St. Leon's lack of progress through the sixteenth to the eighteenth centuries, whereby the age of sentiment proves a dead end. If we are tempted to take seriously the hope embodied in his son Charles' companionate marriage to Perdita on the last page of this novel, *Fleetwood* steps in to dash it.[54]

The reading scene in *Fleetwood* can be read as a corrective to the companion scene in *Wrongs of Woman*, with *Wrongs* highlighting reading's role in initiating love and *Fleetwood* its role in terminating it—a point announced in the title of the second couple's choice of text, *A Wife for a Month*. By referencing Fletcher, *Fleetwood* shifts the focus to the act of reading when informed by male sensibility. For while Mary's walking out on the reading scene on one level expresses her sheer otherness to Fleetwood, on another level it enacts a rejection of his assumption that she is fused with him—especially when it comes to her reading—though his assumption that they should be fused is ratified generally by the world of his reading. This scene is fraught with tension from the start. Some relates to the anxiety that arises from never knowing for certain what another is feeling, especially in moments of closeness. "She *seemed* to enter strongly into the feelings of the poet" (198). But more stems from the fact that only one party is directing the reading and that all the authorities on it are male. "After dinner *I* proposed reading with Mary a play of *my* favourite Fletcher." "She *agreed with me* that no poet of ancient or modern times, *as far as her acquaintance with them extended,* was able" to give such a lively picture of male heroism. We "coincided in opinion with Dryden" about the excellence of Fletcher's use of the English language. Though we have "no need of words," when we "have recourse to their aid, I instruct at once, *and am* instructed" (198–99). The reading intensifies its imposition on woman once Fleetwood claims to be reading the text on Mary's face. "I read the sentiments of the royal speaker" in the "animated eye and glowing cheek of the charmer who sat beside me." "I was delighted with the effect of my experiment. . . . It is a pleasure that should be husbanded" (199).

To the extent that we read Mary's textual *interruptus* as intentional, this is a remarkably feminist scene that, on the one hand, goes beyond even Wollstonecraft in decrying the gender asymmetries that mark a couple's reading life and, on the other, marks the only sphere in which any of Godwin's novels affirm the rights of women. Otherwise, his novels grant little sympathy or, with the exception of *Deloraine,* narrative space to the situation of women. They never characterize a woman engaged in public service, nor are they ever narrated from a female point of view. It is as if these novels cannot yet imagine and thus inhabit the mind of a woman who has thinking powers. The inability seems related to Godwin's marked preference for composing novels of romance over sentiment, a preference visible as well in his positive ascription of "nobility" to feelings tied to domesticity even in novels set in the eighteenth century (especially in *Cloudesley*). It is linked as well to his eventual endorsement of chivalry, developed during composition of *Life of Chaucer,* and his retreat from pursuing gender equality after 1799.[55] *St. Leon* is the last text to entertain as a serious hypothesis the notion that a wife and "consort" should be an equal.

Yet this assessment of a failure of imagination in Godwin's representation of female characters can cut a different way. For one thing, Godwin's chief project in his novels is reform of male character, the necessity of which reform is linked to the severity of the problem understood in virtually every text. Each focuses on a particular passion that unmans its protagonist—curiosity in *Caleb Williams* and *St. Leon*, jealousy in *Fleetwood, Cloudesley, Deloraine*, paranoia in *Mandeville*, remorse in *Deloraine*.[56] Taken together, the verdict seems to be that men have major problems connecting. In this regard, we might say that Godwin continues to work with Wollstonecraft as an authorial team, employing a novelistic division of labor along gender lines. Perhaps, too, Godwin is taking up Wollstonecraft's implicit challenge to Rousseau to get working on a new Abelard for the woman with thinking powers also in the making. A second qualification is that these novels are *staging* men's failures at relating in order to direct some much-needed attention to the problem. They suggest that women would do well to follow Mary in turning their backs on male attempts at literary entrapment.

A brief look at how the novels consigned to the period of "Oblivion" depict marriage underscores the persistence with which Godwin connects advances in women's status and marital possibilities to advances in the literary domain. At first glance, these later novels appear to represent a marked retreat from Wollstonecraft's in their conventional affirmations of sexual difference. *Deloraine* asserts that men and women are "two different species of being; or at least the distinction of sex divides us no less effectually" and stipulates that they are separate and unequal: "Man is the substantive thing in the terrestrial creation; woman is but the adjective, that cannot stand by itself" (14, 29). These accounts are often supplemented by highly traditional, and idealized, descriptions of marriage. "I invite her to enter into my soul, and to possess the 'crown and hearted throne of my love.' We are truly united; she is 'bone of my bone, and flesh of my flesh'; and for this obvious cause 'shall a man leave father and mother,' comparatively estrange him from all other living things, 'and cleave to his wife' " (14). But these assertions are not only voiced by male characters whose moral characters are presented as suspect; they are also presented as perceptions filtered through conventions of romance and sentiment. The narrator, Meadows, in *Cloudesley*, admits that he saw in his beloved Isabella "all that I had painted to myself of an angel, a celestial missionary. . . . The lambent fire that played in those eyes had no alloy of any thing gross or of a frailer sort. It was wholly unearthly" (26). Arthur asserts of Irene sentiments that Deloraine voices about his beloved wife, Emilia: "Beauty never appears so beautiful, as when it is under the dominion of sorrow. Beauty, in its hour of exultation and pride, has a tendency to arm the spectator against its inroad and usurpation. . . . But beauty in sorrow . . . no longer defies us to conquer its prowess. It is the weak and tender flower, illustrious in its lowliness, that asks for a friendly hand to raise its drooping head" (79; see *Deloraine*, 91, 10, 90). Even then, both novels admit how far short of the ideal even good marriages fall, and the narrator in *Cloudesley* articulates why. When men are in love, "we ascribe to the favoured she the most unparalleled and super-human excellencies. But, if we enter into the engagement deliberately and in cool blood, we well know that it is a compromise"—a compromise, moreover, composed of two facts. First, "The creature that our exalted imagination has figured to us, does not exist on the face of the earth." Second, "of those that do exist, only a small number are accessible to us, or are such as we have the smallest chance to win to favour our addresses." Consequently, "we contentedly give up some of the qualifications we should have desired in the partner of our life, and accept of such as are within our reach" (43). Deloraine highlights the inverse problem: "I never have the imagination that we can have separate interests" (13).

The supposition that Godwin is criticizing, rather than endorsing, conventional courtship patterns and ascribing their popularity to romance literature is strengthened if we consider the curious choices of book that his couples read in the process of sealing their love, books that are always brought to his beloved by the male suitor. As we have seen, Fleetwood somehow deems the most appropriate text for his posthoneymoon outing with Mary the "admirable" *Wife for a Month*, a title that seems to stipulate the desired length of a marriage. (The title actually refers to a bargain struck between the evil king, Frederick, and noble Valerio, by which Valerio agrees to be executed at the end of the month if in the meantime he can enjoy sex with his wife, Evanthe.) In the event, Fletcher's Evanthe gets a better deal than Godwin's Mary, whose marital bliss, once she has wounded her husband "in the point where he is most alive," is over by day two. Subsequent choices of courtship texts predict even worse fates for the woman. In *Cloudesley*, Arthur is said to court Irene through the "story of Bireno and Olimpia in the Orlando Furioso," a tale that "at first sight" might seem "little appropriate to his suit to Irene." "Proving himself the falsest and most worthless of his sex, he [Bireno], instead of conducting his mistress in safety to the place of their destination, . . . left her to be devoured by wild beasts, or to fall into the hands of savage freebooters" (81). Later, Arthur's brother (the central protagonist of *Cloudesley*) not only identifies as the distinguishing trait of "lover" someone "perhaps always prone to adopt the character of a relator and an historian" but also explicitly models himself on Othello in his courtship of Selina: "She loved me for the dangers I had passed, / And I loved her, that she did pity them" (113).

It is hard to say exactly what Godwin had in mind by foregrounding these texts as part of a male lover's courtship ritual. At the least, they offer warnings that marriage is hazardous, more often than not damsels are distressed by their romance heroes, and a long history of writing has both naturalized and sentimentalized male betrayals. Perhaps they level a generic critique: happy marriages are delusions of sentiment; tragedy tells a more realistic story. Or again, forewarned is forearmed; start taking more seriously the lessons that classic love stories deliver. Specific references to *Othello*, one of Godwin's favorite texts, suggest that, like Wollstonecraft, he conceived literary texts as at once reinforcing constraints on women and offering possible escape routes. *Othello* not only stages the predictable outcome of jealousy, murder of the woman, but also jealousy's favored means to fuel its passion: fabrication (a process strikingly depicted in the wax effigies in *Fleetwood*). By foregrounding protagonists in the throes of jealousy, Godwin's novels recognize sexual love as a major impediment to that "going out of heart" that links attachment to the pursuit of justice. Hard enough for any parent to foster that "going out of heart" in one's child, it is virtually impossible for a spouse to facilitate the natural curiosity or adventurousness of one's partner. As *Deloraine* asserts, the death of one's lover is far preferable to having to witness her desire to be elsewhere. A second insight associated with *Othello* offers a productive route toward reform: tell stories that open out new horizons and initiate transport to wider worlds.

This seems to be the function ascribed to marriage in *Cloudesley* and *Deloraine*, although they divide up the route that *Othello* considers together. The union between Irene and Arthur in *Cloudesley* explores attraction to racial difference, whereas Deloraine's two marriages foreground the transports resulting from story. In *Cloudesley*, the "happiest consequences" are expected from bringing together within the "compass of one family" citizens from "the most eminent and highly endowed nation of ancient" and of "modern" times— Greece and England. This is because their union disrupts the tendency "for different races to sequester themselves in a sort of sullen disunion from each other"; whereas "benevolence prescribed, and improvement required, that this supine monotony should be abolished, that the prejudices of different tribes should be brought into collision, and their various accomplishments made to encounter and combine, for the common advantage" (83). *Deloraine* returns to the topic of coupled reading and ascribes unprecedented agency to the female partner in the literary domain of marriage. The text states that, precisely because of the difference between the sexes and, implicitly, the effacement of this difference by the literary critical tradition, evaluative input from both

genders is necessary before any pronouncement on a work of art is "consummate." Indeed, input from the woman is deemed superior. "In the female
bosom in particular, there is a quickness, a truth, an intuition of feeling and
taste, by which I was specially the gainer, and with which no individual of the
sterner sex may ever hope to compete" (18). While the qualities ascribed to the
"female bosom" appear essentialist and conventionally "feminine" (though
also conventional traits of genius), they are also portrayed as essential to an
accurate assessment of books and to the comprehension of human character.
What distinguishes Deloraine and his first wife, Emilia, as a couple is their
"advantage in studying the inmost recesses of human character, which perhaps
no other human creatures ever possessed in an equal degree" (19). This is
because Emilia reads in the manner of Wollstonecraft—with a "quickness, a
truth, an intuition of feeling and taste, by which I was specially the gainer"—
and because their conversations are characterized by the "most perfect unreserve" (18, 19).

This assertion of hetero-ality in *Deloraine* has its heterosexist and hetero-
normative elements. Still, it is an achievement that marks both a nonhomo-
phobic limit to Godwin's general idealization of male-male friendship and a
nonsexist advantage in advocating women's right to declare on works of literature. *Deloraine* is exceptional as a Godwinian novel in granting not only
significant narrative space to women but also thinking powers to at least two
of them. *Deloraine* is the only one of Godwin's novels that characterizes a
woman as a writer, a fact about Emilia that we only discover after she dies. "I
doted on the desk at which she had been accustomed to write, and the inkstand
which had afforded her a medium for recording her thoughts. . . . Her hand-
writing to my eyes was the masterpiece of the creation" (32–33). In marked
contrast to Mary in *Fleetwood*, women in *Deloraine* are active parties in the
reading scenes. Emphasis is on mutuality, not imposition, and how partnership
transforms work into pleasure.

> To the solitary reader his books are indeed a dead letter. To feel that the
> conceptions and images imparted to the mind from the unliving and uncon-
> scious page strike at once on the sensorium of two, enhances the gratification
> tenfold. The eyes of both parties meet. A smile of approbation, or a glance of
> censure springs up on either side, and gives new life to their common occupa-
> tion. . . . When a difficulty presents itself to a solitary reader, he either slurs it
> over with indolence, or he investigates it with a sullen perseverance, stripped of
> the true intellectual charm. But, when two persons bring together the force of

their combined intellect, and contribute the stores of their several observation and experience, while even the difference of their humours and temperament sensibly adds to the light collected in the common focus, then the question is pursued honestly and in good faith, and neither party lays aside the weapons of his warfare, till he has achieved a common victory over the difficulty towards which their efforts had been directed. (236–37)

A model of scholarly collaboration, the passage goes on to stipulate the erotic payoff of such pursuits. "Sometimes, too, with our graver studies and more serious disquisitions we would intermix 'grateful digressions, and solve high dispute' with sportive interruption, and [conjugal] caresses" (237, 17; also *Fleetwood*, 299–300). In other words, textual study leads to sexual dalliance, and literature elicits both.

Invoking this citation, which occurs twice in this text, is not without hazard, since referencing *Paradise Lost* evokes an entire history of associating woman with sin, fallenness, and illicit desires for knowledge. Here, however, Godwin invokes Western culture's originary parents to affirm instead a relation among knowledge, couple-life, and sexual-textual pleasure—a quite stunning assertion of the role of reading in the origins of life. In this rescripting, he pursues what Bahar describes as Wollstonecraft's characteristic approach to Eve in focusing on her "postlapsarian" struggles "with worldly cares," thereby responding to the "word in [his] ear" dropped long ago in a letter to him, wherein Wollstonecraft promises "not [to] be very angry if you sweeten grammatical disquisitions after the Miltonic mode."[57] *Deloraine*, then, extends this revision of Eve as scholar to women writers and readers and suggests how to loosen the stranglehold of the literary tradition on them. One route appears to circumvent the tradition altogether through recourse to nature; another disrupts the "all the world" of books by having them read by a couple whose all-the-worldness to each other loosens the confines of both domains.

The first route is associated with Emilia, the "late incomparable companion" of Deloraine's early days, who is said to have a "truly original mind." "She was naturally learned; she studied not the world through 'the spectacle of books,' or the teachings of her instructors; . . . *She was in this respect as if there had been no such thing as literature*" (33, emphasis added). The emphasis on "intuitive discernment," though problematic in dissociating woman and reason, guarantees her independence from tradition, written authorities, and ensures that "all her conclusions were her own" (33). This echoes Wollstonecraft's proposals in "On Poetry" (not to mention those in Wordsworth's "Preface to *Lyrical Ballads*") to revivify a world that has been deadened through a literary writing so congealed that it produces "men of stone; insipid figures, that never convey to the mind" the "idea" of "life."[58] In *Deloraine*, Emilia's originality lies in this rejection of servility. And when this type of thinker talks or writes, the world is "sure to hear from her something new; new in the substance of what she reported, or new in the manner in which she saw the things she described" (33).

The second way underscores a new benefit of coupled reading, by which reading together allows each partner to gain some distance on the text. That one is reading not only the author's words but also one's partner's reaction to them means that one is detached from the narrative, witnessing as well a critical (and gender-differentiated) perspective on it. This process externalizes the dynamic interplay between books and readers who, in pursuing trains of thought other than those of the author they are also reading, preserve a measure of agency and autonomy that keeps them from blindly repeating the same old love plot or features of homicidal heroism. Moreover, rereading when alone a text that had formerly been read with one's beloved re-evokes his or her presence and serves as the medium through which now-separated lovers reunite. "If they read, they each imagined the other to be at hand, and did not so much consider how the reflections and paintings of the author affected themselves, as how they would be received by the other" (45).

It is tempting to read these passages autobiographically, as expressing what Godwin prized most in marital relations and what he lost in losing Wollstone-craft, a partner with whom he studied "the inmost recesses of the human character," the capacity of doing so "which perhaps no other human creatures ever possessed in an equal degree." They also suggest how Wollstonecraft stayed alive for him after all these years in his ongoing commerce with books—whether with those she wrote, those he wrote about or in collaboration with her, or those that they read or discussed together. Such depictions cannot be fully appreciated apart from consideration of Godwin's mourning practices, a topic explored more fully in chapters 2 and 5. They also must be viewed as part of an intense dialogue with Shelley's later novels and as Godwin's belated homage to Shelley's eventual mourning of Percy. But in the current context, as depicting the role of reading in strengthening women's agency in marriage, *Deloraine* adds a surprising twist to the exploration in *Othello* of pathological jealousy. Here homicide is the outcome of Deloraine's jealousy over his second wife, Margaret's, prior history of couple-reading, one that not only excludes him but also occasioned "conjugal caresses" between her and another partner.

Actually, imagined caresses are not the major problem. For while, as her husband, he now possesses "her body, all outward duty, honour and observance," he knows that "her mind was another's," that is, William's, her first love and the partner of her earliest shared reading (138, 106, 45).

The only solution to the remorse that threatens to corrode Deloraine's vitals after he murders William comes through the literal fruit of his textual-sexual commerce with Emilia, his daughter Catherine, who ultimately heals his mind. Not only is Catherine an embodiment of Emilia ("The mind of Catherine was . . . full of sensibility and taste [237]) but she takes her mother's place in the shared-reading relation. A striking repetition of *Matilda*, in which daughter Mathilda is conflated with her dead mother, Diana, and requested by her father to pick up the reading of Dante "at the place where [his wife / her mother] left off," this father-daughter coupled-reading scenario is a first in Godwin's novels. Even more striking, *Deloraine* avows but domesticates the incestuous overtones by altering only slightly descriptions of their reaction to shared reading. "Sometimes too with our graver studies and more serious disquisitions we would intermix 'grateful digressions, and solve high dispute' with sportive interruption, and affectionate caresses, such as might best beseem the father and his daughter" (273).

The role that Shelley's comprehension of textual incest plays in Godwin's version (and final admission) of the topic must await exposition of Shelley's novels in chapter 3. For now, my main point is that these final novels do not radically revise Godwin's position on marriage and domestic affection and that, while less interested in championing equality between the sexes generally, they esteem both wives and daughters as full reading partners. This is the sphere in which Godwin's women are granted agency and autonomy, even as that sphere is shown to bear a complicated relation to both qualities. Echoes of *Othello* in *Deloraine* suggest as much, as do the lines ascribing originality to Emilia. For the same passage that states how she communicates "as if there had been no such thing as literature" is the most densely citational of any in all of his works. The "immedia[cy]" of her communication rests on this evidence: there "was to her no medium, no 'seeing as through a glass darkly' " or "through 'the spectacle of books.' " Her talk was "not a lesson, 'learned and conned by rote; set in a note-book' "; her letters, however "evanescent," were "precious to me" for "contain[ing] some fragment of the soul of this 'divine perfection of a woman' "; hers was "prompt eloquence, a rapid and unimpeded stream, 'more tuneable than needed lute or harp to add more sweetness.' It was a stream that enlivened its banks, while 'with fresh flowerets field and valley smiled.'" In brief, "she was indeed and in truth, 'fancy's child,' while to your astonished sense she 'warbled her native woodnotes wild'" (33–34). It would be hard to miss the point that there is no unwritten space available from which to begin anew, even for women. A more liveable strategy would involve expanding the province, meanings, and associations of words so that they do not prove so confining.

Poor Reception

> [Godwin's] folly in thus making himself a mark for abuse is incon-
> ceivable. Come kick me—is his eternal language. Yet is the man a
> good creature—brimfull of benevolence—as kind hearted as a
> child would wish.
>
> Robert Southey, 17 August 1801

Godwin's novels did not so much fundamentally alter his reservations regarding the domestic affections as probe them by questioning the nature and consequence of human attachments. His are some of the most profoundly skeptical treatments of cohabitation on record and are useful precisely in showcasing how the cult of the bourgeois individual, particularly in its possessiveness about its associations, makes marriage a pathology-producing proposition. The next chapter explores Godwin's alternatives to domestic affection, his calculations of the optimum distance required between persons to circumvent the "excessive familiarity" that makes domesticity despotic for all its members. But Godwin's engagement with this topic, particularly during the years between 1797 and 1805, when he was fighting to salvage his reputation, taught him valuable lessons about the importance of avowing love for family if one wanted to maintain viability as a public intellectual and about the vehement resistance that publics show to those who seek to divulge family secrets. In the public eye, such activity discredited an individual from the humanity that he deemed himself in the service of perfecting. One general difficulty with sustaining a revolutionary vision is that, by definition, one is out in front and therefore without hope of immediate support. Godwin's struggles on this score were especially intense because they pitted against each other two of his most crucial tenets—integrity and a self-postponing self. For while integrity remained central to his conceptions of autonomy and sincerity, it came to be ascribed to a truth (and a self) growing ever more provisional. The difficulty of maintaining this position, especially when the public read it as rendering him at once inhumane and nonhuman, is visible in the enervation characteristic of his increasingly isolated protagonists. But during this period, when he was still struggling to retain a public to reform and affront, he tried a variety of tactics to regain their esteem.

By 1798, because of his status as "one of the most hated men in the country," whose name (along with Wollstonecraft's) was synonymous with atheism, treason, adultery, bigamy, licentiousness, and infanticide, Godwin faced a daunting task.[59] To the extent that he met it by publishing more positive feelings for family, marriage, and children, he occasioned a further charge of inconsistency. Relatively speaking, this charge was easy enough for Godwin to dismiss, since, compared to other notorious apostates of the time, his change of heart was tame. "Not that I see cause to make any change respecting the principle of justice, or any thing else fundamental to the system there delivered" (*St. Leon*, 11). Still, at times he conceded the change while browbeating the opposition into admitting their small-mindedness in leveling the charge. "Some readers of my graver productions will perhaps . . . accuse me of inconsistency." "In answer to this objection, all I think it necessary to say on the present occasion, is . . ." (11). "Certain persons, who condescend to make my supposed inconsistencies the favourite object of their research, will perhaps remark with exultation on the respect expressed in this work for marriage" (*Fleetwood*, 14). More fundamentally, he made "the alleged demerit of inconsistency" the measure of honest enquiry, the sign that the writer is motivated by truth, not self-concern. The "cheapest plan for acquiring reputation" consists in "conforming ourselves to the prejudices of others," whereas the "active and independent mind" will "inevitably pass through certain revolutions of opinion" (*Enquirer*, 220, 195, 220; also 207).

Attacks on his humaneness and humanity were harder to handle, for they "wound[ed]" him "at the point where he is most alive." In general, Godwin served the cause of (his) humanity by redefining justice as an issue of morality that is uncoupled from religion, state sanctions, or sentimentality. This entails altering fundamental tenets of humanity, which in turn requires honest inquiry into those dark "secrets of the heart" that compose the subject and object of his fictional and nonfictional thoughts on man. Yet these thoughts estrange him from his public and prompt him to question the advisability of "expos[ing] one's] character to the world," especially when "for the most part it is a disclosure made to enemies."[60] Some of his attempts to address this paradox mark the limits to Godwin's detachment and impersonality, as he strives to vindicate himself as a family man. "Good God! And so you heard me gravely represented in a large company yesterday as an advocate of infanticide." "To come immediately to the point in question: Am I, or am I not, a lover of children?"[61] Others flaunt both traits by stressing how he "stands alone" while other former "champions of the French Revolution" are now "floating" on a self-interested "tide."[62] His most extensive public attempt to counter the "flood of ribaldry, invective and intolerance which has been poured out against me and my writings," his "Thoughts Occasioned by the Perusal of Dr. Parr's Spital Sermon [of April 15, 1800]," shows the depth of his woundedness and his apparent attraction to it (165).[63] For at the same time that Godwin aims to clarify his support for the domestic affections (once again requoting the preface to *St. Leon*, among other things), he invites renewed attacks.

"Thoughts Occasioned by the Perusal" is truly impressive in the number of ways that Godwin hoists himself on his own petard. Affirming that he has stood firm while most have capitulated, he also confesses his errors without actually portraying them as errors. Expression of his concession, that in *Political Justice* he underestimated the positive motive force behind filial affection, only strengthens the impression of his antipathy to it. "The most ignorant parent, whose lips were never refreshed from the well of knowledge" will "scarcely ever fail to love his child," even though said child "should be an idiot, deformed and odious to the sight; or imbued with the basest and most hateful propensities." Indeed, that parent "will perhaps rather consent that millions should perish, than that this miserable union of his dotage should suffer a moment's displeasure." In brief, "I do not regard a parent of this sort with any strong feeling of approbation" (182–83). Nor, unstoppably, "do I regard a newborn child with any superstitious reverence. . . . I had rather such a child should perish at the first hour of its existence, than that a man should spend seventy years of life in a state of misery and vice" (199). Besides, infanticide is "an expedient perfectly adequate to the end for which it has been cited" and, moreover, more humane than the situation "in this country," where children are "half destroyed by neglect" and "perish miserably without any chance of approaching maturity" (200, 203).

The experience of publicly reconsidering his position on domestic affection apparently reconvinced Godwin of its initial justice, although it converted few others. The *British Critic* retitled the essay "The History of the Rise, Decline, and Fall of a second-hand Sophister, who, after having written himself into some notoriety, by stolen paradoxes, has written himself down by original nonsense."[64] But Godwin's specification within those "Thoughts" of how acknowledging the "beauty and utility" of the domestic affections affects the case of "Fénelon and his valet" introduces two considerations that prove fundamental to subsequent thoughts on man and revisions of the interrelation between writing and truth. First, Godwin exposes as "deception" the assumption of Dr. Parr and his supporters that, "if the father is saved, this will be the effort of passion," whereas "if Fenelon is saved, the act" arises from "cool, phlegmatic, arithmetical calculation" rather than, as is truly the case, equally from passion, but passion in the service of "improvement of millions" rather than self-preservation (187). Second, Godwin admits as his one serious miscalculation his own assumption that the merit of a writer is self-evident to the British public. "If I had put the case of Brutus," "if I had put the case of Bonaparte," rather than of the writer-philosopher Fénelon, "few persons" would have experienced "any difficulty in deciding" to save the public benefactor over a family member (187–88). But "the benefit to accrue from the writing of books is too remote an idea, to strike and fill the imagination" and thus the "prejudices and habits of men" prejudge in favor of saving one's parent (187). Now *this* really wounds him at the point where he is most alive.

Oddly, both of these considerations re-emerge in his *Essay on Sepulchres* (1809), a text that teaches survivors to acquire the "craft" of compelling the earth to "give up its dead alive," in part by redefining what is cold and making the case for writers as a nation's truest benefactors. Meanwhile, what this experience caused him seriously to rethink was the easy transfer posited in the *Enquiry concerning Political Justice* between writing and truth. This process he now conceived as a topic *for* enquiry, not the unproblematic grounds of it, for, as his relations with the public prove, positive reception of writing is in inverse proportion to the singularity of its truth. Plus, print as the medium of enlightenment impedes one of the chief features of Godwinian truth —mutability, revisability, change as one's circumstances change one's ideas. Growing insight into the intransigence of print, let alone print culture, troubled Godwin's writing, his confidence regarding the future effected through writing, and the projected future of his own writing. It influenced the advice he offered would-be reformers, like the young Percy Shelley, against rushing not only into action but also into print. "I see no necessary connection between writing and publishing, and least of all with one's name. The life of a thinking man who does this, will be made up of a series of Retractions. . . . I have myself, with all my caution, felt some of the effects of this."[65] This is deeply hard-won but finally ineffectual advice, because it pits one truth—write but do not publish—against another—revise public opinion before instituting change. It also addresses precisely the audience whose heedlessness of such advice is central to their efficacy. For radicals are known to rush in where wiser men fear to tread. It's just that when they do so at the wiser man's presumed invitation, no one is sure where he stands.

CHAPTER TWO

Forms of Attachment

The portrayals of domestic arrangements in the novels of Wollstonecraft and Godwin are valuable for posing as a relevant question, What is the value of family? Is family or the values conventionally associated with family life the arrangement most conducive to life, independence, and the pursuit of justice? Wollstonecraft's answer is more affirmative than Godwin's, in effect assuming its value but under conditions yet to be realized. Those conditions focus on making family life more accommodating to women but involve cultivating the mental lives of each of its members, for the enhancement of women's minds depends on and improves upon the minds and happiness of husbands and children. Godwin's concerns over family remain fundamental. Family life not only weakens individual autonomy or, more to the point of his novels, is no match against male oversensitivity but also sanctions as humane the propensity to care most about one's blood relations, a propensity that Godwin finds immoral on two counts. By substituting instinct for reasoned judgment, family feeling mistakes the basis of true attachment. By constricting rather than enlarging the sphere of one's relations, it mistakes its aim and final end. At best, family life provides incentive and opportunity for individuals to exercise their feelings, but once they have attained sufficient strength, those feelings should head outward into the world.

But what are the alternatives? Part of the sticking power of family is its presumed naturalness and indispensability as the origin of human attachment, apart from which a self would be alone, unsocialized, bereft. Intriguing about this family's efforts to reform family from within is that they theorize the self as an object-in-relation, which for them encompasses relations to other persons and other things. Even their approach to the topic of self is relational—that is, associational. None addresses selfhood in its own right but only as other concepts—justice, equality, women, truth—occasion reflections on it (witness Godwin's *Thoughts on Man,* or Wollstonecraft's *Thoughts on the Education of*

Daughters). Moreover, none comes to view self apart from a relation to books or the forms of dissemination that their commitment to writing and truth entails. At first, recognition of the self's proximity to writing stemmed from the reformist energies that drove Godwin's and Wollstonecraft's political writings, whereby change in society depended on changes to the conventional plots, genres, and institution of writing. But gradually these writers could not think reform—that is, could not posit a future—apart from a personhood disseminated by writing

There are powerful disincentives to embracing Godwin's views on attachment. The priority he ascribes to reason in his accounts of either the individual or human modes of attachment has been discredited on general grounds by virtually every recent account of subject formation. The chief objection of feminist and poststructural schools of critique concerns the affirmed indifference of reason, both as the objective aim of its concept of self—that is, the grounds of its claims to universality—and the privileged trait of its psychology. As philosopher and personality, Godwin has long been seen as epitomizing the negative features of the latter aim. Most accounts of Godwin have some difficulty warming to his coldness, especially his reactions to other family members' pain—famously, Mary's anguish over the death of her children but also the misery that prompted Fanny to take her life.[1] Some also consider his personality a chief cause of that pain. My reason for re-examining Godwin's "thoughts on man" is to show how his reason is more postenlightened and attuned to difference than he is normally given credit for and how his psychological indifference underlies a type of humanity intimately tied to justice. Promoting the two together underlies his lifelong efforts to theorize attachment apart from sentiment and to perceive the subject as an object that is at once drawn toward others on the model of magnetism and linked to others in a causal—even signifying—chain. This object-subject, moreover, is not overly defensive about maintaining its difference from things. Godwin describes "person" as a "vessel," a "mechanism," a "link," a "stone," not so that it can be used by or use others—Godwin's remains one of the strongest voices against instrumentalizing others—but so that "person" can be disarticulated from "feeling," "depth," "interior," and aligned more with books.[2] Even in his own day, Godwin's thoughts on this subject got submerged by the alternate models that flanked them: on one side, the cult of sentiment and sensibility, with its privileged "femininity," as well as the sympathy theorized by Scottish Enlightenment thinkers with its "impartial spectator"; on the other, imagination as a faculty of perception, creativity, and morality that gives rise to idealization of the "poet."[3] Moreover, to the extent that his thoughts are classified correctly as necessarian, they are portrayed in Coleridge's *Biographia Literaria* as necessarily superseded by imagination. Later critics and biographers of Godwin humanize his necessity in the process of softening his attack on domestic affection.[4]

Renewed interest in Godwin, spurred by the recent editions of his collected writings and the impending publication of his diaries, should allow for a reassessment of the difference that Godwin both embodies and theorizes.[5] More than any of the well-known writers of the period, including Wollstonecraft and the Shelleys, Godwin lacked personality. His diaries support this assessment, which is why no one has been in a hurry to publish them. So do his own fragmented autobiographical writings—"I became, by the operation of circumstances, reserved, insulated and timid"; "I was, it seems, uncourtly and repulsive in my manners, and exhibited symptoms of a pride that was both immeasurable and past endurance"—even as they record the impressive number of persons that he encountered on a daily basis, encounters that he prized highly but in the same manner as he prized his daily encounters with books.[6] Indeed, encounters with friends or books were valued precisely for providing the "stimulus and excitement" lacking in him and deemed essential to "successful composition."[7] Even still, renewed interest in Godwinian psychology is more likely driven by current antipathy to models of sameness grounded in imagination or sentiment than to new enthusiasm for his personality.[8] For his times, Godwin remains different in his opposition to conformity and similitude as well as in his skepticism over human sympathy. This does not keep him free from bias, but it keeps his writings surprisingly receptive to alterity. Think of the aberrations that mark his protagonists and that block easy identification with them. Think of his lifelong scholarly pursuits of the paranormal, the mechanical, the necromantic, and the fanciful. Godwin's coldness, then, marks an advantage for conceiving the human apart from sentimentalism or idealism. His chief goal for the humanities is fostering a reading practice attuned to the tendency, not the articulated moral, of a work, which necessitates forms of inquiry that are prolonged, dynamic, unstable, and open to change.

Alternate Conceptions

Are all the kindnesses of the human heart to be shut up in the
paltry limits of consanguinity?

Fleetwood

Both Wollstonecraft and Godwin foreground the category of friend when
envisioning what a good relation entails, which is attachment based on merit
that facilitates further openness to others.[9] Moreover, both partners esteem the
category because they find the relational aspects of friend well-suited to the
kinds of social revolution that each is promoting. For Wollstonecraft, friendship provides the optimal model for adult heterosexual relations. As is well
known, *A Vindication of the Rights of Woman* not only characterizes a good
marriage as friendship but also devalues those aspects of marriage that are
conventionally seen to surpass friendship: chiefly sexual intercourse, but also
retreat from the public sphere and a strict division of labor within the private
sphere. Somewhat paradoxically, the advantage for feminism of envisioning
wife as friend is clearest in woman's role as mother, for that kind of wife has
every reason to fulfill her duty to the next generation by educating them
properly. In so doing, she ensures a more equitable future for women and has a
hand in shaping domestic policy in the meanwhile.[10] The wife conceived as
lover has little incentive for perceiving her duties as public service, since
managing her children's education detracts from her amatory pursuits, aligns
those pursuits with prostitution, and puts her at a disadvantage in competing
with her daughters. Whatever instruction she manages to convey, moreover, is
likely to retard women and society by reinforcing passive, mindless, or captivating manners in girls. Estimations of the value to the future of envisioning
wife as friend to her husband have been debated, since many critics judge her
promotion of marital friendship to be hostile to sex, female pleasure, and
physical appeal and thus less likely to result in reproduction.[11] Her promotion
indeed underestimates the desire of both sexes at times to be captivated and
captivating, but it also showcases how seldom her readers construe as sexy a
couple's compatibility of mind or taste.

Godwin employs the category because his version of friend entails the kind
of affection that is central to justice. His most famous critiques of domestic
affection coincide with his campaign to be a "friend of man," the new philosophical definition of which stressed not the irreplaceability but the replenish-

ability of friends. The goal of universal benevolence has as its affective requirement a conception of attachment as rational, transferable, replaceable, and
multiple. William Hazlitt characterizes the mentality well in his *Memoirs of
the Late Thomas Holcroft*, Holcroft being, among other things, one of Godwin's best-loved replaceable friends. Under the "modern philosophy," Hazlitt
writes, "family attachments would be weakened or lost in the general principle of benevolence, when every man would be a brother. Exclusive friendships
could no longer be formed, because they would interfere with the true claims
of justice and humanity, and because it would be no longer necessary to keep
alive the stream of the affections, by confining them to a particular channel,
when they would be continually refreshed, invigorated, and would overflow
with the diffusive soul of mutual philanthropy, and generous, undivided sympathy with all men."[12] In other words, true friends of man are friend to no
particular man (not to speak of woman) because attachment to a part violates,
by neglecting, the whole.[13]

It is hard to distinguish idealization from caricature in descriptions of
radical experiments, especially when the perspective is retrospective and the
writer is not only distanced from but is also taking his distance from the
project. But at the least, Hazlitt's description establishes that Godwin was not
alone in defining friendship in this way, that the definition was in fact asserted
by a close-knit circle of radical friends in the early 1790s, who in later years all
came to experience similar doubts over the desirability of this outcome—each
feeling profoundly isolated and betrayed by his respective publics and friends.
The anguished "Have I one friend?" of the final chapter of *Biographia Literaria* speaks at a minimum for Coleridge, Godwin, Holcroft, Lamb, and Hazlitt.
Indeed, much of the pathos of first-generation romantic writing is fueled by
the struggle to locate one's friends after having dissolved the category in one's
youth.[14] But what is distinctive about Godwin's rendition is that, although he
too grows personally dissatisfied with his experiences of this concept of friendship, he never rejects the affective model or grounds of connection on which it
is based. One could even say that Godwin's growing *personally* dissatisfied
with it proved that the concept of friendship was still both valid and working.

The bottom line for Godwin is the conviction that attachment is necessary.
"There is nothing that the human heart more irresistibly seeks than an object
to which to attach itself."[15] "[Man] is linked to his brethren by a thousand
ties; and, when those ties are broken, he ceases from all genuine existence"
(*St. Leon*, 231). What may appear to be a commonplace is actually the result of
a complicated balancing act for Godwin, for central to understanding his

conviction are two tenets that are often viewed as in tension with each other: his concept of person as a social individual and his allegiance to the doctrine of necessity. The priority that Godwin placed on individual autonomy and private judgment does not require that a person eschew sociality or human interaction. From first to last, the Godwinian self is relational and perceived as "an indivisible member of society."[16] This conviction underlies Godwin's notions of psychology, morality, and the kind of society that his writing aims to achieve. His novels explore the near insanity that results from an individual's sense of total isolation, his historical writings foreground the impossibility of separating character from context, and his moral thinking, even when it ascribes more weight to the psychological dimensions of motive, never reduces benevolent actions to pure self-interest. At most, it concedes the co-presence but separability of disinterested and self-interested motives.[17]

Godwin's political commitment to working for the whole is a psychological task and requirement. "We shall never sufficiently discharge our duty [as members of a community], till, like the ancient Spartans, the love of the whole becomes our predominant passion, and we cease to imagine that we belong to ourselves, so much as to the entire body of which we are a part" (*Thoughts on Man*, 204). Precisely this supersession of the self, or what Godwin elsewhere terms positively as "self-postponement," constitutes the distinctive trait of a political leader. "He that would benefit mankind on a comprehensive scale, by changing the principles and elements of society, must learn the hard lesson, to put off self, and to contribute by a quiet but incessant activity, like a rill of water, to irrigate and fertilize the intellectual soil."[18] The primary criterion of leadership but also valid citizenship, then, is the ability to comport oneself as a not-self, a nonpossessive individual. Anything that intensifies the magic of "my" disqualifies one from public service.

On one level, there is nothing unusual about de-emphasizing the self when the discussion concerns achieving social harmony. Moral and religious codes of conduct have as their chief aim restraining the impulses of self so that one can hear and answer to a higher calling. But Godwin aims to formulate this self without enlisting any of the concepts that have traditionally served to keep it in line: heaven, hell, sin, guilt, punishment, conscience, sacrifice, duty. Consequently, he must also devise reasons other than God or prison and incentives other than self-sacrifice or family loyalty for a people's coming together and living together as a group. The characteristic image that Godwin invokes when envisioning connection, links in a chain, an image standard in materialist and necessarian worldviews, underlines its nonpsychological dimension

(*Political Justice*, 165). In his use, this image also indicates the linkages among his philosophical, epistemological, and moral convictions and bespeaks three fundamental realities of human life: self is indissociable from others; attachment is a matter of forging, not assuming, connection; forging connections is how humans acquire knowledge and how they learn to live as a group. Call this a process of association, by which connections of thought also lead to connections among people.

Commentators who explore Godwin's doctrine of necessity have tended to foreground its impact on his theories of causality.[19] The proper understanding of events, as of human character, requires careful analysis of how previously existing causes produce their ensuing effects. One of the major ends of this analysis is also part of its means: reducing the share that sentiment plays in constituting persons or events and in the comprehension and further concatenation of them. One of the best-known aspects of Godwinian morality is its effort to present crime as a matter of ignorance, not guilt, and thus to place moral and cultural improvement in the hands of education, rather than of the law, government, the military, or the church.[20] Less attention has been paid to how Godwin's necessarianism affects his positive understanding of human relations, in large part because his focus on the mechanical and machinelike properties of agency, coupled with his infamous critique of domestic affection, are seen as implying that Godwin discredits the intensity of human attachment. Hardly. Godwin calls attachment not only fundamental to life but also the "life of our life" (*Thoughts*, 167). His novels show how ruptures in this doubling of life unmans his protagonists. But he sees sentimental attachments, like those to family, weakening one's commitment to the broader picture.[21] The value of Godwin's approach to relation lies in its adherence to both components of the conviction that attachment is necessary. For him, the fact that human actions are determined affects the strength and aim of a person's attachments.

Godwin's envisioning of attachment as links of a chain foregrounds several features that work to ensure that one's experience in the chain is not constraining but liberating. This requires that a person perceive herself as a link, whose meaningful existence depends on being linked to others but whose connection to those others also preserves a sphere of autonomy.[22] It also entails perceiving oneself as part of a chain whose aim is infinite extension through space and time, rather than encirclement, whether of family, nation, or even globe.[23] While Godwin's commitment to extending the chain remained consistent, he modified his estimation of the desirable distance, or degree of contact, between links over time. In the first edition of *Political Justice*, his primary concern is safeguarding autonomy by preserving the individual from imposition—whether by government, neighbors, family, or books. By 1798 and thereafter, his concern shifts toward strengthening attachment rather than autonomy—but still as the means to social justice—out of a growing recognition that "too much independence is not good for man" (*Fleetwood*, 167). This means that true friends of man now have the added responsibility of preserving individuals from perceiving themselves as radically alone, for the perception of isolation destroys one's incentive to engage the world. This degree of detachment literally renders the world a "blank" and a person "but one degree removed from insanity" (*Fleetwood*, 164).

Here are the chief constituents of Godwinian attachments. They are earned, not given or assumed, and earned through the concurrence of "right opinions." This process makes attachment a matter of head as well as heart, for consensus in thought and taste is what "casts hearts in the same mould." They entail not a "love of compassion but a love of approbation"—that is, as affection in accord with judgment—one "proof" of that attachment being that both partners are "improved" by their "mutual partialities," a second that each is committed to "executing" the other's projects, especially after one of them dies (*Fleetwood*, 249, 285, 133). Second, attachments expand, rather than contract, the heart. They foster the "going forth of the heart" that characterizes benevolence, true public service, and reading (*St. Leon*, 140). Third, attachment expresses itself in "frankness," "communion of spirit," sincerity, and "unreserve." "The great end of all liberal institutions is, to make a man fearless, frank as the day, acting from a lively and earnest impulse" (*Thoughts*, 211, 213).

Shifts in his specification of the best kind of object to which or to whom to be attached alter in relation to two coordinates of relationality: whether objects are deemed replaceable or irreplaceable; whether in them one seeks similarity or difference. Throughout his life, "friend" remained the category that best satisfied these features of attachment, especially the unreserve and sense of approbation that the experience of being attached fosters. "Friendship is to the loftier mind the repose, the unbending of soul" (*Thoughts*, 194). "The smallest reserve is deadly to [friendship]. . . . Our hearts, which grew together, suffer amputation [when reserved]; the arteries are closed; the blood is no longer mutually transfused and confounded" (*St. Leon*, 131). But who or what best constitutes a friend changed as Godwin experienced and reflected on his losses.

The first shift in object occurred when Godwin was living with Wollstonecraft, which prompted him to include "wife" in the category of "friend," up until then reserved in his writings (though not life) for men. Love letters between the two constantly play on, and play with, their status as friends, and wives portrayed in novels written after 1797 are characterized as friends.[24] In this respect, *St. Leon* does pay homage to "the author of the Vindication of the Rights of Woman" in its linkage of marriage with friendship, marriage and friendship with frankness, and all three with equality between the partners. "Excessive and clandestine advantages" destroy the "equality" that is "the soul of real and cordial society," for a "generous spirit . . . delights to live upon equal terms with his associates and fellows" (*St. Leon*, 176). Even more so does he delight in equality with his wife, for inequality "destroys that communion of spirit which is the soul of the marriage-tie. A consort should be a human being and an equal" (175).

After *St. Leon*, Godwin's attitude changed regarding the role of equality in achieving the frankness of wives as friends. By 1805, Fleetwood is portraying sexual difference as central to heterosexual intimacy: "I had not been aware that nature has provided a substitute in the marriage-tie for this romantic, if not impossible friendship [between men]. . . . The difference of sex powerfully assists the intimacy; similarity of character can never unite two parties so closely, as the contrast of masculine enterprise in one, and a defenceless tenderness in the other" (*Fleetwood*, 191). This specification of difference represents a serious setback for the revolution in female manners that Godwin was supposedly "executing," as proof of his attachment, on Wollstonecraft's behalf. Nor is the assertion simply another indication of Fleetwood's aberrance. All subsequent novels and nonfictional writings specify inequality between heterosexual partners as the condition of unreserved love. *Mandeville* and *Cloudesley* tend to ascribe the achievement of frankness to male friends but describe friendship in the language of heterosexual marriage. *Cloudesley* endorses Julian's need for a male friend by quoting the scriptural sanction for the creation of woman, "It is not good for man to be alone," and invokes the cadences of the marriage ceremony in describing male-male friendship. "They must have been together in sadness and festivity, . . . in difficulties and in plenty, in sickness and in health" (161).[25] *Deloraine* implicitly debates the claims of friend and wife by characterizing both relationships in the same way. Deloraine's first, and ideal, marriage to Emilia Fitzcharles, the love between William and Margaret Borrodale, and the friendship between William and Travers are all said to produce openness, frankness, and communion between partners. But as *Deloraine* asserts, sexual difference produces the "most perfect unreserve" between persons (18).

In the graver and more sentimental communications of man and man the head
still bears the superior sway; in the unreserved intimacies of man and woman
the heart is ever uppermost. Feeling is the main thing; and judgment passes for
little. . . . If I and my male friend agree in a certain opinion, it is well; . . . Still
however we are two. But, with a female, and that female the object of my growing partiality and preference, every new agreement of sentiment and approbation brings us nearer to each other, removes one more brick from the wall
which originally separated us, dissolves our several identities, and, as it were,
melts us, like different chemical substances, in one crucible, and mingles us in
heart and spirit, with a feeling that we can never thereafter be divided. (13)

In contrast, the similarity that characterizes male-male friendships occasions
distance. "There will in reality always be some reserve, some shadow of fear
between equals, which in the friendship of unequals, if happily assorted, can
find no place" (*Thoughts*, 196–97). "Love cannot exist in its purest form and
with a genuine ardour, where the parties are, and are felt by each other to be,
on an equality; but that in all cases it is requisite there should be a mutual
deference and submission" (199).

The psychological profile of the "friend of man" comes up for reconsidera-
tion in the face of growing losses, both the tenet that particular attachments
weaken one's connection to the whole and that friends are, and should be,
nonexclusive and replaceable. *St. Leon* voices dissatisfaction with the latter
tenet. "I felt that human affections and passions are not made of this transferable stuff, and that we can love nothing truly, unless we devote ourselves to it
heart and soul, and our life is, as it were, bound up in the object of our
attachment" (139). This dissatisfaction is visible in Godwin's discussions of
mourning (explored in chapter 5) and particularly discernible in his published
reactions to Wollstonecraft's death. While *Memoirs of the Author of "A Vindication of the Rights of Woman"* admits the irreplaceability of the lost object
("that light is extinguished forever"), it focuses more on the ways that "the
author" never belonged to him in the first place. His attachment to "Wollstonecraft" is portrayed largely as nonparticular and impersonal and, in fact, a
connection as much to the "public welfare." Exploring the "calamity of death,"
Essay on Sepulchres (1809) revisits loss in a more general fashion that, paradoxically, specifies in some detail "all that is lost" when a "great man" dies,
especially if he is the "wife of my bosom" (8, 9).

Godwin's subsequent writings adopt several strategies for dealing with the
"calamity of death" because of the threat it poses to maintaining proper object

relations. But even when he stresses the incalculability of the loss occasioned by death, his efforts remain primarily directed at extending the scope and nature of attachments. Despite his reputation for withdrawal, Godwin never retreats on this front.[26] Moreover, he often construes irreplaceability as a feeling, not a fact, about human attachment. Witness his defense of second marriages: "I should hold that in many cases he who entered into a second marriage, by that action yielded a pure and honourable homage to the manes of the first" (*St. Leon*, 241). What does not change fundamentally, even when he grieves, is a second psychological requisite of a friend of man—that, to the extent that he "would benefit mankind on a comprehensive scale, by changing the principles and elements of society," he "must learn the hard lesson, to put off self, and to contribute by a quiet but incessant activity, like a rill of water, to irrigate and fertilize the intellectual soil." A proper friend aids this self-postponing, whether embodied by "man," "wife," or "book." In the case of "wife," it helps if she is an author of books.[27] Otherwise, the con/fusion achieved by sexual intercourse or despair over the loss of it threatens to make the self recongeal, either because sex "is, all through a selfish sentiment, the pampering of weakness" or because loss of it turns one into a "statue of despair" (*Fleetwood*, 220).

One of the most remarkable definitions of friend links it to the impartial spectator posited as internalized by Scottish-enlightened notions of sympathy. A friend thus offers precisely what Godwin's "new man of feeling" lacks—the capacity to view things from a perspective other than one's own, perspective understood not as a point of view, whether compatible or opposing, but as a point from which to view and thus gain distance on the object. Usually associated with male-male attachment, it is accomplished as well when a heterosexual couple reads.

> No man needs a friend, so much as he who is under the slavery of a domineering passion. A friend is like Time, the master of us all, or like boundless Space. He removes us to a due distance from the object, which we see falsely and distorted only because we are too near to it. He makes us view it in the light, in which the generation yet unborn shall view it. . . . I can hardly describe to my friend the thing that torments me, in the wild and exaggerated way in which I view it with closed doors. What I deliver to him, is a compounded notion, made up partly of the impression I have myself entertained, and partly of the temper of his mind, and of my anticipation of the way in which he will regard the facts I have to relate. (*Mandeville*, 145)

This is a striking redefinition of friend and the objectivity as well as borrowed time that attachment to such a friend occasions. This friend eschews the theatricality of the impartial spectator of sympathy by indefinitely postponing the show.[28] S/he also moderates the passions by serving as mediator of them.[29]

But, as this passage from *Mandeville* goes on to say, "how exceedingly rare is this phenomenon, a friend!" Godwin's (and Shelley's) novels repeatedly voice this lament, even as their books come to fulfill the definition of friend as one who "makes us view [objects and passions] in the light, in which the generation yet unborn shall view" them. What impedes male-male friendship for both authors is pride, ambition, the inability to bear an equal. Since their portrayals of the outcome of pride are so dramatic, it is easy to overlook the remedy that Godwin proposes for it. "The true definition of a friend is, he to whom I can bear to speak, and whom I can bear to hear" (145).[30] This definition does not mandate sameness or equality as the grounds for exchange but rather openness to dialogue. Not that this condition is any easier to achieve, as *Mandeville* makes clear, until the final two novels of Shelley. But with this definition, women recover some of the ground they have lost in Godwin's mystifications of sexual difference, since his novels come to prize the home front as the only space where people speak frankly and where a man can let down his guard against constant misinterpretation of him in the public sphere. And this definition not only positions the friend within a more public private sphere but also accentuates the interlocutory feature of friend.

Attached to Reading

> A book is a dead man, a sort of mummy, emboweled and embalmed, but that once had flesh, and motion, and a boundless variety of determinations and actions.
>
> *Fleetwood*

When Godwin or his protagonists come to affirm that books are friends, they are not being rhetorical, sentimental, or misanthropic. Books are friends (and friends come to be books) because interchange with them fulfills the specifications for proper attachment: won or earned, linking head and heart, valuing approbation over compassion, expanding rather than contracting the heart. They also satisfy the proofs: readers are improved and rendered active, committed to executing the other's projects, strengthened in self-diffusion, and made part of a larger whole. "Every man who is changed from what he was by the perusal of th[e] works [of Shakespeare and Milton], communicates a portion of the inspiration all around him. It passes from man to man, till it influences the whole mass" (*Enquirer*, 40). Moreover, the conviction itself that books are friends was not only earned in the case of Godwin, but hard-won.

Godwin connects the topics of friendship and reading whether he is treating books in a negative or positive fashion. In *Political Justice*, the friend of man links his reservations regarding cohabitation and marriage to reservations regarding reading, for the ways that both activities threaten the autonomy of man. "Every man that reads the composition of another, suffers the succession of his ideas to be in a considerable degree under the direction of his author" (452). Although this subordination does not "form a sufficient objection against reading" (as compared to marriage, which is a distinct "evil"), Godwin's initial ambivalence toward books emerges in discussions regarding the relative merits of conversation and reading. At issue is the degree to which books are dead or alive. At first, and up until 1797, Godwin treats books and conversation as opposing categories and states his clear preference for the vitality offered by conversation. Books, he writes in *Political Justice*, "have a sort of constitutional coldness" and, to the extent that they advance new trains of thinking, provoke "sullenness" in readers "unwilling to stretch [their] minds" or "strik[e] into untrodden paths" (121). In contrast, conversation is lively, animates its members, and "gives freedom and elasticity to our mental disquisitions" (121). Late in life, Godwin can still oppose the "abstraction" of a "book" to "the living human voice" that "shoots through us like a stroke of electricity," but this is meant to express his "regret" that people "but imperfectly" perceive when reading that a "being of flesh and blood like ourselves" is "address[ing] us" (*Thoughts*, 176).

Around 1796–97, Godwin softens this opposition, as evident in *The Enquirer*, which "evinces a more constant respect for the importance of the printed word as the chief force of enlightenment."[31] He begins to portray books as plausible substitution for conversation with friends and as adequate compensation for the loss of it. "Senseless paper! Be thou at least my confidant! . . . It is no matter that these pages shall never be surveyed by other eyes than mine. They afford at least the semblance of communication and the unburthening of the mind; and I will press the illusion fondly and for ever to my heart" (*St Leon*, 137).[32] The Rousseauistic Ruffigny in *Fleetwood* combines the two attitudes, first by opposing books, described as "the cold, insensible, mechanically constructed pages and sheets that have been produced by my fellow-creatures," to "the living volume of nature," but then by defending books as dead men with whom one can nonetheless converse. "Let no man despise the oracles of books! A book is a dead man, a sort of mummy, emboweled and embalmed, but that once had flesh, and motion, and a boundless variety of determinations and actions. I am glad that I can even upon these terms, converse with the dead, with the wise and the good of revolving centuries" (*Fleetwood*, 69). By 1809, conversation with the dead is the most vital thing going. According to *Essay on Sepulchres*, not only are "Milton, and Shakespear, and lord Bacon, and sir Philip Sidney . . . not wholly [dead]," but they "live as my friends, my philosophers, my instructors, and my guides" (22). They are in fact so alive and productive of life that the *Essay* advises the present generation not to "hold a more frequent intercourse with the living, than with the good departed" (22).

The implications of this shift from prizing conversations with one's live friends to those with the illustrious dead are wide-reaching; they entail corresponding changes in the category and evaluation of "life" as well as the writing of biographies, topics explored in chapter 5. For now, my interest is in what conversation and books have in common as modes of enlightenment— that is, their sociability—and the differing ways that conversations and books attain the same end: that "collision of mind" that Godwin deems essential to the activation, dissemination, and renewal of ideas.[33] "Indeed, if there be such a thing as truth, it must infallibly be struck out by the collision of mind with mind" (*Political Justice*, 15; also *Political Justice Var.*, 151–52). "For all that [man] has, he is indebted to collision" (*Enquirer*, 234).

Mark Philp's explanation of what motivated Godwin's softening of his rationalist position in the second and third editions of *Political Justice* is relevant here. He claims that the weakening of the circle of Radical Dissenters and, especially, the loss of the frank exchanges that characterized radical dinner parties of the early 1790s forced Godwin to spell out more fully what the first edition, in its primary address to a Dissenting audience and set of principles, could assume: not simply the power of truth but the belief that truth has inherent power.[34] Godwin's having to envision a wider audience for his enquiries, the consequence both of a more realistic conception of authorship and a change in his social life, meant devoting more attention to the factors that motivate persons to embrace truth once they discover it. This involved specifying how, why, and to what persons get attached. In this respect, we might establish as a linkage what Philp sets up as an opposition in his claim that love for Wollstonecraft should not be viewed as primarily responsible for

motivating the revisions to *Political Justice*.[35] For both the waning of the
radical dinner parties and the gaining of Wollstonecraft—not to mention the
subsequent losing of her—invited slippage in his life/writings between being
attached to ideas and persons that was then consummated in loving books.

Godwin's descriptions of reading similarly support the goal of sociality and
the initial benefits ascribed to conversation in achieving it. They have as a
chief aim ensuring the going forth of heart that expands one's world, activities,
and sphere of relations. "True reading is investigation, not a passive reception
of what our author has given us, but an active enquiry, appreciation and
digestion of his subject."[36] What this requires, first off, is that one read more
than one book at a time in order not to fall "under the control" of a single
perspective or author or to remain isolated in one's reading. A "judicious reader
will have a greater number of ideas that are his own passing through his mind,
than of ideas presented to him by his author." "A true student is a man seated
in his chair, and surrounded with a sort of intrenchment and breastwork of
books. It is for boarding-school misses to read one book at a time."[37] Such a
student values projects that lead him "from author to author in wide succession, and [that take] away the oppressive feelings of passiveness which frequently pursue us, when we resign ourselves to the simple and direct reading
of a single work" (*Fleetwood*, 139–40). Such activity of mind is especially
visible in the reading of history, which not only necessitates comparison and
evaluation of sources but also has as its goal inspiring through example "whatever of noble, useful, generous, and admirable human nature is capable of
designing and performing."[38] Like conversation, proper reading makes minds
and ideas collide. Like timely friends, it lessens the opportunity for head-on
collisions occasioned by impetuosity or over-reaction. "The book does not
deserve even to be read, which does not impose on us the duty of frequent
pauses, much reflecting and inward debate. . . . It is with the intellectual, as
with the corporeal eye: we must retire to a certain distance from the object we
would examine, before we can truly take in the whole" (*Thoughts*, 115). But
what distinguishes books from conversation is the wider scope and access they
grant to the dissemination of ideas. "Without books" one remains a "mere
novice" in life, because "the life of a single man is too short to enable him to
penetrate beyond the surfaces of things." In this regard, books are friends who
add years to one's life (*Enquirer*, 103).

This extension of sociality through reading has two, somewhat paradoxical
but interrelated, consequences that work to counter self-absorption. Godwin's
goal of diffusing enlightenment as widely as possible leads to the formulation

of a self that is itself diffused through reading. For the goal of reading is not simply self-reform or the alteration of character—though what Godwin wants it to achieve on these scores is highly ambitious, since he specifies the reading of Shakespeare, Milton, *Caleb Williams,* and *A Vindication of the Rights of Woman* as "constitut[ing] an epoch in the mind of the reader, [such] that no one, after he has read [them], shall ever be exactly the same man that he was before."[39] Reading extends the reader's grasp on the world by putting "every thing within his reach," which in turn expands the mind both in terms of knowledge and incentive to grow ever bigger (*Enquirer,* 95, 237). It also enlarges a person by "doubl[ing] one's existence" through "familiarity" with a cherished author (95). Ultimately, reading is transformative of the concept of the human.

This process is evinced in Godwin's editing of Wollstonecraft, which under-scores how discerning the tendency of a work diffuses the personhood or identity of an author. It keeps an author always in process, whose "life and ideas are unfinished," as Rajan writes, and places that author "into history" in such a way "as to initiate the uncertain process of her future reading."[40] Godwin works to achieve this version of immortalizing authors by specifying what reading "in a proper spirit" entails (*Enquirer,* 238). It affects which authors get canonized, those being most praiseworthy who have the "talent to 'create a soul under the ribs of death'; whose composition is fraught with irresistible enchantment; who pour their whole souls into mine, and raise me as it were to the seventh heaven" (140). It heightens a reader's receptivity to "the consequences that do not cease to flow fresh from what" these authors wrote and thus continue to write (*Sepulchres,* 23). Reading in this spirit also works to insert live readers into history and the uncertainties of it. It inspires them to become "heroes," according to the performative logic of history's inseparability from romance: through the "contemplation of illustrious men," readers "insensibly imbibe the same spirit" and "kindl[e] into a flame the hidden fire within us" ("History and Romance," 293). It also dissolves readers as well as authors into air. "Every man who is changed from what he was by the perusal of [Shakespeare's and Milton's] works, communicates a portion of the inspiration all around him. It passes from man to man, till it influences the whole mass." Indeed, the inspiration released by such authors is so powerful that it reaches those who have never read them. "I cannot tell that the wisest mandarin now living in China, is not indebted for part of his energy and sagacity to the writings of Milton and Shakespear, even though it should happen that he never heard of their names" (*Enquirer,* 141). The importance of this notion, by which reading at once diffuses personhood and affects peoples around the globe, is evident in the repetition of this passage twelve years later in *Sepulchres* (29). It assumes a more sinister cast in *The Last Man*, whereby one author's inspiration is another's contagion.

This dissemination of enlightenment through reading has as a second consequence the formulation of a new sphere of sociality, one vastly under-recognized in assessments of Godwin but one that puts in a clearer light under what conditions he can be said to have valued home. Those conditions involve conceiving home as a public house or coffeehouse where ideas are read, discussed, composed, diffused. Godwin never advocates this home renovation explicitly (he takes it a step further by making his home a publishing house, aptly named the Juvenile Library), but it can be apprehended through the combined effect of his separate restructurings of family, public opinion, and reading. For if, on the one hand, family is opened out to embrace all friends of man and, on the other, the public nature of opinion must be consolidated apart from organized political groups, then the home space becomes the optimal germinal space of the Godwinian public sphere.

Godwin's arguments against political associations—indeed, organized groups of any sort—arose out of his critique of modernity as fostering partiality, divisiveness, and sectarianism coupled with contemporary discussions of how to conduct political reform, especially during a time of revolution. Godwin's attack on divisiveness coincides with his objections to family but encompasses larger forms of organized group life as well, all of which forms he castigated for the way that adherence to a collectivity "make[s] a part stand for the whole" (*Political Justice Var.*, 142). Godwin's antipathy to groups is stronger than his reservations regarding self-absorption, even granting the near insanity that he claims results from perceiving oneself as alone. Group life incapacitates the mind altogether, blunting its activity, sensitivity, and freedom of enquiry. It survives by placing an injunction on thinking so that members conform to the party line.[41] The unthinking nature of groups is exacerbated by the growing complexity of modern life, which makes the drawing of distinctions, boundaries, and divisions a necessary part of thinking and of social organization. Such skills of segregation damage the coherence and cohesion of society and even render more unlikely the prospect of finding a friend. Whereas "the savage man probably" encountered "a companion" wherever "he encounter[ed] a being of his own species," the "civilized" man, owing to the "artificial distinctions of civilized life," claims as his "companion" "one man picked out of ten thousand" (*Mandeville*, 214). This accounts for the "reserve" and "coldness" that characterize modern society.

Modern disharmony is intensified by the "present irritated and unnatural state of political affairs," which in turn gives rise to an increase in political associations, factions, and clubs. These organizations, however, only heighten current agitation because they violate virtually every tenet of Godwin's model of political reform. "True reform" is a gradual and sequential process, whereby the "public mind" is first "enlightened," then "unequivocal" in voicing "public sentiment," which results in a "grand and magnificent harmony" felt through "the whole community" and manifesting itself in a "consent of wills" that no leader can "withstand."[42] The "true instruments" for effecting this transformation are "argument and persuasion," which disseminate new ideas throughout society but without recourse to compulsion, dogmatism, or demagoguery (*Political Justice*, 115). Political associations, however, by leveling "all understandings into one common mass," inflame rather than inform auditors, "propagating blind zeal, where we meant to propagate reason," because truth is "swallowed up" both in the "insatiate gulf of noisy assemblies" and when "any species of publications is patronized by political associations" (*Political Justice Var.*, 144; *Political Justice*, 115, 122; *Political Justice Var.*, 143). The "harangue and declamation" characteristic of public speaking are even less likely than patronized publications to convey truth, since they foster the cult of personality and the likelihood of things getting violent (144).[43] As a measure "intrinsically wrong," then, political associations are especially reprehensible in revolutionary times. "Moments pregnant with so important consequences" demand leaders who are "untainted" by the "headlong rage of faction," who can "judge, with the sobriety of distant posterity," and who are "happy enough to make [their] voice heard, by all those directly or remotely interested in the event."[44] They temper headlong rage by conducting what Godwin calls "familiar discussion," a process through which innovative ideas grow familiar to the public through a series of free and spontaneous discussions among familiars (*Political Justice Var.*, 145).

John Thelwell captures well the still-current frustration regarding Godwin's antipathy toward groups by characterizing "Considerations on Lord Grenville's and Mr. Pitt's Bills . . . by a lover of order" as "the most extensive plan of freedom and innovation ever discussed by a writer in the English language" that reprobates "every measure from which even the most moderate reform might be expected."[45] Yet this criticism overlooks one configuration of group life that Godwin deems central to his reworking of the public private sphere: envisioning family as a public-oriented relation and home as a sphere of enquiry among familiars. Godwin gestures toward this solution in specifying what, besides "time, reading, and conversation," is required to render new ideas familiar: "unreserved communication in a smaller circle, and especially among persons who are already awakened to the pursuit of truth" (*Political Justice*, 118, 120). Discussion that promotes something beyond "brute and unintelligent sympathy" occurs "with advantage" in "small and friendly societies" but with optimum "vigour and utility" in the "conversation of two persons" (121; see also *Political Justice Var.*, 144). Even more to the point, such a utopia is potentially pervasive. "Does the fewness of their numbers" imply the "rarity" of these friendly societies? "Far otherwise: the time perhaps will come when such institutions will be universal" (*Political Justice*, 121). Such belief gives added relevance to Godwin's and Wollstonecraft's decisions to direct their social work from and at the home front. Indeed, reform could start and stop there. It also explains their unceasing concern to raise up children in the pursuit of truth.

Several things are necessary to make a home a public house, but foremost is "Wollstonecraft"—not as person, wife, or mother but as public intellectual (the blueprint for which Godwin does provide in *Memoirs of the Author of "A Vindication of the Rights of Woman"*). Only such a female presence mitigates the "excessive familiarity" that, according to Godwin, characterizes the unreconstructed home and impedes "familiar discussion." Such a presence had only become conceivable as exercising a "political voice" within the house since the 1790s, when "Mary Wollstonecraft, and to some extent Mary Hays, Catherine Macaulay, and Anna Letitia Barbauld, began to articulate" claims to women's "political identity."[46] The Wollstonecraftian household favors neither the sentimental nor the concentric remodel of home.[47] It follows enlightened specifications, chiefly of her own devising. The domestic "manners" that "acquire value in social exchange" pursue the "revolution in female manners," by which women are esteemed for their ability to liven up conversation and awaken the next generation, though sometimes they extend to dress.[48] Even evaluated by today's standards, Wollstonecraft's domestic arrangements are impressive in the lengths that they go to make private space open to fostering the thinking powers of all inhabitants. Her concept of a productive household embraces a separation of work spheres that allows her and Godwin to maintain separate residences.[49] Though hers also includes the management of childcare, meals, socializing, and cleaning, it has the specified advantage of considering one's husband a guest. It also envisions the education of children as requiring both instruction at home and attendance at a day school, so that the young learn in the company of peers of both genders but without also learning that home is a space opposed to work, world, ideas, or men.[50]

Disseminating this re/vision of home—or at least the desperate need for it—occurs in Wollstonecraft's fictional writings where the woman of the house is almost never situated within a domestic interior. Usually, she is on the road or high seas (*Mary, A Short Residence*), running from home or a madhouse (*Wrongs of Woman*), working for others as governess or mistress (*Original Stories of Real Life, Wrongs of Woman*), or being educated in a cave, the place from which the education of daughters begins ("The Cave of Fancy"). Her most feminine and sentimental text, composed out of impassioned love letters to Imlay, positions the woman traveling throughout several countries and evaluating each society in relation to the share of mind and taste evident in its domestic arrangements. Nonfictional depictions portray the woman of the household reading, writing, socializing, instructing children, and supervising her and their outdoor activities. These include sports, travel, shopping, and philanthropic and social work, as well as managing businesses, participating in public affairs, running schools for girls, and running for office. A worthy home life also entails acknowledging one's responsibility for women who have fallen outside the bounds of respectable society. This includes assuming responsibility for defending Wollstonecraft herself, a need that the afterlife of her life/writings makes all too clear.

Given the indispensability of Wollstonecraft to the ambitious project of household remodeling, it was fitting that Godwin move into her study and write under her image after her death.[51] For his purchase on these renovations was insecure, especially as they facilitate the liberation of women outside their studies. More to his taste were designs to foster the autonomy of men and children and to lessen power differentials between parent and child, for, as we have seen, after 1799, he deemed inequality between the sexes necessary for partnered intimacy. What qualifies Godwin's household as a public house, besides its forthright adoption of children from other men (whether of Wollstonecraft's or Mary Jane Clairmont's or the many young men he mentored), is the counter it poses to the forms of despotism specifically ascribed to political associations and the unreconstructed home.[52] Despotism of the former breeds mindless adherence to the party line, of the latter an "excessive familiarity" that results in the same thing.

Godwin states that excessive familiarity is "the bane of social happiness" and the cause of the "ill humour which is so prevalent through all the different walks of life." Because the "well-known maxim" is true, that "familiarity breeds contempt," one of "the most important of the arts of life" is ensuring that "men should not come too near each other, or touch in too many points" (*Enquirer*, 118–20). Cultivating this art of life is especially crucial in the home space. Excessive familiarity with one's children occasions the "harsh tones" and "peremptory manner" that stunts a child's faculties and renders him unwilling to pursue intellectual challenges. A "footing of undue familiarity" with one's "wife" prompts men to treat women "as we do children." The "first and most fundamental principle in the intercourse of man with man is reverence," the attainment and maintenance of which quality is in inverse proportion to the degree of sentimental and physical closeness between persons (120). Priority on reverence links Godwin's critiques of political assemblies and family life through the capacity of each formation to reduce individuals to undifferentiated masses. Even when Godwin comes to admit cohabitation as a blessing in the *Enquirer*, it remains a mixed one, owing to the excessive familiarity fostered by current models of domesticity.

Godwin's writings on domesticity aim to counteract precisely this tendency by ensuring that no one at home, not even the children, be treated as a child or be allowed to act like one. Even if Godwin compromised on the desirability of full equality between the sexes, he was fully committed to overturning the "PERPETUAL BABYISM" that, according to Mary Hays, characterized the contemporary situation of women.[53] And even if he expressed qualms about endorsing all the rights of public women, he chose as a second wife another woman with a dubious sexual history and who ensured that his household was a place where ideas were generated, published, and sold. No one disputes the importance of the so-called second Mrs. Godwin in initiating and running the family bookstore—though hardly anyone admires her for it.[54] Though she may have inhibited the (homo)sociality of Godwin's radical dinner parties, by the time she entered Godwin's life, those days were over anyway and he was already viewing books as more efficient than conversation at stimulating and disseminating thought. In any case, whether under Wollstonecraft's or Clairmont-Godwin's supervision, his house facilitated "familiar discussion" in several respects. It welcomed as "familiars" persons unrelated by blood and evaluated the resemblance of its members according to features of mind, not physiognomy. It prized frankness but also set "a guard upon the door of our lips" (*Enquirer*, 120). It perceived women as thinkers, writers, and public figures but also as individuals whose "tact" and sensitivity soften the "sort of men, whom a perfect sincerity disqualifies for some of the kinder offices of society" (*Mandeville*, 121). It characterized the ideal of family life as "so much harmony of interests, yet each member having a different pursuit" (*Fleetwood*, 246). Through these means, home life preserves the "variety" that is central to the ongoing stimulation, generation, and dissemination of ideas and fulfills the "great end of all liberal institutions," to make persons "fearless, frank as the day," and capable of "acting from a lively and earnest impulse" (*Thoughts*, 213). This last goal is the chief respect in which Godwin modified his sustained preference for feudal over bourgeois household arrangements.

The Godwinian house, then, is the social institution that comes closest to satisfying "liberal" ideals in the current age. It is the space where individuals thrive to the degree that they are not smothered and whence ideas are set forth and sent forth into public space and time. For in Godwin's view, frankness is hardly a prominent feature of courts of law, government, or religious institutions. Compared to them, Godwin comes to value domesticity for fostering the frankness that he deems so rare in exchanges in the public sphere and so essential to the development and dissemination of ideas. This may explain why images of domestic life in Godwin's novels feature members engaged in reading and rational converse and then pursuing separate activities, or why they associate scenes of reading with expressions of love. Moreover, the frankness found at home is the counterpart to the male protagonist's brutalizing experiences in the public realm and the antidote to the enervation and depression that they generate in him. Virtually all of Godwin's novels explore this dynamic: that characters cannot pursue their public functions—whether that means bringing others to justice or bringing more just conditions to them—either because their characters are misconstrued and therefore the justice of their actions negated (Caleb, St. Leon, Mandeville) or because their entire adult life is spent trying to keep their "true" character from being revealed (Falkland, Cloudesley, Deloraine). Early on, analysis of class bias motivates this depiction, whereby truly just characters who lack political and economic clout are not given a fair reading, whereas aristocratic men can preserve their honor because they have the means. But even more fundamental is Godwin's sense that public service is nullified by the inability of any public being to find or fulfill the profile of friend: he to whom I can bear to speak, and whom I can bear to hear.

The most controversial aspect of the Godwinian household, what critics deem negative but what Godwin finds highly beneficial about his kind of house, is the detachment that it fosters. Maintaining a degree of detachment is central to the home's capacity to facilitate justice, for that goal depends on sustaining activities that are deemed cold—like scholarship, rational discourse, estimations of merit, personal restraint—and that counter the excessive familiarity cultivated by warmer pursuits, like sex, nurturance, anger, and pity. Indeed, aspiring to be cold is an indispensable art of life which Godwin's life/writings aim to fuel. His most original "thoughts on man" attend to the "dust" that composes the "great man" and entail a deliberate inquiry into the proximity of "human" to "stone" (11).[55] The preface to *St. Leon* clinches its ostensible re-evaluation of domestic affection by asserting that "it is better that man should be a living being, than a stock or a stone."[56] What appears startling in its banality actually marks a significant change of heart, itself already changed—that is, erased—by the time it appears in print. The original manuscript postscript to *Caleb Williams* has Caleb asserting that "true happiness lies in being like a stone." While the truth value of that assertion is qualified by its ascription to "the period of my insanity" and effacement in the published conclusion, the analogy tends to emerge when Godwin is weighing the benefits of attachment.[57]

Caleb invokes "stone" in order to express his longing for the insensibility to pain and misinterpretation that being a stone, or being like stone, offers. Several of the characters in Godwin's novels are turned to stone after hearing some unwanted message, and *Deloraine* has as a subplot the transformation of Borromeo's "heart of stone" into a "heart of flesh" through reattachment to others (156). However, as the emphasis on being *like* a stone suggests, this is a figure of speech that, in protesting the ways that being sensitive, conscious, and mutable means being in constant pain, is not to be taken literally. Yet Godwin's use of the trope is part of a philosophical reflection on the kinship between animate and inanimate substances, and on the desirability of that kinship. As Caleb's initial remark makes clear, asserting this kinship is part of a broader assessment of what—and of how much or how little—separates life from death, sentience from insentience—a topic that Godwin considers throughout the rest of his life/writings. But aligning human with stone is also tied to psychological reflections that are in turn political questions regarding the preconditions of benevolent acts. What is the degree of insensibility required to ensure that one remain responsive and not wholly bereft of attachment? How much insensibility does a socially minded author or life partner need?

Such questions, especially as pursued in irritated times of sensibility and political upheaval, influence Godwin's embrace of coldness as a desirable trait of heart and mind. Even Godwin recognizes that the project requires redefining coldness or, in Coleridge's term, desynonymizing "warmth" from vitality, enthusiasm, feeling and "cold" from frigidity, disinterest, or death—a strategy first ventured in Godwin's reply to Dr. Parr, in which he corrects the misinterpretation that saving Fénelon over a family member is a cold act. A footnote to the *Essay on Sepulchres*, itself concerned with reanimating the dead, describes how this "cant" regarding the heart's temperature misconstrues "human" and "feeling":

> There is, and perhaps always has been, much cant afloat in the world, about *warm hearts*, and *cold hearts:* and no doubt there is a real division of human beings into what may be loosely called the *feeling* and the *unfeeling.* But the division is not exactly as it is vulgarly understood. The hottest fire is not that which on every slight incentive blazes on the surface, but that which is close pent up in the recesses of the heart, and much oftener causes the bosom to glow, than the eye to send forth sparkles of fire. In a word, the sincerest warmth is not wild, but calm; and operates in greater activity in the breast of the [stoic], than in that of the vulgar enthusiast. (21–22n, original emphasis)

Anchored in a "moral" drawn from Greek mythology that associates "chastity" not with a "frigid and languid state of thought" but with a "heat" more "admirable and divine than any other of which an intellectual being is susceptible," Godwin's recalibration of cold is part of his effort to modify current enthusiasm for sentiment by making attachment inseparable from understanding (21n).

Fostering understanding apart from the warmth of sentiment is why Godwin claims that "true happiness" exists in the life of the skeptic, defined in "The Essay on Scepticism" (1797) as the "only consistent lover of truth."[58] Loving truth means being on a constant "voyage of discovery," for the skeptic "never lays up the vessel of his mind in the harbour of opinion," nor does he ever consider his enquiries at an end (309). What impedes the public's embrace of skepticism is the objection "that it is necessarily allied to coldness of character." But this is "a glaring mistake," for skepticism has "two eminent advantages" over the "enthusiasm engendered by deceit," those being "ardour and animation," which is why the skeptic is the "genuine friend" of man (308).

The degree to which Godwin stays in touch with the coldness in humanity, even when he struggles to devise different terms for it, is compelling. The apprehension is central to maintaining optimism about the future, which requires maintaining an unsentimental approach to human life. Even if he has a predisposition to coldness—he identifies the "two leading features" of his character as "sensibility and insensibility"—this does not exempt warmer hearts from striving to attain it.[59] Available methods include directing one's passion toward scholarship, women authors, and the illustrious dead, and conducting social revolutions according to these principles. There is obviously a degree of self-defense in this project and a life's worth of frustration over vindicating himself on the scores of insensitivity, withdrawal, and indifference.[60] Even when anti-Jacobins accuse him of licentious behavior, they also harp against his lack of feeling as a philosopher and a family man. But the project also means to cultivate the type of person who will remain steadfast in the cause, no matter what amount of resistance or misinterpretation he or she faces. And this means devising persons who perceive themselves as links in a chain or rills of water "fertiliz[ing] the intellectual soil" and thus who acknowledge their afterlife as the most substantial part of their life.

Godwin's reflections on writing as activity, media, and technique intensify the coldness that the content of his life/writings is designed to promote. At first, he regretted the deadness associated with books but then he began to prefer books over most of the living, whose sullenness toward thought impedes life and retards progress on any level. In contrast, books remain vital, alive, and capable of change. This view influenced his practice of composing *Lives*, which, in their linkage of history to biography and fiction to fact, restore vitality and romance to the illustrious dead. It motivated his attachment to books for the ways that such attachment models the forms of understanding and connection-making that underlie his view of rationality and sociality. The problem is that reception of writing is a group-identified and group-identifying process, which reduces complexities and favors conformity. This is where being indifferent to misreading, attack, and public censure is crucial to fostering new writing and the futures it seeks.

Insight into the mortifying capacities of writing is what the daughter of these writers picks up and extends. She not only inherits parents who are deemed cold for different reasons, but she inherits one whose frankness about the warmth of the other is keeping her life/writings dead. Shelley's own writings are far more anxious than Godwin's about the mortifying capacities of signification as well as whether any audience will read or abide her words. She lives with a profound sense of the ability of a single word to alter one's fate or turn one to stone. Yet Godwin's experiences with public reception, too, suggest the sticking power of first words and first editions. *Thoughts on Man* instances as "the glory of man" and proof "that we leave our improvements behind us" that often "the multitudinous sea is incapable of washing away" a "single sentence, a single word" (143). Other thoughts, also of daughters, perceive this as a major burden—that, once uttered, words can never be retracted, owing in part to their existence in a chain. Contemporaries, like Coleridge and Thelwell, are troubled by slippages in signification, the inability to stabilize conflicting meanings contained within the etymology of a given word.[61] For these two, worrying over a sliding signifier might provide relief from the fixity resultant from being declared dead by the press or of thinking one's own words brought death to another. Still, even when set in stone, words set everything in motion. "Here lies what was once a man!"[62] "Shadows, arise, and read your fall! Behold the history of the last man" (*Last Man,* 364). Here lies M-A-R-Y.

CHAPTER THREE

Family Relations

The novels of Mary Shelley have long been seen as having an almost obsessive relation to the topic of family relations.[1] Some, like *Matilda* (1819), *Lodore* (1835), and *Falkner* (1837), arguably have no other thematic or plot interest. All three feature a young female protagonist (Mathilda, Ethel Lodore, Elizabeth Raby) whose sole activity involves effecting the shift in a life of devotion from father to husband. Those novels that address more public matters do so through commentary on or plot investment in marital and family arrangements. This is true of the historical novels, *Valperga* (1823) and *The Fortunes of Perkin Warbeck* (1830), both of which not only unfold their specific political concerns within a central male protagonist, Castruccio and Richard, but also externalize the tensions within him in a pair of women (Euthanasia and Beatrice, Katherine and Monina), both of whom love the male hero. It also applies to those novels that are beyond history, *Frankenstein* (1818, 1831) and *The Last Man* (1826), which situate their investigations of the beginning and end of human life within sustained commentary on domestic arrangements.

Shelley's relentless focus on family has often been construed as a conservative rejoinder to her parents' radical critiques of family, her radical husband's indifference to family life, and a sustained protest against the bad parenting that she received from all of them.[2] Staying with the parents for now, her novels' repeated explorations of domestic arrangements are read as countering her father's polemic against the my-ness or selfishness that allegiance to family fosters and as ignoring her mother's efforts to dissociate "woman" from "sentiment" by advocating futures other than marriage or motherhood for women. *Frankenstein* is read as epitomizing both charges, even now that critics are discussing other works, as if *Frankenstein* inverts Godwin's reservations in its emphasis on how neglect or avoidance of family fuels the egotism and Prometheanism of men. Victor is the first in a series of men whose unconscious misogyny pushes them to extremes, whether that means creating life apart from women or journeying to the ends of the earth to avoid dealing with them. Shelley at times also vastly extends the scope of the isolation that characterizes almost all of Godwin's male protagonists. The desolation ascribed to Caleb, Falkland, St. Leon, Fleetwood, Mandeville, Cloudesley, and Deloraine affects each of them and their nearest and dearest, but that associated with Victor, Mathilda's father, Castruccio, Lionel, or Perkin Warbeck encompasses vast public territories, if not the entire world. The extensiveness of Shelley's portrayal of male hubris could be viewed as expressing allegiance to her mother's feminist aims, except that her female characters are so invested in heterosexual love. Even the few who exercise public, or history-making, functions (like Euthanasia, Katherine, and Monina) are depicted as motivated solely by love.

It would be foolish to deny that Shelley's accounts of family relations either stem or differ from the life/writings of her parents, for they do both in significant ways. But assessments of their reactionary nature are complicated by two simple facts. First, what seems to preoccupy these novels is the perversity of family relations. Her parents' assessments of marital and familial despotism are tame compared to the feelings that Shelley explores as normal constituents of family life. Family feeling in her novels is almost always incestuous, usually necrophilic and, in the early days, homoerotic.[3] It expresses itself in homicidal and suicidal fantasies that often produce the melancholic going-it-alone that Shelley calls life. Even in the so-called sentimental fictions that characterize Shelley's later, allegedly conformist, years (*Lodore* and *Falkner*), the most eroticized domestic relation is always that between father and daughter. From start to finish, the fiercest attachments are those between living and dead. A second preoccupation further modifies the conservatism of her novels, namely, their insistent foregrounding of the performative status of reading and writing. In my view, *this* coupling, of familial and literary relations, expresses Shelley's allegiance to the revolutionary projects of her parents and constitutes the radicalism of her approach to family.[4] Her novels question what persons love in their relations as well as how literary relations affect them and this love.

Shelley begins her life-long treatment of domestic affections at the place where her father ends up and her mother leaves off: linking discussion of the nature and reform of family to discussion of the nature and reform of writing. For Godwin, as we have seen, recognition of this connection was belated and hard-won. Frustration over the public's inability and unwillingness to read him sympathetically forced him to confront the opacities of writing and the impediments that print poses to change. From the start, Wollstonecraft perceived writing, and certainly the history of Western writings, as a mixed blessing, and she always linked her vindications of the rights of women to the cultivation of new writing practices, authors, and readers. But only her last, and unfinished, novel explicitly connects its discussion of the prospects for women's happiness to the importance of female storytelling and portrays literature as the only existing social institution that is not simply invested in retarding the progress of women. Shelley's writing career begins from this insight. Indeed, affirming the point is her strongest and most sustained contribution to political reform over the course of her life, even as her later novels work less hard at foregrounding the fact and process of their narration. The affirmative version conceives of writing as the best means for effecting the changes in public opinion that are the precondition to achieving institutional reform, and the only means that women have to do so. But this affirmation depends on maintaining a skeptical view of the possibilities associated with writing, which involves staying mindful of the unpredictable movement from word to world and the varying receptivity or even existing reality of an audience. In her works, words have the power to make reality as well as prophecy the future; but they also are shown to have no discernible effect on the course of human events or feelings and themselves are frequently arrested, lost, and delayed.

The primal scene of her parents' coupling, which links the creation of life to the creation of texts and the forms of re-creation that they offer, is formative of her identity as "Mary Wollstonecraft Godwin," "Mary Wollstonecraft Shelley," and "Author of *Frankenstein.*" The *Memoirs of the Author of "A Vindication of the Rights of Woman"* establishes her parents' coming together as facilitated by a book. *Memoirs,* as well as Godwin's journals and their correspondence, go on to mark, and (mis)calculate, daughter Mary's conception as "William."[5] Then *The Wrongs of Woman; or Maria* sets into play the novel depiction of sexual love being solidified through coupled reading, which the original William perpetuates in ensuing novels. Shelley's novels extend this tradition—several of their scenes of reading being some of the best-known parts of her works (especially in *Frankenstein* but also in *Matilda, The Last Man,* and *Falkner)*— but in ways that already forecast fundamental differences in her approach to familial and literary relations. For one thing, her scenes of reading are usually composed of either a solitary person or a group. When the parties are a pair, they are invariably father and daughter. For another, reading together is no guarantee that the persons reading will stay together or that the solitary reader will come together as a unified self. Nor does the reading portrayed necessarily grant access to better, or more ideal, worlds. For a third, what distinguishes "book" from "friend" or one's attachment to either is even harder to discern than in her parents' works. For, in Shelley's world, the *precondition* of attachment is how one is related, whether as person or story. As *Frankenstein* makes clear, attachment is contingent on whether a creature or story is read in a sympathetic fashion.

Given her familial-literary background, it is surprising that Shelley's novels never portray heterosexual lovers engaged in acts of mutual textual intercourse. *Matilda* narrates such acts as a thing of the past, as characterizing the love that existed between Mathilda's father and mother and between Woodville and Elinor (8, 23, 49). *Falkner* asserts that Neville "opened" the world of the poets to Elizabeth Raby but does not portray the two engaged in reading them together (223). Perhaps this is because such scenes so embody the reality of Mary and Percy's love life that they feel redundant, are presupposed, or are being jealously preserved for that scene. If Shelley and her subsequent biographers disagree over the intensity, persistence, longevity, and exclusivity of this love, all are united on the comparative harmony and consistency that characterized their reading and writing lives as a couple. The facts of this accord are recorded in the journals of their coupled lives, which indeed initiate that record. The editors of the *Journals* note that Mary and Percy use "a new book to celebrate the beginning of a new life"; they purchase a green notebook as soon as they arrive in France and begin "Shelley and Mary's Journal Book" with a description of the day on which they eloped (28 July 1814), written by both parties (*Journals*, xv). As is well known, Percy's contribution to the journals waned fairly quickly, leaving it to Mary to record their daily activities. The editors portray this asymmetry as a critical advantage in providing "a reflection of Mary's development over the years which is seen nowhere else in her letters or her published works." Their next sentence specifies the advantage as providing evidence to counter, or modify, her reputation as "a reserved woman," one frequently "accused of coldness," though the editors also concede that the vast majority of the entries are hardly self-revealing (xv). "She may have doubted the wisdom of using the journal as a place to record too many of the details of their private lives, but she was certain of its importance as a record of their movements and the books they read; often she noted their reading when the entries for long periods contain little other information" (xviii).

It is standard in characterizations of the *Journals* to maintain this opposition between Mary documenting her feelings and documenting her reading.[6] Entries that detail Mary's feelings are seen as revealing her subjectivity, whereas those detailing her (and Percy's) reading are deemed factual or contextual, construed as relevant to interpreting her or his publications. This is a curious way of approaching the lives of professional writers. Plus, it radically dilutes this family's understanding of personhood, always in part fiction. Intercourse with books makes up a huge portion of the life of writers, and it is hard to distinguish what in one's reading pertains to one's private or public life or one's affections or reason. This is even truer when each of the lovers is an author and when their love life is so famously grounded in literature. To this day, "the Shelleys" remain one of Western culture's most romantic images of the passion that exists between intellectual couples, a view facilitated by the journal entries that, taken together, highlight the tenets that governed Shelley's public private life. First, books are a major part of her and Percy's personal lives and intimacy. Their love for books strengthens and perpetuates their love for each other. Second, recording their reading activity gives insight into their private lives as well as their professional lives as authors. Third, because their interior lives are shaped, marked, and marred by the books that they read, recording those titles is crucial to knowing what is going on with, between, and within them. Fourth, love for books is what both partners wish to bequeath to their compatriots and future generations. Indeed, extending love for books was their favorite, and only shared, plan for social amelioration.

The record of the *Journals* highlights other features of this couple's love for books and their love through the medium of books that do affect characterizations in Shelley's novels. Pillow talk never engages one other person only; expressions of intimacy always encompass a third party. Consciousness of this third party is heightened in the Shelleys' love life by the "ever-present Claire" in their married, domestic, psychic, and reading lives (xvi). This constant presence is visible in the circumspection and secret coding devised by Mary (here, her father's daughter) to exclude Claire from the "private" written exchanges between Percy and Mary, and their attempt to placate her by giving her one of Percy's notebooks for her journal. As it happens, their relative success at excluding Claire makes the journal the only real private sphere for this couple. But the (omni)presence of a third party is evident in their repeated references to passages, titles, characters, or scenes from the literary love tradition when they or her characters try to express their feelings of love. Their consciousness of future third parties is also discernible, according to the *Journal* editors, in all that this couple leaves out of the "private" record. From early on, this couple records their lives with an eye toward shielding themselves from the scrutiny that their lives and writings about family also invite. Shelley's novels, then, often draw attention to the crowd that attends a pairing. Sometimes the triangulation involves a discernible threesome, as, for example, when the creature in *Frankenstein* learns to read by eavesdropping on Felix's instructions to Safie or when Mathilda's father requests that Mathilda start reading in Dante's *Purgatorio* at the spot where his wife, Diana, left off sixteen years ago. More frequently, characters learn to love in the presence and with the spirit of the dead, whether those dead are family members, illustrious members of the literary tradition, or both.

These portrayals of the opening out of couple love in Shelley's novels arguably mitigate the self-involvement or claustrophobia that a passionate married life, especially between writers, often entails. They may also seek to counter the openings that Percy's activities instigated. In any case, they are motivated by two different sets of concern that relate to Shelley's notions of selfhood as expressed in her fiction. The literariness of the Shelleyan character, especially in the early novels, shows selfhood to be self-divided, multiple, from the start. Frequently portrayed as composed in relation to the books s/he reads and the fictional characters that s/he loves, the Shelleyan protagonist is also often "read" or interpreted like—and sometimes as—a literary text. Moreover, explicit allusions to specific texts within a given novel serve to reveal the "unconscious" desires and intentions of certain characters, especially in the case of Mathilda but also of Lionel in *The Last Man* and Gerald Neville in *Falkner*. Such portrayals accentuate the ambivalence regarding couple reading that each of Mary's parents' novels explore in different ways, Wollstonecraft's highlighting how reading traditionally stymies women's fantasy lives and life options, Godwin's suggesting how one's love for books or a particular author can both intensify and block human relations. With Shelley's protagonists, the twoness often resides within the character, the self coupled to his or her fictional forebear.[7] This characterization makes it difficult for "character" to assume identity, responsibility, or human agency because it is unsure of what is motivating its acts.

A second concern is how gender affects the not-one-ness of Shelleyan selfhood, further dispossessing the female character of identity and autonomy in legal, social, and economic terms, especially in marriage. By taking as her usual protagonist (after *Frankenstein)* a female whose first love often includes books, she composes characters who must confront a relation to autonomy and love that is irreducibly vexed. Like Wollstonecraft's novels, hers foreground writing as the means for changing female dispossession. But unlike Wollstonecraft's, hers do not—cannot—begin afresh but instead seek to revise classic Western myths, especially pertaining to female sexuality.[8] Several of her texts reconfigure the features of classical figures: Prometheus, Proserpine, Beatrice, Mathilda, and Midas. Others follow Wollstonecraft's lead by portraying "new" women, whose novelty resides in their thinking powers (Euthanasia, Katherine, Fanny Derham). These new women take one of two forms: women whose love for a man is shown to be reasonable and supportive of the wife's reasoning powers or women who love to read by and think for themselves. But even here, her novels remain skeptical about the progress or emancipation inherent in women's access to literature. The means to a better future, reading keeps women engaged in and by the past.

The novels that have the most elaborate framing devices (*Frankenstein, Matilda, The Last Man*) are also those that place the greatest emphasis in their narratives on the importance of reading or of literary culture in the formation of individual and group identity. They are also the novels with the most explicit *commentary* on family dynamics, although all her novels feature characters that are related to each other as family. I begin with *Frankenstein* and *Matilda* in order to highlight their renditions of how a character's foundation in fiction affects the reformation as well as deformation of family relations.[9] These are the two texts that go the farthest in accentuating scenes of writing and reading that in effect probe the humanity of literature—*Frankenstein* exploring the extent to which reading can humanize a creature, and *Matilda* questioning one's responsibility for the desires that classic literature implants within readers. Understanding these inter-relations requires that we distinguish between Shelley's "radical" and "feminist" investments. Critics tend to collapse the two, while they often read her focus on family as at once conservative and feminist because female-identified. But both *Frankenstein* and *Matilda* are less feminist than her historical or sentimental novels, generally viewed by most critics as conformist and conservative.[10] Certainly, the latter are less edgy or adventurous and less experimental formally, but they are more concerned with portraying female characters and addressing the status or future of women. They are also prophetic in a subtler, less spectacular, way. Both in her historical and sentimental fictions, female characters are portrayed less as readers than as characters who have made, or will make, the future—and who, in so doing, create new possibilities for female character. Her early radical texts clear space for this future by exploring how and whether familial or literary relations are successful at humanizing individuals.

Literary Creatures

> I became myself capable of bestowing animation upon lifeless
> matter.
>
> *Frankenstein*

Critics have often noted the connections asserted in *Frankenstein* between
fathering and authoring or bestowing life and writing books, a dynamic especially visible in the relation between Victor and the creature, Victor described
variously as father and author of the creature's being.[11] The linkage is usually
noted as implying Shelley's protest against fathers and authors who do not
take responsibility for the lives that they have engendered, an implication read
back into her dedication of *Frankenstein* to "William Godwin, Author of
Political Justice, Caleb Williams, &c,"—that "&c" including her own beget-
ting. This alleged judgment constitutes the "feminist" component of the novel,
understood as involving a critique of Prometheanism, male hubris, science,
and the penchant of all three to ignore the attractions of home in their zeal for
penetrating nature.[12] But if we extend this coupling between bestowing life
and authoring or reading texts to the entire novel, several things shift in
standard assessments of its aims. First of all, the foregrounding of scenes of
narration becomes related to the text's investigation of the nature of familial
and literary relations and the status of the creature in relation to both. It also
stresses the creature's status not only as bookish but as a book—composed as it
is out of pieces of the dead and animated through the eyes of another. This
raises the question of how recognizing the literary component of this "new
species" affects how it is read and evaluated by readers within and of the novel.

This double focus on narrative and human relations complicates the opposition between private and public spheres that is often said to structure the
novel's analysis of and solution to Prometheanism—granting sufficient respect
to domestic affections; grounding one's public enterprises in love of family or
home. The frame narratives themselves (not just the stories they frame) merge
the two categories by publicizing private feelings and addressing this writing
to familiars. For example, the outer frame, which has the most explicit commentary on the composition, receipt, and destination of writing, stages this
discussion between a brother and sister whose medium of writing is letters.
Victor's narration to Walton, with its ostensible warning against adventure,

isolation, male egotism, occurs as storytelling around the kitchen ship-stove, discourse that is then committed to writing by the listener and subject to the speaker's editorial revisions. The creature's narrative to Victor relays information that only a parent, and precisely not the baby, should know, just as the creature's knowledge of Victor's status as its "father" comes from reading Victor's journal, a fact that it should have learned from its father. The accounts that these frames frame also nullify the separation of spheres in ways indicated by the novel's subtitle. For *Frankenstein*'s probing of interiors, thematized in its investigation of the psychological disposition of Prometheanism as men wary of domestic and female interiors, takes its cue from one of Western culture's oldest myths disseminated through print culture. And *Frankenstein* modernizes this classic myth while portraying it as internalized by a group of men: those poet-voyagers (not yet legislators) whose realm encompasses the far reaches of the globe and mind and whose imaginations are fueled by ancient romantic mariners.[13]

Acknowledging this subversion of private/public distinctions invites us to strengthen Kate Ellis's reservations regarding the endorsement of domesticity in *Frankenstein*.[14] The alleged endorsement stems primarily from an analysis of Shelley's depiction of Victor's creation and lack of relation to his creature. But one could say that Victor's failure to parent his creature is already accomplished in the process leading up to its creation, which not only removes woman from the site of re/production but also isolates Victor from all prior relations—to nature, family, friends, or books. The creature's eventual murder of Victor's relations, then, is only the visible manifestation of what Victor has already achieved and is the necessary outcome of the creature's origin in (and, ultimately, status as) a nonrelation. Ascribed to either party, these murders clearly warn against "procrastinat[ing] all that relate[s] to [one's] feelings of affection" (38). But while *Frankenstein* articulates Shelley's founding convictions that being or feeling connected precedes the ability to act benevolently and that sympathy is indispensable to virtue, it does not equate feelings of connection with domesticity or imply that home is the space where hearts come alive (or even are kept alive). In fact, returning home means entering the house of mourning, a fact stressed by the absence of home births.

Consider those maxims usually cited as affirming the desirability of home. "Learn from me, if not by my precepts, at least by my example, how dangerous is the acquirement of knowledge, and how much happier that man is who believes his native town to be the world, than he who aspires to become greater than his nature will allow" (36).[15] "If the study to which you apply yourself has a tendency to weaken your affections and to destroy your taste for those simple pleasures in which no alloy can possibly mix, then that study is certainly unlawful. . . . If no man allowed any pursuit to interfere with the tranquility of his domestic affections, Greece had not been enslaved; Caesar would have spared his country; America would have been discovered more gradually; and the empires of Mexico and Peru had not been destroyed" (38). Invariably construed as statements regarding *Shelley's* position on the primacy of domestic affections, they are asserted by Victor, who is a famously unreliable narrator, especially at those moments when he interprets, rather than relates, his narrative, and who never himself adopts this position. Their structure is similarly revealing, for such passages stand in an oppositional relation to the story proper, not only by disrupting the narrative in order to comment retroactively on it but also by contradicting both its tone and content. In this, they resemble the strategy of both versions of Coleridge's *Rime of the Ancient Mariner* (one of the presiding genii of *Frankenstein*), the validity of whose moral is undercut by the sheer counterweight of the narrative, not to mention its supernatural content and the repetition compulsion that keeps recharging it. Furthermore, the statements themselves are patently absurd—in themselves and in the contexts of *Frankenstein* and Shelley's positions on relations generally.

The comparison that structures the first maxim is both false and misleading when read as asserting that happiness is likelier to be found at home than abroad, within one's native sphere rather than out in the world. But that opposition (home/world) is contained *within* the first half of the comparison —"How much happier that man is who believes his native town to be the world"—which is then contrasted to the ostensibly opposing, but actually simply different and, in several ways, incontestable condition—"than he who aspires to become greater than his nature will allow." And what makes the man happier is that he finds the world *in* his native town rather than choosing to reside in it in order to avoid the world—an imaginative or performative dimension that is crucial to Shelley's version of fictional reality. The second claim is even harder to reconcile with the ambiguities that permeate a Shelleyan worldview. Where in *Frankenstein* or Shelley's life/writings do we find "simple pleasures in which no alloy can possibly mix"? Where would the world or the home be—indeed, where in the world would we be—"if no man allowed any pursuit to interfere with the tranquility of his domestic affections"? A provisional answer also reveals Shelley's position on domesticity. We would be with the dead, arguably the primary occupants and (pre)conditions of home.

The actual portrayals of domesticity and family life in *Frankenstein* suggest as well a more equivocal evaluation of this sphere. Marriage is associated with the "decline of life" for men and the termination of life for women. Victor and Elizabeth's hands are joined over their mother's deathbed, Elizabeth's wedding bed is her deathbed, and the required preparation for her wedding day includes "becom[ing] grave" (23, 29, 69). Domestic life is described as "quiet" (25, 70, 111), "tranquil" (70), and "monoton[ous]" (111), a mode of living that requires men to "relinquish" their "public employments" and "pursuits" and that sanctions male perceptions of females as "insect[s]," the treatment of whom resembles tending "on a favourite animal" (23, 24). After they are grown, males leave the home and "delay" returning for as long as possible. Considerate men at least wait to marry until the decline of life, but others ensure the decline of their fiancées by traveling for years, "slacken[ing] their progress" as they approach home, and associating the act of marriage with being "tied" down, "bound close," and sitting "down for life within the walls of [their] native town" (53, 146, 117). Nor does the plot ever confirm the assertions of the "tranquility" and quiet found at home, except in death. Each time that Victor crosses a threshold, he reproaches the person he meets for destroying his calm with their anxiety. He implores Earnest to "try to be more calm, that I may not be absolutely miserable the moment I enter my father's house after so long an absence" (56). He whines to Elizabeth on their wedding day, "Ah, if you knew what I have suffered, and what I may yet endure, you would endeavour to let me taste the quiet, and freedom from despair, that this one day at least permits me to enjoy" (148).

Far from rejecting her father's critique of domestic affection for blocking justice by exacerbating selfishness, then, Shelley broadens his analysis in several ways. In effect, *Frankenstein* addresses the topic in the spirit of Godwin's second-stage approach to domestic affection, when he begins to promote affiliation over autonomy as the relational structure most conducive to achieving justice. Several critics have noted resemblances between the texts and the eponymous heroes of *St. Leon* and *Frankenstein*.[16] By stipulating as the "chief concern" of *Frankenstein* demonstrating the "amiableness of domestic affection" and the "excellence of universal virtue," the 1818 Preface (written by Percy) adopts the aims and the strategy of *St. Leon*, often read as the most "autobiographical" of Godwin's novels in its positive treatment of marital and domestic relations but, as I argued earlier, more appropriately read as recognizing the importance of affirming domestic affection to gaining a fair public reception. St. Leon and Victor not only pursue the same magic—the "search of the philosopher's stone and the elixir of life" (*Frankenstein*, 26)—but claim that by doing so they are benefiting humanity, while in fact they end up cutting themselves off from all human connection (in this inadvertently acquiring their aim). But *Frankenstein* pushes to extremes two ramifications of Godwin's efforts to cultivate the public features of family. It presents the foundational human connection—a parent's to its offspring—as a matter of justice. "Oh, Frankenstein, be not equitable to every other and trample upon me alone, to whom thy justice, and even thy clemency and affection, is most due" (74; also 104). It details the possibilities and liabilities of being raised on books.

The creature represents Shelley's strongest case that benevolence depends on being (well) related and perceiving oneself as such. As the creature maintains, "I was benevolent and good; misery made me a fiend," and that misery is the product of "being alone, miserably alone," which is in turn the consequence of having its character repeatedly misread (74, 75). This portrayal amends the necessarianism of Godwin, whether conceived as a moral or an epistemological system, by construing as idealized the view that every living thing is inevitably linked in a chain. The fact that the creature perceives itself as unhooked to others, as existentially alone, occasions the actions that place it outside the bounds of the human (the position from which it began). In this regard, the creature poses a challenge to necessity that is reinforced by its claimed kinship to Adam and Prometheus. Which comes first: the first of a species or sympathy for it? For as the creature points out, only when one "live[s] in communion with an equal" and "feel[s] the affections of a sensitive being" does one "become linked to the chain of existence and events" (110). One can be alive and yet not exist, for existence in *Frankenstein* depends on two conditions whose necessity remains unaltered throughout Shelley's works —imagination and love. Imagination is necessary to existence, and love is a rational need—indeed, the (universal) foundation of justice.[17]

This linkage between love and justice affects the opening out of the nuclear family that is enacted in *Frankenstein*. Victor includes in "this description of our domestic circle" his closest friend, Henry Clerval, "for he was constantly with us" (24). Also, Justine Moritz, though technically a servant, is "received" in "our family," "beloved by all the family," and recognized as acting toward the youngest "as a most affectionate mother" (46, 60). Changes made in the characterization of Elizabeth's parentage also bear out this impulse. Critics tend to construe her refiguration in the 1831 edition, where she is an orphan of a Milanese nobleman, as working to erase the implications of incest ascribable to her presentation in the 1818 edition as Victor's first cousin. But, as Betty T.

Bennett asserts, marriage between first cousins "was not regarded as incestuous in England in that period," and, as Katherine Hill-Miller points out, suggestions of incestuous desires between Victor and Elizabeth persist in other forms.[18] Arguably, then, the shift in parentage is meant to stress the breadth of reach of possible family relations—an emphasis accentuated by the international and intercultural love between Felix and Safie and by the Orientalism in the attraction of Victor to Henry.

Another means of opening out the family gets at the heart of the issue of whether the family is ever, or ideally, a relation of blood. It concerns the function and status of books in *Frankenstein* and the degree to which they are portrayed as constituents of family life (in the twin senses that idealized scenes of De Laceyian domesticity revolve around reading and that what is read delineates the features of family) and adequate substitutes for it. Critics have emphasized the importance of reading in *Frankenstein* on the formation and development of Victor and the creature.[19] This is not surprising in a story about human development, except that in this text reading is what initiates and then fleshes out the development of a new species of in/humanity. Victor describes reading as the chief "event" that "led by insensible steps to my after tale of misery," by which he means both that he read the wrong books— antiquated rather than up-to-date accounts of natural history—and received inadequate paternal supervision of his reading. If, instead of dismissing the works of Cornelius Agrippa and Paracelsus as "sad trash," his father had bothered to explain why their "wonderful facts" were neither "real" nor "practical," the "train of my ideas would never have received the fatal impulse that led to my ruin" (25). The creature and its misery are even more dependent on reading, for books are said to awaken, not just cultivate, its mind and sentiments. The course of its reading, first an account of social institutions (Volney's *Ruins of Empire*), then of God's creation of man (Milton's *Paradise Lost*), then the lives of men of the classical past (Plutarch's *Lives*), then its own creation, mirrors part of what it is seeking through reading—knowledge not only of the world but also of humankind's and its own position within the world. Acquiring this knowledge is indissociable from the feelings that reading intensifies and the questions that such feelings raise: Am I human? To whom or what am I related? What am I if I am not related? At the same time, the books that the creature reads literally teach it the various relations of family and its desire for them.

The centrality of reading to the creature's development is understandably compensatory, because it is an abandoned child. Since it has no parent or family, books do the best that they can to awaken its heart, inform its mind, and teach it how to forge cognitive and human connections. The inadequacy of books compared to persons as fit companions is asserted in the frame narrative, when Robert Walton laments his lack of a friend and describes writing as a "poor medium for the communication of feeling." It certainly appears to be borne out by the outcome of the creature's reading, where the lack of a live companion, a *semblable*, transforms the creature into a fiend. But this negative evaluation is undercut by several features of the novel that suggest instead the superiority of books over family members, especially in terms of expressing or communicating passion. Percy's 1818 Preface stipulates that great poetry, and even "humble" novels (!), specialize in the delineation of "human passions more comprehensive and commanding than any which the ordinary relations of existing events can yield" (7). Similarly, the creature's reactions to the great works of Western culture reinforce the intensity of their delineation of passion. They also acquaint it with the extremes of human feeling—for death as well as life, evil as well as good. More fundamentally, the characters in these books are the first "beings" with which the creature identifies, perceives a resemblance, and hence experiences a "personal" connection, because their genesis is similar to its. This humanization by reading cuts both ways. It makes the creature crave "real" human connection, the absence of which prompts it to wipe out the human.

This topic is a subset of the larger theme of the dangers of knowledge and thus the rewriting of the fall that *Frankenstein* presents.[20] Precisely the picture of community that is accentuated in literature makes the creature perceive its difference from humans as well as its ostracism by them. In this, *Frankenstein* raises a topic that is explored throughout Shelley's writings: the degree of conformity between reading and living and the worlds that are encountered in each. At the same time that *Frankenstein* stresses the value of literature for cultivating sentiment and extending one's access to and familiarity with the world, it shows the capacity of literature to underscore a being's alienation, even exile, from humanity. Indeed, the sense of exclusion that literature intensifies provokes homicidal tendencies. *Frankenstein* explores this dynamic as a species issue, as the consequence of the creature being the first of a kind and therefore someone for whom the literary tradition does not speak. Subsequent texts treat this as a gender issue, implied in *Frankenstein* as well by the critical tradition that stresses the creature's feminization.[21] In both cases, literature is valued because it provides the only available means by which marginalized subjects can identify with, even contribute to, culture at the same time that it heightens their sense of alienation from it. What stories speak to me? Which myths find the heroism in femininity? Why does literature make a monster out of my impulses and character? Why do I feel akin to these dead letters? At the same time, access to literacy in *Frankenstein* literally makes a creature immortal, for language and the "science of letters" are portrayed as the only "godlike" substances in creation.[22]

In the case of the creature, its perceived resemblance to textual characters, both fictional and biographical, stresses its own a/humanity. In this regard, fictional characters are closer to its life than the humans it encounters. Recognizing the creature's a/humanity complicates its responsibility for the murders it commits; it occasions, even justifies, the sympathy that humans feel for it, especially when it is allowed to relate its life story. This characterization pushes to extremes the ambiguity that gains prominence in Shelley's texts regarding the ontological and ethical status of fiction. But this a/humanity also reflects poorly on the family, not just in the sense that its father's cruelty occasions its after tale of misery by making it into a monster. It accentuates how family life robs persons, too, of their lives and animacy. For the home is haunted by the dead, especially dead mothers, and the desires of the living are directed toward this end. The portrait of Caroline Beaufort hangs over the hearth in a memorial to mourning, posed as she is kneeling beside the body of her dead father (an image painted at the "desire" of Victor's father) and positioned over a "miniature" dead William. Scenes of betrothal occur on deathbeds, as the portrait of Caroline and the engagement of Victor and Elizabeth make clear. The only thing that brings the family together—and sons back into the household—is the death of one of its members, and the text goes out of its way to place its births either on the road or in a boarding-room laboratory. The 1831 edition specifies that Victor is born at Naples, Elizabeth adopted while the family is "making an excursion" on the "shores of Lake Como," and Earnest is born abroad—whose arrival finally causes Victor's parents to "g[i]ve up entirely their wandering life and fi[x] themselves in their native country" (190, 193). Only William, then, is born by a woman at home, and he is the first to go. With the exception of Justine (whose mother hates her), every family member in *Frankenstein* is motherless: Caroline Beaufort, Elizabeth, Henry Clerval, Felix and Agatha, Safie, and all the Frankenstein children once Caroline dies. And the females in the text all die when they reach childbearing potential.

It is as if families in *Frankenstein* are related by absent or spent blood, blood that gives them life but then stops flowing before they are grown. As a consequence, the passions of these children are at once bloodless and necro-philic. As critics have noted, Victor's passion for Elizabeth is mortifying; in dream and reality, his is the kiss of death and the consummation of it.[23] The creature expresses its desire for connection by strangling others, stressing the point that the demand for love can suck the air out of a person. But it, too, has been programmed this way, by exposure through the *Sorrows of Werter* to the triangulation of desire and its demand that someone must go. This does not imply that *Frankenstein* rejects all domestic affections or the desire to have an interior life. But it underscores the misery of not having one's reading life borne out by reality and the difficulties that arise when beings are s/mothered by books. Though dark, the linkage in *Frankenstein* of narrative and familial relations gives a foretaste of what becomes forward-looking in Shelley's re- and decomposition of family. Family members could use a little more breath-ing room, especially its women. A sense of space can be gained by opening up the family to others who are not related by blood or fixated on it. And this entails perceiving family as the encounter with otherness that it actually phantasmatically is and valuing it for granting such a presentiment of life.

Literary Associations

> Often . . . I have compared myself to Proserpine.
>
> *Matilda*

Welcoming death into the household is one of Shelley's most striking contributions to the history of the novel. Her novels repeatedly portray death as a major component of domestic life and one of its most pressing realities. Stressing this fact is not meant as a denigration of domestic life but as a re-evaluation of the kinds and modes of living available in it. Upbringing in a family can propel youth forward into the world, but it can also bind persons so closely that they can neither move nor breathe. Many go under. Think of the number of characters who die by suffocation in Shelley's novels. William and Elizabeth are strangled, Justine is hanged, and Mathilda's father, Euthanasia, Adrian, Clara, Monina, and Alithea Rivers all drown. Even more innovative is Shelley's forthright admission of incest in family settings, a topic broached in *Frankenstein* as well as in *The Last Man, Lodore,* and *Falkner* and the un-spoken center of *Matilda,* a truly striking investigation of the lethal and incestuous nature of family ties. Here too the admission is not meant merely to discredit domestic affection or overbearing fathers but to identify the challenges that living in a close family raises—among others, the admission highlights literature's contribution to stimulating such desires.

By penning her life story on her deathbed, *Matilda* links writing to death from the start of the novella. Being on the verge of death, Mathilda claims, gives her license to write what she could not say while living about the taboo— and her violation of the taboo—that grounds the family by ensuring that its members head out into the world. In this regard, incest is Shelley's name for the "excessive familiarity" that Godwin contends damages a child's ability to unfold her mind and expand her relations. Nothing unfolds in *Matilda* for Mathilda except misery; and she remains fixated on a moment in time that she hopes to recover through various denials of the movement of time. Critics often read *Matilda* as Shelley's attempt to dramatize, and possibly legitimize, her "excessive & romantic attachment" to her father, an approach that Charles Robinson calls into question by stressing the distance that Shelley takes from her protagonist as an author, narrator, and daughter.[24] But attending to her roles as author, narrator, and daughter also shows how Shelley cannot break free from the incestuous nature of familial and literary relations, fused as they are in her specific history as daughter. This most self-enclosed of Shelleyan texts, both in its publication history and total lack of narrative interest in public life or events, displays the public effects of literary classics on a self's formation. For although guilt forces incest to go unnamed, both guilt and incest boast an illustrious literary history. Indeed, judging from the content of our myths, incest is a primal relation.

This paradox is related to a second explored by *Matilda*. On the one hand, *Matilda* portrays incest as something that profoundly isolates its female protagonist—so much so that she cannot find words for the experience, chooses to feign death rather than face social interaction, flees whatever affection is subsequently offered her, and depicts her existence as a "cold chill" that she casts upon any who approach her (61). Like the creature in *Frankenstein* (and most of Godwin's protagonists), she considers herself the most "solitary" creature in existence, not because her appearance but her "history and the never ending feelings and remembrances arising from it" place her outside human sympathy (*Matilda*, 40). Like the creature, too, she is alive but does not exist. A similar condition is often said to characterize this author in 1819, at once grief-stricken over the death of her last remaining child, William, and so desolated by a series of losses that the world appears a blank. But this kind of isolation is only part of either narrative. For *Matilda* also explores the ways that the topic of incest, and writing about it, place Mathilda and Shelley in good company. Part of Mathilda's story includes her making several allusions to a series of incest texts and literary characters distinguished by their excessively romantic feelings for another family member. Writing *Matilda* not only revived Shelley's spirits but also placed her in the writing company of friends—like Coleridge, whose words the text cites repeatedly, and like Percy and Byron, who were also composing incest narratives around this time (*The Cenci* and *Manfred*).

Matilda is even more insistent than *Frankenstein* in linking human and literary relations. Mathilda is essentially raised on books, since she, like the creature, is an abandoned child. Except for a nurse (who leaves when she is eight) and an aunt who is cold as ice, all her girlhood relations are either fictional or natural. Besides the trees to which she bears "an individual attachment," Rosalind, Miranda, and the lady of Comus are "brought to life" as her girlhood "companions," and she herself credits books with supplying ("in some degree") the "place of human intercourse" (13). After the death of her father and her retreat to the wilds of Scotland, the "study" of books is what makes her "more human" again. Through reading, Mathilda recovers her wish for "sympathy" and her longing for connection (46). Moreover, her affections are always mediated by pictorial or written representations. Her favorite dream-vision as a girl is a reunion with her father, the "idol of her imagination," undertaken in a Rosalindesque pursuit in which she is "disguised like a boy" and wearing his "miniature" "exposed on my breast" (14). That Mathilda's affections are formed on fiction explains her penchant for drama, for staging her feelings, and, particularly, her longings for death. Charles Robinson is right to spotlight "Mathilda as Dramatic Actress" and to detail the numerous ways in which she "feigns" states and "performs" emotions like a "tragic actress."[25] However, his tendency to equate "performer" with "dissembler" and to judge Mathilda harshly for it suggests an oversimplification of what it means to have one's character formed by art. To what extent, *Matilda* asks, is a tragic flaw one's own?

This is not to say that the text portrays Mathilda as bearing no responsibility or taking none for her acts. Nor is it to discredit Robinson's main point, that Shelley distances herself from her narrator through accentuating Mathilda's drama. But it is to say that *Matilda* questions the ability to distinguish fully illusion from reality, especially when characters raised on fiction have books as their first loves, and it then explores why the determination or expiation of guilt in such a world is such a complicated epistemological, as well as ethical, endeavor.[26] To reduce the problem of incest to morality is to ignore the power of the unconscious—"I did not yet know of the crime there may be in involuntary feeling" (24)—and of literature for both fueling and repressing knowledge of such desires. On the one hand, Mathilda *is* innocent of the "crime" and arguably even of the awareness of the crime for which she feels such guilt. Her father says as much in asserting that "I have made your innocent heart acquainted with the looks and language of unlawful and monstrous passion" (32). On the other, she is well versed in the looks and language of this passion through the fictional characters with whom she identifies. The first page of her narrative has her identifying with Oedipus. "It is as the wood of the Eumenides none but the dying may enter; and Oedipus is about to die" (5). At different points, she displays her familiarity with several desirous daughters through allusions to famous incest texts, especially her declared "favorite," Alfieri's *Myrrha,* which, as Robinson notes, casts the daughter as the "sexual aggressor."[27] Others are to Sigismunda, who "was so loved by her father, Tancred, that he killed her lover Guiscardo," to Lelia in Fletcher's comedy, *The Captain,* who "propositions her father and argues that 'tis not against nature / For us to lye together,'" and to Proserpine (20, 19).

These literary allusions complicate determinations of what Mathilda knows about her guilt or desire and expand on two issues that are raised in *Franken-stein.* One concerns the dangers that reading poses in its ability to inspire inappropriate thoughts or feelings. Beyond the specific danger of incest, *Matilda* addresses the capacity of fiction to arouse feelings and desires that are ostensibly beyond the experience of youth, for *Matilda* specifically identifies novels as one of "the various ways that youth in civilized life are led to a knowledge of the existence of passions before they really feel them" (8). More to the point, reading in *Matilda* helps make a daughter into a sexual "monster," the nature of whose desires, in her view, places her outside the bounds of humanity— though squarely within the classical humanities. The other issue from *Fran-kenstein* involves the degree to which life experience is necessary to bring home the truths of fiction. This is figured in two ways in *Matilda.* As Mary Jacobus shows, what makes the father's declaration, "My daughter, I love you," so traumatic is that it repeats Mathilda's "innocent" girlhood wish to hear precisely these words. Hearing them confirmed in reality implicates her in the guilt and desire that she consciously disavows.[28] But consciously, too, she is steeped in this desire through the texts that she reads and loves. The question then becomes, What is the status of feelings that are inspired by literature? To what extent are those feelings "personal"? and thus, What accountability does a person have for feeling or acting on them?

One could say that *Matilda* addresses such questions by exploring the possibility of guilt by literary association. Technically, the "crime" that the text investigates is hearing—in fact, demanding that one hear—a word that, once spoken, changes one's world and, especially, one's sense of the possibility of ever relating to others. After all, the passion between father and daughter is never expressed physically; in addition, the text goes out of its way to portray Mathilda as virtually bodiless. She is characterized as a "nymph," a "deity," a "ministering Angel of Paradise," and is precisely opposed by her father to the "women we meet in dayly life" (33, 34). Instead, what enters Mathilda is a word; this is the "poison" that is "poured" into her ears and that immediately changes all her "blood" into a "cold fountain of bitterness corrupted in its very source" such that it "no longer . . . supports life" (53). In other words, a word— and the text reiterates this struggle over "the word"—can change one's life or even end life as one knows it.[29] In itself, this is a plausible definition of great literature, the effect of whose words are transformational, epoch-forming, especially because such works have as their defining quality the intensification of passions that are out of the ordinary, extraordinary, even sublime. Moreover, the word in question here happens to be *love,* certainly one of the main constituents of literature and also the word that women are allegedly dying to hear.[30] Not just the nature of the crime in *Matilda* but also her expressions of guilt are literary. Mathilda borrows the language of literature and the tragic stage to express her guilt, and *Matilda* positions guilt within the then-contemporary literary scene by specifying as "the worst fiend of all" the "involuntary feeling" of "Remorse" (24).

The word *remorse* introduces a second way in which guilt is figured as a literary association, for the text both cites and alludes to several of Shelley's associates who are also writing on remorse and incest. The text's habit of citing but not incorporating other literary texts into its narrative has been explored by Jacobus and Tilottama Rajan in relation to the unreadability of trauma, a topic that I pursue in chapter 5.[31] The mode of quotation—these passages are left unassimilated in the text—indeed suggests Mathilda's exclusion from the literary community either by virtue of her gender or her crime. But the fact of quotation, and the circumstances surrounding both Mathilda's and Shelley's explorations of incest, imply an unusual level of immersion in the literary community for any person, woman or man. As we have seen, Mathilda's world of relations *is* fictional and her primary reality is illusion, as critics note in order to condemn her for being both otherworldly and disingenuous, but Shelley depicts this situation as a natural outgrowth of the circumstances in which Mathilda grew up. Early immersion in the literary had similar consequences on Shelley's character, for whether she ever finally lived up to her founding reality was *the* troubling existential question of her life.

In *Matilda*, the question is staged in the relation between Mathilda and Woodville, the Percy Shelleyan poet who affirms the writer's twin responsibilities in and to the world: write to improve the conditions of living, and continue to live so that you can write to improve the conditions of living. This in-text debate plays out the opposed positions within the Shelleyean household in 1819 on the question of the support for life found either in language or in literary tradition. The contest is not simply between Percy and Mary but also within Percy, between the "beautiful idealisms" of *Prometheus Unbound* and the "sad realities" of *The Cenci*, whose tragic protagonist, Beatrice Cenci, is unsurpassed in embodying the difficulties of ascribing guilt or owning up to it. In the preface to *The Cenci*, Percy portrays Beatrice as exposing the generic incompatibility between "moral" and "dramatic interest" by inspiring condemnation at the same time that she elicits sympathy. On the score of guilt, the play is darker still in ascribing "innocence" to the period before speech—that is, before language implicates a subject in the guilt and desire of the other. "She is as pure as speechless infancy."[32] *Matilda*, then, in associating Mathilda, Matelda, Beatrice, and Proserpine, and by emphasizing Mathilda's similarity to Percy's Beatrice by showcasing her as an unsuccessful tragic actress, makes the individuality and authenticity of its protagonist difficult to discern. It also casts doubt on the depth of the isolation that she feels. One could say that Shelley depicts the experience of incest as transforming Mathilda from a "real" character into one whose only kin are literary (the place from which she starts her life). This seems to represent a loss for life, except that those literary characters have proved so attractive in intensifying live readers' longings for the heightened and radically life-transforming experiences that belong to the literary.

Recognizing the shaping power of fiction, the capacity of stories to insinuate themselves into a person's blood, dreams, and feelings, is part of the formulation of the subject's formation that *Matilda* explores. This *is* Mary Shelley's story—not that her "excessive & romantic attachment" to her father is incestuous but that her formation as a daughter-subject is informed by literature and by a literary tradition that has little language for characterizing deep connections between fathers and daughters other than incest. Experiencing this set of conditions has implications for how one understands one's life as a set of relations that are both "real" and literary. Like *The Cenci*, *Matilda* activates a restless casuistry in the reader in order to accentuate the contradictory, even self-canceling, nature of literature when a work is evaluated for its discrete moral, dramatic, or literary interest.[33] *Matilda* does not condemn Mathilda or her father (though they condemn themselves) so much as lay bare the paradox that incest is Western culture's grounding taboo and one of the fundamental relations in, and of, its literary culture. To construe having incestuous feelings simply as a moral issue is to weaken, not facilitate, the handling of them "responsibly." Words are never innocent, and those that are deemed unspeakable accrue enormous interest.

Shelley's novels address the matter by treating incestuous feelings as both a fact and a challenge of family life that comes from the excessive familiarity that living in such circumstances breeds. In her account, family members would do well to face this reality directly rather than deny or efface it. The plot of *Matilda* shows the negative consequences of keeping this reality unspeakable; as text it breaks the silence. Subsequent novels, like *Lodore* and *Falkner,* admit the intensity between fathers and daughters but ultimately allow for its redirection to a third party. By so doing, they let both parties live or rest in peace and begin to modify the one-sidedness of literary culture's treatment of the topic, especially its dis/figurations, and consequent condemnations, of a daughter's desires. This is related to another issue that distinguishes Shelley's inheritance—and genius—as daughter and writer. Up until her mother's day, with very few exceptions, literary culture had been incestuous, comprising a shockingly small group of like-minded men. Both of her parents worked to make writing more receptive to difference, more comprehensive and comprehending of the world. At the same time, literary culture thrives on what comes before. The point is not to deny or break the chain but to expand the associations attached to any particular link in, or linkage of, the chain. In this, Shelley recognized her father's necessity by privileging books in the chain of events and circumstances that compose the individual.

New Histories and Sentiments

It seems as if the eternal Lawgiver intended that, at a certain age, man should leave father, mother, and the dwelling of his infancy, to seek his fortunes over the wide world.

Lodore

Subsequent novels are less concerned with making reading an aspect of their plot or books part of a character's motivation. Nor do they frame their stories in ways that call attention to the activity and vagaries of writing, with the exception of *The Last Man*, considered in chapter 5. Instead, Shelley moves on to a second formal innovation in composing historical fiction that displays both the discipline of history and past historical events that comprise past history as embedded in fiction. In her historical fiction, *Valperga* and *The Fortunes of Perkin Warbeck*, and in her later sentimental novels, *Lodore* and *Falkner*, she then explicitly connects possibilities for the future to the characterizations of her female characters. The most obviously fictive element in the histories of Castruccio and Perkin Warbeck are the women that Shelley arranges around them, women who, in their dispositional opposition both to the central male figure and to each other, bear witness to the different paths that history could have taken had it been more receptive to women—alternatives that pertain both to the events themselves and to the ways that these events are composed as history.[34] That is, events of history would have gone differently if male leaders had not pursued ambition at the expense of human relationship, and the probability of such events occurring would have been greater had the discourse of history been less focused on great men and heroic action and more in touch with community, the logic and affect of association, and the quotidian events and sentiments of daily life. In this last regard, the unsensational nature of the plots, characters, and events of her sentimental novels is part of the history that Shelley was composing.

Pursuing alternatives to conventional history affects virtually all of Shelley's writing projects and innovations, including those that remake history by writing and rewriting the *Lives* of illustrious men, among them her father and her husband. They also include revising some of the classic myths of Western culture and subjectivity. For now, I want to focus on the two chief alternatives to the conventional subject of history that these later novels offer, both of which counter male ambition as it attempts to rule the world and affect the future: female friendship and intellectual women. Not only are the two depictions interconnected and instrumental to amending the excessive familiarity of family, but they also highlight what is liberating about the quotidian, even domesticated, nature of Shelley's commitment to women.

One thing that distinguishes Shelley's later novels from her earlier ones is explicit focus on the concerns and prospects particular to women. *Frankenstein*, as many have noted, is almost exclusively concerned with men, male-male relations, and desires to exclude women even from the sphere of reproduction.[35] While *Matilda* features a female protagonist whose misery consumes the entire narrative, that misery is portrayed as individual, not generic (though embedded in literature), and gender is not presented as a major cause of it. Moreover, Mathilda is portrayed as wholly male-identified in her choice of friends and authors. Shelley's historical fictions and sentimental novels start to amend this situation. Female characters begin to look to other women, not just to other female fictional characters who are authored by men, as fit companions; they also start to talk explicitly about the value of having other women, not just books or men, as friends. Readers can easily miss this change and its significance because it sounds so mundane, but the new emphasis on female friendship actually embodies an important solution to several misery-inducing fictional and actual conditions explored in these works. Women need to start looking to other women for comfort and enlightenment when so many of their mothers are dead, so many books ignore or belittle their desires, and so many men prove disappointing in their preoccupations with self or public affairs. Only then, these texts imply, will women improve their emotional situations and start to reform the stories that shape them.

Making this point motivates the structure of Shelley's historical fictions, both of which feature a male hero whose worldly ambitions ultimately override his love for a woman and both of which place around this hero a pair of women, each of whom, through the experience of loving the same man, ends up loving and supporting the other. In *Valperga*, Euthanasia (Castruccio's fiancée and a woman whom he sincerely loves) shelters Beatrice until her death, after Euthanasia's discovery of Castruccio's affair with Beatrice has caused Euthanasia to end her engagement to him and after Beatrice's discovery that Castruccio loves Euthanasia has unhinged her mind. In *Perkin Warbeck*, Richard requests of Monina, the woman who loves him unrequitedly, to promise in the event of his death that she will provide refuge to his beloved wife, Katherine. As it happens, Katherine finds a home and deep friendship with the wife of Richard's arch-foe and usurper of his title, King Henry (who is Richard's sister). Such a deliberate rewriting of the known facts of these men's histories suggests a conscious intervention into history's usual depiction of women in love. First, they foreground as one of the fictions of history the "fact" that a woman's love is all-consuming. Both texts feature heroines whose love for a man also encompasses their civic duty, and both sketch an alternative to female rivalry in love by making the ostensible rivals into friends. This friendship does not deny the pain and disappointment that the women suffer in their experiences of heterosexual love, but it poses an alternative to this suffering and a valuable compensation for it. "Bound by the sweet ties of gratitude and pity," Euthanasia and Beatrice "found in each other's converse some balm for their misfortunes," a balm, moreover, that is not simply the comfort of sympathy or lament but of mental activity. "Though unhappy," they were no longer "wretched" because conversing together kept each "mind active" (*Valperga*, 248). The effect of Katherine's "eloquence" on the unhappily married Elizabeth is even more liberating. "After years of silence, to utter her very inner thoughts, her woman's fears, her repinings, her aversions, her lost hopes and affections crushed: she spent her bitterest words; but thus it was as if she emptied a silver chalice of its gall, to be refilled by Katherine with heavenly dew" (*Perkin Warbeck*, 346). In other words, women find their voice in the company of other women and thereby foster each other's thinking powers.

Such depictions come full circle in applying Godwin's and Wollstonecraft's stipulations for a healthy marriage back onto the source of those stipulations, friendship. The shared circumstances, tastes, and habits of mind that, according to her parents, solidify love and make it equivalent to friendship in its cultivation of thought are now shown to ground the affection between women and to posit female friendship as a desirable outcome of failed marriages. What is new is that activity of mind is now shown to be characteristic of women, at once something they desire and that others find desirable about them. Cultivating shared tastes here means also sharing a taste for the same man, for women who love the same man do find their thoughts moving in similar directions (*Valperga*, 246). Shelley's depiction of this extension poses an alternative to the jealousy, rivalry, and enmity that literature characterizes as the chief, or only, kind of bond that exists between women; in this, it is a complement to Godwin's explorations of jealousy in men. This depiction also affects the nature and outcome of the new definitions of love that are being produced in her historical fictions. As Euthanasia explains, discovering that her all-in-all has loved another not only deidealizes him but also allows her to re-enter human society. "She had separated herself from the rest as his chosen one; she had been selected from the whole world for him to love, and therefore was there a mighty barrier between her and all things else; no sentiment could pass through her mind unmingled with his image; . . . but, the god undeified, the honours of the priestess fell to the dust" (*Valperga*, 190). This is less a full-scale demystification of heterosexual passion than an attempt to make it less of a do-or-die proposition for women. This is "the spirit of love" that Katherine embodies, "now kindling the balmy atmosphere of charity to many, now concentred in one point, but ever ready to soothe human suffering with its soft influence" (*Perkin Warbeck*, 346).

A second revision concerns the implications of flanking a male protagonist with two females. Concerning men the point is fairly basic: they need a lot of shoring up, especially those who are or deem themselves illustrious. Concerning women, the pairing constitutes a less monolithic view of the monomaniacal disposition often ascribed to women in love. This point is reinforced by the nature of the pairing. Because one of the two in the pair has interests other than men, it highlights the possibility of intellectual women having a range of interests, including a strong one in loving and being loved. The pairing also pluralizes gender difference by ascribing both masculine and feminine characteristics to women in love. This difference becomes noticeable when we compare these novels to *Frankenstein*, whose only desired union is between men who embody masculine and feminine principles (Victor being scientific, solitary, penetrating; Henry and the creature being literary, social, and receptive). The historical fictions each focus on female friends, one of whom is thoughtful, public-minded, and cultured (Euthanasia, Katherine), the other wholly absorbed by love (Beatrice, Monina).

The temptation to polarize these women as masculine or feminine and as oriented toward the public or private sphere is undercut by several factors that constitute a different image of the type of woman who loves. The "masculine," or intellectual, woman is far more "feminine" than the woman whose man is her entire reality, for the former is compassionate, loving, sympathetic, and service-minded. She nurses the wounded by lightening, through enlightening, their minds. The conventionally "feminine" woman is fierce, unwavering, sacrificial, in her attachment to him. In short, she is both martyr and hero in her "enthusiastic . . . adoration of one devoted being" (*Perkin Warbeck*, 304; see also *Valperga*, 191). Furthermore, the "new" Shelleyan woman loves with an intensity that does not exclude the world but enhances her service in and to it. Katherine details the logic of this interaction in the "Conclusion" to *Perkin Warbeck*: "We are not deities to bestow in impassive benevolence. We give, because we love. . . . I quarrel not with—I admire—those who can be good and benevolent, and yet keep their hearts to themselves. . . . I am not one of these, and yet take no shame therefore. . . . Permit this . . . heart . . . to reap what joy it can from the strong necessity it feels to be sympathized with—to love" (400). With these words, Shelley asserts the social efficacy of passionate love and thereby rejects the tendency of her father's adherence to necessity to oppose the two categories.

With these words she also underscores the difficulties that women who live by a less conventional code of ethics face in history and in fiction. For Shelley feels compelled to defend Katherine by adding a Conclusion that, she notes, will be "deemed superfluous" by readers who either consider the story over now that its central male hero is off the stage or who judge Lady Katherine Gordon harshly for various acts of her "after life"—acts that are suppressed in Shelley's narrative but that include "acceptance of a pension from Henry VII" and "marriage to three successive men" (394, 395n). Harsh judgment is voiced in the Conclusion by Edmund, Richard's cousin, who accuses Katherine of having betrayed her husband and his cause by agreeing to reside in the court of Henry VII. Stating for the record that "Lady Katherine Gordon is a favourite of mine," Shelley desires that Katherine be allowed to "speak for herself" (and also Shelley for herself) in showing how "her conduct, subsequent to her husband's death, was in accordance with the devotion and fidelity with which she attended his fortunes during his life" (395n). This self-defense entails several propositions that, as chapter 5 explores, occasion major controversy within Shelley's texts. One set involves the duty to mourn, here portrayed in its most affirmative light. Katherine asserts the necessity, and defends her ability, to move on, even while stating that her "present [solitary] existence" is but "the spiritless remnants of" a former bliss, on the grounds that persisting in grief "avail[s] nought to a spirit in Paradise" and violates "the master-law of our lives[—c]all it love, charity, or sympathy" (395, 399, 398). For "must my living heart be stone, because that dear form is dust, which was the medium of my communication with his spirit?" (400). A second set instructs the grief-stricken in how to mourn, by becoming receptive again to "the beauty of this visible universe" and responding once more to the claims of the living (398). This response is portrayed not only as sanctioned by the spirit of Richard in Paradise but also as reforming family and thereby social conditions. In acting like a mother toward the children of her husband's enemy, Katherine believes that she gratifies "the eyes of Richard" and "bestow[s] happiness on" the "England he loved" (400).

Both in content and context, such words are clearly marked as fictional, as possibilities, not actualities, in the world that Lady Katherine inhabits. She says as much in excusing Edmund "for the false judgment you pass on me" but in hoping that "years and quiet thought" will eventually allow him to "read my heart better, and know that it is still faithfully devoted to him I have lost" (398). Strengthening the capacity to read women's hearts better is what Shelley's historical fictions aim to achieve by showcasing the limitations that the cultural reduction of "woman" to "love" places on women and the persons who surround them. Women like Monina and Beatrice, whose entire existence is bound up in a man, are shown to be radically uncivilized. "Methinks," says

Beatrice, "it would please me, that my lover should cast off all humanity, and be a reprobate, and an outcast of his species. Oh, then how deeply and tenderly I should love him; soiled with crimes, his hands dripping blood, I would shade him as the flowering shrub invests the ruin; . . . My intensity of love would annihilate his wickedness; . . . I should be every thing to him, life, and hope; he would die in his remorse; but he would live again and again in the light of my love" (*Valperga*, 250). In contrast, Katherine and Euthanasia make their loving congruent with the claims of humanity. But their fates also suggest that their time has not yet come. In the case of Katherine, acceptance of the non-exclusivity of her love must wait until people are educated to perceive women as complex beings. Until such times, the "Conclusion" claims as a matter of justice the permission to love for beings who have been granted no other occupation or preoccupation in life. The situation (though not the time) is different for Euthanasia, whose quality of mind and right to rule are recognized but not yet allowed to influence the world for the better. Rare minds like hers rest in suspended animation in an ocean cave, awaiting the day when reality conforms to republican, and less masculinist, ideals.[36]

It is left for a novel set in contemporary times to bring forward a female character who expresses no desire for marriage or passionate union with a man. The character Fanny Derham in *Lodore* represents a major innovation in Shelley's writing on two fronts. She is the only one of Shelley's female characters whose love for books and a life of the mind is neither subordinated to nor nullified by a desire for domesticity, and she is the only female in the pair of women that Shelley's later fiction characterizes whose love for her female friend (Ethel) is not grounded in shared love for the same man.[37] Instead, like Christabel and Geraldine, the attraction between Ethel and Fanny stems from their love for their fathers, who were boyhood and lifelong friends. Critics have noted that Fanny is the most Wollstonecraftian of Shelley's heroines in that she "loves philosophy," "pants after knowledge," and cherishes the "independence" that is the hallmark of her father's system of education, based as it is on cultivating "the duties and objects befitting an immortal soul" (79, 213, 218).[38] These features are in marked contrast to the character and upbringing of Ethel, whose father gave her a "sexual education" modeled on "Milton's Eve" and the "romance of chivalry," which taught her to be "dependent," the "prop" of others, and to "seldom" think and "never ac[t] for herself" (218, 19). Whereas the entire plot of Ethel's life involves negotiating a shift from love of her father to marriage with Edward Villiers, Fanny remains single, though not unattached to other women, "need[ing] but her liberty and her books" (218).

Second, the neat summation that happily ends *Lodore*, wherein Lady Lodore is reunited with daughter Ethel, thereby alleviating the couple's financial
hardships, and then rewarded for her sacrifice by marriage to her true love,
Horatio Saville, is explicitly not extended to Fanny. The only Shelleyan character to attempt to claim for herself in this world a "world where there is
neither marrying nor giving in marriage" (the famous ending to *Mary*), her
fate, the narrator of *Lodore* points out, is not easy to describe. "One [character]
only remains to be mentioned; but it is not in a few tame lines that we can
revert to the varied fate of Fanny Derham." Indeed, "it would require the gift
of prophecy to foretell the conclusion" of the life of such a woman, and it
remains for "after times" to be able to present her life as at once "a useful
lesson" and one that others will wish to "imitate" (313). In the meanwhile,
apparently, writers should direct their efforts to revising the conventional
plots of femininity so that a character like Fanny can someday plausibly exist
in the worlds of fiction and actuality and that her happiness as a single
thinking person can be alluded to in a few words rather than requiring an
entire writing career.

The portrayal of Fanny in *Lodore*—as desiring to live independently and as
embodying a story not familiar enough to be captured in a "few tame lines"—
suggests that contemporary times have not progressed much beyond the medieval times of *Perkin Warbeck* in reading women's hearts more accurately.
While Katherine pins her hopes on education for improving women's options
and situations, novels set in Shelley's times do not bear out this optimism. The
concluding lines of *Lodore* level a critique against the treatment of Anglo-
European women that *Frankenstein* had domesticated by ascribing it only to
the Muslim world. In *Frankenstein*, Safie's ability to cultivate "higher powers
of intellect, and an independence of spirit, forbidden to the female followers of
Mahomet" requires that she "marr[y] a Christian, and remai[n] in a country
where women [a]re allowed to take a rank in society" (a "prospect," however,
undermined by the portrayal of all the European women in the novel) (92).
Lodore suggests that the cultivation of a woman's intellect and independence
requires that she not marry at all, a requirement presented in two ways. The
position is affirmed directly in describing a woman like Fanny as "more made
to be loved by her own sex than by the opposite one," given that "superiority of
intellect" in women is "little" in "accord with masculine taste" (214). It is
implied as well through the characterizations of the women who do marry.

Fanny may be the most forward-looking aspect of the novel, the reception
of whom must await "after times," but it is Ethel and her family who are the

center of attention, especially the two men who dictate Ethel's fate and whose fates are themselves intertwined when Ethel's future husband (Edward Villiers) literally stands as second at her father's (Lord Lodore) death by duel. This focus on and characterization of Ethel are in line with the subgenre to which *Lodore* and *Falkner* belong, the silver-fork novel, and, as its name signifies, the conformity and conservatism that critics claim underlie Shelley's enlistment of this genre.[39] Certainly, both of these novels eschew the mythic revisionism that constitutes her early texts and, in their conclusions, appear far more reconciled to the ways—that is, conventions—of the world, especially the social convention of marriage and the literary convention of equating a happy ending with marriage. Certainly, too, this reconciliation can feel like a regression from her parents', especially her mother's, texts, whose final, though unfinished, accounting of *The Wrongs of Woman* indicted several social institutions for keeping women "bastilled for life." But, after more dramatic but less effectual struggle, *Lodore* and *Falkner* attempt to alter marital despotism from the inside: that is, from within the literary and social conventions that cause women to desire marriage and thereby circumscribe their fates.[40] On the literary front, this includes altering the sentimental novel, the marriage plot, the happily-ever-after of an end in marriage, and the forms of semblance ascribed to "polite" society. On the social front, it entails reforming family and the higher classes.[41] In the understated ways that these novels take on these conventions, they get down to the hard work of re/form.

On one level, these polite novels join Shelley's earlier novels in underscoring the perversity of family relations by foregrounding the incestuous nature of father-daughter bonds. But their treatments of this topic mark their difference and arguable "progress" from the psychosocial stalemates explored in *Frankenstein, Matilda,* and *The Last Man.*[42] For both novels present an extremely close relation between father and daughter as a realistic component of family life, especially when so many mothers die in childbirth, and then work to detail the conditions under which this relation can be made conducive to healthy attachments, rather than to stagnation, evasion, and psychosexual arrest. The outcomes of her prior novels display how difficult this process is to achieve. Not only is no one happily coupled but also each of the three novels ends with a scene of total isolation and desolation. In this light, one function of *Lodore* and *Falkner* is underscoring what an unusual achievement, rather than a given, a happy marriage actually is. Another function is showing how to attain it, a process that involves altering social and literary conventions regarding marriage, including some significant revisions to her own parents' lived and literary enactments of it. These changes are registered primarily in the depiction in *Lodore* of Ethel's marriage to Villiers, a marriage that does not conclude the novel but instead occurs halfway into the text, thus granting narrative time to the work required to maintain their marriage as happy, viable, and satisfying to both parties. This work involves clearing away several impediments that stem from the marriage of Ethel's parents, Henry Fitzhenry (Lord Lodore) and Cornelia Santerre, and that include parental interference, the life of high society, and unrealistic expectations regarding marriage. On the level of plot and of psycholiterary history, *Lodore* makes clear that a daughter's happiness in marriage depends on her getting out from under the influence of her forebears.

The project of *Lodore* is to modify understandings and practices of heterosexual love so that it does not exclude fellow feeling and social service or get sacrificed to the "flimsy web" of appearance that constitutes the world of high society. Put a different way, its major aim is to insert some realism into depictions of marriage and romance. To this end, *Lodore* portrays a form of married life in which the love between husband and wife remains passionate and inexplicable yet does not impede recognition of or interactions with society. Achieving this balance entails challenging cultural fantasies that impede both realism regarding love and healthy object choices. Ethel's "idyllic" childhood, spent alone with her father in the wilds of America, is shown to have been bad preparation even for the designedly "feminine" education that her father devised for her (18). For it requires nothing short of "a miracle" to make "into an actual event in life" that "picture of beauty," whereby a "Gertrude or an Haidée, brought up in the wilds, innocent and free," knows how and when to give her heart to "some accomplished stranger, brought on purpose to realize the ideal of their dreamy existences" (74).

At the same time, *Lodore* affirms as realistic desires for the *je ne sais quoi* of passion. Whereas Lord Lodore's "unhappy choice" of a wife results from his resolving to "marry one whom his judgment, rather than his love, should select," Ethel's happy choice in a husband stems from deeming some aspects of love inexplicable. "There was something beyond, that no words could express, which was stronger than any reason in her heart. Who can express the power of faithful and single-hearted love? As well attempt to define the laws of life, which occasions a continuity of feeling from the brain to the extremity of the frame, as try to explain how love can so unite two souls, as to make each feel maimed and half alive, while divided" (217). Yet the "exultation in possession," the delight in the "mine, my own, forever!" that comes from loving single-heartedly, is said to be neither unhealthy nor selfish (199). "Did they love the less for not loving 'in sin and fear'? Far from it. The certainty of being the cause of good to each other tended to foster the most delicate of all passions, more than the rougher ministrations of terror" (198). Moreover, exultation in possession is selfish only under the "reasoning" of "a cold and meaningless philosophy, which gives this name to generosity and truth, and all the nobler passions of the soul" (199). What ratifies the justice, as well as passion, of their love and the happy vision of "the long, long future which they were to spend together" is that this "mutual property" in each other is a "free gift one to the other," a gift that ensures "the right" of "conferring mutual benefits" that then become the "better part" of each partner (199).

In such declarations, *Lodore* adjudges Lord Lodore's rationalist approach to love to be "good in theory, but very defective in practice" (37). Gaining distance from one's parents is further thematized within *Lodore* as moving beyond their generation and the mindset it signifies. For if the revised fantasy and lived reality of love in *Lodore* neither desires nor necessitates a total retreat from society, it also must ensure that conventions of society, especially the hypocrisy of high society, do not "mar and destroy" its chances to unfold (125). *Lodore* counters various forms of semblance that characterize its upper classes and that pit honor, reputation, and appearances against virtue, plain dealing, and truth. When the child (Cornelia) of "a worldly woman and an oily flatterer" such as Lady Santerre meets a child (Henry) of ancestral honor such as characterized the Fitzhenry family from time immemorial, the straightforwardness of their love is compromised from the start (43). Neither is schooled to know or state their feelings directly or to consider affection the highest goal in life. Moreover, the now-grown man of honor idealizes womanhood and thereby views woman "as a vision—a creature from another sphere," whereas his gravity and abstractedness, in her eyes, make it only more likely that he will see through her (7). One consequence, then, of having her existence depend on a keeping up of appearances is that she views with suspicion any effort by her husband to open her eyes to the ways of the world. "Proud in youth and triumphant beauty, . . . the world looked to her a velvet strewn walk—her husband alone, who endeavoured to reveal the reality of things to her, and to disturb her visions, was the source of . . . sorrow or discomfort" (46). Then the "system of society" "increase[s] their mutual estrangement" by offering different avenues for diversion to each gender—for men, "public affairs," for women "fashion" (46–47). *Lodore* states that these impediments to their love are in reality but "flimsy web[s]" based on "an imaginary rather than real bondage." But under current social conditions, they nonetheless prove "insurmountable barriers" to that "outpouring of the heart" that constitutes this text's version of the satisfaction found in marriage (44; see also 123).

Lodore, then, is visionary in connecting the probability of happiness in marriage to a greater realism about it. This is at once a class critique, whereby the upper classes, in their pursuit of appearances, raise impediments to the honest outpouring of feeling; a gender critique, in that a "man is more thrown upon the reality of life, while girls live altogether in a factitious state" (160); and a critique on two levels of the style of romance. At one point, the narrator worries aloud that, "in recording the annoyances, or rather the adversity which the young pair endured at this period," s/he risks offending refined readers by bringing them into "contact with degrading and sordid miseries" and offending "those of a lower sphere of life" for emphasizing circumstances that, in their view, "scarcely deserv[e] the name of misfortune" (201). The narrator defends this practice on the grounds of realism. "It is very easy to embark on the wild ocean of romance. . . . But all beautiful and fairy-like as was Ethel Villiers, in tracing her fortunes, it is necessary to descend from such altitudes, to employ terms of vulgar use" (202). These are precisely the grounds on which Ethel, for all her schooling in femininity, builds a new world in which married love is a reality that is sustainable over the long run and is gained by confronting directly the highs and lows of life.

Even in itself, this portrayal of marriage *is* an achievement, given the major impediments to marriage that exist in society, gender relations, and psychic reality and also in Shelley's and her family's writings up to this point. If those writings counter the literary tradition's general mystification of marriage by detailing the many forms of despotism that marriage enjoins on women (*Wrongs of Woman, Frankenstein*) and men (*Fleetwood, Frankenstein*), then *Lodore* counters that despotism by also modifying aspects of the literary tradition that Wollstonecraft especially holds accountable for further constraining women. Through its patient focus on Ethel and Villier's marriage, *Lodore* both earns and shows how to earn the happily-ever-after that most novels claim for marriage by never taking it as their dominant plot. This display includes an indictment of literature for cultivating false expectations of happiness. "How much happier we are than all the heroes and heroines that ever lived or were imagined! they grasped at the mere shadow of the thing, whose substance we absolutely possess" (233). Possession of substance is also how *Lodore* describes middle-class, or at least plain-speaking, values, thereby modifying from within the subgenre to which it belongs, the silver-fork novel.

The type of happiness *Lodore* claims for marriage is also earned by facing, rather than effacing or demonizing, a substantial psychic impediment to it that is also mishandled by the literary, especially classical, tradition: a daughter's excessive attachment to her father. In moving beyond the equation of close father-daughter ties with incest, *Lodore* undoes the blockage erected in its author's own prior daughter-narrative, *Matilda*, which the first volume of *Lodore* essentially reprises. As in *Matilda*, volume 1 portrays a father and daughter who are all the world to each other in the wilds of Illinois, a potential suitor is a threat to their happiness, and the father's untimely death is said to "poiso[n]" the "springs of life" of the daughter who, now "in love with death," returns to England as a "monument of woe" (*Lodore*, 99). Walking the streets of London, Ethel is virtually indistinguishable from Mathilda. Totally "solitary," each finds "no pole of attraction to cause a union with [her] fellows" and perceives the "moving crowd" as "so many automata" and "shadows of a phantasmagoria" (101; see *Matilda*, 43). But Ethel diverges from Mathilda in her ensuing receptivity to new life, figured in the differing prospects associated with Villiers and Woodville. These prospects essentially concern what share the past plays in any new attachment. Whereas Villiers, like Woodville, arrives with a "heart ready to give itself away in kindness," only Villiers is met halfway by Ethel because, in his having stood second to Ethel's father, she can open her heart to him without feeling that she is betraying her father (103). Put the other way, and in marked contrast to *Matilda*, after meeting Villiers "it had become more difficult to die" (155).

Shelley's final novel, *Falkner* (1837), does not even have to kill off the father in order for the daughter to be able to transfer her affections to a younger man. Even as it admits the "conflicting duties," the "sad struggles of feeling" occasioned in Elizabeth by these competing interests, *Falkner* resolves them, in part by portraying Neville as less worldly and more poetic than Villiers and yet less "gloomy and self-absorbed" than Falkner, and in part by showing that the "poetic fervour" of his "countenance" does not signify that he is out of touch with the complexity of human existence (223, 70). Neville's realism, in other words, is in contrast to the idealism of Woodville's poetic worldview *and* the worldliness of Villiers. Moreover, the "progress" associated with these men, as indicated by the similarity *and* variants of their name, also implies a growing embrace of the city, and civilization, as the realistic scene of life. But sanctioning the love between Elizabeth and Neville ultimately involves ratifying highly unconventional expressions of love and duty, for, before they can marry, Neville has to admit Elizabeth's (surrogate) father into his household—the

man whom, up until then, Neville has devoted his entire life to finding and
punishing for causing the death of his beloved mother. Reconciliation with
this murderous arch-foe ultimately occurs as an expression of loyalty to that
mother, occasioned by a re-evaluation of connection. "There is more real
sympathy between me and my mother's childhood friend—who loved her so
long and truly—whose very crime was a mad excess of love—than one who
knew nothing of her—to whom her name conjures up no memories, no regret"
(295). In this, the last novels of Shelley center their "views and happiness in
the living instead of the dead" but without belying the dead or their ongoing
presence in the living (128). In this, too, they make their peace with Shelley's
legacy as author, lover, and daughter.

The past has to be allowed to rest, even as it is actively shaping the present,
for the younger generation in *Lodore* and *Falkner* to have some kind of life of
its own. But *Lodore* also addresses the future, one in which there is neither
marrying nor giving in marriage, by according its last words to Fanny. This is
important to recognize in a work initially subtitled "a tale of the present time"
and one still frequently judged harshly for catering to conformist standards of
"Victorian" domesticity. The text's last words are literally inspiring, since they
admit that Fanny's current reality and fate cannot be spoken in a few "tame"
lines. New histories and associations need to be forged around the words that
compose her existence before they can be registered as meaningful and worthy
of emulation. Moreover, the radical potentiality of words has already been
associated with Fanny and the social reforms she at once figures and envisions.
"Words have more power than any one can guess; it is by words that the world's
great fight, now in these civilized times, is carried on," but people are "so
afraid to speak, it would seem as if half our fellow-creatures were born with
deficient organs; like parrots they can repeat a lesson, but their voice fails
them, when that alone is wanting to make the tyrant quail" (213). Like saying
"I do not" to marriage or writing to end the wrongs of women.

These words about the power of words to make a better future, when
ascribed to Fanny, also help to breathe the life back into unfinished possibilities of Wollstonecraft's life/writings, extending their influence and tendency
by forming a collectivity speaking out against marital despotism. Echoes of a
road not taken are heard in the name Fanny (not to mention Blood), Wollstonecraft's first love and the source of her interest and training in letters.
Embodied in the fictional Fanny, "more made to be loved by her own sex than
by the opposite one," this Fanny figures what Claudia Johnson sees as one
"logical" conclusion to *Wrongs of Woman* and its full-scale rejection of the

sentimental plot, a female-only household and kind of love.[43] *Lodore* contends that women are "glad" to find a "superior being" in "one of their own sex" since they thereby escape "those dangers, which usually attend any services conferred by men" (214). Shelley's active engagement with this kind of re-directing of the love and marriage plots during the composition of *Lodore* has been documented by Betty T. Bennett in *Mary Diana Dods, A Gentleman and a Scholar*, which describes how Shelley befriended and aided Dods and Isabel Robinson, posing as a "Mr. and Mrs. Sholto Douglas," in their efforts to live together as a married couple.[44] One can fault *Lodore*, then, for ascribing to the future what was a current and known reality for certain women, except that all of Shelley's novels explore how a being's self-perception and sense of options depend on public reception more than on individual conception. Nor has women's pleasure in the superiority of other women been clearly established.

But if the suggestion that Fanny's reality can only be conveyed currently as a potentiality is read as deferring to social convention, there is nothing evasive in Shelley's rewriting of the biblical injunction to marriage—or in the hubris underwriting this revision. Twice the novel instances the wisdom of the "eternal Lawgiver" and the "dispensation of the Creator" in ordaining that, "at a certain age," the "young" should "leave father, mother, and the dwelling of [their] infancy," not to "cleave to" another but rather to "seek [their] fortunes over the wide world" (or "seek some new abode where to pitch our tents, and pasture our flocks" [78, 138]). This dispensation, moreover, is grounded in a "love of change" invariably "planted in the young" (78). A bold rejoinder to the urtext of Judeo-Christian heteronormativity that truly resets the world all before young readers, the rewriting also takes on patriarchs closer to home, though just recently buried. For twice *Deloraine* (1833) cites with approval the biblical sanction of marriage. If in *Lodore* Shelley accepts without demurral *Deloraine*'s conscription of daughters into the coupled reading scenario, even to the point of solving "high dispute" in Miltonic fashion—another father whose literary successes depend on daughters—she does not extend that endorsement to patriarchal restrictions on young women's futures. Here she extends her mother's position in granting wider worlds to the new Eve, Fanny. This path eschews nature altogether and enters the "Paradise" of no giving in marriage through cultivated society (156).

PART TWO

LIFE WORKS

For the stories illustrating the instruction [this book] contains, you will not feel in such a great degree the want of my personal advice.

Original Stories from Real Life

[T]he more fully we are presented with the picture and story of such persons as the subject of the following narrative, the more generally shall we feel in ourselves an attachment to their fate, and a sympathy in their excellencies. There are not many individuals with whose character the public welfare and improvement are more intimately connected, than the author of A Vindication of the Rights of Woman.

Memoirs of the Author of "A Vindication of the Rights of Woman"

Dear Mother, let me kiss that tear which steals
Down your pale cheek altered by care and grief.
This is not misery; 'tis but a slight change
From our late happy lot.

Proserpine

My life & reason have been saved by these "Lives."

Journals of Mary Shelley

Fancy's History

The world for ever is, and in some degree for ever must be, in its
infancy.

Essay on Sepulchres

Life is merely an education, a state of infancy, to which the only
hopes worth cherishing should not be sacrificed.

A Vindication of the Rights of Woman

Whether life works and the degree to which literature improves the
chances of life working are insistent questions in the life/writings of the
Wollstonecraft-Godwin-Shelley family. Both questions stem from two of their
writerly preoccupations: intense engagement with the lifeworks of illustrious
authors, including themselves, and skepticism about progress. The first takes
account of their distinction as canon revisers, their fame as generic innovators,
and their commitment to collecting, editing, disseminating, and deciphering
the life/writings of each other. All three activities raise further questions about
the value of illustriousness, the standards by which it is evaluated, and how
well any one of them can be said to measure up. It also acknowledges their
efforts to devise and promulgate new forms of writing that, in their views, help
change the species for the better and lessen some of the difficulties of living—
efforts motivated by their convictions that history is romance and biography,
that fiction is science and autobiography, and that writing "lives" extends the
life of the author as well as his or her subject, usually also an author.

Their questioning of whether life is workable is raised primarily by their
status as mourners and their family history of depression, in part the result of
the remarkable degree to which tragedy in/formed their lives and animates
their writings. These conditions make their life/writings confront limit states,

such as trauma (also, arguably, bankruptcy), and occasions the skepticism they each at times voice over whether humanity, womankind, or a person ever progresses. But it also occasions two projects that portray literature in a more affirmative mode. One involves the promotion of mourning through writing, enjoined by Godwin as a civic duty on survivors, which Shelley at first vehemently resisted and then came to accept. The other is their commitment to reforming childhood through revising the literature written for and about children as an effort to envision the world someday being able to claim that life works.

Shelley has the most intense relation to both components for reasons of biography and chronology. She is the last of the three to go and thus the one left to decipher and disseminate the remains of her illustrious parents (and husband), a project that affected her characterizations of fictional protagonists as well as her turn toward biography and editorial work, which projects eventuated in a notion of selfhood and creativity *as* a being occupied with remains. Shelley is also the one whose love life was so intertwined with death and a love for it that her life/writings epitomize the interrelations between the arguments of Parts One and Two. That is, whereas Wollstonecraft and Godwin see love as initiated, solidified, eroticized, and revivable through a couple's shared reading and writing, Shelley cannot think of love, life, or writing apart from death and contends that efforts to decouple any of them from familiarity with death leaves persons radically unprepared for living. In part, the intimacy of her life/writings with death stems from her status as one of Western culture's most famous widows—in love with an author even more in love with death than she—whose misery, expressed most insistently in *The Journal of Sorrow* and *The Last Man*, registers the profound insufficiencies of writing *and* mourning. But it is equally twined with her birth and her first lessons in reading, since she learned four of her letters on her mother's tombstone and the rest in Wollstonecraft's unfinished "Lessons," a primer that instructs very young children how to read—as well as how reading can empty one out.[1]

One advantage of Shelley's comprehension of the place of death in life, love, and writing is that she comes to disarticulate trauma from tragedy as a literary practice and psychic reality, in the process making space for more productive— often in the sense of counterproductive—forms of writing about loss. Chapter 5 charts the incredibly complex mourning itinerary of her life/writings, whereby her texts about trauma—*Matilda, Proserpine, The Journal of Sorrow,* and *The Last Man*—give way both to the calmer, more worked-through fictions of *Lodore* and *Falkner* and to a generic shift to biography through her involvement in composing *The Lives of the Most Eminent Literary and Scien-*

tific Men of Italy, Spain, and Portugal and *The Lives of the Most Eminent Literary and Scientific Men of France.* Chapter 6 approaches the life cycle at the opposite end, by underscoring her admission of trauma, but precisely not as tragedy, into children's developmental narratives. This querying of "development" shapes other aspects of Shelley's life story, troubled as it is, and she was, by the charge that her life/writings fail to live up to the radical ideals of Wollstonecraft's, Godwin's, or Percy Shelley's lifeworks, especially as they pertain to the politics of perfectibility. But from early on, she saw commitment to perfectibility as necessitating enquiry into the obstacles to progress—an approach also taken in Wollstonecraft's various vindications and Godwin's post-*Enquiry* enquiries into political justice—and that she claims as what she owes to their legacy. "[My mother's] greatness of soul & my father['s] high talents have perpetually reminded me that I ought to degenerate as little as I could from those from whom I derived my being."[2]

Positioning growth on a decline is a forthright admission that being part of a rising generation or literary movement guarantees nothing about positive change. Like many of her novels, it raises a question about the necessity, validity, or meaningfulness of constantly—or ever—moving forward. Some of this skepticism is characteristic of all second-generation romantics, born into a disillusioned age and thus distanced from the start from utopian promise.[3] Yet, several things distinguish Shelley's inability to perceive the bliss of being alive besides her characteristic realism about the difficulties of living with a revolutionary partner. How could she not identify with a post-bliss syndrome when her fame as an author and a lover peaked when she was a teenager, when no one considered her a revolutionary, when her babies kept dying, and when her husband and friends rejected her for being cold even while respectable society never accepted her because of her illicit past (her elopement and her parents)? These facts of her life sharpened awareness of the impediments to making a fresh start and distinguish her discussions of idealism from those of other second-generation writers, like William Hazlitt and Percy Shelley. Her writings, especially about daughters, highlight a second resistance to moving forward, since so many of them have to occupy the position of lover or mother prematurely.

But much of Shelley's distinctive lack of bliss was bequeathed to her by the life/writings of Wollstonecraft and Godwin, both of whom aimed at perfectibility by chronicling political, cultural, literary, and psychic resistances to enlightenment, including their own. Theirs are dark life/writings, whose path toward light dwells in perversity, heartbreak, the dust of the grave, which

Shelley imbibed before she could write against them and through which she as writer found and made her way. Indeed, their capacity to stay in the dark is what makes them at once visionaries and realists. This capacity, I wish to argue, is inseparable from their penchant for fancy, increasingly being defined during this period as wayward, deadening, and outmoded, and it underlies their most successful generic innovations. Fancy is key to Wollstonecraft's "original stories" of girlhood, Godwin's formulations of history as romance, and Shelley's science fiction as well as interpersonal-intertextual romance, in large part because their "fancy" anticipates Freud's "psychic reality." Recovering their comfort with fancy modifies the reputation of the parents as (inconsistent) rationalists, as if championing women with thinking powers requires ignoring their passions or investigating mind never leads to magical places. It also modifies the reputation of romanticism as the age in which imagination made fancy into a passing fancy of literary culture.

One of romanticism's chief cultural legacies is according to imagination life-giving and life-affirming powers. Coleridge's definition of imagination as the "great I AM" sizes up this position, just as his distinction between imagination (whether primary or secondary) and fancy culminated the process of inverting the traditional hierarchy of fancy over imagination under way in aesthetic and psychological treatises throughout the mid to late eighteenth century.[4] As James Engell has shown, during this time imagination came to be associated with creativity, organicism, unity, and life; fancy with fixity, partitions, mechanization, and death. On one level, the supremacy of imagination and romantic characterizations of it is indisputable, for fancy in our times is effectively a dead term, at least as an honorific. We still know roughly what it means to call someone or something "fanciful," and those meanings rarely include being "imaginative," "creative," or "productive," but we generally find other terms. But on another level, and certainly as a description of the romantic period, the supremacy of imagination is anything but secure. For one thing, the authority of its chief spokesperson, not to mention chapter 13 of the *Biographia Literaria,* is radically unstable, and the entire in/famous distinction is arguably motivated primarily by anger at Wordsworth. For another, the visible gender divisions, not only between "manly" Shakespeare and "effeminate" Spenser or virile poetry and impotent romance but also between their respective male and female champions, suggest that these were fiercely ideological debates, very much in flux during the period.[5] At most, and only in retrospect, the passing of fancy holds as a description of canonical romanticism, circumscribed as it once was by the imaginations of six men, which occluded all those fanciful works by the Della Cruscans, the Hunt circle, the Cockney School, and virtually all women authors that have been coming back into focus in the past two or three decades. As a general point, this process of literary history enacts one of the facts of fancy, its wanderings and waywardness.

Still, what proves unusual about the approach of the Wollstonecraft-Godwin-Shelley family is that each member promotes fancy precisely because of its associations with the dead, the fixed, the mechanical, and the magical. Equally important, they do not view these qualities as rigorously opposed either to imagination or to life but instead treat them as necessary components of life, the repression of which humans perform at their peril. By and large, all three of them use the terms *fancy* and *imagination* interchangeably. Following the logic of romanticism, then, their "fancy" tends to get swallowed up by their (or especially Percy's) "imagination," as, for example, in the index to the collected works of Wollstonecraft, edited by Janet Todd and Marilyn Butler, which lists under the heading "Fancy—*see* Imagination." My aim is not to re-erect a firm distinction between their conceptions of the two faculties (often, they use both words in one sentence) but to explore where their fancies characteristically take them.[6] And generally, their fancy, even more than their imagination, brings them into contact with things that have passed or have come before. Whither that contact leads varies. For Wollstonecraft it heads toward the otherworldly of storytelling, for Godwin the domain of history, for Shelley remains as the material out of, and through which, life is composed. These variations prompt heated debates over the temporality and temperature of fancy as well as its destination or direction. Taken together, however, their treatments of fancy render visible a major aim of the attempts by imagination to make fancy "a passing fancy"—keeping women and the dead in their place. It is fitting, then, that Wollstonecraft situates fancy and initiates enquiry into it at "The Cave of Fancy."

Caves

> I could not resolutely desolate the scene my fancy flew to . . . when
> a knowledge of mankind . . . rendered every other [scene] insipid.
>
> "The Cave of Fancy"

Wollstonecraft initiated the family's interest in fancy by writing "The Cave of Fancy: A Tale" in 1787.[7] She then enjoined discussion of fancy by leaving the tale unfinished, and leaving it to both her husband and daughter to revive when she died in the process of bringing life to both of them. The connection (on both counts) is clearest with daughter Mary, whose birth occasioned her mother's death and who transformed "The Cave of Fancy" into *The Fields of Fancy*, which she then transformed without the frame chapter into *Matilda* (1819), itself consigned to oblivion until its reappearance in 1959. But it also pertains to Godwin, who edited and published "The Cave of Fancy" as part of the *Posthumous Works* only months after Wollstonecraft's death and who, in his own account, had only begun to reap the benefits of daily access to her animating presence before "this light" was "extinguished forever" (*Memoirs*, 141). One of the main things that Wollstonecraft brought Godwin—in all accounts missing in him up to this point—was a combination of traits associated with fancy and imagination, including tact, intuition, taste, even a degree of playfulness. Initially, his rationalist projects and disposition show him suspicious of the operations of fancy, but they began to warm during the year of his marriage, as registered in *The Enquirer* and the essay "Of History and Romance," the former published, the latter composed in 1797. This warming grew stronger later that year, when Godwin edited Wollstonecraft's remains, especially "The Cave of Fancy" and "On Poetry" but also *The Wrongs of Woman; or, Maria*. Other friends, notably Coleridge, contributed to the softening of Godwin's rationalist convictions at this time and are credited, along with Wollstonecraft, with fostering his imagination and poetic sensibilities.[8] But fancy is what keeps Godwin connected to Wollstonecraft not only in fantasy long after she was technically dead.

Intended as a series of tales within a tale, the one completed tale in "The Cave of Fancy" concerns the amatory education of an unnamed female "spirit" who narrates to the young girl Sagesta, rescued from shipwreck by the sage Sagestus, what will become a classic Wollstonecraftian plot. She is poised between two love objects, the more desirable man being conventionally less worthy because he is married but perceived on the score of sensibility as far worthier. In deference to her mother, she marries the man whom she esteems but does not love, thereby consigning herself to a life of melancholy, enlivened only by flights of fancy, described as the "only refuge" she has "on earth" (203). The ostensible lesson of the tale is to school desire toward virtue by pursuing "active benevolence" in the world, a step that the female spirit finally takes at the end of her story, when, emerging from one of her rapturous communions with her dead beloved, she encounters a weeping girl and accompanies her home in order to relieve the child's sick mother—an action portrayed as ratified by the cave. "Here I have discovered, that I neglected many opportunities of be-ing useful, whilst I fostered a devouring flame" (206). Also made clear by her so-journ is that, for most of her life, she "saw through a false medium" that, instead of allowing her to distinguish mortal from immortal so that "earthly love" would lead to "heavenly" (since only the latter can "fill" the "soul"), collapsed the one into the other and thereby destroyed the possibility of both (206).

From the start, then, for this is one of Wollstonecraft's earliest attempts at fiction, "Cave" positions fancy at the heart of her writing projects and the problematic that they explore, how "thinking powers" place a woman at odds with her heart and the ways of the world. (The topic acquires a more frustrated tone as Wollstonecraft's career proceeds: How much longer must forward-looking women wait before they find space in the world?) Even more intriguingly, it places the education of a young girl under the auspices of fancy and equates the acquisition of knowledge with storytelling. Godwin's explana-tory note implies that this equation is more by authorial default than design. Sagestus, "determined to adopt the child, . . . retired to the hut . . . to think of the best method of educating this child, whom the angry deep had spared. [The *last branch* of the education of Sagesta consisted of a variety of characters and stories presented to her in the Cave of Fancy, of which the following is a specimen]" (my emphasis, 198). The tale's status as fictional accompaniment to *Thoughts on the Education of Daughters* also published in this year suggests that a deeper connection is being made among education, women, and fancy.

The tale establishes several facts about fancy that preside over Wollstone-craft's life/writings. First, fancy is on the side of life and is opposed to "the world"—meaning this world and current realities for women. The tale's setting establishes this logic, whereby entrance into the cave of fancy is deemed crucial to the young girl's survival by taking her out of the world, and is reinforced by the pursuits of fancy as portrayed within the tale. That fancy is a life force is signified by its characteristic adjective, "warm," and the object that it pursues: "futurity," variously associated with God, the afterlife, politics, or other hu-mans. Its eroticism is underscored by fancy's habit of "panting" after futurity.[9] What fancy does oppose is coldness, associated not with death but with "the world" of fashionable society. Indeed, sojourn with the dead is often the only way for fancy to regain heat and vitality, having been rendered "torpid" by commerce with the world. "One only refuge had I on earth; I could not resolutely desolate the scene my fancy flew to, when worldly cares, when a knowledge of mankind, which my circumstances forced on me, rendered every other [scene] insipid" ("Cave," 203). The "scene" to which fancy resorts links death to divinity, through their joint share in "immortality." Opposed to the "unmarked vacuity of common life," fancy restores the female spirit's "former activity of soul" by reviving her "passion" for her beloved, now safely dead (203, 204). Such passion rekindles "the eccentric warmth that gave me identity of character" and serves as a "pledge of immortality" through fancy's penchant for idealization (204). What renders the husband of the female spirit unworthy of her is his dearth of fancy and thus lack of interest in perfectibility. "His religion was coldly reasonable, because he wanted fancy, and he did not feel the necessity of finding, or creating, a perfect object, to answer the one engraved on his heart" (201). In contrast, she has "seen the divinity reflected in a face I loved; . . . [and] could not think of immortality, without recollecting the ecstacy I felt, when my heart first whispered to me that I was beloved" (205).

The formative impact of fancy on love is asserted throughout Wollstonecraft's career, but its circumscription in "The Cave of Fancy" by conventional dictates of morality proves it to be in an early stage of formation. The main difference between "The Cave of Fancy" and *Mary, a Fiction* is the latter's explicit challenge to the morality—that is, rationality—of the female spirit's "useful warning" to Sagesta: "Trust not too much to the goodness which I perceive resides in thy breast. Let it be reined in by principles"—namely, thou shalt not commit adultery (200). But *Mary* ponders what kind of God requires the beloved to be dead *so that* the female lover can "indulge a passion" without it being a "crime," especially when the loss of that passion is shown to deaden her soul ("Cave," 204). And it asks what kind of God "forces me to admire the faint image" of his "perfection" in a particular man and then withdraws all means of obtaining earthly satisfaction with or through him (*Mary*, 46). Increasingly, Wollstonecraft's novels come to depict conventional morality regarding love—the "what will the world say?" of the Lisbon ladies in *Mary* and the definition of marriage as a keeping up of appearances in *Wrongs of Woman*—as literally deadening and deadly ("cold dictates of worldly prudence" that turn the heart to "stone" [*Mary*, 30; *Wrongs*, 144]).[10] Such depictions position fancy on the side of reality against the semblance of "the world." Even more importantly, they align fancy with perfectibility in considering "this strong delusion" proof that "I myself 'am of subtiler essence than the trodden clod': these flights of the imagination point to futurity" (*Mary*, 46).

By the time of *A Short Residence in Sweden, Norway, and Denmark* (1796) and the unfinished *Wrongs of Woman; or, Maria*, Wollstonecraft is finding it much harder to perceive any discernible shape to futurity, whether associated with God or the revolution in female manners, that would make life bearable for thinking women. Still, she does not retract her belief in the progressive dimension of fancy, she just uncouples it from confident predictions about what is to come. While Barbara Taylor is right to emphasize the relation of Wollstonecraft's "eroticized imagination" to her "piety" and to criticize current feminists who, by considering religion a "dead letter," miss its shaping role in her views on imagination, she herself underplays the amoral and pre-Christian features of Wollstonecraft's imagination by overlooking its first appearance as fancy in "The Cave of Fancy."[11] As we have seen, "Cave" is already endorsing the process that Taylor identifies as the "Christian Platonism" espoused in *Mary*, by which "the 'deification of the beloved object' in erotic love is a shadowy intimation of our love of the Deity," but that cave is Platonic, not Christian.[12] At the other end of her career, *Wrongs of Woman* is neither Platonic nor discernibly Christian, but it still insists that fancy is the source of hope in life. At most, its piety is portrayed as a thing of the past: Maria "recollected . . . with what fervour I addressed the God of my youth" (143). In other words, while fancy from first to last is a force of life, movement, and desire and is associated with the "progressive" dimensions of life, its "futurity" is not always directed toward God or the Good, nor is the "life" it seeks necessarily a "good" quality.[13] Fancy's other characteristic adjectives speak this amoral truth in being "wanton," full of "caprice" and "exuberance."

The construal as warnings of Wollstonecraft's attention to the role of fancy in love that we explored in chapter 1, whereby the foregrounding of fancy ostensibly puts women on guard against confusing fantasy and reality in their visions of love, stems partially from feminist critiques of idealization. On one level, Wollstonecraft is surely responsible for initiating the critique, committed as she was to exposing the ways that men's idealizations of women, especially in literature, allow them to avoid or denigrate "real" women, whether fictional or live. But she also highlights the role of fancy in idealization and articulates the necessity of idealization as a stage in youth and love. As she explains in *A Vindication of the Rights of Woman*, the chief difference between love as a "passion" and an "appetite" is the presence of fancy in the former (99). Fancy's capacity to idealize its object joins with its characteristic mode of apprehension ("dimness," a dwelling with "shadows") to ensure, literally, that the lover pursues his beloved with a passion. Otherwise, passion "sinks" into "appetite" when "its object is gained" and, all too frequently, ends in "disgust" (30).[14] Fancy's modes of "pursuit" are not synonymous with Lacanian desire, but they share several features. Fancy acknowledges the essential lack in man, depends on object confusion between the other and Other, and perceives its drive as at once imaginary and mobile.[15] To a certain extent, its object is sheer forward motion, what Wollstonecraft depicts as a "bring[ing] forward of the mind" (177).

Contrary to then-current views that idealization is demeaning to women, Wollstonecraft argues that fancy's idealizing tendencies are useful even when directed toward women. The indistinctions of fancy ward off, or at least defer, one complaint against idealization: objectification of women. A second—dehumanization—is more ambiguously avoided through "deification of the beloved object," which, though admittedly a mixed blessing on the score of enjoyment, is essential for affirming the autonomy (if not humanness) of passionate women. But Wollstonecraft sets certain preconditions on the proper operation of fancy in love. Adoration must be directed at a particular woman, not the entire species, and should constitute only the initial stage of love.

> It is natural for youth to adorn the first object of its affection with every good quality, and the emulation produced by ignorance, or, to speak with more propriety, by inexperience, brings forward the mind capable of forming such an affection, and when, in the lapse of time, perfection is found not to be within the reach of mortals, virtue, abstractedly, is thought beautiful, and wisdom sublime. (*Rights of Woman*, 177)

> Devotion, or love, may be allowed to hallow the garments as well as the person; for the lover must want fancy who has not a sort of sacred respect for the glove or slipper of his mistress. . . . This fine sentiment, perhaps, would not bear to be analyzed by the experimental philosopher—but of such stuff is human rapture made up. (194)

Even more importantly, the stage of idealization is essential to the progress of youth, for without an initially idealized view of "the world," the "ardour of youth" would be "deadened," the "luxuriancy of fancy cut to the quick," and all powers of growth and maturity stunted (176).

Here is where the frame and inset tale of "The Cave of Fancy" start to cohere, but not as a unity. The one completed tale with its focus on a girl's amatory education exemplifies "the best method of educating" youth under the logic of fancy. The first step toward "knowledge" and an "enlarged social feeling" requires idealization. For "if, in the dawn of life, we could soberly survey the scenes before us in perspective, and see everything in its true colours, how could the passions gain sufficient strength to unfold the faculties?" "Stripped of all its false delusive charms," the world looks, well, senseless. It also provides no incentive for progressing. From such a demystified perspective, "the sons and daughters of men" appear to be "pursuing shadows, and anxiously wasting their powers to feed passions which have no adequate object; . . . And love! . . . To see a mortal adorn an object with imaginary charms, and then fall down and worship the idol which he had himself set up—how ridiculous!" (*Rights of Woman*, 180). In other words, the young should not stay in this stage of worship, but they will not get very far if they do not begin from it. Nor should adults think that they are helping by providing cynical, or even realistic, assessments of the world before a child has gained some familiarity with it. Young people must "mix in the throng, and feel as men feel before [they] can judge of [men's] feelings." "I may be told, that the knowledge thus acquired, is sometimes purchased at too dear a rate. I can only answer that I very much doubt whether any knowledge can be attained without labour and sorrow; and those who wish to spare their children both, should not complain, if they are neither wise nor virtuous" (181–82). What they instead produce are "cold" and "prudent" beings, incapable of "rapture" and unwilling to move or be moved. Such beings truly are lifeless; for "when an unwelcome knowledge of life produces almost a satiety of life," the "days of activity and hope are over" (178). Only those who cultivate "powers of the soul that are of little use" in the world know that "life is merely an education, a state of infancy, to which the only hopes worth cherishing should not be sacrificed" (178–79).

Initially idealized views of the world, crucial for the progress of youth generally, are especially important for the unfolding of female minds. This is why her increased insight into the coldness of the world does not cause Wollstonecraft to renounce the operations of fancy. *The Wrongs of Woman*, though deeply pessimistic about the will of social institutions to advance the cause of women, promotes fancy as a necessary stage of female life, once it and previous texts have defined the usefulness of fancy as nonutilitarian. Such texts offer three correctives to the "warning voice" from "The Cave of Fancy," which advises Segasta to rein in her passions with principles. First amendment: "Regulation of the passions, is not, always, wisdom," *especially* in girls, and even granting how harshly "the world" punishes them for falling. For "going astray" is one of the chief means of "enlarg[ing]" the mind (*Rights of Woman*, 179). Indeed, having been granted a wider margin for error is the only reason why men are superior in reasoning. To redress this situation, females must be accorded a similar field for error, provided that the period of straying is a stage that they, too, outgrow. As Maria explains, "There are mistakes of conduct which at 25 prove the strength of the mind, that, ten or fifteen years after, would demonstrate its weakness; its incapacity to acquire a sane judgment. The youths who are satisfied with the ordinary pleasures of life, and do not sigh after ideal phantoms of love and friendship, will never arrive at great maturity of understanding" (*Wrongs,* 104).

Second amendment: Once acquired, knowledge should lead to action, even if that action violates former vows or social conventions. "Had I not wasted years in deliberating, after I ceased to doubt [about the necessity of leaving my husband], how I ought to have acted—I might now be useful and happy. For my sake, warned by my example always appear what you are" (123). Though fraught with difficulties, appearing as one is, in Wollstonecraft's vision, means refusing to dissemble one's feelings once their object proves unworthy of affection. For passion is on the side of life until the forced repression of it robs a person of animation and the will to live. Though love often leads to women's misery, especially under then-current conditions, it also provides one of the few chances women have to enjoy life's "genuine blessings." This right is higher than marriage vows, for it involves the right to life itself.

Third amendment: Seek the blessings of love in this world (though not in "the world"), not in the next. The female spirit's recognition in "The Cave of Fancy" that she "saw through a false medium," which led her to confuse divine love with earthly, becomes in *The Wrongs of Woman* a recognition that imagination, precisely because "delusive," "procures" some of the "solid comforts of life." "We see what we wish, and make a world of our own—and, though reality may sometimes open a door to misery, yet the moments of happiness procured by the imagination, may, without a paradox, be reckoned among the solid comforts of life" (173). This recognition is a key element of sexual love, as we saw in chapter 1, whereby fantasy is seen as crucial to maintaining belief in the fidelity of one's partner, which is presented as a precondition of deciding to engage in sex in the first place. This is the sense in which love is most like literature, not simply formed on it—this recognition that happiness comes from fictional as much as real pleasures. The point is not to crave delusion or seek to preserve it but rather accept that the half-created aspect of love leaves lovers open to errancy.

For Wollstonecraft, then, fancy's role in love is a fact regarding the necessity of fantasy to sustaining love. To describe its share in the formation of love is not a warning against fancy or love or, even more importantly, against the role of fiction in the constitution of love and life. Instead, the warning concerns how the world—the so-called real world and the world of fiction—limits women's choices in life to love and their choices in love to romance heroes. The only hope for changing this reality for women rests in the capacity of fancy and imagination to envision other worlds. Effecting this hope in turn requires altering the literary tradition and expanding the vision of the world that has been depicted by the fancy of "poets." For the poet, in painting a "heaven of fancy," encourages unrealistic expectations of life and love. Always "fencing out sorrow" in their "scenes of bliss," they exclude "all the extactic emotions of the soul, and even its grandeur" (177). Those who wish to pursue life with a passion and find happiness in this pursuit must not model their actions on the versions of reality that former poets have depicted. That reality is too ideal in its exclusion of sorrow, too depressing in its "insipid uniformity" (177).

Such vindications of the right of women to life, love, and happiness suggest that the melancholy that suffuses *A Short Residence*, such that the narrator "dreads" to "unfold" her daughter's "mind" lest, in so doing, she pit her heart against her principles and thereby consign daughters to misery, is not Wollstonecraft's last word on these topics. Though virtually hopeless about the willingness of social institutions to advance the cause of women, hope remains in *The Wrongs of Woman* in the power of fancy to change hearts and heads. This hope is embodied in Jemima, whose own life story expands the content and protagonists of canonical literature and whose response to Maria's and Henry's stories displays the capacity of literature to transform people and worlds. Maintaining hope in this possibility is the promise of Wollstonecraft's life/writings, devoted as they are to lifting the "pall" that the fancy of poets has placed on women's spirits. The effort that this entails is still audible in her words from the grave that hail those "few" readers who, "surely," "will dare to advance before the improvement of the age and grant that my sketches are not the abortion of a distempered fancy" (Author's Preface, *Wrongs*, 83).

Dust

> To a mind rightly framed, the world is a thousand times more
> populous, than to the man, to whom every thing that is not flesh
> and blood, is nothing.
>
> *Essay on Sepulchres*

That Godwin's fancy came after Wollstonecraft's is a fact of chronology and desire. Or one should say that the topic of fancy in Godwin's oeuvre underscores the desirous aspects of nonchronological history. For on one level, God-win's writings began with fancy and in the time of fancy. As Pamela Clemit reminds us, one of his earliest compositions is a fiction, *Imogen: A Pastoral Romance* (1783–84), that uses romance conventions to enlighten the world.[16] In this regard, his literary-political aims required a merger between reason and fancy from the beginning of his writing career.[17] But the desirous and desirable aspects of fancy in the history of Godwin's life/writings, particularly as they relate to the discipline of history, are attributable to his romance with Wollstonecraft. Before, his history writings, social commentaries, and fictional compositions were largely separate projects. Around 1796–97, Wollstonecraft's life/writings encouraged him to treat more directly and positively the topic of fancy (also imagination) in *The Enquirer* and an essay composed for its second volume, "Of History and Romance."

This period of Godwin's fancy manifests several of the same features as Wollstonecraft's. Fancy is now deemed a necessary part of life and of a rational mind, it is opposed to convention, and its goal is futurity. The fact that, by the mid-1780s, Godwin's "futurity" has become divorced permanently from Christian concepts of immortality affects the type of futurity his fancy is after. Put schematically, Wollstonecraft's fancy heads upward and onward. Even when it communes with the dead, it envisions its beloved's approving downward gaze or a future meeting of both in the heavens (*Mary,* 73; "Cave," 202). And even when it despairs over the will-to-progress of the world, it continues to move on. In contrast, Godwin's fancy primarily looks backward and downward in pursuing its goal of reforming the world. Its domain is history, its afterlife the dust of the illustrious dead, whose lives fancy is able to revive.

Fancy in the late 1790s is a precondition of Godwin's sense of aliveness, especially as aliveness and animation are tied to his notions of history (them-selves tied to biography). In "Of History and Romance" (1797) and the Preface to *Life of Chaucer* (1803), Godwin identifies fancy as crucial to his historical method and critique of current historians and present times, and he shows how these views on history are intimately linked to his concept and practice of romance. Most obviously, romance here refers to the generic designation for fiction that also bespeaks its antiquation in being the form of the Middle Ages and its progress into the novel. But these topics also coincide with two aspects of Godwin's and Wollstonecraft's personal romance: the role that the genre of romance plays in their varying support for the revolution in female manners; the role of fancy as remedy for depression. Godwin's experience of these various linkages between history and romance in turn affects his understanding of the nonlinear and unprogressive aspects of historiography and current times. These are the places where enlightened historiography confronts its other in the in/fancy of romance.

Unpublished until 1987, "Of History and Romance" was composed in early 1797, during the time that Godwin was seeing *The Enquirer* through the press. Because both of these publications serve to widen the sphere of rationality as initially conceived in the first edition (1793) of *An Enquiry concerning Political Justice*, Godwin's thoughts on history are closely tied to his thoughts on the nature and perfectibility of human life. The essay's first sentence rates the "study of history" as "among those pursuits which are most worthy to be chosen by a rational being," while subsequent sentences (as well as the title) specify the inseparability between fact and fiction ("History," 291). Achieving this merger, moreover, is important for the ways that the study of history affects futurity. The prospect of more perfectible days depends on a form of history-writing that, in combining fiction with fact, makes "dry bones live."[18]

Actually, Godwin's chief aim in "Of History and Romance" is to reanimate the "dry bones" of the discipline of history. He seeks to revive history, an effort necessitated by the torpidity produced by current historians, whose writings threaten the vitality and mental lives of their readers. This goal entails reprioritizing the twin branches of history, the "study of mankind in a mass" and the "study of the individual" (291). Godwin endorses "study of the individual" precisely because it will restore liveliness to current practices of history-writing, which slight this branch because of several misconceptions regarding the status of fact. First, the study of society, because it deals in abstractions and does not "descend" to particularities, is admired for its "dry and repulsive nature" owing to a general correlation among fact, "difficulty," and "excellence." Current readers of history "disdain the records of individuals" because those records, in "exciting [their] feelings," "disturb" not only their claims to objectivity but also the "torpid tranquility" of those readers' "soul[s]" (291). Second, statements of fact, Godwin asserts, are rarely completely factual; in fact, "*nothing* is more uncertain, more contradictory, more unsatisfactory than the evidence of facts" (297, emphasis added). Nor are facts the quintessence of history. Those who "know only on what day the Bastille was taken and on what spot Louis XVI perished" profess "the mere skeleton of history. The muscles, the articulations, every thing in which the life emphatically resides, is absent" (297). Third, study of the individual is a more productive branch of history because it literally ensures the future. The end of this branch is not "knowledge of the past" (the aim of "general history") but "a sagacity that can penetrate into the depths of futurity" (293). Those different ends in turn produce different habits of mind, the former seeking "dull repetition," the latter "aspir[ing] to something more animated and noble" (292). In fact, *only* the knowledge attained through study of the individual gives "energy and utility to the records of our social existence" (294).

This aim, of producing history that facilitates futurity by being more conducive to a reader's or a people's ability to stay alive, depends on several methodological principles that are each linked to preconceptions about life. First, the "happiness" of mankind depends on the exploration of "new and untrodden paths," which in turn entails study of the individual, not "society in a mass." Therefore, historians must "scrutinize the nature of man" before they can "pronounce what it is of which social man is capable," and this scrutiny is best achieved by focusing on the life of an individual (293). Second, those individuals who are worth "becoming intimately acquainted with" are "men" of "great genius" or those who manifest "bold and masculine virtues" (295). Third, such individuals should be studied in great "detail," never in "abridgement," and in their roles as "friend" and "father" as well as public thinker, speaker, or "patriot." For "it is in history, as it is in life. Superficial acquaintance is nothing" (294). These methodological principles also influence Godwin's evaluation of various periods of history and history-writing, all of which he judges according to whether or how well they bring the past alive. On every score, "ancient history" proves more generative than "modern history." Its subjects are "giants" in comparison to modern "degenerate" "pygmies," who, whether as subjects or authors, are "weighed down" with "prejudices and precedents" and "disciplined to dull monotony" (295). If modern readers want to gain some stature, then, they need new practices—that is, a return to the fabulous practices—of history.

The "science" of "true history," consequently, must reshape itself on and as romance. Only in this way can aspiring historians mitigate the "falsehood and impossibility of history"—falsehood, because, owing to the fabular nature of facts, even so-called objective history is "little better than romance under a graver name" (298); impossible, because "the conjectures of the historian must be built upon a knowledge of the characters of his personages. But we never know any man's character" (300). The closest any individual can come to knowing anybody's character, including his own, is when that character is "the creature of his own fancy"—that is, a fictional character of his own creation. These are the grounds on which Godwin positions the "writer of romance" on "higher grounds" than the writer "formerly called the historian" (300). For "true history consists in a delineation of consistent, human character," which entails showing how "such a character acts under successive circumstances" and, more basically, how character grows as well as "decays" (301).

Commentators often note the curious about-face at the end of the essay, where, precisely in detailing in what the true delineation of character consists, Godwin appears to cede back to the historian part of the ground that he had granted the writer of romance. As Jon Klancher shows, the reversal underscores the necessity of factoring contingency into the comprehension of character, of recognizing that the smallest circumstance can alter the course of an individual's moral, like the world's natural, history.[19] Training readers to foresee the consequences of contingency is what is beyond the capacity of the romance writer, not because of the fictive status of his reality but because of the logical impossibility of an author scripting what is to him truly unforeseen into his own creation. Unforeseeability only comes from elsewhere—from God, natural law, trauma, or the events of history, which the historian does not have to foresee because, in already having happened, they "are taken out of his hands" (301).

The "truth" value of history, then, resides in the mundane fact that the events that it narrates have occurred. But this does not change the priority of romance on the score of truth or vitality, for the historian, and certainly contemporary historians, neither focus predominantly on individuals nor understand the character of individuals when they do. On the other hand, it is standard to evaluate novelists according to the degree that their characters cohere and come alive. Godwin reaffirms this assessment of the truth-value of fiction when he prints the same defense of romance more than thirty years later as part of the preface to *Cloudesley* (1830). "However paradoxical it may seem, fictitious history is more true and to be depended upon, when it has the fortune to be executed by a masterly hand, than that which is to be drawn from state-papers, documents, and letters written by those who were actually engaged in the scene" (6). Even more apparently paradoxical, the "science of history" depends on romance because novels are at once more scientific in their study of man and more truthful about it. They are more scientific, as we have seen, because the novelist understands his characters and is thus able to display the causality—the concatenation of cause and effect that forms a character—in ways that history usually does not and probably cannot. For "man is a more complex machine, than is 'dreamed of in our philosophy': and it is probable that the skill of no moral anatomist has yet been consummate enough fully to solve the obscurities of any one of the great worthies of ancient or modern times" (7). Precisely because novels are more truthful about the fact that consistency of character is fictional, readers of fiction will be less undone than readers of history or philosophy by the contingencies of life, those "unlooked-for phenomena, which, in the history of an individual, seem to have a malicious pleasure in thrusting themselves forward to subvert our best digested theories" (7–8).

Such views explain and arguably justify Godwin's habit of calling his own novels "histories of man." They also help to resolve another apparent paradox between Godwin's disinterest in the kind of individuality associated with sentiment and his habit of focusing in his novels on a specific individual— signified by his choice of title for every novel. For the generic applicability of these admittedly aberrant individuals lies both in what can be gleaned about human nature from the comprehension of their character and in their own composition as literal composites from a wide array of sources, experiences, and records ("History," 299). When Godwin turned to writing history after 1797, he embraced these principles. His history works describe a particular time period, frame of mind, national culture, and intellectual milieu through focus on the life of a specific, historical individual. In this way, biography becomes a history and history a *Life*, or *Lives*.

The first of his "fictitious histories" to elucidate Godwin's "true" "science of history" is his *Life of Chaucer*, in 1803. The Preface states Godwin's "wish" as historian to "carry the workings of fancy and the spirit of philosophy into the investigation of ages past," in the current instance, an age of fancy (xi).[20] It stipulates as well the interchange between biography and history, arguing that the comprehension of Chaucer's "mind" demands an "extensive survey of the manners, the opinions, the arts and the literature" of the fourteenth century and that the "biography of Chaucer" provides a "portion of the literary, political and domestic history of our country" (viii, ix). The role of fancy is to animate Chaucer and thereby enliven contemporary readers, who have been "stupif[ied]" and deadened by the "phlegmatic and desultory" methods of contemporary historians, who are "men of cold tempers and sterile imaginations" (x). By contrast, historian Godwin turns necromancer, "rescu[ing] for a moment the illustrious dead from the jaws of the grave" and making "them pass in review before me" (xi).[21] The goal of this reanimation is not merely to enhance readers' comprehension but also to encourage readers to emulate Chaucer and his historian by turning historians themselves, now that their appetites for scholarship have been whetted by fancy and then directed to the relevant archival sources (x).

Godwin terms his fanciful-philosophical mode of history-writing a "work of a new species" (x). If he was overstating his novelty as historian, as the work of Mark Salber Phillips indicates, he was certainly distinguishing himself, and consciously distancing himself, from those contemporary historians who hailed the birth of historiography as the eradication of romance.[22] Enlightened literary history charts the development of mind by describing various periods of history in terms of their varying proportions of darkness and light. Just as romances are said to wane in popularity as the magic they reflect becomes antiquated, so minds affirm their rigor by taking their distance from fancy. The linearity of Bishop Hurd's account is only the most familiar version of the necessary dissolution of romance. "Thus at length the magic of the old romances was perfectly dissolved. . . . Reason in the end drove them off the scene and would endure these lying wonders, neither in their own proper shape, nor as masked in figures."[23] Such accounts are part of the process by which history establishes its credibility by manifesting its incredulity toward superstition and magic. It announces itself as a "stern," "severe," and "impartial" discipline that counters the pleasures of fiction *and* of former practices of history (like those of Herodotus and Thucydides).[24] Even their expressions of nostalgia for the lost world of "fine fabling" do not alter their view of the facts—that facts put fancy to flight as the sign of enlightenment. In contrast, Godwin protests such dispiriting accounts of the progress of mind.[25]

Fancy's role, then, in ensuring that history resemble romance and in re-animating the history of romance associated with the Middle Ages (the literary romances of which Godwin identifies in *Life of Chaucer* as our best records of the actual circumstances of the period), has a complicated relation to the history and practice of Godwin's and Wollstonecraft's "personal" and literary romance. Certainly, fancy's capacity to reanimate and to maintain ongoing "intercourse" with the illustrious dead worked wonders on their relationship after 1797. The presence of fancy also suggests their ongoing accord over the various ways that fiction can make life come alive, if not now, then in the future. Indeed, the remedy for depression that Godwin identifies in his version of history is not simply opposition to the torpid effects of current historiography. His version of romance history also cured his own depression, and those of readers like him, who are lonely not only because their illustrious friends are dead but also because the so-called living are either deadening or lethal as interlocutors.

The sociality provided by the so-called dead of history receives its fullest expression in the *Essay on Sepulchres* of 1809. Here Godwin describes proper history as enlightened necromancy, a public raising of the dead in the service of national mourning and renewal, by proposing to Parliament that it "erect some memorial of the illustrious dead in all ages on the spot where their remains have been interred" (the essay's subtitle). Erecting these memorials is essential to making "dry bones" live not as "cold generalities and idle homilies of morality" but as friends, "brother-men" (22; *Chaucer*, 2:16). The aim is intercourse with the dead as a form of sociality purged of Gothicism, for God-win welcomes these spirits "around my path, and around my bed" (*Sepulchres*, 22). In this regard, fancy vastly enlarges one's social sphere. Why "converse only with the generation of men that now happens to subsist" when we can "live in intercourse with the Illustrious Dead of All Ages" (22)? To "a mind rightly framed, the world is a thousand times more populous, than to the man, to whom every thing that is not flesh and blood, is nothing" (23).

While the fancy in history promised to keep Wollstonecraft alive for God-win, they parted company over fancy's association with romance. It is curious how often the romances of Chaucer are implicated in Godwin's courtship of women after Wollstonecraft's death. Even before he composed *Life of Chaucer*, his first proposal of marriage was to Harriet Lee, coauthor (with her sister Sophia) of a series of modern stories of the *Canterbury Tales*. The only surviving letter during his courtship of Mary Jane Clairmont, in which he confesses the "animal magnetism" that draws him to her, was composed at Woodstock, where he had gone with his publisher to visit the home of Chaucer. Composition of the *Life* began within days of his second marriage.[26] Thus, efforts to start afresh in his middle age ("I am not a boy," he assures Lee) were tied to a romance revival of a personal nature. In other words, fancy's role in Godwin's concept of romance places love in the Middle Ages as a fact of Chaucer's and Godwin's biography.[27]

The chivalry associated with Godwin's middle-age romance heightened the distance between him and Wollstonecraft. Wollstonecraft's image remained over the hearth in his study but its spirit of gender equality did not survive a second season. For fancy's association with romances of the Middle Ages affirms an unequal relation between the sexes. As we saw in chapter 1, by 1803 Godwin endorses this inequality as vital to heterosexual love. "I think, quite contrary to the vulgar maxim on the subject, that love is never love in its best spirit, but among unequals. An excellent invention of modern times [here meaning chivalry], that, while woman by the nature of things must look up to man, teaches us in our turn to regard woman, not merely as a convenience to be made use of, but as a being to be treated with courtship and consideration and fealty."[28] In contrast, Wollstonecraft's fancy never looks back, certainly not to the Middle Ages or chivalry as offering better opportunities for women. On that score, Wollstonecraft remains an Enlightenment thinker whose passion requires an enlightened outlook and social circle so that it does not continue to constrain or demean women. Moreover, the pleasures of sociality promised by history are minimal when the illustrious dead are perennially speaking against one's interests. The idea of intercourse with such company left Wollstonecraft cold, whereas it warmed Godwin's spirits, especially when castigating the "cold tempers" of contemporary historians.

But beyond Wollstonecraft—or, more precisely, when confronting the broader ramifications of the "calamity of death" associated with her passing—Godwin's fancy put him in touch with the least enlightened aspect of its drive toward truth: that, owing to this calamity, the "world for ever is, and in some degree for ever must be, in its infancy" (*Sepulchres*, 10). Paradoxically, this state of infancy results from distinctive qualities of Godwin's rationalism, namely, his acknowledgment of all that is lost in humanity's march toward modernity and his emphasis on the necessity for individuals to find their way, and their truth, for themselves. Contrary to popular belief, Godwin has a keen eye for the undesirable features of rationality. In his view, modern individuals, in eschewing romance for reason, turn their backs on wonder, excess, times and modes of magic, and they deny any pleasure in their work/ethics. This antipleasure principle stunts those who live in "these days of the dull and the literal," the monotony, conformity, and chill of which days "blight in the bud every grander and more ample development of the soul" ("History," 364, 365).[29] Precisely as "slaves of an uncontrollable destiny," humanity's ancestors had more freedom and more fun; they did not have to comport themselves with the "perseverance and moral courage" enjoined on those who live in more enlightened times.[30] Whereas "advanced ages" are chained to necessity, as an economic and logical condition, "infancy" is "lawless" in its novelty. To infant eyes, everything is as fresh, vibrant, and full of wonder as are the words ostensibly spoken in the earliest ages of the world. No wonder infant(ile) voices question why they should move on.

Even more surprising is Godwin's consideration of whether individuals *can* progress beyond infancy. In part, this question stems from death's truncation of life projects, not merely that death ends them but that it also ends the potentialities and contingencies of living. In part, it arises out of the nature of learning. By requiring that persons acquire knowledge and conviction for themselves, each person and, more importantly, each generation must begin again from scratch. "The world is much like a school," whose studies are "perpetually beginning: and though much is acquired, and great and earnest efforts are made after improvement,—one decade, and one century of years, passes away and another comes, and everything is nearly in the same posture" (14n). This commitment to free thought likewise restricts in advance the growth anticipated in Godwin's characterizations of history and political science as "sciences" in their "infancy," sciences that are even less likely to progress owing to the forces aligned against enlightenment. In a word, youth; what Godwin calls the "ever-young infatuation, inexperience, and temerity" that "perpetually disturb the profoundest designs and maxims that can be framed for general advantage" ("History," 361; Preface to *Political Justice, Sepulchres,* 14n). This is a startling picture of the world according to Godwin and of the world of Godwin—this world in which nothing progresses. Acquaintance with such a world spurred his writing, underwrote the project of the Juvenile Library, and informed the infancy and enlightened fancy of the child of his and Wollstonecraft's romance. It also came back to haunt him in the object choices of her wandering fancy.

Fields

> But when before have I not followed your slightest sign and have
> left what was either of joy or sorrow in our world to dwell with
> you in yours till you have dismissed me ever unwilling to depart?
>> *The Fields of Fancy*

Shelley's fancy fed on remains. Remains are all she had in the case of her mother, and they were crucial to the forms of animation and coldness that she inherited from her father, who wrote that *"the great man himself"* is "simply and literally" the "dust that is covered by his tomb" (*Sepulchres,* 20; original emphasis). The remains with which Godwin conjured respond to the science of history conceived as enlightened necromancy. They addressed his loneliness and peopled his world, at least the world of his study. Shelley was chiefly preoccupied with reassembling the remains of her parents and husband, but from early on she found ways to create new species of life from remnants. Most famously, remains of the dead gave rise to a creature still stalking popular imaginations, while another set (the leaves in the Sybil's Cave) predicted the end of human life altogether. More than her parents, perhaps more than any of her contemporaries, Shelley's writings bespeak the death-in-life. They not only declare themselves "in love with death" but also perceive "death the skeleton" to be "as beautiful as love" (*Fields,* 394). The spectral nature of that voice is strengthened by the series of tragedies that mark her life/writings and by her familial-historical status as second-generation and secondary to all the major figures in her life. The voice is triggered by another favorite scene of her girlhood, one that depicts young Mary behind a sofa transfixed by hearing Coleridge recite the *Ancient Mariner.* No wonder Shelley's life/writings have so often been construed as impeding progress, whether in failing to carry through on her family's passion for reforming or in dampening Percy's spirits with her "dreary reality." Less perceptible has been the influence of Coleridge on the arrested character of her life/writings, but his mariner haunts her "wandering fancy" and quest for meaning in life.

Struggle over the meaning of life is particularly visible in *The Fields of Fancy*, 1819, recomposed as *Matilda* with significant revisions, the most important being the repression of the initial frame narration.[31] This text represents Shelley's most explicit treatment of the role of fancy/imagination in negotiating death-in-life and her most explicit engagement with her mother's fictional writings. Critics have often read *Matilda* as a coming to terms with the impact of her father in her life and writings, especially her "excessive & romantic attachment" to him.[32] Even those, like Pamela Clemit, who argue against "psychobiograph[ical]" assessments of the text and instead view as Shelley's "primary concern" "not so much . . . family personalities as . . . family writings," still narrow those to the "themes and techniques" of Godwin and Percy Shelley.[33] One exception is Mary Jacobus, who draws attention to the mother, Diana, as at once prefiguring and informing the melancholy of Mathilda and *Matilda.*[34] Intriguing to me is the significance of Shelley's original title, which echoes "The Cave of Fancy," and then her decision to repress the titular, but not substantive and structural, echoes of "Cave" in the text of *Matilda.*[35] In this, *The Fields of Fancy* both modifies and confirms Charles Robinson's point about the "surprising" absence of "direct references to (or even echoes of) her mother's works in the works of Mary Shelley."[36] Perhaps it begins to identify a characteristic mode of dealing with her mother in her life/writings, a presence that is shadowy from the start, given that that life is only captured in writing.

Given the predominant plot of *The Fields of Fancy*, it is easy to view this text as heavily male- and father-identified, despite its having a female protagonist. Mathilda's obsession with her father, coupled with the gender of her only significant, though never fully actualized, friend (Lovel/Woodville), is one reason why, in chapter 3, I located *Matilda* in the phase of Shelley's radical, but not explicitly feminist, writings. Yet aspects of the narrative, and especially the frame, suggest that *Fields* is not only in explicit dialogue with Wollstonecraft but that it also marks a definite advance over the forms of male-identification characteristic of *Frankenstein*. The only arguably Wollstonecraftian stand-ins there, the signatory female letter-writer, MWS, of the first frame or the decidedly undomestic Safie, at the heart of the novel, are not able to effect a discernible change in the novel's correlation between men and adventure. Even the references to fancy are ascribed to a masculinist world-view, since fancy is presented as the source of Western science and of Victor's desires to create life without a woman. If Mathilda is not portrayed as wholly adventurous, at least in the sense of being curious about, or receptive to, the world, she is remarkably adventurous within her limited environs—starting with her childhood fantasy life through to her actions after her father's death, both of which show her to be highly inventive and resourceful and, for all her depression, quite capable of maneuvering literally around the world. She is even bolder in her relations with her father, totally apart from the question of her complicity in incest. For Mathilda is dogged or, as Clemit says, Caleb-like in satisfying her curiosity regarding her father's secret and is wholly emancipated in addressing him as "a friend & equal" (*Fields*, 370).[37]

Three issues govern this discussion of what does and does not remain of *The Fields of Fancy* in *Matilda*: the relation of these texts to "The Cave of Fancy" and its author; depictions of fancy's relation to life in both Shelley's versions; and the implications of fancy on Shelley's notion of writing as remains. The "broad parallels" between "Cave" and *Fields* that Clemit instances concern Sagesta's education by a spirit who "presents the story of her earthly life as a 'useful lesson,'" the "didactic structure" of which is adopted in chapter 1 of *Fields* and is aimed at the unnamed female narrator. The "useful lesson" directed at Sagesta pertains to the proper channeling of "adulterous passion" into "a life 'enlivened by active benevolence,'" which in *Fields* is applied to Mathilda's incestuous passion by the lessons of Diotima and Lovel and in *Matilda* by Woodville.[38] A more fundamental parallel, in my view, concerns not only the sheer focus on a female protagonist and the direction of her mind but also the placement of female education under the supervision of fancy, in both cases a new departure in Shelley's life/writings and decidedly not one "of the many conventions of the fictional model that Godwin originated."[39] Moreover, the relocation of the spirit of fancy from cave to fields suggests Shelley's comprehension of the tendency of Wollstonecraft's fancy in subsequent works. Indeed, Shelley's own repression of the explicit didacticism of chapter 1 of *Fields* enacts the movement of Wollstonecraft's fancy from "Cave" to *Mary*, which, as I argued earlier, questions the morality of the "useful lesson" that enjoins females to rein in passion by conventional or biblical principles. It follows the spirit of these directives to their new un-Platonic locale, those wider fields for straying that are essential to the unfolding of a girl's mind.

Although the emphasis on fields gets buried in the narrative's reshaping as *Matilda*, the spirit it signifies remains in ways that imply a fuller internalization of Wollstonecraft's less use-driven principles. To put it a different way, *Matilda* refers to the mother text in a more shadowy, less directly confrontational manner than *The Fields of Fancy*, an assessment supported by two other changes from draft to fair copy. The entire frame narrative, with its explicit personification of fancy as the female spirit, Fantasia, is deleted. Inserted into *Matilda* is the steward's observation to Mathilda, "you are like her [Diana] although there is more of my lord in you" (23). Taken together, these changes characterize the nature and extent of Shelley's allegiance to her mother's fancy in her own version of fancy. This estimation entails calculating the distance that separates both Shelley's from Wollstonecraft's and both of theirs from the fancies of their men.

The frame narrative explicitly raises an issue that both versions of the narrative proper also confront. What is the role of fancy in intensifying and mitigating suffering or, as a broader question, What is the proper balance between realism and idealism in life? The frame intensifies these questions through its setting and form—a Socratic dialogue within the Elysian Fields.[40] In this, it fleshes out the Platonic implications of the setting of "The Cave of Fancy" and ascribes wisdom to females, not only in the "prophetess" Diotima (who, after all, is the instructor of Socrates in the *Symposium*, a crucial pretext for *Fields*) but also in the personification of fancy as the female spirit Fantasia and the gender of Diotima's and Fantasia's special charges (who all get merged into Mathilda in *Matilda*). It also accentuates the life-or-death consequences of proper education for women—indeed, it suggests that their education continues after they have died and determines their postmortem futurity. For the unnamed "captive" of Fantasia is brought to that part of the Garden that is reserved for those dead who are seeking wisdom and virtue through "contemplation" and who, though "still unknowing of their final destination," have a "clear knowledge of what on earth is only supposed by some": their "happiness now & hereafter depends upon their intellectual improvement" (*Fields*,

53). In this regard, one could say that *Fields* addresses the other end of life from that presented in "Cave," the young girl in "Cave" being rescued from death and educated for life—that is, for love—in the world, the young maiden of *Fields* exiting life as a result of illicit love and entering an afterlife of "meditation" on the memories of "the traces of our feelings" (359).

The classical setting suggests the influence of Percy and also Godwin, a field of study that is of comparatively little interest to Wollstonecraft. But distance from her mother's fancy is most readily measured in the grieving narrator's reaction to Fantasia (doubled by the young woman's skepticism regarding the wisdom of Diotima). Though formerly devoted to Fantasia, this narrator, presented at the beginning of chapter 1 as submerged in grief, resists her offers of transport, because Fantasia's mode of diversion betrays the narrator's "only reality"—misery. "As to follow her was to leave for a while the thought of those loved ones whose memories were my all [,] although they were my torment[,] I dared not go" (352). Such proffered transport also belies her physical condition, the "weight of grief" being so overwhelming that she simply cannot move. Distance is also evident in the explicit lessons drawn from fancy's differing locales. The female of "Cave" learns that, by fanning her passion, she neglected the active benevolence that "enriches" life and "sweetens" death. The female of *Fields* concludes that one "moment" of oblivion is worth "a life of painful recollection." The cave's wisdom is further countered by the young woman's response to Diotima, that knowledge is no match for misery. "My passions were there my all to me and the hopeless misery that possessed me shut all love & all images of beauty from my soul" (358). Even the language of the cave's fancy belongs to another world. "Are there in the peaceful language used by the inhabitants of these regions— words burning enough to paint the tortures of the human heart?" (359).

Shelleyan reactions to fancy in 1819, then, put the alleged depths of Wollstonecraft's melancholy into perspective. Wollstonecraft may "dread" but she continues to "pant" after the unfolding of mind that constitutes fancy's hope and futurity. For Shelley, the hopelessness associated with that "tragic year" of 1819–20 renders life, especially a life of learning, a total blank. Suffering can so absorb one's being that the entire external world is lost. The "dreary realities" of that year colored her fancy and depiction of Fantasia by posing this question from the field: Is all this suffering necessary to the prospect of better times?—a prospect that, for Wollstonecraft, required an initial idealization of reality so that minds would desire to unfold; a prospect that made Godwin unrealistic about the all-consuming reality of a person's pain. From the perspective of *The Fields of Fancy*, there is a point after which pain is wholly unproductive. Present-day theorists call this traumatic knowledge; Shelley in this period termed psychic arrest a reality of life.[41]

Traces of this debate regarding the adequacy of fancy to suffering remain in the narrative proper of both versions. Here they are tied to the characterization of the poet, Lovel/Woodville, and the debates he and Mathilda hold over the responsibilities of the living to live and to thereby improve the conditions of living for others. This debate has two components that correlate to separate, though interrelated, audiences: one concerns the proper response of the grief-stricken, whose misery has curtailed all interest in life; the other concerns the special responsibility and efficacy of the poet to ameliorate suffering and enliven the world. In his "personal" grief and universal acclaim as poet, Lovel/Woodville exemplifies the connection between the two themes. On the face of it, then, these traces seem to confirm Clemit's sense that the fair copy intensifies Shelley's reliance on the "themes and techniques" of Godwin and Percy Shelley, not just for the obvious reason that Lovel/Woodville is patterned on Percy—and on Shelley's fantasies about him, especially the claim that "the multitude extolled the same poems that formed the wonder of the sage in his closet" (389). Closer inspection reveals the extent to which this fancy—even as imagination—follows in the wake of Wollstonecraft.

In effect, Mathilda attacks the exemplarity of Lovel/Woodville on two grounds: his status as mourner, and the realism of his idealism. His successful mourning, as compared to her melancholy, raises doubts in her mind about the quality of his love, since he is able to move beyond the loss of someone who once (apparently) was all the world to him. This in turn makes her suspicious of "this boasted friendship" he is offering her, since "he got over his grief for Elinor" and was then "glad to find even me for an amusement," so that, granting the less intense connection between the two of them, Mathilda would be wise not to base even the dimness of present happiness on him (396). For Mathilda, total misery *is* the proper—that is, the only adequate—response to the loss of the person who is the "life of my life." What kind of "life" lives on when the life of it is gone? Let's talk about cold.

This question is linked to the idealism expressed by Lovel/Woodville as it relates to "active benevolence," a discussion prompted by Mathilda's proposal that he fulfill the only condition that would "prove" his friendship, accompanying her in death (396). Lovel/Woodville's response echoes several of the key propositions of Wollstonecraft's and Godwin's futurity and the kind of selfhood (that is, nonselfhood) on which it depends. "We have been placed here & bid live & hope . . . if the labours of those who cast aside selfishness & try to know the truth of things are to free the men of ages now far distant . . . from the burthen under which they now groan [;] . . . if this free them but from one of the evils that now so heavily oppress them—cheerfully do I gird myself to my task" (398). To this affirmation of self-postponement, Mathilda poses two relevant questions. Why am I born an individual, with all my particular sensations and passions, if my highest purpose is to merge with—indeed, get submerged by—the world? And why should I give up the misery that concenters my being if this is the only access to self-coherence available to women, whose history and life roles feature nothing but submergence?

The stakes are even higher when these questions are directed to Lovel/ Woodville in his function as poet. For given the extensive influence that poets have on the world, they have a greater responsibility to keep hope, and thus the future, alive. "Let us suppose that Socrates or Shakespeare or Rousseau had been seized with despair & died . . . when they were as young as I am; do you think that we and all the world should not have lost incalculable improvement in our good feelings and our happiness by the destruction[?]" (398). Yet this higher vantage of poets also gives them greater opportunity to do harm, especially to those whose reality is deemed too foreign or uninteresting to be noticed, and thus represented, by them. Here Mathilda's skepticism is directed at the otherworldliness that so often characterizes the poet's dealings with the world. This includes his penchant to view reality, including other people's sufferings, as rich material for his imaginative projects; also his success at promoting a form of sympathy that, by identifying with the other's pain, allows him to focus on himself. Mathilda voices these charges, as Jacobus states, with the "ring" of an "authentic marital complaint."[42] The first charge is well known, especially as it applies to this year when Percy was composing a tragedy and opposing it to his lyrical drama: "Perhaps he is already planning a poem in which I am to figure—I am a farce & play to him but to me this is all dreary reality—he takes all the profit & I bear all the burthen" (395). The second expresses disappointment over the poet's unfulfilled promise to "speak peace" to her "vext soul" (394).

The reservations that Mathilda voices here are not applied to all aspects of fancy or to all imaginative writers, but to the false reality of the worldview of overidealizing poets—those who feel untouched by, or hold themselves aloof from, the harshness of living. In this regard, Shelley endorses Maria's sentiment voiced in *The Wrongs of Woman*, that, by "fencing out sorrow," the world envisioned by the fancy of poets is both "insipid" and precisely not useful (141).

While the depths of misery Mathilda feels rule out her finding any "solid comfort" other than misery in life, Mathilda's *is* a limit case (that is, a case of trauma) and does not voice Shelley's general, or even the unnamed female narrator's only, position on fancy. That narrator describes herself as a former devotee of Fantasia, until her bereavement renders her totally unresponsive to any one or any thing. Moreover, the portrayals of Fantasia (in the frame) and of fancy (in the narrative proper) stress the palpable reality and vitality of the fictional, or otherworldly, world that she and it inhabit. The narrator stresses this vitality in her uncharacteristic rejection of Fantasia's offer of transport: "But when before have I not followed your slightest sign and have left what was either joy or sorrow in our world to dwell with you in yours till you have dismissed me ever unwilling to depart?" (*Fields*, 352). Moreover, the locations "under [Fantasia's] command" include the "many lovely spots" which "poets of old have visited" as well as other spots both "beautiful" and "tremendous," said by Fantasia to be kept "in reserve for my future worshippers" (352). The characterization of Fantasia as well stresses the mobility of her moral character, at once "wanton" and "consolatory," though always "lovely" (351). In other words, Fantasia is transporting but decidedly not ideal.

Within the narrative, fancy's effects are similarly real and aligned with realism about life's complexities. As Mathilda states, the "various images" of fancy bring "now consolation and now aggravation of grief to my heart" (365). This recognition, that fancy both fuels and mitigates grief, is what makes it "lifelike," especially in the tragic year of 1819–20. Neither life nor literature is a consistent source of happiness, and neither can prepare a person fully for the misery that comes from living or reading. The ongoing allegiance of *this* fancy to Wollstonecraft is recognized in *Matilda* by the preservation not of its titular location but of its characteristic mode: a "wandering fancy." Wandering implies the presence of those fields necessary for straying but removes the mandatory idealism of the Socratic frame.[43]

Allegiance is especially visible in the biggest shift from *Fields* to *Matilda*: Mathilda's new status as writer. *Fields* frames Mathilda's narrative, portraying it as told to Diotima by a young woman in the Elysian Fields and overheard by the grief-stricken unnamed narrator (a young woman, by the way, described as "about 23 years of age in the full enjoyment of the most exquisite beauty[,] her golden hair float[ing] in ringlets on her shoulders—her hazle eyes . . . shaded by heavy lids and her mouth . . . seem[ing to] breathe sensibility" [355]). In *Matilda*, Mathilda pens her life story on her deathbed, finding in the prospect of dying courage—indeed, license—to "unveil" her "tragic history" (6, 5). Now uniting in herself the grieving subject and the writer, Mathilda perhaps feels herself more equal to the task of acknowledging Woodville as "friend," the only one "who will receive [these pages] at my death" but nonetheless whose specificity she annuls by "relat[ing] my tale as if I wrote for strangers" (5–6). Returning the depersonalizing favor of poets to Woodville, she nonetheless also writes in the spirit of Wollstonecraft, whose final unfinished narrative framed Maria's dreary reality with a staging of writing to two "strangers," her baby and then Henry, both of whom, like her writing itself, hold the promise of futurity. Dark as is Mathilda's reality and happy as she now is to die, her unveiling of the despair of her life is addressed to a future in which such misery may be redressed, at the least by not being not-spoken by virtue of the "fencing out" of sorrow characteristic of idealist poetry. In this regard, the shift in titles accurately indicates the shift in the province of fancy, from external to internal, from nature to woman, from *Fields* to *Matilda*.

If, as Clemit rightly argues, we should perceive in *Matilda* Shelley's conscious artistry and detached engagement with the "family writings" of Godwin and Percy Shelley, then we need to include engagement with the writings of Wollstonecraft as part of that artistry. For Wollstonecraft's life/writings, as I argued in chapter 1, promote the form of active reading that Clemit associates with Godwin's narrative strategies. And if we perceive Shelley taking distance from Wollstonecraft's and Percy Shelley's fancy in reactions to Fantasia and Lovel/Woodville, then we might also ask what it is about Godwinian fancy that Mathilda rejects, beyond Clemit's specifications of Godwinian candor, shown to have disastrous consequences in this novella. Clemit's pointing to the date when Shelley began the fair copy, 9 November 1819, suggests that she began rewriting *Fields* "on the very day she heard that Godwin had lost a lawsuit concerning his house in Skinner Street and was required to pay back rent of £1500," for Shelley "planned to publish *Matilda* for Godwin's benefit."[44] Talk about "he takes all the profit and I bear all the burthen"; Mathilda's lament is an accurate reckoning of the financial history of Shelley's life/writings in relation to Godwin. Yet, even here, Shelley does not present herself or her protagonist as simply victimized by paternal demands. The burden is considerably lightened through the aggression voiced in both daughters' writings and readings.[45] Only *Matilda*, the text being rewritten for Godwin's profit, includes this reference to the resourcefulness of Mathilda's fancy. When asked to choose a text from which to read aloud once her father has revoked his initial request that she take up Dante at the place "where [her mother] left off," Mathilda "took up Spencer and read the descent of Sir Guyon to the halls of Avarice" (23). (In *Fields,* she picks up Ariosto's *Orlando Furioso* at the point where Isabella, to save her honor, tricks the "cruel King, Rodomante," into beheading her [368n]). Indeed, let Godwin have all the profits when this level of burden gets lifted. In the event, only Shelley cashes in, since Godwin withheld *Matilda* from publication and thus gained nothing from it other than insight into one daughter's psychic accountings. They may not be financial, but Shelley's fancy reaps enormous profits in remains.

So does Mathilda's fancy. For all her misery and unsuitability for life, Mathilda is quite resourceful in orchestrating her life and death more than once. Moreover, the narcissism of her remorse ensures that she give an account of herself only when it will do her no harm and might do future daughters some good. This strategy necessitates writing from a deathbed that positions her life story as remains left for "strangers," who may or may not ever "peruse these pages," to decipher. On one level, a life story that, in the sheer fact of its narration, alters the unspeakability that, until then, has characterized its contents and passions, on another, in being addressed to strangers, voices both this writer's alienation from any current readership and also her claims to one in the future. Envisioning one's readers as strangers implies that more than one's acquaintances will be engaged by one's works. Mathilda has it both ways, in assuming that only Woodville will read her pages but composing them for a wider, unfamiliar audience. For she and her author know that the reception of stories, especially those pertaining to formerly unspeakable matters, is hugely precarious, but that time is on the side of remains.

CHAPTER FIVE

Living Off and On
The Literary Work of Mourning

Of the many "revered" books written by her parents which Mary, Percy, and Claire read as guides to and sanctions of their youthful experiences, *Essay on Sepulchres,* according to William St. Clair, was "one of Mary's favourites." Presented to her 14 May 1814, on the occasion of her half-sister Fanny's birthday and "also the day [Godwin] recovered from his latest attack of fits," *Essay on Sepulchres,* St. Clair speculates, "may have been intended to prepare her for the day when he too would lie in St Pancras Churchyard" (549n). In the event, the *Essay* oversaw a striking number of intervening deaths before Godwin was finally laid to rest on 7 April 1836, of natural causes. These intervening deaths all lay outside the "natural" course of things, by occurring either to a very young child, at one's own hand, or by an unnatural act of nature, and they substantiate the image of Mary Shelley as a perpetual mourner. They include the death of a premature daughter (6 March 1815), Fanny's suicide (9 October 1816), the suicide of Percy's first wife, Harriet Westbrook (10 December 1816), the death of one-year-old Clara (24 September 1818), the death of three-year-old William (7 June 1819), the death of five-year-old Allegra, Claire and Byron's daughter (20 April 1822), and the deaths by drowning of Percy and Edward Williams (8 July 1822). If St. Clair's speculation is correct, one can say that Mary was certainly well practiced in, if not prepared for, the day when Godwin would finally lie in St Pancras Churchyard.[1]

A second detail from St. Clair strengthens the image of Mary as perpetual mourner. Whereas he depicts the three recently returned "runaways" in 1814 reading several of Wollstonecraft's and Godwin's books "curled up together in front of the fire" in their newly rented home in Margaret Street, St. Marylebone, the *Essay on Sepulchres* singles Mary out. This text "she would take with her to St Pancras Churchyard and read alone as she lay on the grass by her mother's grave" (366–67). Already carrying within her the (ill-fated) fruit of her and Percy's fabled former lying together on this very site, Mary is hardly alone in this act of reading "alone" to and with the spirits of her mother, lover, and fetus. Indeed, the very book she is reading, as we saw in the last chapter, is telling her just how populated this spot is as well as how well-befriended she is when she sojourns by it. "To a mind rightly framed, the world is a thousand times more populous, than to the man, to whom every thing that is not flesh and blood, is nothing." For "dry bones" live as "friends" who surround one's "path" and "bed" (81–82, 79). Just how well did this book prepare Shelley for the many deaths that at once populated and emptied out the paths and beds of her young-adult years? What did she imbibe from this book of mourning that, in delineating the "duty" of "survivors," depicted as a national duty the mourning of her own mother? How did this form of duty complicate Mary's "personal" reaction to the many unmournable losses in her life, the repeated retelling of which preoccupies her life/writings and biographies of her?

Relatively little attention has been devoted to this scene of Shelley's literary-psychic formation as compared to that lavished on prior scenes of her tracing the tombstone letters that spell Mary (one as two) and her necrosexual union with Percy (two as four as one). This neglect is odd, since biographers and critics are inclined to dwell on the misery, rather than bliss, that allegedly makes up her life/writing history and that is said to distinguish her from Percy. Some of this inattention may be the product of scholarly ambivalence toward adolescence, even though everyone agrees that Mary's most exciting years belong to this allegedly transitional period. But it stems also from critical neglect of *Essay on Sepulchres,* a vastly undercelebrated work in the Godwinian canon, both in its day and ours.[2] This critical neglect is reinforced by the widely held view that Godwin is a poor authority on the topic of mourning, owing to the perception of his relative absence of human feeling coupled with his totally inhumane responses to his daughter's grief and suffering. The argument of this chapter runs counter to this received wisdom. For not only was *Essay on Sepulchres* one of Shelley's "favourite" parental texts, but it initiated the terms, passions, and tensions that underlie her many textual accounts of mourning and the work of mourning that those accounts are said to accomplish (or not). It also set in motion her various generic approaches to treating the fact and affect of death. After *Frankenstein,* a text more invested in investigating writing's share in generating life and death than in responding to death, Shelley's writings probe the capacity of writing to accomplish the work of mourning in fictional, editorial, autobiographical, and biographical forms. When considered together, these texts make visible Shelley's obsessive challenge to writing to clarify the terms by and on which writing—her own as well as the classics—is said to conquer death. Shelley goes farther than Godwin in posing this challenge, but *Essay on Sepulchres* lays a crucial foundation. More precisely, *Sepulchres* directs the question of the status of death to survivors, whereas Shelley's writings direct the status of surviving to writing. But the two approaches converge ultimately to make peace with the illustrious dead.

Facing the Calamity of Death

It is much to lose such a man.

Essay on Sepulchres

The main goal of *Essay on Sepulchres* is to examine "the effects flowing from the mortality of man to human affairs, and the feelings and sentiments it becomes us to cherish respecting the Illustrious Dead" (preface, 6). The formulation is striking, both in its two-pronged approach to the topic of death and for the ways that it invites misunderstanding. The little commentary that exists on this text has essentially focused on the second phrase at the expense of the first, giving rise to the claim that *Essay on Sepulchres* is "of a very different character from some of the earlier productions of the same pen" because its remarks are "too sentimental and romantic."[3] The best recent commentary, by Mark Phillips, follows this tradition. Foregrounding Godwin's interest in the "associational" logic of historical commemoration, by which a simple marker in the landscape evokes a flood of memories, Phillips characterizes the project itself as promoting "an essentially spectatorial and inward," "essentially private," and "sentimental" response to history.[4] Godwin's proposal to mark with a simple wooden cross the graves of the illustrious dead "and to leave the rest to the mind of the spectator" evokes in the "sentimental traveler" passional and private associations that are "nostalgic" and "elegiac" in nature (*Sepulchres*, 18).[5]

Emphasis on the uncharacteristically sentimental and romantic tone of *Sepulchres* is encouraged by its first several pages, which describe feelings of overwhelming loss that arise when a "great and excellent man" dies. "My friend, as long as he lived, was in a certain sense every thing to me. His society was my delight. To anticipate the seasons when I should enjoy that society, was the balm of my life. His presence, his countenance, what a solid and substantial good I derived from them! . . . My personal knowledge of him, was the sustainer of my faith, my antidote against misanthropy, the sunshine which gilded the otherwise gloomy and cheerless scenes of this sublunary state. It is much to lose such a man" (8–9). Owing to the suddenness and totality of this loss, all of the personal effects of this friend become invaluable, talismanic. "His ring, his watch, his books, and his habitation" acquire an "empire over my mind," making me "happy or unhappy," "tortur[ing]" or "tranquillis[ing]" my spirit. Not only this, but "if this friend were my familiar acquaintance, if he dwelt under the same roof with me, if (to put the strongest case) I were so fortunate that the person worthy of all this encomium were the wife of my bosom," then this "greatest of earthly calamities, and the most universal" is the "most terrible" of all (8–9).

Un-Godwinian as they sound, these comments should not be read in a vacuum. They constitute Godwin's second attempt at public mourning, after the outcry over his extreme insensitivity in "stripping his dead wife naked" in the *Memoirs* of 1798, whereby these first pages work to re-establish Godwin's credentials as a mourner, as someone who has experienced firsthand how devastating it is "to lose" a friend, particularly the "wife of my bosom." But they also occur as preparation for examining the "effects flowing from the mortality of man to human affairs," effects that profoundly influence Godwin's understanding of death, life, history, and mourning, the chief of which effects is "that the world for ever is, and in some degree for ever must be, in its infancy" (8). Key to perceiving Godwin's unsentimental approach to mourning is discerning the double sense in which the calamity of death keeps the world in infancy, one sense we already touched upon in the last chapter. Recognizing this reminds us that one's attitude toward mourning depends on one's concept of death and that associational logic is part of the culture of necessity, not only, as Phillips suggests, of sentiment.

Both ways in which the calamity of death keeps the world in its infancy acknowledge the severity of the challenges posed to life by death in order, ultimately, to overcome them. In the first, more common, sense, Godwin calls the death of an (eminent) individual a "calamity" that is "greater" to the survivor than to "him that dies," the "effects" of which "are beyond all the powers of calculation to reach" (8). What is incalculable about this calamity is the loss not so much of the person who was "every thing" to the survivor but of all the unrealized potential within that person that, with his death, will now never be brought to fruition. "The use and application of his experience, the counsels he could give, the firmness and sagacity with which he could have executed what he might have thus counseled, are gone" (8). Even with the most accomplished men, far more is lost—that is, far more remains in potentia, now never to exist—than has been gained or realized by that individual in the world. In this calculation, then, the more eminent the person, the more his death retards intellectual progress because the yet-to-be and might-have-been of him is always far greater than the "is." The second form of calamity is even less personal. Here death keeps the world in its infancy because survivors not only quickly forget the dead but also periodically seek to obliterate history. "We cut ourselves off from the inheritance of our ancestors; we seem to conspire from time to time to cancel old scores, and begin the affairs of the human species afresh" (14). This desire to start afresh, coupled with the fact of ending too soon, whether envisaged as a child or a generation, keeps the world from moving forward.

Addressing both of these challenges informs Godwin's proposal to mark the graves of the illustrious dead throughout England. In practical terms, marking individual graves allows survivors to find where the illustrious un/dead still reside on this earth, visit them, and commune with—actually imbibe—their presence.[6] Such a practice allows visitors to "indulge all the reality we can now have of a sort of conference with these men" (12). Compiling an atlas of where these graves exist allows the current generation to plan their commemorative travels and ensures future generations that a record of these "records of past ages" will never be obliterated. "Though cities were demolished, and empires overthrown, though the ploughshare were passed over the site of populous streets, and the soil they once occupied were 'sown with salt,' the materials would thus be preserved, by means of which, at the greatest distance of time, everything that was most sacred might be restored, and the calamity which had swallowed up whole generations of men, might be obliterated as if it had never been" (29). For the goal of this proposal, as Godwin "plead[s]," is to "paralyse the hand of Oblivion," both in the case of the individual's very short-term memory—indeed, general "apathy"—in commemorating the dead and in the case of history's tendency to erase itself periodically (22, 17).

These marked graves dotting the landscape serve as a constant visual reminder to survivors that the past is part of their current reality and thus not to be forgotten. Even more central to paralyzing the hand of oblivion is altering modes of perception so that things that are not "flesh and blood" are still perceptible. The illustrious dead are "shadows . . . no more than we are shadows"; by removing the "grosser film" from our eyes, humans "might live and sensibly mingle with Socrates, and Plato, and the Decii, and the Catos, with Chaucer, and Milton, and Thomas Aquinas, and Thomas à Becket, and all the stars that gild our mortal sphere. They are not dead. They are still with us in their stories, in their words, in their writings, in the consequences that do not cease to flow fresh from what they did" (23). "Inestimable benefit" will flow from "our attaining the craft and mystery" by which each of us, in our "several sphere[s]," learns to "compel the earth and ocean to give up / Their dead alive" (6). The benefit is a "composure of spirit" that is favorable to "elevation of mind," "generous action," and "virtue." In other words, learning to see the dead as existing among the living, as capable of converse, and therefore of still influencing events—and learning to view this as a desirable state of affairs—is crucial to Godwin's efforts to produce a benevolent and well-focused citizenry. Such "vivid recollection of things past" but not gone ensures "the boldest improvements" in the future. "The genuine heroes of the times that have been, were the reformers, the instructors, and improvers of their contemporaries; and he is the sincerest admirer of these men, who most earnestly aspires to become 'like unto them'" (6). Indeed, emulating these dead helps the world start to progress beyond infancy.

For Godwin, then, the impediment to successful mourning is not resistance to surmounting one's losses or to cathecting new objects but envisioning death as a radical antithesis to life. The *Essay on Sepulchres* works to mitigate humanity's resistance to mortality by making death less removed from life and depicting the dead as our familiars. Familiarizing death—literally, making the dead part of the family—is meant to ensure that, when a beloved dies, grief does not incapacitate survivors and that surviving does not require obliterating all memory of the dead. Indeed, the capacity of death and the dead to disrupt the living directly correlates to an individual's ignorance, denial, or repression of the dead. "He must be a man of feeble conceit and a narrow soul, to whom [the dead] are like the shadows of a magic lantern. Shadows certainly they are, no more than we are shadows" (23). The "duty" of survivors is not simply to remember the dead but to "acquire the craft" by which to "compel" the earth and ocean to "give up their dead alive" (6). Attaining this craft involves revising one's notions of nature, history, and the constitutive presence of the dead in both.

Godwin's depiction of nature in *Sepulchres* demonstrates the profound materialism that underlies his imminent transcendentalism. To the extent that it appears wild, uncivilized, natural (as it does, as he says, in "new countries"), nature actually impedes a person's ability to see, and thus live in, the world correctly. The advantage of living in an "old country" is that there is no getting around the dead, who compose the earth of such countries and account for its "admirable fertility." The "clod (such it is now)" citizens of old countries "know formerly to have been" some part of its eminent individuals, the knowledge of which bears fruit in "sentiments and virtues, of those thoughts which make man the brother of them 'that have none to help them,' and elevate him to a God" (18–19). In other words, the "renovating virtue" that stems from an experience in Godwinian, as contrasted to Wordsworthian, nature vastly expands the duration that constitutes the past accessed by any individual's memory—extending from one's childhood years to the earliest periods of one's national community, figures from which times still exist as "guides, instructors, friends" to the living (19).[7] Dwelling in such a landscape, rich in community and history, in turn enlivens the "reading of history," for readers in this nature more readily flesh out the "cold and uncertain record of words formed upon paper" (21).

This kind of fleshing out of the records of history links the *Essay on Sepulchres* to stipulations in "On History and Romance" and the preface to the *Life of Chaucer* explored in the previous chapter. All three texts view familiarity with an eminent individual as the best way to comprehend a historical period and to envision a better future. All three see such study as crucial to acquiring the craft of making the earth give up its dead alive or, as the preface to *Chaucer* puts it, of "rescu[ing] for a moment the illustrious dead from the jaws of the grave" and having "them pass in review before me" (xi). But *Sepulchres* also stipulates a new tenet, which underlies these earlier writings and profoundly influences the life/writing practices of Godwin and Mary Shelley.[8] It explicitly connects the topic of survival to literary lives—both the living of and the composition of them.

While "vulgar minds" think that "military and naval" heroes are a nation's truest benefactors and thus most worthy to be commemorated, higher minds see that the "benefit or glory of their accomplishments" is only "temporary" and thus look to "literary men" for lasting inspiration (28). Here *Sepulchres* publicly censures the faulty thinking responsible for the public's poor reception of his defense of Fénelon, as delineated in his "Thoughts occasioned by the perusal of Dr. Parr's Spital Sermon" (1800), and specifies several reasons why the lives that literary persons lead and leave behind them are the most conducive to strengthening the public's welfare. For one, lives of literary men, as compared to military heroes, remain "whole" long after the person has passed. Cimon and Scipio have "dwindled into a name; but whole Plato, and

Xenophon, and Virgil have descended to us, undefaced, undismembered, and complete" (28). The wholeness of these remains keeps such lives as close to alive as possible, the study and imbibing of which is crucial to keeping or making the living more alive. "I can dwell upon them for days and for weeks: I am acquainted with their peculiarities; their inmost thoughts are familiar to me; they appear before me with all the attributes of individuality; I can ruminate upon their lessons and sentiments at leisure, till my whole soul is lighted up with the spirit of these authors" (28–29).[9] For another, these remains themselves are said to live, alter, change with the times through what Godwin elsewhere terms their "tendency," or, in *Sepulchres*, the "consequences that do not cease to flow fresh from" their words and deeds (23). That is, "new" eyes alter and update, according to their historical conditions, the truths that these past lives are articulating. Third, this transmission of life and new life through imbibing the remains of Western culture's most illustrious writers can be felt around the globe and imparts "energy and sagacity" to "the wisest mandarin now living in China" even if he has never heard of Shakespeare and Milton (29). Because "every" person who is "deeply impressed by the perusal of their works communicates a portion of the inspiration all around him," Plato, Chaucer, Shakespeare, and Milton are literally part of the air that we breathe as well as the earth that we tread (29). Such a palpable "reality" means that *willed* blindness keeps one from affirming one's neighborship with the worthy dead of all ages.[10] It also means that persistence in grief is a refusal to acknowledge not only that death is part of life but also that the dead are among the most vibrant and attractive parts of it.

Debilitating grief, then, is not part of Godwin's reality or comprehension of it. This is not just because he does not view death as wholly foreign to life or the living but also because denial of the alterity of death is central to his commitment to justice. *An Enquiry concerning Political Justice* already seeks to annul the otherness and permanence of death by affirming that the perfectibility attendant on reason will one day eradicate human mortality. Later, Godwin comes to confer on writing, rather than reason, the power of extending life and certain eminent lives indefinitely, but he still retains the emphasis on justice. Avoiding the incapacitation of grief is crucial to attaining an equable and perfectible world. For the calamity of death already represents such a challenge to perfectibility that things should not be made worse by rendering survivors dead to the world and its objects, even temporarily. Mitigating such indifference to life underlies Godwin's redefinitions of self, attachment, marriage, and family, the purpose of all four being the strengthening of one's connection to objects *by* resisting (rather than insisting on) the magic of "my." This means that the loss of a child in Africa should affect a just person as intimately as the loss of one's own child. But it also means that the devastation that Godwin *acknowledges* in the loss of a beloved is not denied but is understood as one consequence of our being "creatures of circumstance" rather than sentiment. "The good thing I have long enjoyed, by habit has become necessary to me, and I cannot be resigned or patient under the privation of it. This remark applies more acutely to the loss of a human friend and associate, than to any other calamity" (9). Defined in this way, the sheer passage of time diminishes calamity because time brings new circumstances, which alter, and thus come to constitute a new, reality. Meanwhile, the loss of all the potential that makes death a calamity is lessened in the case of eminent writers. The potential within the reality of their written words (that is, their tendency) continues to unfold over time, so long as there are new eyes to read them.

A decade after *Essay on Sepulchres* and certainly by 1822, Mary Shelley was wholly familiar with death and thus well positioned to evaluate the "inestimable benefit" of Godwin's reformulations. The account is not a ringing endorsement. One would be hard pressed to hear "composure of spirit" in the voices of Mathilda in *Matilda* (1819), Ceres in *Proserpine* (1820), the "I" of *The Journal of Sorrow* (1822–24), or anyone except Lionel in *The Last Man* (1826). Nor could one claim that any of these texts surmounts loss to re-engage with reality or even values that endeavor. The grieving protagonist of *Matilda* desires only blankness from the world, and the sole survivor in *The Last Man* finds nothing but blankness in his efforts to communicate with humanity. According to these voices, having the dead as one's familiar provokes stasis, melancholy, anxiety, or rage, which causes many of them to question the optimism and sexism of Godwin's position. Why focus only on illustrious men? Talk about the calamity of a child's death, which under any definition is loss of the virtually all-potential. And what about one's beloved? Just what kind of love *wants* to survive the loss of the love of one's life?

Such questions are raised by texts from Shelley's most profound period of grieving, 1818 to 1826, which acquaint readers with a degree of devastation that is unparalleled in the history of letters. *Matilda, Proserpine, The Last Man,* and *The Journal of Sorrow,* stunningly bleak texts about the capacity of death to render one's world, and the entire world, a total blank, constitute the strongest possible counter to Godwin's dispassionate approach to death, mourning, and surviving. Exploring them within this familial dynamic, however, yields two claims that deepen critical appreciation of Shelley's, and her parents', contribution to mourning and trauma studies.[11] One is that these texts ultimately give rise to successful mourning in a manner that is faithful to the method and solutions posed in *Essay on Sepulchres*. The fact that Mary Shelley is generally perceived as expert at mourning has impeded critical perception of how she achieved that expertise, a process that was deeply hard-won, tenuous, and belated and that was central to her acceptance both of her worth as writer and of the value of the literary tradition. A second claim is that the dynamic that this series of texts enacts demonstrates their relevance to contemporary trauma studies. Not only do they stage an acting out of trauma (both within protagonists and as texts) in order ultimately to work through to an affirmation of mourning through writing, but the life/writings of Shelley constitute a detailed charting of this process for the first time in literary history. Moreover, by situating her life/writings within the mourning strategies of Godwin, usually viewed as her antithesis in this register, we come to see the centrality of illustrious writers to both of their understandings of survival.

Positing the relevance of Godwin's writings to trauma studies seems to be invalidated by my prior assertion that debilitating grief is not a part of Godwin's reality because of his rationalist approach to surmounting loss. For, despite significant variations in the definitions of trauma, contemporary trauma theorists, often taking their cue from post-Shoah philosophers like Levinas and Derrida, view trauma in Freud's sense as undermining enlightened notions of identity, memory, mimesis, and history. Emphasizing the permanent loss *to* memory and subjectivity of the traumatic event, the "reality" of trauma is evident only through the repeated re-enactment that is the sign of the irretrievability of the event that, by having caused a permanent breach, hole, or gap within the protective shield of the psyche, threatens the subject's capacity to integrate by re-presenting the hurtful experience in normal consciousness.[12] Indeed, one paradox of trauma is that there is no there there, in the place to which one's symptoms keep returning the traumatized subject.

Nor is Godwin's relevance to trauma studies exactly genealogical in Ruth Leys's account of that history. As Leys points out, modern understanding of trauma began in the 1860s, as an investigation of the physiology of shock, and then acquired its psychological and psychoanalytic dimensions at the end of the nineteenth century, when trauma was conceived as a "wounding of the *mind* brought about by sudden, unexpected, emotional shock."[13] What Godwin brings to the topic is twofold: a powerful engagement in several of his novels with the traumatic effects of historical events on various protagonists, especially Mandeville but also St. Leon; and a profound sense of the impediment to historical progress posed by the two scales affected by the calamity of death—personal devastation coupled with humanity's desire periodically to efface the record of the past.[14] For him, both of these conditions lead to a world arrested at infancy, and the combination of the two perpetuates injustice and global inhumanity.[15] An intriguing genealogical linkage does exist in Leys's reminder that hypnosis is "historically central to the genealogy of trauma," an assertion, for her, that both accounts for and may help to circumvent the theoretical impasse between mimetic and antimimetic approaches to trauma and that, in the case of Godwin, recalls his early, and lifelong, fascination with mesmerism.[16] For Godwin's reason does not repress but emerges out of his awareness of the ways in which one often is, and should be, beyond, if not beside, oneself.

Shelley's vehement challenges to Godwin's tenets during her period of trauma are useful for indicating what critics of Godwin, unlike herself ultimately, have not gotten beyond: the view that there is something inhuman/e about not being incapacitated by loss of a loved one. Shelley's writings frame the charge by stressing how the grieving person's "life" depends on remaining occupied by the (not yet fully) lost object, voicing what is still a valid problematic of grief, that moving on feels like a betrayal of those one has loved.[17] Critical responses to Godwin display an often-unacknowledged linkage between value and feeling, as if one responsible consequence of analyzing the "effects of mortality on human affairs" should not be striving to inculcate a greater acceptance of the inevitability and survivability of others' deaths. This is not to assert that realism or rationalism adequately addresses the psychic and physical realities associated with loss or with its treatment—nor does Godwin assert this. His efforts to stress the interconnections between history and romance, person and context, magic and science, human and machine indicate a more complex picture of the mind than views of his rationalism tend to credit, a picture, moreover, which his insistence on education and cultural enlightenment sought to inculcate, not simplify. The fact that daughter Mary initially rejected Godwin's consolatory strictures fits the favored image of her as rebel daughter *and* sentimental reactionary. But such an image arrests her at a stage that her life/writings show her to have outgrown.

Blank Desertion

> Even when we think we are creating, we are always being worked
> by foreign messages.
>
> *Jean Laplanche*

A critical truism about *Matilda* is useful for framing one argument of this investigation of *Matilda, Proserpine,* and *The Last Man.* The truism associates *Matilda* with exploration of Shelley's "excessive & romantic attachment to my father," which this section construes against the grain as attachment to his theories and practices of mourning. It extends the richest critical commentary on *Matilda* to all three texts to take up suggestions offered by Tilottama Rajan and Mary Jacobus regarding their treatments of trauma and what Rajan deems the "unreadability" of *Matilda.*[18] A second strand of argument identifies a temporal dynamic within these texts' own probings of the literary work of mourning. Here I suggest that texts are paired, in the sense of opposed, in the emphasis they grant to the consolatory ends of writing. Their pairing also stages the revisionism that characterizes Shelley's accounts of her own periods of grieving, by which she revises former assertions of the total blankness of her world in the light of new misery. In the immediate wake of William's death, Shelley writes that "I no sooner take up my pen than my thoughts run away with me—& I cannot guide it except about *one* subject & that I must avoid. . . . I never shall recover that blow—I feel it more now than at Rome—the thought never leaves me for a single moment—Everything on earth has lost its interest to me."[19] Yet in the wake of the new trauma of the drowning of Percy, such desolation comes to feel partial, even remediable, for the writing of *Matilda* was "sufficient to quell my wretchedness temporarily" (*Sorrow,* 442). This dynamic is repeated in her account of the new desolation associated with the move back to England, in whose light (i.e., darkness) the period in Genoa immediately after Percy's death now appears productive. "My grief was active, striving, expectant." "I could have written something, been something. Now I am exiled" (470). Precisely this question of the im/possibility of survival generates the composition and content of these fictions.

Readers acknowledge some working through to an acceptance of death and mourning in the later fictions of Shelley's oeuvre. From the perspective of *The Fortunes of Perkin Warbeck* (1830), *Lodore* (1835), and *Falkner* (1837), texts like *Matilda* and *The Last Man* certainly sound grief-stricken, arrested, traumatized, and they are invariably read in this way. The present argument does not dispute this perception but wishes to emphasize the status of the grieving texts as themselves transitional, as themselves literally working through to the position that comes to be accepted by the later novels as the working through of grief through writing, and to underscore a less complete but equally oppositional structure within and among the fictions of this middle period. As I hope to show, each of these texts debates the validity of the necessity to mourn, a position first affirmed, not accidentally, by the male-poet figure, Woodville. Not surprisingly, either, female figures voice the strongest objections to this duty, with Mathilda, Ceres, and Perdita all staking their survival on not moving anywhere. But, for reasons that begin to reveal Shelley's linkage among gender, writing, and dying, Proserpine, the archetypal daughter of trauma, is shown to turn a deaf ear to prior women's objections to mourning. Proserpine initiates the perspective that Shelley's life/writings will belatedly come to affirm in the form of the duty of writers to live on.

The content and critical reactions to *Matilda* make visible the more obvious connection of Shelley's life/writings to trauma studies. The topic is father-daughter incest, the life progress of the narrator is arrested, the past is her only reality, and her psychic state and physical *goal* is dissociation. Also, her actions represent a near-perfect case of acting out, by which Mathilda stays gripped by the past and her desire to reunite with it, such that she attempts to stage a suicide pact with Woodville. Jacobus explicates the quite striking convergence of Shelley's and Freudian treatments of trauma. Given that the kind of incest depicted is not physical intercourse but invasion by the word *love,* what constitutes Mathilda's experience of incest as a trauma is how Mathilda's girlhood fantasy of recovering her father through his declaration, "daughter, I love thee," resignifies that past event: "Even before her father's incestuous disclosure, Matilda had read the illicit idyll encrypted in her unconscious girlhood phantasy. Matilda is possessed by a concrete event (a word, a look) where once there had been an ordinary Oedipal phantasy. This, rather than any attempt at physical seduction, turns out to be Mary Shelley's definition of incest trauma and its wretched after-effects."[20] Jacobus goes on to explore the *literary* symptoms of trauma as depicted not only in Mathilda's narrative but also in her form of narration—an early instance of what Dominick LaCapra calls the "risky symbolic emulation of trauma," a "writing of terrorized disempowerment as close as possible to the experience of traumatized victims without presuming to be identical to it," which he deems "prevalent" since the end of the nineteenth century.[21] The crucial textual symptom, which for Rajan constitutes the unreadability of *Matilda*, involves how quotations from other literary texts are unintegrated, unassimilated into the voice of the narrative, as if, in Jacobus's words, they intrude from "an unmanageable archaic underworld" and resist symbolization.[22] One major effect, then, of the "unspeakability" that *Matilda* ascribes to the topic, as well as the word *incest*, is the exclusion of Mathilda from the worlds of social relations and literary transmission.

However, Jacobus also views *Matilda* as partially moving beyond the negativity of this textual diagnosis of trauma by instancing the positive dimensions of Mathilda's recourse to writing. The missed event, the "unknowable 'beyond,'" in *Matilda*—that is, the death of her mother, Diana—is accessed through an act of "literary rememoration" that is legible as "an attempt at literary self-cure."[23] Moreover, Mathilda's refusal to read herself as a "tragedy," the reading of herself that she imputes to Woodville, prompts her to "writ[e her] own version of the story," to "upstage" him by becoming a "lyric monodramatist of despair."[24] Still, Jacobus shows, signs of trauma remain evident in several features of Mathilda's relation to the literary tradition and the "despair" associated with it. First, Mathilda projects the eloquence and idealism of poetry onto Woodville and vests them in the "'elsewhere' of quotation from Dante, Spenser, and Wordsworth."[25] Second, Mathilda's enlistment of Dante's *Purgatorio* serves regression rather than transformation, for what she takes from it is "the longing for paradisal reunion."[26]

Such observations position *Matilda* as a textual treatment of trauma and a traumatized text and thus establish it as the benchmark against which to measure Shelley's subsequent depictions of trauma. Its linking of trauma to the question of literary transmission also provides the connection that will ultimately move Shelley and her protagonists beyond the stasis *and* acting out embodied in this text. Establishing this connection happens on two levels. In debating the duty to mourn, *Matilda* introduces a thematic topic that is taken up in the other two texts, by which the all-or-nothing status of love is linked to the acceptance or rejection of the consolations associated with literature, a debate staged between Mathilda and Woodville. As is her wont, Mathilda affirms the extremes, depicting the loss of the "all" of love both as "sudden and entire" and as resulting in a "love" for "death" (19, 58). She also rejects the kind of love embodied by Woodville, both in his relation to Elinor and in his articulation of the idealism of poetry, as suspect and disingenuous because it is capable of transference, substitution, change—and also because it mystifies reality.[27] For her, then, the only "proof" of love resides in Woodville's agreeing to accompany her into the all-and-nothingness of death. To this offer Woodville famously opposes his defense of poetry as mandating the duty to surmount one's losses in order to live for the betterment of the world.

Woodville's rendition of this duty stresses two components that are usually ascribed to the life/writings of Godwin and Percy Shelley. The first involves the self-postponing nature of the truly benevolent person, understood here as the duty to live for the future, no matter how dark is one's current reality: "If the efforts of the virtuous now, are to make the future inhabitants of this fair world more happy; if the labours of those who cast aside selfishness, and try to know the truth of things, are to free the men of ages, now far distant but which will one day come, from the burthen under which those who now live groan, and like you weep bitterly; if they free them but from one of what are now the necessary evils of life, truly I will not fail but will with my whole soul aid the work" (59). The second emphasizes the paramount value of writers and thus the absolute necessity for them to survive. "Let us suppose that Socrates, or Shakespear, or Rousseau had been seized with despair and died in youth when they were as young as I am; do you think that we and all the world should not have lost incalculable improvement in our good feelings and our happiness thro' their destruction?" (59). Texts after *Matilda* moderate the outcome but not the essential poles of this debate as occurring between the all-or-nothing of human love and the future of writing.

The second level on which the connection between trauma and literary transmission is played out directs attention to the dynamic by which debates over the duty to mourn are modified or inverted through textual pairings. Apprehending this dynamic helps to weaken the tendency to anchor any particular expression of inconsolable grief, mourning, or trauma in details of Shelley's "personal" situation. Often couples in these texts, usually heterosexual couples (whether lovers or parent and child), express opposing views on the topic, as if to suggest that gender and generational position affects one's ability or desire to mourn, especially when mourning entails seeking consolation in literature, itself often painfully selective in what it considers worthy losses or gains. Moreover, extending the debate over a series of texts makes readers undergo an experience similar to Shelley's in perceiving how reactions to death change, vary, and are never finalized and how such reactions are often influenced by reading.

The major changes undergone from *The Fields of Fancy* to the fair copy of *Matilda* illustrate both of these levels. As we saw in chapter 4, *Matilda* deletes the frame narration of *Field of Fancy*, in which Diotima ultimately affirms the value of mourning but without denying the power and reality of despair, and instead inserts the content of her account into the body of the text by splitting it into sides assigned to opposing genders. Even more importantly, *Matilda* shifts from third-person to first-person narration. In both *Fields* and *Matilda*, Mathilda hangs firm in articulating the "despair" attendant on surviving, but by now narrating her story, Mathilda moves beyond the unspeakability of the trauma of incest, even if she is composing her story on her deathbed. As a writer, then, she now claims a certain kinship with Woodville, though she denies this kinship by stressing the differences between them and addressing him as "stranger." An even larger step forward is made in the movement from *Matilda* to *Proserpine*, texts separated by only a few months in their composition. For *Proserpine* not only eschews the status of "tragedy" ostensibly imposed on Mathilda by Woodville (and by Percy on Mary in this year) but suggests that moving on, and moving beyond certain forms of trauma, has everything to do with revising the literary heritage.

There are several ways in which *Proserpine* moves beyond the trauma, and the literary symptoms of trauma, discernable in *Matilda*, the most striking of which underscores Shelley's characteristic recourse to literature to navigate reality. For if, as Jacobus asserts, Mathilda's insertion "into a prior romance" (the father's conflation of Mathilda and her mother, Diana) becomes "explicitly literary when her father asks her to read Dante" at the place where her mother "left off," Mathilda's *consciousness* of her identification with a prior female legend is evident when she compares herself to Proserpine. "Often . . . I have compared myself to Proserpine who was gaily and heedlessly gathering flowers on the sweet plain of Enna, when the King of Hell snatched her away to the abodes of death and misery" (19). But whereas the Proserpine in *Matilda* is invoked to confirm that Mathilda's reality lies in "the abodes of death and misery," the Proserpine of *Proserpine* moves elsewhere and thereby moves beyond Mathilda's traumatized approach to texts and living. The reaction of this Proserpine to her abduction and rape by Pluto suggests how. "Dear Mother . . . This is not misery; 'tis but a slight change / From our late happy lot" (act 2, ll. 264–67). Whereas Mathilda clings to her misery through a textualized refusal of metaphor and ingests the fantasy of paradisal reunion in Dante's *Purgatorio*, whereby the "nevermore of loss becomes the evermore of imaginary repossession," Proserpine ensures generational and literary transmission through her capacity to change and accept change.[28] Indeed, part of her legendary meaning is the necessity of seasonal change. Both in its content and as a text, then, and even granting its fidelity to the

main outlines of the legend, *Proserpine* is avowedly nontraumatic and un-
traumatized. Its content affirms the reality of incest but as something capable
of being survived, and its status as a reworking, not a repetition, suggests a
characteristic mode of working with and through trauma. Part of that working
through in *Proserpine* involves the "missed event" in *Matilda*. The unmournable loss of the mother there is here transformed into rejection of the mother's
fixation on loss.

The few critical works to explore *Proserpine* consider both the classic
legend and Shelley's revision of it as expressions of feminism.[29] Generally the
legend is viewed as depicting the origins of patriarchy as a violent disruption
of mother-daughter union by the intervention of phallic authority and desire.[30] It portrays maidens as innocent, fathers as rapacious, and maternal love
as so unconditional that it considers annihilation of the earth nothing when
compared to a daughter's recovery. Feminist interpretations of Shelley's *Proserpine* present equally sentimentalized versions of the mother-daughter relation, often in homage to the mother of liberal feminism and her grieving
daughter-author. The feminist spirit of these interpretations is valid, especially when it accentuates Shelley's multiplication of female poets and narrators in her version as a way of reinserting women into the literary heritage.
But a crucial part of the feminist message lies in its representation not of
patriarchal disruption as a tragedy but of pre-Oedipal union as a myth that
often leads to tragedy. In Shelley's version of *Proserpine* and literary history,
that is, tragedy follows on the myth, or cultural fantasy, of a kind of oneness
that makes loss antipathetic to aliveness.

The very first words of *Proserpine* connect the presence of the mother to
her absence and both to narrative. "Dear Mother, leave me not! I love to rest /
Under the shadow of that hanging cave / And listen to your tales" (1.1–3). It
associates tales, not milk, with the daughter's demand for sustenance at the
same time that it depicts the daughter's craving for deanimation, for rest. Both
features place storytelling beyond orality, in symbolic and mortal territory, and
stress a textual origin in Ovid and intertextual proximity to Wollstonecraft.
The daughter loves to rest under the shadow of that "hanging cave," which
echoes "the cave of fancy" of her mother's text. The feminist implication of
linking mother and tale arises through the multiplication that disarticulates
creativity from re/productivity. Maidens and nymphs have reached maturity
as poetic figures, testifying to what Alan Richardson rightly terms Shelley's
"feminist mythic revisionism."[31] Act 1 characterizes Ceres, Ino, Eunoe, and
Proserpine all as "weavers of 'tales and songs,' of 'poesy,' of 'verses sweet,' "

foregrounding a "community of mythmaking women" that occasions celebratory accounts of feminist solidarity within the play.[32] Susan Gubar reads *Proserpine* as depicting "a pastoral time of communality between all women, young and old," a line that virtually all of the few commentators on the drama adopt for several compelling reasons.[33] With the exception of a brief appearance by Ascalaphus, no male personage ever enters this drama. We do not view Pluto's abduction or rape of Proserpine or come into the presence of Jove, who, as Jeffrey Cox points out, enlists Iris (usually associated with Juno, not Jove) rather than Mercury as his messenger to earth.[34] Act 1 dwells solely on relations among women, and act 2 is stunning for the reason that Richardson explores: "The communitarian nature of the female deities' resolve" to accompany Proserpine to Hades, thereby subverting patriarchy's attempt to come between women.[35] Against all odds and precedent, these females deem themselves capable of creating an "Enna" out of "Elysium." Ceres vows to transfer earth's fertility to Erebus and "feed the dead with Heaven's ambrosial food," while Arethusa predicts that Earth by degrees "will fade & fall / In envy of our happier lot in Hell" (2.207, 218–19). Clearly, in Shelley's version, male power over female bodies does not imply their exerting corresponding power over women's fates, for these women can make residence in hell enviable through their spirited force of mind. But it hardly renders female community paradise, either.

Critics who read *Proserpine* as the tragic myth of "female sexual initiation" fail to account for the text's insistence from the start on the spaces within and between all the female characters.[36] The play opens with separation, the surprising explanation for which establishes the mother's phallic desires: Ceres leaves Proserpine because Jove "commands" her service at the celestial dinner table, and "none will eat till I dispense the food" (1.22). Moreover, by identifying both Ino and Eunoe as perfectly acceptable substitute nourishers of Proserpine, Ceres herself portrays the maternal realm as symbolic. One female is as good as another when it comes to filling empty spaces.

> Eunoe can tell thee how the giants fell;
> Or dark-eyed Ino sing the saddest change
> Of Syrinx or of Daphne, or the doom
> Of impious Prometheus, and the boy
> Of fair Pandora, Mother of mankind. (1.24–28)

Initial emphasis on the substitutability of women is reinforced by the rivalry on display throughout the first act. Eunoe is catty about Ino's tale-telling abilities, Ino is a tattletale, and all three maidens cannot wait to get away from each other and thus out from under the mother's only parting command, to "Depart not from each other" (1.30). In coming after Proserpine's abduction as well as these initial fractures, the communitarian resolve in act 2 is precisely a girls' reunion. It suggests that one function of patriarchy is less to rupture than to facilitate bonding among women, granting them license to ascribe to men the aggressions that constitute persons. Even after her abduction, Proserpine does not fully embrace sisterhood or her mother, who is now depicted in the daughter's position of pleading, "Leave me not, Proserpine, / Cling to thy Mother's side!" (2.233–34). Though hardly enamored of Pluto, Proserpine finds in Hades something that the maternal realm seeks to rein in: the pleasures of wandering, more spaces to stray.

Versions of the verbs *wander* and *stray* occur seventeen times in a two-act play, giving some indication of why this daughter is not eager to "cling to" her mother's side.[37] Doing so is a losing proposition, fixed as the mother is in stasis, rage, and obstinate calculations of loss. Shelley's Ceres does not undergo the adventures and ludic self-transformations that attend Ovid's version of Ceres in search of her daughter.[38] Nor until the very end does she acknowledge *any* gain in having a daughter restored to her for six months out of every year— quite an enviable proposition from any grieving subject's perspective. For Ceres insists on the all *of* nothing and on gain as involving a full recovery of loss (the "nevermore" and "evermore" of *Matilda*). Proserpine's calculations are more accepting of the something within loss and gain:

> Dear Mother, let me kiss that tear which steals
> Down your pale cheek altered by care and grief.
> This is not misery; 'tis but a slight change
> From our late happy lot. Six months with thee,
> Each moment freighted with an age of love:
> And the six short months in saddest Tartarus
> Shall pass in dreams of swift returning joy.
> Six months together we shall dwell on earth,
> Six months in dreams we shall companions be,
> Jove's doom is void; we are forever joined. (2.264–73)

The weight of that "freight" of love, especially compared to joy's fast-forward in hell, shows how far removed is Proserpine's "forever joined" from being a mere "sucker [on] the parent stem" (2.235). Precisely what "forever joins" also forever separates mother from daughter—the words of the stories that often tear them apart. "Or dark-eyed Ino sing the saddest change / Of Syrinx or of Daphne" (1.25–26). Or *Memoirs* of one's mother record that she "had nothing to communicate" from her deathbed regarding the future care of her daughters.[39]

Emphasis in *Proserpine* on the separation that attends even the closest human relations is meant as an affirmation of life and preparation for it. The classic legend stresses Proserpine's lack of preparation for what eventuates— whether that pertains to her abduction, premature sex, loss of sorority, or time spent in hell. The issue of preparation is suggested by the emphasis in *Matilda* on the suddenness of the change that causes Mathilda to identify with Proserpine, where in a heartbeat one's entire world is altered. Shelley's additions to the legend suggest how standard means of preparation for living, whether through parenting or literary storytelling, prove inadequate to extreme circumstances, especially when both parents and literature are promoted and valued as being capable of averting, of warding off, such extremities. That is, *Proserpine* links the status of mother to storytelling in order to address both sides of inadequate parenting: when a parent impedes a child's wandering, growth, and change and when s/he forces the child to mature prematurely, whether by dying, leaving, or initiating them into sex.[40] But rather than presenting literature as wholly remedial, *Proserpine* presents stories as themselves also enacting parental inadequacies. Hearing stories can widen a daughter's range of experience but also can arouse passions within her before she has the wherewithal to handle them.

Tales in *Proserpine* are shown as both describing and stimulating lust, seduction, rape. The sexualizing of story becomes audible when we compare accounts of Alpheus's pursuit and rape of Arethusa. In Ovid, Arethusa describes her rape to mother Ceres only after Ceres has learned of and accepts Proserpine's fate. Arethusa also dwells on the chase, not its end in rape, in fact stopping at the point where Diana cleaves the earth to facilitate her escape. In Shelley, Ino sings Arethusa's song to Proserpine immediately after Ceres departs to host Jove's dinner party (the song is Percy's composition), and she details both pursuit and aftermath—though, as Richardson notes, not the means by which Arethusa comes to find their "watery task" so desirable.[41] It is as if Arethusa's song in *Proserpine* generates the subsequent events, positioned as it is at the very beginning of the mythological drama. Certainly, the hearing of it is eroticized. In asking Ino to repeat the song, Proserpine desires not information but transport, the being "entice[d]," "enchant[ed]," "beguile[d]" by sound—in a word, carried away.[42] Such transport gets Proserpine beyond the maternal demand to "depart not" and "cling to" the mother's side, but it also causes her to confront sexual realities before her time.

This latter question, regarding the sufficiency of literature to prepare one for traumatic eventualities, was a heated topic in the Shelleyan household during 1819–20. As I noted in chapter 3, it is visible in repeated intertextual discussions of the meaning and outcome of incest, debated through female protagonists who mirror each other in revealing ways. Mathilda, Beatrice Cenci, and Proserpine are all cast as "victims" of incest who also explicitly occupy the mother's place prematurely, either by coming before the mother in the father's affections (Mathilda and Beatrice) or coming between so-called adult sexual partners (all three). But while *Proserpine* shares the focus on incest with these other texts, its treatment of this trauma results neither in unspeakability nor death. The untraumatic status of abduction and incest ("this is not misery") results from its survivability ("'tis but a slight change") and sets Proserpine apart from her sisters. What makes Proserpine a survivor is not her refusal of guilt, for in this she is joined by Beatrice Cenci, but her relation to language. Proserpine turns a deaf ear to the invasion of a word through the ear as well as to the consequences that are said to follow from it.

The curious eruption into *Proserpine* of aspects of the trial scene from *The Cenci* illustrates these texts' differing perspectives on the kind of responsibility entailed in language. Upon her return to earth, Proserpine initially adopts Beatrice's mode of asserting her innocence: she lies. To Iris's question whether Proserpine has eaten "such Tartarian food as must for ever / Condemn [her] to be Queen of Hell & Night," Proserpine replies in Beatrice's terms: "No, Iris, no—I still am pure as thee: / Offspring of light and air, I have no stain / Of Hell!" (2.156–62). But their differing use of the lie suggests more categorical distinctions. Beatrice persists in avowing her innocence by ascribing guilt to the patriarchal language that names it: to

That which thou hast called my father's death
Which is or is not what men call a crime,
Which either I have done, or have not done;
Say what ye will. I shall deny no more. (*Cenci* 5.3.78–86)

In contrast, Proserpine immediately recants once Ascalaphus "call[s] to [her] mind your walk last eve, / When as you wandered in Elysian groves . . . you plucked its fruit, / You ate of a pomegranate's seeds" (2.176–77, 183). Her admission denies *that* guilt lacks a name by denying the suitability of guilt to her situation. "If fate decrees, can we resist? Farewell!" (2.191).

The ease of Proserpine's "farewell" compared to the strain audible in Beatrice's "Well, 'tis very well" suggests why only Beatrice is a tragic heroine. *The Cenci* associates innocence with a pre-Oedipal time before language, a position ratified by Cardinal Camillo's remark that Beatrice "is as pure as speechless infancy" (5.2.69). When Proserpine revokes her lie, she does not situate innocence before speech or indict language for an inability to speak female desire or innocence. Instead, she sees fate's decrees as necessary and therefore as absolving her of guilt while she also uses language to reframe the terms that have silenced women. From this position, incest proves less of a trauma in *Proserpine*. The play's temporal location as pre-Oedipus facilitates the absence of guilt and also foregrounds the daughter's desire to move beyond the mother's fixations. It is Ceres, not Proserpine, who employs Beatrice's second mode of defense at her trial—mesmerizing Marzio so that he recants and expires on the rack—and turns it on Proserpine:

> Sweet Proserpine, my child, look upon me.
> You shrink; your trembling form & pallid cheeks
> Would make his words seem true which are most false.
> Thou didst not taste the food of Erebus;—
> Offspring of Gods art thou,—nor Hell, nor Jove
> Shall tear thee from thy Mother's clasping arms. (2.285–90)

Proserpine eludes the mother's mortal clasp by affirming her part-time residence in Hades, in whose fields she is free—that is, fated—to wander.

The breakthrough that is represented in *Proserpine* highlights several dimensions of the working through of trauma that Shelley comes to associate with writing. One mode entails rewriting those stories that link traumatic events to unspeakability and thus withhold one means of dealing with their aftermath. While by definition nothing can prepare one for trauma, precisely because what makes an event traumatic for one person and not for another is one's total lack of preparation for it, several things related to symbolic representation can aid one in alleviating traumatic effects.[43] Shelley's approach to the Proserpine legend suggests that if certain life tragedies were not always portrayed as traumatic, they might not always be experienced as such. Knowing that many others have undergone the same kind of misery can keep one from experiencing the radical isolation that stems less from the nature of the misery than from the unspeakability that has been associated with it. In contrast to Mathilda, Proserpine speaks her reality and affirms misery as a condition that can be survived, gotten through. In so doing she disconnects incest from trauma by characterizing her fate not as tragedy but as mythological drama.

As a literary project, Shelley's treatment of Proserpine also redresses some of the symptoms of trauma manifested through Mathilda's alienation from the poetic tradition. Shelley's recourse to myth highlights at once her indictment of the literary tradition for severely restricting what counts as an estimable life and her undying support of writing for perpetuating life. Recourse to myth suggests that guilt and its association with tragedy does not inhere in language but in a literary tradition that is guilty of silencing, of keeping the "voices of life" from certain subjects, whether topics (like incest, homosexuality, or death) or categories of person. Through the setting of Proserpine, Shelley reverts to the time before writing—literally, to an oral culture unmarked by Oedipal configurations or timing. In so doing, she endorses the conventional connection between orality and women but without condemning woman to the conventions that have thus far defined her, including those that cast her as prehistoric and ahistorical in her demands for oneness, merger, and fusion.

The moving on that Proserpine accomplishes by redefining "misery" as "a slight change" indicates the kind of transformation Shelley believed the literary tradition had to undergo before it would stop curtailing life by traumatizing readers. More kinds of people have to be able to tell more kinds of stories so that life's eventualities become less capable of rendering anyone's reality a total blank. One of the stories that needs rewriting concerns the finality and alterity of death. The literary tradition can only hope to serve progress, and thus move the world beyond the infancy entailed by the calamity of death, if it is alive and capable of transformation. This means not only that what constitutes a tradition must be able to change with the times by including more kinds of story but also that the tradition itself must remain open and alive to its internal transformation by new eyes. Shelley pursues the latter project with a vengeance, affirming the necessity *and* creativity of revision rather than originality, renovation rather than preservation, the capacity to make an entirely new species out of disposable parts. The urgency stems from her awareness that subjects can be silenced not only by history but also by a futurity that is not receptive to discovering their tendency, thus postponing indefinitely the efficacy of those marginalized voices on behalf of whom she speaks. Her texts are riven and driven by the prospect that no one in the future, let alone the present, will be able to read their message. It is as if she envisions and attempts to counter the perpetual infantilizing of a people that is achieved in the name of culture. Fathers protect and mothers nurture their young.

This effort to render the literary tradition less traumatizing on certain subjects has major implications for Shelley's literary practice. In my view, it underlies her proclivity for generic engineering, both in what she constructs and what she avoids. For Shelley's bias toward hybrid forms can be seen as facilitating a less idealized or holistic view of what composes life and death.[44] As a writer and mythic regenerator, Shelley is no purist; she describes her mode as parasitic (*Frankenstein*), her task as collecting and deciphering (*The Last Man*), and her aim as revival, both of herself and of the dead (*Journal of Sorrow*). Likewise, her refusal to write in the forms of tragedy or elegy suggests conscious avoidance of the canonical genres of mourning, which, in her critique, mystify rather than ratify the complexities of death and life. As content and form, *Proserpine* speaks against the binary format that characterizes Percy Shelley's writings of the prior year, his effort to confine the sad realities of life to a historical tragedy that is then enveloped by the beautiful idealisms of lyrical drama, to lift the veil that transforms death into its opposite, or to situate love in a realm that transcends earth, time, and death.[45] From the point of view of *Proserpine*, these are all strategies to avoid, rather than surmount, the desolation of grief, either by claiming that death is synonymous with life or finding nothing in the world worthy of love (the position of the "tender heart" in "Lift not the Painted Veil"). *Proserpine* asserts its antipathy to such mystifications by calling Prometheus neither "unbound" nor a more "poetical character" than Satan or Beatrice because "exempt from the taints of ambition, envy, revenge, and a desire for personal aggrandizement" but simply "impious" (1.27).[46] Possibly the author of *Proserpine* considers the author of *Prometheus Unbound* bi-polar.

A second ramification on her literary practice is visible in the status of Proserpine as heroine. Though mythic and legendary, Proserpine is hardly ideal. Described from the start as "heedless" rather than innocent, her aim is to gain a little freedom to stray (1.310). Moreover, her status as legendary but not ideal contributes to her cultural-reformist appeal. For unlike Mathilda or Victor Frankenstein, Proserpine is neither wholly fictional nor the creation of one individual author's fancy. Instead, she is an extremely well-known, indeed legendary, fictional individual whose existence is a fact in Godwin's sense of the term as well as a fact of literary-cultural history. Moreover, she remains one of Western culture's foundational images of the passage from maidenhood to womanhood. Shelley's choice of such a heroine suggests the cultural power of her characteristic form of reform. By revising a myth of femininity, rather than inventing a new species, she engages with the classics—literally the literary underworld—but in a manner that demystifies them and therefore alters standard interpretations of them.[47] The errancy of this Proserpine is synonymous with forward movement as cyclical change—a valid image of the generations. Through this re/vision of daughterhood, Shelley not only dis-associates trauma from incest and parental abandonment but also modifies, in the spirit of her mother, the status of virginity as an all-or-nothing affair. The loss of *this* myth, she implies, is truly not misery but also probably only a slight change from some daughters' late unhappy lots.

Two years later, life—again in the form of death—intervenes in the form of the death of Percy, severely curtailing the forward motion achieved in her life/writings through the birth of Percy Florence and the composition of *Proserpine*. The formulation of "misery" as "slight change" in *Proserpine* is now recast as global devastation in *The Last Man* and propels readers back into the barren psychic landscape of *Matilda*, now extended over the entire globe. Depicting the end of humanity from the perspective of the sole survivor, Lionel Verney, *The Last Man* challenges every consolation or strategy associated with overcoming death, the extreme darkness of which view occasioned evaluations of the novel as nihilistic, antipolitical, and a full-scale assault on masculine romanticism.[48] These traits have long been viewed as commentary on Shelley's "personal" situation—as expressions of the profound nature of her grief and rejection of the unrealistic tenets of the men in her life.

The extent to which the two are causally related is best evaluated by considering *The Last Man* as the most extreme of Shelley's explorations of the "effects flowing from the mortality of man to human affairs, and the feelings and sentiments it becomes us to cherish respecting the Illustrious Dead." For *The Last Man* links the reality of grief to the status of illustrious men both as a "personal" matter, depicted in the relationships between Perdita and Raymond, Idris and Lionel, and Adrian's friendships with all of them, and as a global problematic, by which grief over the death of humanity challenges the cultural value of illustrious men to such an extent that the last man, in dedicating his memoirs to the Illustrious Dead, envisions their second demise through this reading of their end. *The Last Man* thereby explores both types of the "calamity" of death outlined in *Sepulchres:* the devastation associated with the loss of the individual beloved and the total effacement not only of humanity but also of its history. The latter in fact seems to inspire the plot and historical dare of *The Last Man*. Is it really true that, "though cities were demolished, and empires overthrown," the "materials" would remain by means of which "everything that was most sacred might be restored," and the "calamity which had swallowed up whole generations of men" would be "obliterated as if it had never been" (*Sepulchres*, 29)?

The indebtedness of *The Last Man* to *Sepulchres* is indicated by the decision of a recent editor (Anne McWhir) to affix the *Sepulchres'* frontispiece, with its motto "Life is the Desert and the Solitude!" to her edition of *The Last Man*. This decision accentuates the intertextual nature of the view of character and reaction to death embodied in the text as well as the relevance of these tenets to Shelley's mourning practice. As McWhir notes, Godwin's frontispiece to *Sepulchres* quotes half of the line from Edward Young's *The Revenge*, "Life is the Desert, life the solitude; / Death joins us to the great majority," to which Shelley alludes in a journal entry of 15 May 1824 and in her notes to Percy's poems of 1821, where she writes, "When those we love have passed into eternity, 'life is the desert and the solitude' in which we are forced to linger— but never find comfort more."[49] This logic, and the comfort it ostensibly offers, is explored most explicitly in Lionel's and Perdita's reactions to the death of Raymond that take up various components of *Sepulchres*. In an effort to allay the "killing torpor of [Perdita's] grief," Lionel speaks of the comfort of knowing that Raymond has now "become one of those, who render the dark abode of the obscure grave illustrious by dwelling there," in a formulation that reverts to death's share in the world's infancy (*Last Man*, 161). "When the world was in its infancy death must have been terrible, and man left his friends to dwell, a solitary stranger, in an unknown country. But now, he who dies finds many companions gone before to prepare for his reception. The great of past ages people it, the exalted hero of our own days is counted among its inhabitants, while life becomes doubly 'the desert and the solitude.' . . . Thus to honour him, is the sacred duty of his survivors" (161).

Perdita performs "the sacred duty of survivors" by first finding the "earthly dwelling of my beloved," then moving "this treasure of dust" to Athens, where she plans to establish permanent residence by the "treasure house of Raymond's dear remains" (162, 164). But her commemoration belies the spirit of *Sepulchres* and Lionel's invocation of it by communing *as* the dead with the dead. "Look on me as dead; and truly if death be a mere change of state, I am dead. This is another world, from that which late I inhabited, from that which is now your home. Here I hold communion only with the has been, and to come" (166). Lionel attempts to deny Perdita this communion, under the

Woodvillian logic that the only "solution to the intricate riddle of life" is to "improve ourselves, and contribute to the happiness of others," to which Perdita responds by drowning herself (167). Implicit in that response is Perdita's view that those who are deadened by the loss of their beloved should be left in peace and that the precondition for enjoying a sense of neighborship with the dead is being dead.

The scenario introduces a second, more sustained, feature of the indebtedness of *The Last Man* to *Sepulchres:* the perspectival structure and psychology of its depicted reactions to death. In *Sepulchres,* this is marked by the contrast between the tone and content of the first pages, which dwell in loving particularity from the point of view of the grieving survivor on all that is lost when a great friend dies, and the later deflations of death as a leveling and wholly quotidian reality that transforms all citizens into mourners and reduces even the greatest men to dust. *The Last Man* adopts this structure and inverts its proportions, with volumes 1 and 2 giving rich descriptions of the daily projects, plans, books read, conversations held, and affections formed in a small group of well-delineated individuals, followed by the epic and underpsychologized scope of volume 3, as the little platoon watches itself, and the population of the entire world, become reduced to a sole survivor. But while *Sepulchres* implicitly offers the second part as a solution to the bereavement delineated in the first part, by desynonymizing death and loss as philosophical and affective realities, *The Last Man* is far less sanguine about the applicability of this solution to the reality of death or living. True, a survivor lives on by identifying with the larger whole, but if s/he does this wholeheartedly, by actually dissolving selfhood into eternity, s/he is often divested of any specific reason or impulse to live. One aspect of the thought experiment of *The Last Man* is to evaluate how, or whether, one in fact survives as a "person," committed to projects, people, and culture, when one lives in the full knowledge and reality of death—that is, when one actually envisions everything living as imminently, if not actually, dead and learns to view substance as shadow. In this regard, the plot of *The Last Man* pushes to extremes the consolations offered by the view of death in *Sepulchres.* How does one commit oneself to heterosexual attachment, the psychic experience of which is depicted in volumes 1 and 2 (as in *Matilda*) as the beloved being all the world to the lover, when one envisions from the start the death of love and of one's beloved? What good is identifying with "man" as a species, if there is no humanity left, in both senses, with which to identify?

In posing these questions, *The Last Man* is the darkest of Shelley's probings of the duty to live and the value of the illustrious dead in promoting and fulfilling that duty. From the point of view of mortality, all human affairs appear chimerical, senseless; the striving after excellence so much vanity or dust. The usual consolation found in belonging to a species—the self-postponement of Godwinian/Woodvillian benevolence, here described positively as "losing our identity"—is rendered void when humanity is totally effaced. In other words, the prospect from which we "learn to regard death without terror" depends on the assurance that "though the individual is destroyed, man continues for ever" (182). The loss of this certainty affects the status of life, love, and the illustrious dead, as Lionel's reactions to the death of Idris and then all of humanity make clear. When Idris, who once filled his entire world, dies, Lionel feels "as if the visible world had grown as soulless, inane, and comfortless as the clay-cold image beneath me" (279). As he watches all the people in the world die, he recalculates the meaning and merit of culture. "One living beggar had become of more worth than a national peerage of dead lords—alas the day!—than of dead heroes, patriots, or men of genius. There was much of degradation in this: for even vice and virtue had lost their attributes—life—life—the continuation of our animal mechanism—was the Alpha and Omega of the desires, the prayers, the prostrate ambition of human race" (229).

The Last Man is explicit, then, in evaluating life from the point of view of radical mortality in order to contemplate what, if anything, remains. It tries to imagine living in the awareness that "death is among us," "the earth is beautiful and flower-bedecked, but she is our grave," and that "because you are gifted with agility and strength, you fancy that you live: but frail is the 'bower of flesh' that encaskets life; dissoluble the silver cord that binds you to it" (206, 189). At the same time, it attempts to envision the something of spirit that survives death. "Was that my child—that moveless decaying inanimation? . . . I turn from this mockery of what he was. Take, O earth, thy debt! . . . Either thy spirit has sought a fitter dwelling or, shrined in my heart, thou livest while it lives" (337–38). In this, it does not reject but extends queries in the texts of both parents that attempt to image and imagine what remains once the life spirit in a person has gone out. Is the dust of remains all that remains? "We had called ourselves the 'paragon of animals,' and, lo! we were a 'quint-essence of dust'" (309). Or as the narrator of *A Short Residence* puts it, "it appears to me impossible that I should cease to exist, or that this active, restless spirit, equally alive to joy and sorrow, should only be organized dust—ready to fly abroad the moment the spring snaps, or the spark goes out, which kept it together. Surely something resides in this heart that is not perishable—and life is more than a dream" (281). Given Shelley's existence within this particular family, it is not surprising that *The Last Man,* too, connects the question of remains to writing, for what remains to and of the last man is his memoirs, *The Last Man.* More startling is this text's effort to depict what it means to live *as* remains and to survive by being occupied by them.

The vision of writing depicted in *The Last Man* has the same perspectival structure as the depiction of life, love, and death. From the point of view of an aspiring individual, access to the world is extended immeasurably through reading, and the decision to turn author is characterized as promising maximum benefit to humankind.[50] But from the point of view of the one who witnesses the end of humanity, the "giant powers of man" that are associated with "man's imagination" appear vain, "senseless," "cold" (252, 335). They are cold not only because no one exists to receive them but also because their afterlife or tendency is envisioned as terminated. This is the import of Lionel's decision to dedicate his memoirs to the "illustrious dead," who, in reading his history of the end of man, will be finally, permanently, laid to rest. For, as Barbara Johnson and Steven Goldsmith have argued, in envisioning the end of humanity, *The Last Man* puts a period on humanism and the Western humanities.[51]

Still, something remains in (the) writing. Even from this ahuman and nonhumanist perspective, Lionel describes the act of writing as valuable, as long as notions of that act are severed from fantasies of influencing, or even apparently addressing, humanity. As Lionel writes, writing is an "opiate," the "occupation" that is "best fitted to discipline" his "melancholy thoughts" because, in reviving the past and reanimating all the associates and associations coupled with it, writing literally occupies him, both in the sense of inhabiting, repopulating, and animating him and giving him something to do (208, 361). This doing of something suspends temporarily the reality of the loss, grief, and death he is narrating through the distance gained by re/presentation. This is precisely the affect and effect ascribed to writing by the "I" of the frame introduction, who answers its own query, "Will my readers ask how I could find solace from the narration of misery and woeful change?" by asserting that "excitement of mind" is "dear to me" (8, 9). Moreover, suspension of pain is linked to the "ideality" that is ascribed to the writing, here, of fiction and, within the narrative proper, of history, an ideality that in both cases is gained by writing from a prospect that allows the retrospect to be free from contingency or the "mosaic of circumstance" that so often brings misery because it cannot be anticipated (209). But whenever one suspends the activity of writing, the misery that was temporarily suspended resumes with all its intensity. "[My companions] have been with me during the fulfillment of my task. I have brought it to an end—I lift my eyes from my paper—again they are lost to me. Again I feel that I am alone" (362).

This vision of writing as occupation, diversion, and company divorced from concerns over content or reception is connected to the last man's choice, upon completing his memoir, of a "future career" as "wanderer." The choice entails a minimal "hope of amelioration" that is similarly decoupled from any specific prospect but that arises from a "restless despair and fierce desire of change" (363, 365). It is as if *The Last Man* empties out all possible content of futurity in order to ascribe to writing a mode of ensuring the future simply through keeping it open and potentially occupied. This ascribes to a life of writing the barest, but only remaining, possibility of hope or forward motion. The minimalism of this activity is tied to its lack of goal-directedness, its indifference toward the to-what or to-whom it is heading. In this, as Samantha Webb argues, *The Last Man* moves beyond a notion of writing as interaction or "transaction" with other humans to writing as self-consolation and the "written manuscript as a memorial or monument" to what remains.[52] It leaves behind the equation of "author with social agency," instead redefining writing and the writer as a being-occupied.[53]

The introduction to *The Last Man* connects these two aspects of writing—the being occupied with writing as remains—in ways that accurately frame the narrative and Shelley's subsequent literary works of mourning. "Whenever the world's circumstance has not imperiously called me away, or the temper of my mind impeded such study, I have been employed in deciphering these sacred remains" (8). The form of decipherment that follows as *The Last Man*, especially the distinctiveness of the narrative voice, illustrates a crucial component of the "being occupied" by writing that also circumvents humanist notions of authorship. As McWhir characterizes it, "identity" in this novel is not "personal" but "intertextual"; it is composed "out of fragments of text." Consequently, character is "less important than voice"; "in other words, who speaks may be less significant than what is said."[54] As the voice of the last man, then, these words are beyond human, both temporally and ontologically. Severed from personality, identity, wholeness, they are literally fragments, echoes, remains—exactly the status, as Johnson claims, of the non/person who is the last to remain.[55] This scripting of the posthuman has been seen as expressing Shelley's nihilism and deep skepticism regarding political or any other type of progress, as if justice does not enter into the form of being that Derrida calls "hauntology."[56] Her positing writing as directionless but mobile not only does not foreclose possibilities but also holds open the space necessary to face, without effacing, the other.

This accommodation of the wanderings of writing moves *The Last Man* closer to the world of *Proserpine*. In dealing with grief, it too comes to affirm the "slight change" that does not define "misery" but its remedy—hope in minimal movement. In this, *The Last Man* represents the most lopsided version of the sometimes "consolation," sometimes "aggravation of grief" brought by Mathilda's "wandering fancy," in the sense that the occupation associated with writing is the *only* aspect of Lionel's reality that is experienced as mitigating, rather than aggravating, his grief (*Matilda*, 19). Even reading is not helpful, for it does not change but only intensifies the mood from which the reader commences reading: "As if in the same soil you plant nightshade and a myrtle tree, they will each appropriate the mould, moisture, and air administered, for the fostering their several properties—so did my grief find sustenance, and power of existence, and growth, in what else had been divine manna, to feed radiant meditation" (361).[57] As a remedy to the trauma entailed by literary transmission, then, *The Last Man* joins *Proserpine* and the urtext of *Matilda*, *The Field of Fancy*, in affirming that persons can return from the underworld to life, that survival is linked to remains, and that the best chance for altering the misery of reality and the reality of misery is to occupy oneself with writing. Only this activity redresses constraints on reality by revising the forms that inform us.

The Last Man, then, marks a conclusion to the series of fictional texts that debate the function of literature in allaying grief and death. Subsequent fictional texts, even when depicting remorse, sadness, and death, are neither anguished nor fatalistic. Moreover, female characters for the first time voice the Woodvillian position regarding the duty to mourn, even when this includes remarrying. As we saw in chapter 3, the next depicted survivor after the last man, Lady Katherine in *The Fortunes of Perkin Warbeck*, affirms this possibility—though not yet the historical reality—for grieving female subjects. "And must my living heart be stone, because that dear form is dust, which was the medium of my communication with his spirit? . . . I quarrel not with—I admire—those who can be good and benevolent, and yet keep their hearts to themselves. . . . I am not one of these, and yet take no shame therefore" (400). The result of several years of textual struggle, this reconciliation with grief seems to clear fictional space for the envisioning of a long happy marriage (*Lodore*) and a successful transfer of attachment from father to husband (*Falkner*). But *The Last Man*, I wish to argue, also concludes the anguished questionings of the "I" of *The Journal of Sorrow*, who is dealing with the loss of her illustrious man. Many critics have linked these two texts, invariably by quoting the I's depiction of itself as the "last relic of a beloved race" and indicating the ways that characters in *The Last Man* are patterned on various components of Byron, Percy Shelley, Mary Shelley, and Claire Clairmont, but also by appreciating its treatment of the "relation between private grief and the public realm of literary fiction."[58] My claim is that reading *The Last Man* in conjunction with *The Journal of Sorrow* indicates the precision of the novel's treatment of the journal's sorrow and the relation of that grief to the "feelings and sentiments it becomes us to cherish respecting the Illustrious Dead." For both texts clearly struggle over the satisfactions gained by conversing with the illustrious dead as well as the legitimacy of coupling "illustrious" with the dead and the way that that linkage impedes living, especially in the case of a living female writer. But reading *The Journal of Sorrow* indicates just how unnecessitated *is* the assertion in *The Last Man* of the specific consolation of writing, the being-occupied by it. For *Sorrow* expresses the im/personal anguish of attempting to have intercourse with the illustrious dead. Are you really here? Do you feel me? Wherein lies the satisfaction of this?

It is striking the extent to which *The Journal of Sorrow* associates Percy with mental stimulation and his death with Mary's troubles with writing. At times she addresses him as "lover" (more frequently as "beloved"), but his chief claim on her heart is as "guide, teacher, & interpreter," the one who stimulates and improves her mind (461, also 429). Loss of him renders the "external" world a blank, but even more worrisome is how it threatens to render blank the pages of every book except *The Journal of Sorrow*, itself uncharacteristically voluble and revelatory about her feelings. More precisely, what threatens to negate all future writing is her inability any longer to envision Percy reading her writing. "I write—& thou seest not what I write— Oh my own beloved—let me not be so deserted. It seems to me that while I live & talk & act—all this may go on & you not be here. But you ought to be acquainted with every mental exertion—or I am indeed alone" (441–42; 482–83). Losing this one reader threatens the entire future of her audience because it makes "all my many pages" "future waste paper," in a word, "trash" (489). Nothing, in all the vast misery of this period, weighs on her more than her inability to write anything worthwhile. "Nothing I write pleases me. Whether I am just in this, or whether [it is] the want of Shelleys . . . encouragement," "double sorrow comes when I feel that Shelley no longer reads & approves of what I write" (476, 483).

The consequences of this felt loss of Percy's readership extend beyond the inoccupation that threatens her aliveness and ability to make a living by writing. It threatens to ensure a permanent separation between Mary and Percy in the forfeit of her claim to join the ranks of the illustrious dead. Repeatedly, the *Journal* voices Mary's concern over being or becoming "worthy" of Percy, and thus "worthy to die" to be with him (438). While her expressions of unworthiness are usually construed as connected to remorse over her infamous coldness (about which these pages do worry), they are more frequently occasioned by vacillations in her commitment to "study" (see, e.g., 441). In fact, the passages most often quoted from this *Journal,* her self-perception as a relic and the writing of *Matilda* as sufficient to "quell my wretchedness temporarily," both occur in contexts that lament Percy's inability to read and thus encourage her writing (476, 442). It is as if Mary needs the felt presence of Percy in order literally to recognize herself as writer, the condition that separates composition of *Matilda* from *The Last Man.* His dying before this conviction is solidified in her own mind causes her to lose not only confidence in her powers but also the assurance of her future fame. This threatens her afterlife and ongoing claim to Percy's love.[59]

Proving herself worthy of partnership with Percy motivated the several projects at hand: not only the "mere tear" that constitutes *The Journal of Sorrow* but also her redoubled commitment to intellectual improvement and collecting, assembling, and editing Percy's life/writings. The *Journal* editors make clear that "almost immediately" after Percy's death, Mary began "assembling and transcribing his unpublished writings," which she planned to publish, first, in the *Liberal* and then in a volume of complete works in order to "keep him alive in the minds of his admirers" and to prove herself alive (434n, 444). This was no easy project; simply recollecting his widely scattered materials (in England and Italy) and accurately transcribing them required extraordinary, what Michael O'Neill calls "heroic," efforts.[60] Moreover, the *Journal of Sorrow* shows the extent to which Shelley's proud assertion of herself as a "reflection" of Percy is not as self-effacing as it sounds. It illuminates an existence that otherwise feels precarious and provides incentive for self improvement. "And I am then moonshine, having no existence except that which he lends me, . . . known & sought through the light he bestows upon me.

Thus I would endeavour to consider my self a faint continuation of his being, & as far as possible the revelation to the earth of what he was. Yet to become this I must change much" (436). It also complicates the coldness ascribed by Percy to her through his imaging her as moonshine in several of his poetic texts. Not only does *her* depiction of herself as moon reflect only what is directed at it, but so does her careful superintendence of Percy's writing prove an undying devotion to his "sacred remains" (*Last Man*, 8).

Deciphering Percy's sacred remains ended up occupying Mary for the rest of her life/writings. Besides collecting, editing, and deciphering his many notebooks, letters, and manuscripts in preparation for the 1824 *Posthumous Poems* and the four-volume 1839 *Poetical Works*, the project included disseminating his poems and ideas through fictional personae in her writings, using lines from his work as epigraphs to various chapters, and referring to his writings in her nonfictional texts. It also involved Mary's continual efforts to compose his *Life*, even granting Sir Timothy Shelley's injunction against it, and to decipher for others and herself the meaning of his life, love, writings, and character. The writing desk, found at Mary Shelley's death and containing "her journals and Shelley's heart wrapped in the pages of Adonais," remains a haunting image of these efforts—this being the very desk that was returned to her on 7 October 1822, having been left in Marlow in 1818, and bringing with it the voices and associations of the dead retained in letters and journal entries of when they were all living. "What a scene to recur to! My William, Clara, Allegra are all talked of—They lived then—They breathed this air & their voices struck on my sense, their feet trod the earth beside me—& their hands were warm with blood & life when clasped in mine. Where are they all? This is too great an agony to be written about" (435). The forms of life and writing that the desk figures and contains (heart, *Adonais,* journal) remain the essential question of Shelley's subsequent life/writings, in their struggles to decipher to what that heart, those writings, and writing itself tends. They find their calmest resolution, I will argue, in Shelley's turn to biography in the latter stages of her life/writings, but they underlie two functions of writing depicted in *The Last Man* that helped to get her there. One concerns the equation between editing and creativity; the other the kinds of legend-making that both activities inspire.

The obvious link between the initial pages of *The Journal of Sorrow* and the introduction to *The Last Man* is a reference in the latter to the loss of the "selected and matchless companion of my toils" (8).[61] "We" began the visit that resulted in the discovery of the sacred remains of the Cumaean Sibyl, but only "I" was left to decipher them and present them in "a consistent form" (5, 8). The nature of this loss is also the same as that depicted in *The Journal of Sorrow*, for the "dearest reward" that is "also now lost to me" is the ability to "frondi altro lavoro / Credea mostrarte (show you some other work of my young leaves)," which some "fero pianeta (cruel planet)" has now rendered impossible (citing Petrarch's Sonnet 322 [8]). But unlike in the *Journal*, this loss is immediately portrayed as having some compensation, as the Wordsworthian echoes in "that time is gone" imply (8). Not just the compensation of consolation gained by "clothing these fictitious [sorrows and endless regrets] in that ideality, which takes the mortal sting from pain" but also the independence that comes from composition, even when one presents one's task as reflection, adaptation, and translation rather than original creation (9).

With independence comes a self-assertion that complements one's derivative status. "Sometimes I have thought that, obscure and chaotic as the[se verses] are, they owe their present form to me, their decipherer" (8). The hubris and aggression that characterize Shelley's ostensible expressions of authorial/self-effacement have been noted, and they preceded as well as followed her husband's death.[62] But that event intensified both dimensions of the pose. Loss of her best instructor, encourager, and collaborator weakened her confidence in her writing abilities—that is, in her and their capacity *or desire* to stand alone. From a post-Percy position, the inspiration from writing *Matilda was* sufficient to quell her wretchedness because in those days she could still count on his commentary and fidelity as a reader. Indeed, that tragic year of 1819–20, including the heartache caused by Percy's wanderings, was also the year in which their writing lives were most intimately paired. Each separately wrote coupled texts—*Prometheus Unbound* and *The Cenci*, *Proserpine* and *Midas*—that themselves depict the vagaries and missed timing of heterosexual couples. They each collaborated with the other, Mary as translator and scenic consultant for *The Cenci*, Percy by providing the songs for *Proserpine*. Loss of such a valuable collaborator caused a huge diminution of her creativity and output, anguish over which loss should not be minimized. But loss of him also made Mary's characteristic stance as writer—that is, decipherer, adapter, translator—primary, not just in purveying his works to the world but in rendering them less chaotic and obscure. "My only excuse for thus transforming them, is that they were unintelligible in their pristine condition" (8).[63] On such grounds, as Susan Wolfson notes, editor Shelley considered herself a "kind of co-author" and "co-owner" of Percy Shelley's *Poetical Works*.[64]

The second consolatory function of writing takes off from the connection between the classical frame (the cave of the Cumaean Sybil) and the auto-biographical lure (we/I). Not only does this second fictional descent to the underworld, as in *Proserpine,* mean to address by circumventing personal and literary traumas; this time it does so by making a legend out of "real" historical personages. *The Journal of Sorrow* already depicts the initial phase of this process in ways that complicate, even reverse, some of the "progress" associated with the wanderings of *Matilda* and *Proserpine.* Responding to death has a way of shoring up boundaries and binary logic that Shelley's characteristic realism about life's complexities had been working to diffuse.[65] As *Sorrow* makes clear, realism is not what a griever needs or craves, especially when the beloved dies in a period of emotional turmoil and perceived estrangement and when all other close survivors deem that griever inadequate in her manifestations of grief and unworthy of the beloved's intellect or affections. The I of *Sorrow* shares the sense of its inadequacy, at the same time that it struggles to make a legend out of the beloved and their love. Aspects of the former process aid the latter, particularly through the etherealizing of Percy, now invoked as "lost divinity," "blessed spirit," "a spirit of the elements" who only assumed an "earthly dress," "one of the wisest, best, and most affectionate of spirits" (443, 445, 473). One way to assert the constancy of their love is to sever lover from body, to perceive Percy as beyond the flesh.

Another is to adopt the poet's idealizing tendencies and direct them at him. *Sorrow* does this in two ways, by elegizing Percy in the mode and words of his poems and by characterizing him in the idealized terms of *A Defence of Poetry.* The two poems most often cited or referenced in this journal are *Adonais* (464, 467) and "Lift Not the Painted Veil" (446, 485), both of which characterize death as life, either because the best are dead or because death is now dead. They are invoked in order to express Mary's longing for a resumption of her life through dying. "I was not born to repose or enjoy; but to suffer—to die—& in death to find my life" (463; cf. 483: "O never shall I live again, never, never more"). The characterization of the Poet in *A Defence of Poetry,* as one whose sins are "redeemed" by the "mediator, Time," becomes the new truth of the character of "beloved Shelley." In "a fit of inspiration," Nature "planted this seed—a flower grew transcendant in loveliness. . . . Brave, gentle, wise; soft as a woman; firm as the star of night—there was no fault in him" (463). Such idealizing ultimately spills over to their love, at one point described as the stuff of legend. "When did before did [sic] a spirit of the elements, taking an earthly dress, select one of this world for its mate? There are traditions of such events & the chosen one was by that choice lifted if not above yet apart from her fellows. I feel thus" (445). It also extended to revising the record of their writing relationship, which, though more in sync than their emotional and sexual lives, was not always the picture of accord that it now appears. This revisionism is clearest when Mary announces frustration, not over Percy's advice to write a tragedy, but over the absence of his encouraging presence on her desire to write one. "I said I would write a tragedy . . . my labours are futile—how differently did I commence an undertaking with my loved Shelley to criticize and encourage me as I advanced" (475).

As active in *The Last Man*, this legend-making assumes two forms. It is enacted through the responses of Perdita to the loss of Raymond and is embodied in the novel's new type of fictional protagonist. The "lost one" and beloved of Raymond, Perdita is a classic example of the legendizing of love. Initially, her love for Raymond is all the world to her. By definition (and in explicit rejection of the logic of love in *Epipsychidion*), her love can suffer no diminution, partition, or reserve. "Take the sum [of love] in its completeness, and no arithmetic can calculate its price; take from it the smallest portion, give it but the name of parts, separate it into degrees and sections, and like the magician's coin, the valueless gold of the mine, is turned to vilest substance" (102). The breach in confidence occasioned by discovery of Raymond's love for Evadne ruptures their oneness and therefore cannot be repaired. "There was no remedy. . . . That which had been was written with the adamantine pen of reality, on the everlasting volume of the past" (97). Raymond's efforts to "establish a renewal of confidence and affection" are an affront to the "singleness," the perfect union, of love (110). "It is not a common infidelity at which I repine. It is the disunion of an whole which may not have parts" (111). Though she declares herself dead in this rupture of love, death now *is* fearful to her because, in being linked by "the chain of memory with this" world, death can bring no relief because no resumption of that former time (111).

But when Raymond actually does die, in effect fulfilling what already Perdita perceives to have been her and his reality while he was alive, everything about the permanence of this rupture, and the oppositions that structure the truth of her former view of love, changes. At news of his possible death, she immediately journeys to "the land which was to restore her to her first beloved, 'Her dear heart's confessor—a heart within that heart,'" where she plans to "begi[n] life again" (129, 133). At confirmation of his actual death, she vows to take up permanent residence beside his tomb, and, when Verney betrays her wishes by carrying her unconscious on board a ship returning to England, she commits suicide by throwing herself overboard. This love that cannot bear any diminishment in life but then recovers—indeed, discovers—its full intensity through the beloved's death is one tragedy of living, but it is not the full story, either of the paired Shelleyan personae (Perdita and Lionel) in *The Last Man* or of Shelley's life/writings. It is the story of the I of *The Journal of Sorrow*, struggling to compose itself through this re/vision of their love.

Legend-making is also visible in the type of fictional personae presented in this novel. Unlike Proserpine, who is a well-known legendary protagonist, and unlike Mathilda, who is wholly fictional but also has intentional autobiographical affinities with its author, the protagonists in *The Last Man* are fictional personages whose biographical and autobiographical resemblances to recently alive persons were meant to help constitute them as legends in the making. This is especially the case with the fictional depictions of Byron (Raymond) and Percy Shelley (Adrian), and not simply because they had the clearest claims on being dead and becoming illustrious. The characterization of Adrian was part of Mary's early efforts to broadcast features of Percy's personality, poetry, and political philosophy that were under way in her editing of *Posthumous Poems*, announced as in progress in December 1822 and meant to include some of his prose writings, which were then truncated by Sir Timothy's threats to disown Percy Florence if Mary persisted in that project (434n1). Characterizing Adrian as a governor and world-changing fictional personage aided in establishing the illustriousness of Percy (arguably as poet-legislator), as did portraying him as a close friend of Raymond, Byron's popularity being well established by this period. It didn't hurt that in this version Adrian is portrayed as asexual. Certainly splitting her own character between the lost one (Perdita) and the last one (Lionel Verney) was useful for simplifying her feelings about the person behind the legend that she was composing and perpetuating.

Lives of Eminent Men

My life & reason have been saved by these 'Lives.'
Lives of Eminent Men of Italy, Spain, and Portugal

The splits occasioned by Mary Shelley's occupation with Percy Shelley's remains inhabit her life/writings and are visible in various splittings in her fictional personae (Perdita/Lionel Verney) and self-characterizations (derivative and primary, collector and inventor, realist in adopting idealism). But nowhere are the generic and "personal" splittings so visible as in her turn toward writing biography, the composition of which healed her and them in significant ways. From 1833 to 1839, Shelley made substantial contributions to the three-volume *Lives of the Most Eminent Literary and Scientific Men of Italy, Spain, and Portugal* (1835–37) and the two-volume *Lives of the Most Eminent Literary and Scientific Men of France* (1838–39), which are included within the Cabinet of Biography (one of five cabinets) of Dionysius Lardner's 133-volume *Cabinet Cyclopaedia* (1829–46).[66] Long construed as money-grubbing hackwork or, at best, respite from the difficulties of imaginative composition, the entries that compose Shelley's *Lives of Eminent Men* are important documents in their own right and a fascinating testimony to her successes and failures at mourning. Even the reasons generally given for the longstanding neglect of this phase of her life/writings acquire a different significance in light of the conclusions about mourning reached in and embodied by *The Last Man*. The detached, impersonal voice of these *Lives* and the text's status as a work of amalgamation rather than original research are hallmarks of her approach to remains. They also link the annotative, fragmentary approach that she necessarily took to Percy Shelley's *Life* to these coherent entries in *Lives of Eminent Men*.

   As contributions to the art of biography, these entries are not as marginal as their relative brevity and generalist venue might cause them to appear. They extend the generic merging of public and private that defines the genre of biography—as a history of an individual who is deemed a worthy subject in proportion to his or her capacity to represent a particular historical period—in characteristic Shelleyan ways.[67] First, like Godwin's *Life*-writings, hers privilege private, accidental, or youthful propensities as more revelatory of character than a person's major deeds or accomplishments. Though she credits "Dr. Johnson" with sanctioning the "bringing forward of minute, yet characteristic details" as "essential" to the "true end of biography," the stated goal of understanding through such details "the *mechanism of being* that rendered him the individual that he was" is clearly Godwinian (*Italian Lives*, 226, my emphasis).[68] Second, she draws so many "facts" regarding their lives from authors' fictional writings that she worries "how Lardner will like" it that "the book will be more of literature than of lives" (*Spanish Lives*, xix; cf. 247). At the same time, she makes out of such fictional fragments coherent forms of life. "We can always fancy at least that we trace something of the man himself in his works, and so form a tissue of some sort from these patchwork materials"

(179). "There is nothing so attractive to a biographer as to complete the fragments of his hero's life," which she does by "fixing the eye on salient particles" in official records and the writer's works (265). These features, along with her inclusion of distinguished women within *Lives of Eminent Men*, allow Greg Kucich to characterize Shelley's biographical writings as forerunners of feminist historiography—as well as significant efforts to educate a new class of female readers.[69] Her desire to "vindicate" rather than castigate writers, especially those who have been "misrepresented and reviled," suggests additional private interests in the publicizing and disseminating of these lives.[70]

In such an approach to writing biography, we discern Shelley's ability to make a (Wollstonecraftian) virtue out of (Godwinian) necessity. As Crook explains, "Lardner preferred straight biography" to "*Westminster Review*–style literary criticism" and to the insertion of "too much autobiography." While this "edict against the ego was a clog on a writer like Leigh Hunt," it was a spur to Shelley's mode of authorship: "adept at circumvention," skilled at "insinuating the highly personal under a mask of impersonality" (*Italian Lives*, xxvii). In this regard, her turn to biography represents a further extension of her penchant to create fictional personae (Mathilda, Proserpine, Perdita, Lionel Verney; Woodville, Adrian) who consciously solicit identification as auto/biography, as well as the penchant of her fiction, starting with *Frankenstein*, to probe the capacity of kinds of writing to facilitate, perpetuate, or terminate life. Interestingly, in describing his initial turn to authorship, Lionel Verney in *The Last Man* announces this next stage of generic engineering and the hubris underlying the self-effacing authorial persona. "My productions . . . were sufficiently unpretending; they were confined to the biography of favourite historical characters, especially those whom I believed to have been traduced, or about whom clung obscurity and doubt. As my authorship increased, . . . I became as it were the father of all mankind. Posterity became my heirs" (122). Through the "quieter" work of composing biography, understood as a "work made out of other work," then, Shelley comes full circle on Victor Frankenstein's claim to benefit humanity by extending the means of life. Quieter, but no less hubristic: "which I think I do *much* better than romancing" (*Italian Lives*, xxi). "The honour of *invention* is due to those who seize the scattered threads of knowledge which former discoverers have left, and weave it into a continuous and irrefragable web" (*French Lives*, 79 my emphasis; cf. 3:415).[71]

Lisa Vargo rightly claims that the detachment of the authorial voice should not obscure "how deeply felt the project was for Mary Shelley" (*Spanish Lives,* xxvi). Her biographical writings represent a crucial stage in her im/personal history of mourning and, both in content and tone, show how far she had come in accepting mourning as a duty. Acquiring capacity to mourn, moreover, is shown to be inseparable from a life of study and writing, a connection that her account of writing these *Lives* confirms and that she saw confirmed by this wide survey of European writers, many of whom found recourse to study the best "resource and consolation" in times of trouble (235). While suffering is sometimes ascribed to the loss of a beloved, *Lives* focuses more frequently on the heartache that "so often" attends "the life of a literary man of high reputation" through critical neglect, misinterpretation, or the absence or loss of his readership (*French Lives,* 304). It redresses such losses not only through acquainting current readers with their lives and writings but also by portraying the then-current neglect as a spur to their eventual fame. On the basis of such depictions, Shelley draws two uncharacteristic conclusions. First, "Man was born to be happy," a state acquired through mobilization of the "affections," sensitivity to nature's "beauty," "delight in the exercise of [one's] faculties," and the "fulfillment of [one's] social duties" (71). Second, writers who facilitate acquisition of this happiness, also called "moral courage," are the most worthy to be read and perpetuated. Put the other way, the writers she deems least worthy of an afterlife wrote in support of suicide (including Foscolo, Goethe, Byron, and de Staël).[72] For "sorrow is rife with desperation; we fly to the pages of the sage to learn to bear; and a writer fails in his duty when he presents poison instead of medicine" (481).

Comments on Goethe's *Werter,* by way of contrast to *Ortis* in the entry on Ugo Foscolo, suggest how the duty to live is aligned with highly topical public realities. Both *Werter* and *Ortis,* in portraying the attractions of suicide, present "a picture which, a few years ago" (the 1770s–80s), was the "model by which the youth of Europe delighted to dress their minds"—that is, a "morbid shrinking from the woes of existence." The outbreak of the French Revolution, by giving youth "an hope, an aim," overturned their "total want of fortitude" and "gave new life to these natural instincts," which disappointment over Napoleon's despotism unfortunately soon "blighted," leaving youth in an even more precarious state of mind (*Italian Lives,* 340). Here, *Lives of Eminent Men* makes a bold intervention into contemporary history by declaring this period of disillusionment, and thus of mourning for the failed ideals of the revolution, officially over. "Since then, a better day has dawned, and men are glad to live for the morrow, since each day is full of spirit-stirring expectation" (340). "The world, in the days succeeding to those of revolution and preceding those of reform, was much divided between those who despaired and those who hoped. The latter now triumph" (329). This resurgence of hope means that sufferers now have stronger incentive to live and thus more reason to seek out better ways of living in works of literature, which also means that readers generally need to do everything in their power to lessen the sufferings of writers. "No people need so much sympathy as poets. The interchange of thought and feeling, the fresh spirit of inquiry and invention, that springs from the collision or harmony of different minds, are with them a necessity and a passion" (299; cf. 330; *French Lives,* 306). Even more essential to expanding the hopes and prospects of new readers is giving "encouragement" to women writers, who, especially "when young," are "open to such cruel attacks" that they rarely make it to maturity as writers (*French Lives,* 491–92).

The confidence that underlies these assessments of the times and of the optimal conditions for living suggests that Shelley's *Lives of Eminent Men* and "art" of biography represent a substantial achievement in her life/writings and her acceptance in both domains of the value of living a literary life. From the 1830s on, her writings affirm with more conviction than ever the power of words to reform the world, in large part because this conviction had been tested severely by a misery brought as often by writing as by life events. The conviction is also linked to having words wielded by long-silenced voices, as the speech given to Fanny Derham in *Lodore* makes clear. But *Lives of Eminent Men* also supervises highly "personal" issues related to the ongoing mourning of Percy and perpetual preparation for the mourning of Godwin, under way, we recall, since he presented her *Essay on Sepulchres* in 1814 in anticipation of his death, which finally occurred on 7 April 1836—that is, after she had completed the lives of men in Italy, Spain, and Portugal and before she began those of France.[73] Read in this context, *Lives* can be seen as allowing Shelley to engage the company that her beloveds are now, or soon will be, keeping, to know them better and help perpetuate their afterlives. They also help her envision her future destination among the illustrious, confidence in this project finally earning her the right to join her husband in death—"& which I think I do *much* better than romancing." But read in the context of her failure to compose a *Life of P. B. Shelley* or to complete the *Life of William Godwin*, it is arguable that *Lives of Eminent Men* also marks the limits of her ability to mourn—or, especially, memorialize—the two men who most enjoined this project on her. Equally possible, however, is that *Lives* memorializes them in a way that is faithful to those writers' notions of living on—as remains that are diffused, disseminated, im/personal, and thus capable of transformation. At the least, the two forms of *Life* projects together stage the fundamental challenge of mourning, by which success represents betrayal of the person—in this case, the writer *and* the concept.

Of the two, and for general reasons that the epilogue's focus on Percy Shelley takes up, *Lives of Eminent Men* is more informed by the memorializing of Godwin than of Shelley. Godwin set the parameters of mourning that occupied Mary Shelley throughout her life/writings (whereas Percy offered the primary occasion); Godwin theorized and wrote *Lives* as antidepressants and ways to reanimate the dead (whereas Percy found the discipline of history "hateful" and never wrote biography);[74] and Godwin died while the project was in process. Godwin's greater presence also stems from the fact that critics read the prefaces and extended biographical notes to Mary Shelley's editions of Percy Shelley's poetical works as a necessarily truncated and fragmentary version of her *Life of P. B. Shelley* (owing to Sir Timothy's injunction), whereas they see the uncompleted "Life of William Godwin" as an ultimately failed act of memorialization. Besides the obvious relevance of her "personal" struggles over the loss of Percy Shelley to the general achievement marked by and promulgated in *Lives of Eminent Men*, whereby writing and study are the best consolation for grief, memorializing of him is visible in *Lives* primarily through its articulations of the true features of "ideal" poetry and a certain idealization of the "sweetness" of a poet. "Ideality is the soul of lyric poetry" which is to be rigorously distinguished from "the poetry of circumstance" (*Italian Lives*, 288). The greatest poets are known by "higher flights of the imagination," "fairy hue," "the sublime transfusion of the material into the immaterial" (294; *French Lives*, 250). "A poet alone could translate Calderon" in ways that capture "his fantastic machinery" and "his incomparable sweetness" (*Spanish Lives*, 251). "[Racine] had not that higher power of the imagination which allies the emotions of the heart with the glories of the visible creation and creates, as it were, 'palaces of nature' for the habitation of the sublimer passions" (*French Lives*, 176). At the least, such depictions worked to establish the taste by which the poetic works of Percy Shelley would be better appreciated. One can also say that Mary Shelley promoted the value, and thus the afterlife, of writers by adopting Percy Shelley's mode of defense in *A Defence of Poetry*—if not whitewashing the "sins" of the poets, then at least putting the most sympathetic construction on them. She asserts that poets require the greatest degree of sympathy of any category of person and that, in judging of poets' lives, readers should beware the mote in their own eyes. This means that the truth biographers serve is not so much literal as productive: "If what comes to light is discreditable, then to publish it risks the disfigurement of an illustrious moral exemplar."[75]

For understandable reasons, few critics have commented on the enveloping of the intended two-volume "Life of William Godwin" within the *Lives of the Most Eminent Literary and Scientific Men of France* other than to note the relief from "poignant memories" and personal conflict provided by the latter in contrast to the former.[76] As Pamela Clemit, who edited Mary Shelley's uncompleted "Life of William Godwin," points out, Shelley's and Godwin's "joint attempt to ensure the posthumous survival and prosperity" of his writings had begun in the early 1830s "with the reprinting of three of his novels," in one of which Shelley wrote an anonymous celebratory "Memoirs of William Godwin" and a prospectus (1832) for a new edition of *Political Justice* ("Life of Godwin," xiv). Clemit then looks further ahead to find in Charles Kegan Paul's two-volume commissioned biography, *William Godwin: His Friends and Contemporaries* (1876), the "future" of Shelley's efforts realized "in a carefully modified form" (xviii). For Kegan Paul's work followed in the spirit of Godwin's notion of a literary life as necessitating discussion of his friends and associates (evidenced by his inclusion, within the *Life of Chaucer*, the *Memoirs of His Near Friend and Kinsman, John of Gaunt, Duke of Lancaster*). If Kegan Paul covered the friends and contemporaries, we might say that *French Lives* handles the second branch, by treating the "manners, opinions, arts, and literature" of the nation and period that unleashed Godwin's writerly productivity and marked the height of his fame. This is not to say that *French Lives* can be equated with the "Life of William Godwin" or that it provided an adequate substitution for it, even in Shelley's mind. But writing it soothed her grief over his loss and accomplished the intention that Clemit ascribes to the "Life of William Godwin" in providing not just "commemoration" but "inspiration" along Godwinian lines—doing "justice" to the "illustrious dead" by providing "animation and encouragement to those who would follow them in the same career" (xiii). It also sets the context for all three of the topics that Syndey Conger characterizes as composing the "generalizable" content of the "Life of Godwin" and that provoked Shelley's anxiety while composing it: "A portrait of Godwin based on and extending his self-portrait in the short autobiography, a discussion of Godwin's part in the English events surrounding the French Revolution, and an account of Godwin's marriage to Wollstonecraft."[77]

Understanding Godwin's part in the English events surrounding the French Revolution is the only obvious point of contact with the second volume of *French*

Lives and only in a displaced fashion. It is perhaps most visible in Shelley's uncharacteristic decision to include four "revolutionary personalities" who are "political actors more than, or as much as writers," as Clarissa Campbell Orr remarks in her introduction, and that allows her to "disassociate the early ideals of the French Revolution from its subsequent extremism and state-authorised bloodshed" (*Spanish Lives*, xlvi–xlvii; the four are Condorcet, Mirabeau, Mme. Roland, and Mme. de Staël). We know from "Life of Godwin" that Shelley was at similar pains to disassociate Godwin's writings and politics in the early 1790s from endorsement of violent or radical change and that effecting this disassociation was key to declaring *Political Justice* an "important era in Mr. Godwin's life—and one also it may be said, in the history of the world" ("Life of Godwin," 59). A "book for all times," *Political Justice* is especially relevant to current times, for it establishes the "purest standard" toward which the "excellen[t]" of all ages should "aspire," including "we . . . children of a calmer day" (64, 63, 59). But it is not simply in providing the rationale for a *renewed* belief in perfectibility and thus re-establishing Godwin as a "public benefactor" by focusing on its prerevolutionary version that *French Lives* speaks to concerns in the "Life of Godwin" (63). Deeper parallels exist that work to alleviate, not simply by disseminating, the anxiety evoked by attempting to justify Godwin's involvement in the French Revolution and his marriage to Wollstonecraft.

How else to understand the stunning assertion that opens the last entry in the first volume of *French Lives* that "there is no name more respected in the modern history of the world, than that of Fénelon. In the ancient, that of Socrates competes with him" (3:198)? For Fénelon epitomizes Godwin's critique of domestic affection as what impedes political justice, the notoriety of which assertion then impedes open acknowledgment, by Godwin or Shelley, of his marriage to Wollstonecraft. The entry, which Orr describes as bridging volumes 1 and 2, gets at these issues through specifying what has never been fully clear: why *Political Justice* deems *Fénelon*, an archbishop and vindicator of Catholicism, *the* most eminent candidate for survival. Commentators have always stressed that it is Fénelon as author, not cleric, that Godwin championed, specifically, the author on the eve of writing *The Adventures of Telemachus*, a vastly popular book on the education of a youth—as if that explains everything. But in describing the object of this book, which was written to shape "the mind and character of his pupil," the "young and ardent prince, who was destined to succeed Louis XIV," Shelley underscores the tendency of *Telemachus* in several of the ways that Godwin promoted through this approach to reading (*French Lives*, 206n). Judged as a text meant to in/form the character of a youth soon to occupy a position from which he will be able to shape the mind and character of an epoch, it is "the best book that was ever written" (otherwise, it is "pedantic, almost childish," and its "monitorial tone" inexcusable [206n]). Unfortunately, it missed its mark. The "early death" of the prince "destroyed the hope of France; and hence ensued the misrule which the revolution could alone correct" (206).

Writing such a book, even with the possibility it signified of an alternate history for France and Europe, and thus also for Godwin's writing career *if* the prince, enlightened on such principles and possessing "none of the ordinary kingly prejudices in favour of war and tyranny," had lived to rule, does not alone substantiate Shelley's initial claim. It also rests on the disinterestedness of Fénelon's character, visible in his "abnegation of self" and "extensive" philanthropy: " 'I love my family,' he said, 'better than myself; I love my country better than my family; but I love the human race more than my country' " (230, 225). More telling still, it is heard in his eschewal of "those chilling words *thine* and *mine*" (231, original emphasis). Even more crucial, Shelley's characterization of his posthumous reputation illustrates how a text's temporal failings and limitations are transcended through the ensuing course of history that that text and writer have helped bring to fruition. While *Telemachus* no longer speaks to contemporary nations, except "despotic" ones "like Turkey and Russia," because the "welfare of nations" now rests on "another basis than the virtues and wisdom of kings," the "spirit of the man" preserves his works from "perishing," even granting that "the science of politics is changed" (232). "His soul, tempered in every virtue, transcends the priestly form it assumed on earth; and every one who wishes to learn the lessons taught by that pure, simple, and entire disinterestedness, which is the foundation of the most enlightened wisdom and exalted virtue, must consult the pages of Fénelon. He will rise from their perusal a wiser and a better man" (232). Composing the life of Fénelon, then, not only allows Shelley to praise the dispositional features that are characteristic of Godwin's mind and writings but also to characterize the tendency of Godwin's writings as prepared by writers like Fénelon. Given that the welfare of nations now rests on "knowledge, and morals of the people," the "proper task of the lawgiver and philanthropist is to enlighten nations," especially in "England and France," where the "influence of the people is so direct as to demand our most anxious endeavours to enlighten them" (232). This assertion describes Godwin's motivation as writer and confirms the method of the tendency that, according to Godwin, keeps a work and writer vital.

The problem that "Fénélon" raises for justifying Godwin's marriage to Wollstonecraft is addressed indirectly in consecutive entries on Rousseau and Condorcet. Initial attempts in "Life of Godwin" show Shelley's working to demonstrate how this decision conforms to his principles and moral character. While the "fervour and uncompromising tone" of the author of *Political Justice* "made his followers demand a rigid adherence" to its principles, which in turn made his decision to marry appear "absolute apostacy" to many, this charge represents a misunderstanding of his character. Since "in fact all Mr. Godwin's inner and more private feelings" were wholly opposed to "vice or libertinism" and "all strongly enlisted on the side of female virtue," he "would readily have proved if questioned that it was only misapprehension of the former that could lead anyone to suppose that they were opposed to it" ("Life of Godwin,"105, 100, 105). The obscurity of this syntax, as compared to the relative clarity of Godwin's explanation, which she cites in a footnote, suggests how fraught the question remained for Shelley's understanding of her father's—and thus her own—life and character, especially as they related to sexual activity. "The doctrine in my Political Justice is, that an attachment in some degree permanent, between two persons of opposite sexes is right, but that marriage, as practiced in European countries is wrong. I still adhere to that opinion" (100n).

Tandem entries in the second volume of *French Lives,* Rousseau and Condorcet both epitomize the "independence" that is the "basis of true genius" and the opposing sexual and domestic behaviors to which independent genius gives rise. Rousseau is reviled for "ruthlessly sacrificing" little children to the "Moloch" of his sexual freedom, while Condorcet is praised for an independence that "holds fast by duty" (335, 375). As commentators note, Shelley loses the balanced and forgiving tone that characterizes most other entries, enjoining readers to "turn with loathing" from a "revolting and criminal" scene (335), expressions of ire often interpreted as voicing a proto-Victorian domestic sensibility. Even here, however, we should note that loathing is expressed over Rousseau's irresponsibility regarding the consequences of his frequent sexual activity, not over having sex itself. This distinction holds true even for Shelley's comments on the women with whom Rousseau has "connections," whose characters are evaluated on the basis of virtues other than chastity. "It is not to-day that we have learnt, that it is not true, that when a woman loses one virtue she loses all" (330). While Shelley goes on to endorse parental "self-sacrifice" and nurturance, those virtues are presented as the means to exonerate a "fallen" woman from "error" (i.e., not as essential femi-

nine qualities) and as enjoined equally on men. "Personal fidelity is the puri-
fier and preserver of the affections; and whoso fails in this, either man or
woman, degrades human nature—the glory of which is to ally the sensations
of love to the emotions of the heart and the passions of the soul" (331).
Rousseau is the most "unnatural" of "natural" men, according to Shelley,
because his independence leads him to treat "duty" to others as "an unwelcome clog" (365). This separation not only "mars many of his views" but
also misconceives the nature of primitive and civilized society.

The nature of this indictment of Rousseau exonerates Godwin's marriage to
Wollstonecraft in two ways. First, by invoking Wollstonecraft's intellectual
and moral authority ("it is not to-day that we have learnt"), Shelley indirectly
validates the wisdom of his choice of partner. Shelley also details as Godwin's
"inner" and "private feelings" a "sense of duty" that does not permit him to
"indulge" in the "practise" of activities that, though he might deem "unjust"
the "laws of society" pertaining to them, would occasion either "deception" or
"injury" to the woman involved or any "loss of usefulness" to either party
owing to the "stigma" indulgence in such activities imparts. Furthermore, the
"natural ties of children" entail "duties" that "necessitate the duration of" the
connection between adult parties, "tamper[ing]" with which "must end in
misery" ("Life of Godwin," 100). This profile of "moral courage," as opposed to
Rousseau's total want thereof, positions Godwin as a friend to women and
mitigates whatever censure might accrue to his unmarried sexual activity—
though his character already absolves him from what is "the case with a
number of men" (though "seldom, if ever," of women), that they "cultivate a
love of pleasure destitute of sentiment" (*French Lives*, 327, 348). But this
exoneration raises a new (old) problem for Shelley's efforts to satisfy Godwin's
"passion for posthumous fame": showcasing his dispositional coldness impedes
readers' affection for him. For as Shelley states elsewhere and learns through
the contrast in her two men, the "truth is that, though in theory and absence,
we may approve the unblameable, the torpid, and the coldly good, our nature
forces us to prefer what is vivacious, exhilarating, and original" (407).

Condorcet proves especially useful for addressing this potential harm to
Godwin's afterlife, owing to D'Alembert's description of him as a "volcano
covered by snow" (371). The image allows Shelley to distinguish between two
kinds of political reformers, "men of great personal susceptibility, uncontrol-
able passions, and excitable imaginations, who have the same power over their
fellow-creatures that fire has over materials cast upon it," and men of "great
but regulated enthusiasm of soul;—which enthusiasm, derived from abstract

principles and founded on severe reason, is more steady, more disinterested, and more enduring than that springing from passion; but it exercises little immediate influence over others, and is acknowledged and appreciated only in hours of calm" (371). From this, Shelley makes the somewhat unexpected observation that a "philosopher" of the latter sort (call him a new philosopher) "was destined to have great influence at the commencement of the French Revolution," while men still acted out of a "virtuous desire to found the changes they brought about on reason, justice, and the good of mankind" (371), although such philosophers soon lost their influence when events grew more combustible. Even more suggestive, Shelley claims that their day has once again come to "we children of a calmer day."

Besides restoring Godwin's readership, the entry on Condorcet works to prolong it indefinitely by recalibrating the heat of fire. Picking up on that footnote in her earliest mourning manual that rejects of the "cant" regarding warm and cold hearts, Shelley enlists Godwin's observation there of the two kinds of fire associated with Vulcan and Vesta to ends other than a distinction between gods of metal-forging and of chastity.[78] "If philosophers like Condorcet did educate their fellows into some approximation of their rule of right, the ardent feelings and burning imaginations of man would create something now unthought of, but not less different from the results he expected, than the series of sin and sorrow which now desolates the world" (376). In other words, calmness, even apparent coldness, of soul is capable of igniting the world, but to what *that* flame tends is as unpredictable as the fire cast by more incendiary spirits. Still, this unpredictability does not invalidate "upright efforts" to "improve [one's] fellows," while it does discredit "any endeavour of government to bind the intellect in chains" (371). A similar coldness in Godwin not only won him a mate but one whose success at unlinking the chains binding female intellect made her epoch-changing. Their joining forces, then, reforged the meanings of "necessity" and "chastity" in ways that continue to enliven children of calmer or of tempestuous days.

This displaced and often subterranean treatment of the lives of Godwin and Percy Shelley (and, occasionally, Wollstonecraft), as registered variously but similarly in her fiction and nonfiction, indicates the path, method, and possible limit of Shelley's mourning itinerary. The uncompleted *Lives* of these writer—family members indicates a failure or, perhaps, a *refusal* to make the lives of her nearest and dearest cohere—perhaps also because they kept raising the status of her coldness. One can view the fragmentary, annotative, and intertextual approach to composing the *Lives of Eminent Men* as a sign of her fidelity to her family's life/writings *and* status as remains. One can also see it as a refusal to mourn, and thus to move on completely from them. In either case, Shelley's life/writings show the special benefits and difficulties of mourning persons who are conceived and beloved as a text. Does it speak? Does it regard me? What does it want with me? Or, as the I of *The Journal of Sorrow* puts it, "What is it then that wanders up & down my heart chilling its blood? . . . Will you not aid me to deserve you?" (469, 470). What *is* clear is that Shelley viewed her custodial approach to remains as her claim to genius and the ranks of the illustrious dead. "The capacity of gathering materials, lying barren but for the life he puts into them, is the great attribute of genius. He might gather the fuel from others, but the fire was his own" (*French Lives*, 415). In this, the afterlife of the author of *Frankenstein* is one of its hideous progeny.

CHAPTER SIX

A Juvenile Library; or, Works of a New Species

The book as child is a standard trope and male authorial ruse that the 1831 preface to *Frankenstein* pushes to extremes when it bids its "hideous progeny to go forth and prosper." Linking book and creature, it humanizes both and declares what few parents or authors ever admit, that their progeny is hideous and that something went terribly wrong between conception and realization. At the same time, this progeny is being *re*issued, given a second chance under hopefully better conditions, even as it is said to represent former happier days for its progenitor—a powerful parental and authorial fantasy that is not often satisfied by reality. Critics have construed this image and text in countless ways that underscore the relation between parenting and artistic creation, irresponsible invention, fear of female re/productivity, or nostalgia for domesticity. This chapter interprets the address to hideous progeny as accurately characterizing three components of the Wollstonecraft-Godwin-Shelley family's life/writings: their prodigious engagement with books for children as well as books as children; their recognition that, since certain books make new species of person, authors might consider the consequences on that new creature as well as on the world of such creations; lived experience of how one's progeny—child, book, or new-creature-in-the-making—can lengthen, strengthen, or deaden one's future.

Even in its most basic sense, as referring to natal children, the issue of progeny poses problems for this family. In Godwin's household, none of "his" progeny had the same set of birth parents and several did not outlive their progenitors. In Shelley's, not only did progeny keep dying but determining whose child was whose remains vexed, especially with Elena Adelaide Shelley. Then there are confusions stemming from the family's deliberate extension of the sphere of family, by which adequate parenting was a question of mentoring more than blood affiliation and familial resemblance a matter not of physiognomy but of shared habits of thinking. Construing their books as their progeny is no less conclusive, since this family saw writing as a form of living and wrote books whose characters are read as surrogate selves or wholly generic beings. Moreover, owing to the strong family resemblance in their authorship, determining whose idea or character is whose or what is original is impossible to delineate. Nor is the connection predictably reassuring, since their books, like their children, often failed to outlive these authors, fell "dead-born" from the press, and were deemed hideous as well as illuminating. In fact, the longevity gained through child or book for each of the three is fairly equal, since all three are basically known for one book and one child (*Enquiry concerning Political Justice/Caleb Williams, Vindication of the Rights of Woman, Frankenstein;* Mary Godwin Shelley, Percy Florence Shelley). How to identify their progeny and then ensure its survival remained radically open questions for all three.

Usually, viewing a book as one's progeny expresses a way for oneself and one's ideas to live on after death and have a longer-lasting effect on the future. The life/writings of this family intensified that dynamic because all three members produced *children's* books intended not only to educate the next generation but also to alter the preconditions of that future by re-forming the child. We have yet to take seriously the sheer volume of work these writers composed on the topic of education, and the number of texts that each wrote explicitly for children—Wollstonecraft's *Thoughts on the Education of Daughters, The Female Reader,* and *Original Stories from Real Life;* Godwin's *Bible Stories, Fables, Ancient and Modern, The Looking Glass, Lady Jane Grey, The Pantheon,* and five histories of different nations; and Shelley's *Proserpine, Midas,* and *Maurice; or, The Fisher's Cot.* Even more serious was the attempt through these texts to produce what they described: a female reader, a male artist, a wandering child. Like many other writers for children in the period, Wollstonecraft, Godwin, and Shelley accentuated the linkage between child-rearing and inscribing a child's mind and stressed the centrality of proper reading to the child's development and sense of connection to the world. But their books for children also explore not only the effects of reading and writing on mental and emotional development but also how the "world of books," especially the world of children's books, predetermines a child's reality.

By the time that Wollstonecraft (in the 1780s) and Godwin (in the early 1800s) started writing books for children, the genre of children's literature and the market for children's books were well established, as was the implicit connection among writing, reading, and rearing a child. A distinct market for children's literature is usually said to have begun in the 1740s, with the work of three publishers, Thomas Boreman, Mary Cooper, and, pre-eminently, John Newbery, whose publication in 1744 of *A Little Pretty Pocket-Book* established "in a stroke, as tradition has it, the juvenile book trade and children's literature in England."[1] Up until then, the argument goes, literature for children fell into two categories, that devoted to religious instruction or to a "mixed bag" of teaching materials, including Aesop's fables, chapbook romances, early courtesy manuals, and a "large body of previously communal literature enjoyed by adults and the young of virtually all classes."[2] After the 1740s, a distinct business in children boomed, initiating a series of debates regarding how, when, whether, and with what a child's mind might best be filled. According to most historians of the topic, the question of what type of book to produce was dominated from the 1740s to 1770s primarily by trade interests in what would sell, with the debate then restricted and intensified in the 1780s, when "socioreligious reformers" such as Sarah Trimmer, Ellenor Fenn, the Kilner sisters, and M. M. Sherwood began to critique fantastic and supernatural reading as harmful to a child's mind and development.[3]

The founding text of this entire movement, John Locke's *Some Thoughts on Education* (1693) (along with his *Essay concerning Human Understanding* [1699]), provides the foundational image for the development of the industry in children's books and the necessity of it: the mind at birth as a tabula rasa or blank slate, on which gets written the impressions and thus evolving record and character of a being's experience. Besides depicting the process of mental development as an activity of inscription, this image erased the until-then ruling assumption of the child's innate depravity and instead literally produced a newborn as a fresh start. Consequently, thoughts on education also began afresh, concerned not with overcoming pre-existing tendencies but with educing from the ground up a mind that is best-suited to perceiving and receiving the world. Moreover, as Alan Richardson argues, the "presumed textual nature of the child's mind" elicited fictional strategies that "brin[g] child and book into a peculiarly intimate and specular relation." With the "growing sense" that the children's text is "both analogous to and potentially contiguous" with the child's mind, the "thematization of reading in children's books t[ook] on a new intensity."[4] Both the newly textualized mind and textual reactions to it in pedagogical discourse and books for children elicited an outpouring of writing during the eighteenth century that crystallized in several controversies revealing essential paradoxes regarding education that the writings of this family place in high relief.

One basic paradox is that the new freedom or sense of possibility associated with the earliest stages of childhood was accompanied by a highly goal-directed, gender-specific, and class-delineated concept of the kind of person that the unscripted period of childhood is supposed to be educing. Debates about education heightened the broader confusion within emergent capitalism regarding what is useful versus fanciful, productive versus wasteful, economic in the sense of expedient versus market-driven. Texts regarding the proper means of educating a child sought to legislate these distinctions in curious ways. For example, the two most widely read and recognized authorities on education in the eighteenth century, Locke and Rousseau, voice skepticism regarding the wisdom of young children reading books at all in their efforts to promote free thought and to preserve for as long as possible a child's ostensibly unmediated relation to nature and experience.[5] Theirs is not the voiced objection of a later decade to the alleged uselessness of fantasy-world novels but a wholesale rejection of books—Locke making an exception for Aesop's Fables and Rousseau advising against any reading until the child reaches the age of twelve and, after that, only *Robinson Crusoe*.[6] On the other hand, those many, but less famous and usually female, writers on education from the 1770s on promote childhood reading but are said to instigate a debate over the claims of reason versus fantasy and imagination to best stimulate and inform a child's mind. Often opposing the moral tale to fairy tales, didacticism to escapism, such discussions sought to determine whether the fantastic or the realistic is most useful in activating a mind.[7]

As Jerome McGann famously noted in a more general context, these distinctions are crucial to the formation of a romantic ideology that links imagination to freedom as a political as well as a literary and an epistemological reality.[8] First-generation canonical poets are key to this affirmation of imagination, just as they, especially Wordsworth and Blake but also Coleridge and Lamb, are said to champion the special imaginative insight of the child, that "seer blest" whose proximity to nature or a pre-existent state grants it access to a deeper, purer, less encoded, encumbered, and enlightened kind of truth. But as James MacGavran, Mitzi Myers, Alan Richardson, William St. Clair, and others have shown, romantic idealizations of the child, and of its mind as a site of free play or acquaintance with the vast, is a mystification not only of the child but also of these poets' own disciplinary and conformist, even imperialist, aims in countering the alleged "goodyness" and didacticism of childhood pedagogues in the name of a nature or imagination that stifles, rather than educes, growth, challenge, or change. After all, as Richardson notes, their endorsements of childlike imagination came after they had seriously revised their assessments of the bliss consequent on living in a dawn of radical possibilities. Increasingly, Wordsworthian imagination became invested in "a sort of primitivism, which closes off the prospect for intellectual development," a closing off that Richardson then finds instrumentalized quite literally in the monitorial Madras system associated with Andrew Bell and endorsed so enthusiastically by Wordsworth and Coleridge.[9] Moreover, as Myers and Norma Clarke point out, such views on imagination are sexist in lumping together, in order to discredit, a host of women writers as the "cursed Barbauld Crew, those Blights and Blasts of all that is Human in man and child" and by grossly underestimating the novelty, importance, and feminist aims served by and through women's entry into this debate.[10] They are equally sexist, I would argue, in the male privilege that they expose through being in a position to be dismissive about the value of reading books—thereby closing off a whole new world only beginning to open to less entitled youth of both sexes.

Hardly revealing a view of mind as a tabula rasa, the poets' campaign against books in general and rationalist books by female pedagogues in particular essentially served to keep these fresh starts safely enclosed in a Burkean second nature.[11] Such dismissals also worked to keep their imaginations free from aspects of reality that posed a challenge to their notions and exercise of freedom, including a whole host of female pedagogues working to in/form different kinds and modes of mind. Moreover, the coupling of Rousseau with Locke as the second undisputed authority on childhood education shows how the constructivist framework of the Lockean yet-to-be-written-upon mind, born free but then enslaved by dicta of government, literature, religion, and formal education, elicited, paradoxically, a form of gender essentialism—not in the sense that gender difference is essential, God-given, and therefore immutable but in the sense that constructing and maintaining gender difference is the essential work of childhood education. This is the basic message of *Émile*, whose rigidity on the score of gender implies that girls could be formed differently—that is, more like boys rather than simply to be liked and validated by them—a possibility that all of its directives regarding Sophie's education worked to foreclose and that the "cursed Barbauld Crew" in all its variety were united in reopening.

Richardson and Myers have gone the farthest in showing at once the falsity and the functionality of the opposition posed between reason and imagination or fairy tale and moral tale as it relates to debates about childhood education. Not only was this opposition erected during the same period that juvenile fiction was producing "calculatedly different books for girls and boys," but new possibilities for female advancement apparently could not win for winning: the new association of girls with "reasonable creatures" was then seen as making them even less adventurous ones.[12] By way of undermining these oppositions, Myers and Richardson also suggest in different ways the advances to this debate that Wollstonecraft and Godwin present in their nonbinary and more systematic approaches to the topic. According to Richardson, Wollstone-craft's educational program is "virtually unique" both in its advocacy of public coeducation and in its recognition that, on its own, "educational reform will do little" without full-scale societal renovation, for the "advantages of education and government are not separable."[13] Myers goes on to show the continuity between Wollstonecraft's conformist writings on the education of girls and her revolutionary *Vindication of the Rights of Woman* by way of demonstrating generally how poorly the opposition between conservative and progressive suits writings by women in this stage of educational reform.[14] Godwin, in Richardson's view, deserves far more credit and attention than he has received, even by Richardson, for seeing no contradiction in advocating both fairy tales and rationalist instruction in the early stages of a child's reading and for seeking neither to idealize nor subjugate children but instead conceive them as "individual being[s], with powers of reasoning." "I do not say that a child is the image of God."[15] In different but fairly unique ways, then, both Wollstonecraft and Godwin conceived the child as text and children's texts as spaces of rational possibility that should be as free from censorship *and* illusory notions of freedom as possible.

My argument for the specific possibilities evident in this family's re/ writing of childhood concerns their fancy-driven understanding of the child as fresh start. Their hospitality to fancy complicates the poles of the rationalist-imaginative debate in ways that affected the rationalist camp even more than the imaginative. No work surpasses Shelley's *Frankenstein* in situating scien-tific discovery and invention in the domain of fancy, as illustrated by the books of medieval alchemy that form Victor's intellectual background and impulse toward science. But that book also pushes to its farthest extent a problematic and a methodology that underlie many, if not most, books for children in the period and that Wollstonecraft's and Godwin's writings explicitly highlight: the function of fancy and fantasy in promoting rational, that is, empirical enquiry. Whether fairy or moral tale, the assumption is that story, image, or mental picture is crucial to ascertaining and internalizing any precept. Whether on the level of cosmos or gadget, the chief question is, How does the world, this thing, this I, operate? The association of empiricism with science and both with the age of reason has severely obfuscated the role of the "inventive," that is, fanciful and imaginative, faculties in scientific invention. Conversely, the association confuses characterizations of the new province of child's play: Are toys useful or playful, products of reason or fancy? What about the uses to which children put them—fantasy or reality? Is learning one's ABCs an exercise, a lark, or a song? Is the mode primarily aural or visual? nominal or representational? an open or a closed system?[16]

My claim is not that the Wollstonecraft-Godwin-Shelley family is unique in merging or blurring these increasingly separated spheres. Indeed, the value of writings on childhood education in this period is the emphasis that they place on fancy's role in escorting a child into the world of fact, science, or moral thinking. My claim instead is that their version and interpretation of this merger explains fundamental paradoxes in educational thinking *and* sheds new light on issues that have hampered reception of their own adult formulations. The merger between fancy and fact is key to forming an enlightened being, the goal and pace of whose forward motion is impossible to predict. It also plots or conceptualizes progress not as linear or even cyclical but as working by fits and starts. Some children surpass their parents, even as young children, others die before their time, others have a burst of activity and then fade slowly, others fail or refuse to move forward at all. Moreover, none of these writers eschews books in early childhood development or posits a prediscursive natural state, whether of physical nature or the natural innocence of childhood. All three advocate books as often more reasonable surrogate parents than their biological progenitors, reasonable in the sense of being both more predictable and more desirable.

Perception of their fanciful-rational approach to children's writing alters reception of their adult writings in various ways. Serious engagement with Wollstonecraft's early writings for girls, whose voiced social conformity and religious piety make many feminist critics either ignore them or slight them as juvenilia, provides an important enactment, as Barbara Taylor argues, of the centrality of fancy and imagination to Wollstonecraftian faith.[17] While Taylor's concern is to show from that how Wollstonecraft's feminist imagination retained, and cannot be thought apart from, its Christian underpinnings, my claim is more "developmental," in terms of both fancy and the status of

Wollstonecraft's belief: fancy is key to arousing religious speculation and faith for reasons similar to its success at awakening young minds to any "big" question. For, as Taylor's own book concedes, Wollstonecraft did seem to outgrow her religious conviction even as her fancy remained aimed at futurity. Godwin's writings for children stress the centrality of fancy and imagination in instructing the mind in ways that run counter to characterizations of his rationalism. The fact that he published such assertions under several pseudonyms (William Scofield, Edward Baldwin, Theophilus Marcliffe) excuses to some extent ongoing oversimplifications, but those assertions are consistent with adult writings that emphasize the centrality of fancy to history-writing and to inspiring individuals to make a better world through conscious emulation of the illustrious dead.

Shelley's investment in the re/writing of childhood accentuates the second major way that fancy affects debates regarding children's books stemming from the rationalist camp and affects any child's progress. The "wandering fancy" that characterizes her Proserpine, written in 1820 but ultimately published in 1833 in a journal produced explicitly for youth, *The Winter Wreath,* foregrounds the importance of desire in the cultivation of knowledge, both cognitive and sexual—and the interconnections between the two. The prominence of desire, or what they more commonly termed passion, in the writings and rationalist agendas of all three writers should not be underestimated, despite a long history of doing so. Passion for scholarship is particularly visible in Godwin's and Shelley's editorial and biographical writings, through which they remembered and re/animated beloved friends. But it also underlies their feminist pedagogies and agendas in stimulating a passion for scholarship in girls as the means of making them less conventionally passionate beings, or perceived as such. Oddly, these writers' embrace of passion in their treatments of sexual knowledge has been slighted even more in critical commentary than their passion for scholarship. The slight takes various forms: it denies the existence of sexual passion (in Godwin), its importance (in Wollstonecraft's feminist writings and Shelley's later novels), or its coherence (in Wollstonecraft's life/writings). The publicity of young Mary's sexual activity allowed perception of her passionate nature to get off on a better foot, though it faltered in her adult life/writings. Promising in this regard as well are considerations of her chief objects of desire, Percy and Godwin, her desire for whom foregrounds the con/fusion in kinds of knowledge that her wandering fancy seeks.

Precisely this con/fusion distinguishes Shelley's writings for children, which are less extensive than her parents' and focus more on the period of youth than early childhood. In her writings, young people learn early certain fundamental facts of life: loss initiates life; fantasy is an essential component of reality; parents and books prove inadequate preparation for living; moving forward is neither as simple or desirable as people say. Like, but even more than, her parents, Shelley's life/writings on childhood exemplify a less optimistic stage in the generally celebratory accounts of the child's mind as blank slate rather than as inherently depraved. Perhaps no child on literary record has given such an elaborated account of the damage wrought by the cultural fantasy that equates "new life" with "unlimited possibility," an equation that denies the extent to which even the most fortunate infant has only minimal possibilities for truly radical growth or change. Infant Mary is hardly fortunate on the score of freedom, even though she is the offspring of the period's most revolutionary parents and pedagogues. For one thing, the predetermination implicit in any new being assuming its family's name is enormous in her case, in which, to hear stepsister Claire tell it, anyone in the family who does not produce an epoch-changing book is deemed worthless, or, as Mary comes to feel, many of the most important events, feelings, and persons in her life have already been prescripted. For another, her given name, the alleged signifier of her singularity, is split, doubled, and deadened from (before) the start: hailed as s/he is in the womb as "William" and then ushered into the world of reading at and on the tomb of "Mary."

Perception of this radical limit to possibility, by a subject who continues to posit writing as the best and, at times only, possibility for change, is voiced in a more general fashion in her parents' writings and remains the most valuable dynamic of their approaches toward children. On the one hand, owing to their comparative freshness or blankness, children *do* constitute the best material on which to revise or recompose the features that make up society—which is why the history of Wollstonecraft's writing for girls shows her trying to catch them at an increasingly younger age. On the other hand, the world stays in its infancy because young people, in assuming their independence, by definition cannot conform to the program, even of their liberation through deprogramming. This is part of what Godwin means by comparing the world to a school.

> The world is much like a school; and to make the parallel complete, little more is necessary than to put one year in the latter, for ten years in the former. The pupils, we will suppose, are placed on an average for seven years; some for a shorter, and a few for a longer term: and the director and guide of the insti-

tution sees one set of learners succeed after another, who are no sooner tolerably accomplished, than they are dismissed from the scene: the studies that are entered on, and the instruction that is given, are perpetually beginning: and though much is acquired, and great and earnest efforts are made after improvement,—one decade, and once [sic] century of years, passes away and another comes, and every thing is nearly in the same posture; while ever-young infatuation, inexperience, and temerity perpetually disturb the profoundest designs and maxims that can be framed for general advantage. (*Sepulchres*, 141)

The wisdom of this family's writings on childhood rests in their comprehension that what is essential to educing a thinking being—independence, a wandering fancy—makes enlightened progress virtually impossible to achieve. For them, there is no going back on this promise or any going back to a time of sheer promise, but there is also no guarantee that the world will ever get very far in this way.

Wollstonecraft: The Child Is Woman to the Mother

Of the three writers, Wollstonecraft's involvement with children and with the topic of child-rearing has received the most critical attention and has generally been viewed as an important component of her life/writings, both theory and practice. With one exception (*Mary, a Fiction* [1788]), her earliest published writings are all explicitly devoted to the topics of children and child education, and they are all seen as drawing directly upon her work experiences as girls' school teacher and governess. *Thoughts on the Education of Daughters*, begun in 1786 and published in 1787, was composed in the aftermath of the closing of the school at Newington Green, which Wollstonecraft had started with her sister Eliza and Fanny Blood in 1784. *Original Stories from Real Life* (1788) and the unfinished "The Cave of Fancy" were written during the period (October 1786 until August of 1787) when Wollstonecraft worked as governess for the Viscount Kingsborough family of Mitchelstown (County Cork) in Ireland, and *The Female Reader*, published under the pseudonym of Mr. Cresswick in 1789, was the first publication undertaken after her return to London and entry into the literary Dissenting circle of Joseph Johnson (who published all of these books). Often, the critical narrative regarding her writings on this topic supports the developmental model of child education being articulated in the period, whereby these are deemed intellectually immature texts whose tone and content, if not orientation, Wollstonecraft subsequently outgrew.

Overly didactic, overly domesticated and conventional, even prissy, these writings hardly suit the Amazonian feminist who will burst onto the intellectual scene in just a few years.[18] If some critics also underscore telling similarities between these early conduct books and *A Vindication of the Rights of Woman*, especially in the degree to which both affirm motherhood, domesticity, and their attendant restraints on female sexuality, almost everyone agrees that by the time of *The Wrongs of Woman* Wollstonecraft and her protagonists have shed the conventionality that characterizes a figure like Mrs. Mason, the tutelary spirit who guides her two young female charges in *Original Stories from Real Life* and whom many readers find unbearable in her self-righteousness.[19]

Even this wholly standard description of Wollstonecraft's textual itinerary occasions some interesting observations that one project of this section aims to unfold. First, all of her original texts on and about children focus exclusively on girls—an unremarkable observation in light of her subsequent writings and the situation of girls in the period but nonetheless noteworthy given the usual gendered pairings in fictional texts about children and her own later arguments in favor of coeducation.[20] Second, the transformation in her expressed attitude toward the chief aims and constituents of femininity, evidenced in the shift in views from these early texts to the *Rights of Woman* and *Wrongs of Woman*, models the process that these early texts describe and advocate for girls. For the bottom line in *Thoughts on the Education of Daughters* and all subsequent thoughts on that topic is "I wish them to be taught to think" (11). The corollary also always follows: "I recommend the mind's being put into a proper train, and then left to itself. Fixed rules cannot be given, it must depend on the nature and strength of the understanding" (21).

Contemporary scholars tend to regard too cavalierly one consequence of the educational situation for girls, and thus also for women writers, living in the 1780s and '90s, who, with rare exception, acquired their literary education in the process of becoming authors.[21] Certainly, in the case of Wollstonecraft, her entry into the Johnson circle marked not only the end of her employment in the few respectable, and to her mind humiliating, positions open to (lower-)middle-class women other than author but also the beginning of her serious schooling as a reader, for what enabled her now to earn a living solely from writing was reviewing books for the *Analytic Review*—a process that resulted in remarkable on-the-job training. By 1791 she was already "well-read in English theology, moral philosophy and *belles lettres*" and moderately familiar with the "major continental philosophes, particularly Rousseau."[22] This means that one way of understanding the "consistency" of her early writings on girls with subsequent writings is that the premium they place on independent thinking necessitates the changes, even contradictions, to follow. Circumstances pointed Wollstonecraft's train of thinking in a particular direction—how to better educate girls for the world—and thoughts on the topic took her from advocating thinking for girls even as they are being groomed for marriage and proper domesticity to thinking about the number of ways that the entire structure of Western society, especially regarding marriage and childbearing, impedes independent thinking and lives for girls.

My third observation concerns the remarkable success of this process as manifested not only in Wollstonecraft's own development but also in her female progeny. Later we will explore this unfolding in her most famous daughter, but here I allude to its effects on generations of feminist readers and, especially, on her first "daughter," whose series of names already (fore)tells the story: Margaret King, Lady Mountcashell, Mrs. Mason. No name evokes the performative nature of Wollstonecraft's textual and pedagogical strategies more powerfully than "Mrs. Mason," the name given to Wollstonecraft's best-known fictional pedagogue and surrogate self, whom Margaret King subsequently adopts in order to pursue new careers in loving and writing. And no other name signifies more clearly the complicated legacy that these writings bestow, especially for girls seeking freer ways of loving and living.

Those familiar with the early phase of Wollstonecraft's writings are well versed in the details of this story. Wollstonecraft's favorite charge while she was governess for the Viscount Kingsborough family was fourteen-year-old Margaret King, who later adopted the name Mrs. Mason from *Original Stories from Real Life*, a text that is based largely on Wollstonecraft's experiences working for this family. She assumed it in the process of leaving her husband Stephen, Second Earl Mountcashell, thereby renouncing her status as countess as well as her claims to her seven children by him, to live on the Continent with her lover, George Tighe, in 1807. Under this name she also wrote and published several books for children for Godwin's Juvenile Library, one of which, her *Stories of Old Daniel*, was one of the Library's biggest successes, followed by *Continuation of the Stories of Old Daniel*. Then, in 1820, Mrs. Mason re-entered the picture by befriending the grieving Mary Wollstonecraft Shelley, encouraging her to begin writing stories for children, one of which Shelley wrote for Mrs. Mason's eldest daughter (by Tighe), Laurette.

Even in its barest outline, this narrative highlights the highly performative effects of Wollstonecraft's writings and tendency that, according to Cora Kaplan and Sonia Hofkosh, are still being enacted today.[23] Wollstonecraft's first good reader, Margaret as Mrs. Mason in effect heeded the call voiced in *Wrongs of Woman* (also apparent in *Rights of Woman*) to follow the law of her heart rather than debase herself through a legal but "immoral" alliance that kept her enslaved to childbearing and aristocratic fashion, one fruit of which daring was then to make a living as a writer. In this choice, Margaret / Mrs. Mason expressed her allegiance to the surrogate mother-author who "impressed her deeply" as a girl (so deeply, apparently, that Wollstonecraft was soon fired by a jealous biological mother) and whose "mind appeared more noble & her understanding more cultivated than any others I had known."[24] But those who rehearse this history seldom pause over the irony of Margaret assuming that name as the presiding spirit over her mental and sexual emancipation. Mrs. Mason has long been deemed tyrannical, overbearing, even sadistic, in her censorious dealings with her two female charges and the book seen as having "a strong claim to be the most sinister, ugly, overbearing book for children ever published."[25] Of course, one could read adoption of the name as merely signifying Margaret King's lasting affection for the person who preserved in print their early association together under the fictional names Mrs. Mason (Wollstonecraft) and fourteen-year-old Mary (Margaret, also age fourteen). But it could also mean honoring the person who instilled in her the seeds of thinking that blossomed into full sexual and intellectual knowing—in which case, we could say that Mrs. Mason successfully read the tendency of Wollstonecraft's "Mrs. Mason," meaning both the textual (Mrs. Mason in *Original Stories from Real Life*) and authorial (Wollstonecraft's pedagogical voice in all of her writings) embodiments of her.[26] Affirming this in turn uncovers what I would argue is the most intellectually emancipatory aspect of these early writings. They teach young girls not only how to think but also how to recognize that fiction composes a sizable portion of reality, especially pertaining to love and sex.

Myers' and Gary Kelly's explications of Wollstonecraft's early brand of rationalism in writing for children, combined with Barbara Taylor's delineation of Wollstonecraft's feminist imagination, show the extent to which Richardson is right in suggesting that rationalists and fantasists are not that far apart in their views of, or designs on, the minds of children. Wollstonecraft stresses the interaction between reason and fancy/imagination several times in these texts. *Thoughts on the Education of Daughters* puts it baldly in stating that "reason strikes most forcibly when illustrated by the brilliancy of fancy" (20), and the introduction to *The Female Reader*, a compendium of selections devoted to the education of girls, gives a developmental account of when and why this is so. Given that "reasoning" is "tedious and irksome to those whose passions have never led them to reason," teaching by example rather than precept is a more effective way to impress the mind. Therefore, *The Female Reader* follows "the simple order of nature" in selecting "tales and tables" that are "addressed to the imagination" rather than reason because the former "tend to awaken the affections and fix good habits more firmly in the mind than cold arguments and mere declamation."[27]

From the start of her writing career (as we saw in chapter 4), Wollstonecraft emphasized the role of fancy in activating a child's rational powers and highlighted the efficacy of story in educating and disciplining young minds. Reconsidering "The Cave of Fancy" in the context of these early writings for girls highlights Wollstonecraft's insistence on the rational(ist) dimensions of fancy/imagination. By this she means several things: (1) fancy/imagination and its products (story, daydream, fantasy) activate thought; (2) fancy and imagination are the faculties associated with futurity, both the power to envision it and the means through which to make a better future; (3) they are especially crucial as the means through which to realize better futures for the female sex, because writing fiction is one of the few avenues of social influence open to women, and because (4) understanding the operations of fancy is key to making more reasonable choices in love. These early texts are usually more dogmatic and moralistic in making these assertions than subsequent writings, but, oddly, that didacticism manifests a greater degree of optimism regarding the realization of such assertions than her later, less preachy writings.[28]

The optimism is telling because Wollstonecraft states explicitly that present times are not at all favorable to educating children properly. Even granting more humane theories regarding a child's original disposition and thus possibilities, cultivating a child's reason is hindered by the deplorable mental states of most of the adults responsible for shaping the minds of children. "To be able to follow Mr Locke's system (and this may be said of almost all treatises on education) the parents must have subdued their own passions, which is not often the case in any considerable degree. The marriage state is too often a state of discord; it does not always happen that both parents are rational, and the weakest have it in their power to do most mischief" (*Daughters,* 9). As the preface to *Original Stories from Real Life* puts it: "These conversations and tales are accommodated to the present state of society; which obliges the author to attempt to cure those faults by reason, which ought never to have taken root in the infant mind. Good habits, imperceptibly fixed, are far preferable to the precepts of reason; but, as this task requires more judgment than generally falls to the lot of parents, substitutes must be sought for, and medicines given, when regimen would have answered the purpose much better" (359). Given that the minds of both children and adults are infantile, education has to occur on two fronts at once.[29] And since young minds are more ductile, less set in their ways than those of adults occupied by "their own passions" and "fastidious pleasures," educators have no choice but to "pour premature knowledge into the succeeding [generation]; and, teaching virtue, explain the nature of vice. Cruel necessity" (359).[30] At the same time and in the process, those mothers who bother to read children's books to their children acquire a remedial education through imbibing the monitory strictures of the truly adult, usually female, narrator, which explains why the "sentiments" uttered are not always "quite on a level with the capacity of a child" (360). In this case, the adult instructor has to spell out the lesson for adult pupils reading it before they can explain the conclusion properly to the (so-called) child.

This double instruction affects the content of these texts and their efforts to find a happy medium between example and precept, imagination and reason, in several ways. All of them advocate early childhood reading and writing as the best activities for stimulating, cultivating, and expanding the mind. "Reading is the most rational employment, if people seek food for the understanding and do not read merely to remember words. Judicious books enlarge the mind and improve the heart" (*Daughters*, 20). "In reading, the heart is touched, till its feelings are examined by the understanding, and the ripenings of reason regulate the imagination" (*Original Stories*, 415). In fact, they promote the activity of reading as itself requiring and therefore modeling the balance of faculties that its content also advises. For this reason among others, books for children are indispensable to the current times in counteracting the kinds of live examples that children are likely to encounter and internalize in their immediate surroundings, where fathers tend to be elsewhere and mothers self-absorbed. "The Cave of Fancy" embodies this trend by having the sage Sagestus employ as the "best method of educating" the orphaned Sagesta her listening to the life story of a female spirit and thus by having the "live" model be someone who is dead. It also makes clear that good stories are preferable to bad mothers in raising a young child. "On observing" the features of Sagesta's dead mother "more closely, [Sagestus] discovered that her natural delicacy had been increased by an improper education, to a degree that took away all vigour from her faculties. . . . He was now convinced that the orphan was not very unfortunate in having lost such a mother" ("Cave," 197, 198). Especially damning is his deduction that the mother is a poor reader, who weeps over "fictitious, unnatural distress" but ignores "real misery" (197).

Original Stories from Real Life extends the trend, first, by portraying the proper instructor of the two young girls as not their mother but a friend, Mrs. Mason, whose chief means of instruction involves telling stories or providing live examples from which the girls are to draw their own conclusions and, secondly, by having Mrs. Mason present as her parting gift to the girls a book "in which I have written the subjects that we have discussed." Both in transcribing for the record their recent live experiences and advising the girls to "recur frequently to" this book, Mrs. Mason suggests the substitutability of teacher and book, life and story, and, more importantly, affirms the palpable personality that resides in stories. "For the stories illustrating the instruction it contains, you will not feel in such a great degree the want of my personal advice. Some of the reasoning you may not thoroughly comprehend, but, as your understandings ripen, you will feel its full force" (*Original Stories,* 449). This explanation alters the distinction, and the impulse underlying the distinction, between rational stories and fairy tales. In educating girls, Wollstonecraft advocates the narration of "stories" over "improbable tales" in order to retain the accent on fancy/imagination and make story approximate real life, which, in turn, will help real life to become more reasonable and a more satisfying story once there are more female *adults* who have life stories that are being told and heard (*Daughters,* 10). For, judging from "The Cave of Fancy," girls need to hear the life stories of *female* spirits for a change, the hearing of which father-figures should facilitate by not conjuring up more male spirits to instruct them.

Granted, these Mentorias draw fairly restrictive and submissive moral lessons from their life stories.[31] The female spirit in "The Cave of Fancy" tells Sagesta to "listen to my warning voice, and trust not too much to the goodness which I perceive resides in thy breast. Let it be reined in by principles, lest thy very virtue sharpen the sting of remorse," principles that Mrs. Mason then obligingly spells out: "Avoid anger; exercise compassion; and love truth. Recollect, that from religion your chief comfort must spring, and never neglect the duty of prayer. Learn from experience" to trust "the wisest and best of Beings" with the "issues, not only of this life, but of that which is to come" ("Cave," 199, *Original Stories,* 449). But the process through which the moralizing Mrs. Mason of *Original Stories from Real Life* turns into the real-life author and lover, Mrs. Mason, is embodied in the method that at once underlines and undermines the content of Wollstonecraft's next publication for girls, *The Female Reader: Miscellaneous Pieces, in Prose and Verse: Selected from the Best Writers, and Disposed under Proper Heads; for the Improvement of Young Women* (1789). Explicitly patterned on William Enfield's *The Speaker* (1774), the first anthology designed for elocution practice that employs a "methodical order in the arrangement of the pieces" rather than being a random miscellany, *The Female Reader* similarly aims to "impress habits of order on the expanding mind" through arranging its material under proper headings.[32] "By this means the surest foundation of virtue is settled without a struggle, and strong restraints knit together before vice has introduced confusion" (55). Its contents build on this sure foundation by inculcating piety, devotion to God, a retiring presence, and inner beauty as true requisites of an educated female, who then is deemed well equipped to encounter vice.

But the short title, *The Female Reader*, also tells a more dynamic story, whereby method starts to undermine content. Accent on the "female" reader underscores the gender and class entitlement of Enfield's ostensibly generic "speaker," who is actually a "gentleman scholar" at one of the "English Dissenting academies." Accent on the female "reader" introduces the ambiguity between reader as thing, book, and container of content and reader as agent, imbiber, and interpreter of it. Compared to *The Speaker*, *The Female Reader*, even as agent, not object, advocates training in more retiring and self-effacing prospects than public speaking, as its selections specify. By and large, they train the female reader to acquire proper femininity, though with a marked emphasis on cultivation of mind. But selections relating to mental cultivation, coupled with the process and definitions of a Wollstonecraftian "reader," show how this female reader grants girl readers the tools to analyze and question the content that informs either category. At once book and person, container and agent, *The Female Reader*, by teaching logical thinking, allows the female reader (and its compiler) to expand the content, rigor, and independence of her mind (a process that Wollstonecraft makes central to chapter 6 of *Rights of Woman*). Indeed, precisely through becoming an avid reader, in which case she is not "entirely dependent on the senses for employment and amusement" or on habit for guides to virtuous behavior, the female reader learns to question the nature and content of the "virtue" that she is being schooled to attain.[33] Defined by Mrs. Mason as a term coming "from a word signifying strength," she states that the "basis of every virtue" is "fortitude of mind," and "virtue belongs to a being, that is weak in its nature, and strong only in will and resolution" (*Original Stories*, 437). If this is so, questions arise as to how virtue can be divisible into specific gendered components and then to why female virtue so often revolves solely around a woman's sexual conduct. More to the point, if female readers take this definition seriously, how can they take seriously the views on gender articulated in the book from which Mrs. Mason is quoting, Rousseau's *Émile,* whose express purpose is to define women as subordinate to men and desirable precisely in their mindlessness and ignorance of their own desires? *The Female Reader,* then, marks a decisive shift in Wollstonecraft's thoughts on the education of daughters. She has moved from thinking primarily about how to inculcate virtue in girls—whether through story or precept, imagination or reason, book or person—to thinking about why virtue as defined for girls is so hostile to their bodies and minds.

The consequences of becoming this kind of female reader in Wollstonecraft's life/writings are not to be underestimated. Within a mere two years, her reading led her to level a systematic critique of the misogyny that underlay virtually every aspect of female socialization and to rally women to assert their rights to write their dreams and realities. Subsequent reading motivated further revisions to her initial fictional as well as nonfictional writings. *Mary, a Fiction* (1788) already expressed her commitment to a new form of female inscription that features "a woman who has thinking powers."[34] Andrew Elfenbein claims that this fiction is unprecedented in portraying a female genius in a sympathetic light, and Wollstonecraft herself advertises her method: fictional realities create new possibilities for real life.[35] But she does not rest with this portrayal. Wollstonecraft's subsequent texts—*A Short Residence* (1796) and *The Wrongs of Woman; or, Maria* (1798)—elaborate the process and consequences of the ongoing education of *Mary* as female reader and writer (one reason for the continued choice of variants of the name *Mary* and the metafictional emphasis on writing: these are books that stage the writing of "Mary"). As we explored in Part One, one result of that education as female reader is diminished confidence in the will of male powers to alter social inequality, which also means diminished confidence in the will, and ultimately the existence, of God. But this diminished confidence in men entails a heightened effort to educate girls and to start the process at an earlier age. Once directed at "infant minds" embodied in girls aged twelve to fourteen (and their mothers), instruction in her later texts addresses daughters who are not yet two (Fanny, in *A Short Residence)* or only a few months old (the baby to whom Maria's memoirs are addressed in *Wrongs of Woman*). The posthumous "Lessons" speaks at once to a four-year-old daughter and a "stranger" still in the womb.[36]

These girls who are scripted as female readers-in-the-making display the desired attributes of potential women of virtue. The only fictional aspect in *Wrongs of Woman*, which is otherwise a fairly daunting depiction of the grim realities of women's existence, is that Maria's baby is depicted as in a position to acquire its earliest lessons from example, not precept, because her mother, unlike all the real mothers pursuing their passions and pleasures, is a true model of virtue—that is, in a position if the baby had lived and Maria had not been confined to a madhouse. No Mrs. Mason in dicta—indeed, her only dictum is that her life story educe, not influence, her daughter's mind—Maria Venables models a life that is open to experience and open to reflecting on and learning from experience, a life that seeks to be independent of law, convention, or orthodoxy of any kind. From such a model, this baby would be able to imbibe, even before she acquired language or reading skills, that a mother's quest for autonomy neither makes her unattractive nor necessarily isolated and that thinking can be a passionate, even voluptuous, activity that leads to more satisfying sexual activity. Moreover, cultivation of the interior does not mean total disregard for the exterior any more than it mandates "plain" as the only style. Cultivation simply begins with and from the mind and, by so doing, enhances by rendering less insipid one's carriage and visage.[37]

Once such a child is old enough to read, new benefits follow. As the early texts spell out, the main advantage of early reading, or intellectual accomplishments generally, is the help they give in gaining some distance on empirical reality. This means not only that a child goes beyond sense and sensual experience but also that she is not dependent on her immediate environs—her sense experiences—for information, models, or guides. Reading provides the necessary mentorship by granting a child independence from the contingencies of her social and physical surroundings. Moreover, once the judgment has been formed, there is no need to censor books, for "every thing will then instruct" (*Original Stories*, 415). This independence is strengthened by Wollstonecraft's stipulations regarding writing at an early age in *Thoughts on the Education of Daughters*. "Children should be led into correspondences, and methods adopted to make them write down their sentiments, and they should be prevailed on to relate the stories they have read in their own words" (18). That is, at an early age children should cultivate their own voices by writing down their sentiments, make received texts their own by rewriting them in their own words, and develop their own opinions regarding even the most canonical texts. "I am sick of hearing of the sublimity of Milton, the elegance and harmony of Pope, and the original, untaught genius of Shakespear. These cursory remarks are made by some who know nothing of nature, and could not enter into the spirit of those authors, or understand them" (*Daughters*, 21).

The process through which girls transform book knowledge into their own experience through a combination of reading and rewriting is the chief insight of the female reader—and the chief method of producing one. Literally, the process involves incorporation, internalization, and inscription whereby a young person is in/formed and fleshed out by her reading. From the start of her authorship and girl-re/production, Wollstonecraft makes little distinction between a "life" and a "story." As the title and method of *Original Stories from Real Life* display, story is the favored means of preparing a child for real life. At the same time, that child is being taught to perceive her life as a story, as something she can narrate, revise, and expect to have heard—even as something original, as something without precedent. This slippage between life and story also accounts for the similarities that characterize the protagonists of these early writings, which feature a fictional Mary, a fictional factual Mrs. Mason, a fictional beyond-this-life female spirit, and a real-life Mary Wollstonecraft, all of whom not only showcase their thinking powers but also anchor those powers in a female character that connects fancy to melancholy to benevolence and hope in God. Understanding the point of this merger helps to account for a standard criticism of Wollstonecraft's fiction—that it is too didactic, too unimaginative, too clear in its designs on the reader, too much like a conduct manual. For her, the goal is different: to underscore the role of fiction and of what we now call psychic reality in real life.

The goal works in both directions. The material for good fiction is women's lives, their daily extraordinary experiences, their dreams and thoughts, because these are the stories that have not been told as literature. Reading them helps shape real lives and better futures, in the sense that young people will have more kinds of material on which to feed, through which to grow. Wollstonecraft's fiction, then, eschews the fantastic, the supernatural, and the improbable because its fancy is trained on futurity. Her fiction adopts the mode of a thought experiment: What do women with thinking powers need in order to love and live more happily? Increasing insight into the intractability of social conditions forces her in her late fiction both to critique major social institutions and to address girls at ever-younger ages. One of the texts that she left unfinished at her death is a reading primer, "Lessons," that teaches the very young not only how to read but how to have a new relation to language. Sonia Hofkosh convincingly depicts "Lessons" as feminist epistemology, teaching children how to read and think in a relational context and teaching them that reading and thinking are fluid processes.[38] Body is not divorced from mind, or girls from boys, on the score of enhancing either, and knowledge is mastered through learning that it is a provisional, and at times painful, never-ending process. The same goes for family life and relations: father is ill, mother needs quiet, baby is on its way. No one is alone; no one's experience belongs only to her; language speaks us, we speak it, and, in so doing, sometimes create new realities. As Hofkosh notes, "woman" is missing from the series of words in which she should appear: "Man. Boy. Girl. Child"("Lessons," 468). But the seeds are planted in the "boy girl child" out of which that new creature will emerge.

Mentor Godwin

> By these different publications it is evident that there is an inten-
> tion to have every work published for the Juvenile Library that can
> be required in the early instruction of children, and thus by degrees
> to give an opportunity for every principle professed by the infidels
> and republicans of these days to be introduced to their notice.
>
> A report by an anonymous government spy to the Home Office, 1813

Scholars have long recognized Godwin's deep investment in education, his extensive efforts to mentor boys, and his writings on how best to activate, shape, and inform minds.[39] Many acknowledge his twenty-year involvement with the Juvenile Library and the M. J. Godwin Bookstore, which specialized in children's books, and several recognize the number of books that he himself wrote for children as well as others that he commissioned or published by associates and friends—the most famous being Charles and Mary Lamb's *Tales from Shakespeare* and M. J. Godwin's translation, *Swiss Family Robinson*. Still, this branch of Godwin's life/writings is understudied and vastly under-appreciated for reasons that go beyond the usual prejudices against children's literature or that pertain to prejudices regarding Godwin's treatment of "family," the "second Mrs. Godwin," and family business ventures.[40] Gender bias, too, motivates harsh assessments of a career move that is usually viewed as signaling (1) a decline in his reputation, judgment, and radical commitments; (2) a selling-out to the commercial aspects of intellectual work; (3) a knuckling under to his "philistine" and "money-grubbing" (second) wife; and (4) motivated by the need to feed an expanding family.[41] Reviewing this material from a less-biased position suggests how essential the Juvenile Library and bookstore were to Godwin's efforts to "feed" his progeny—"his" understood as an affiliation of mind, not blood, and "feed" as encompassing mental nourishment. Reading the books that he composed for children shows his truly groundbreaking efforts to rewrite history. For him, the future depended on revising not only what counts as history but also traditional accounts of British and world history, and doing this was instrumental to forming new subjects who embody more creative approaches to re-creating their worlds.

The Juvenile Library, which, after all, spanned the period 1805–25, was an integral phase of Godwin's ongoing critique of family and his effort to perfect society through recomposing the next generation. It published and disseminated to a wider audience the instruction that Godwin was well known for providing to various protégés while trying to make a living that benefited himself, his marriage, his family, and his friends. Moreover, Mary Jane Godwin had impressive credentials for proposing this business venture, owing to her editorial work at Benjamin Tabart, a publisher of children's books, before she married Godwin—a firm with a reputation for addressing the imaginative side of children.[42] Surely some of the venom directed at her role in this career shift stems from not wanting to envision Godwin pairing up with another woman writing partner, not wanting to perceive "Mrs. Godwin" as an adequate replacement of Wollstonecraft on this score. Similarly, Godwin's enlistment of friends in his publishing venture, whether as financial or authorial contributors, is of a piece with his reformulations of family and can even be viewed as a less tangible, but no less sociable, phase of the Dissenting dinner parties of the previous decade. Perhaps it is also an effort to get some of those minds back on the same page through getting a whole generation of new minds thinking along the same lines.

In any case, Godwin's own writings for the Juvenile Library—in all, some dozen books published under two pseudonyms—deserve critical attention for their efforts to implement many of his most innovative ideas from scratch. As is true of Wollstonecraft's, these texts for children are some of his most popular, and most frequently reprinted texts, several of which were classroom standards for decades.[43] *Bible Stories* (William Scofield, 1802), his first work for children that predates institution of the Juvenile Library, was a commercial success, with a new edition issued the following year, at least two pirated editions in the United States, and was still listed as in print in 1831. His three works of history, of England, Rome, and Greece (pseud. Edward Baldwin, 1806, 1809, 1822) were adopted for the curriculum of a number of schools, including Charterhouse and Christ's Hospital, and were reprinted many times. So were *Fables, Ancient and Modern, The Pantheon,* and his *Outlines of English Grammar,* the last two being very influential classroom textbooks, *The Pantheon* already in its fourth edition by 1814. As William St. Clair sums up the matter: if "numbers of readers are a measure of influence, Edward Baldwin did more to promote human progress than William Godwin."[44]

What characterizes Godwin's writings for children is a no-nonsense emphasis on first things first. Prefaces to these works criticize prior children's books for misunderstanding how children learn and what they need to know in order to develop into thinking individuals. The ensuing text revises what has counted as knowledge or truth regarding scriptural, classical, and British history. This re/visionary principle is nowhere more evident than in his *Bible Stories,* otherwise in danger of being perceived as a blatant marketing strategy to curry favor with the "socioreligious" reformers who are cornering and policing the market (via Sarah Trimmer's *Guardian of Education,* a soberminded review of children's books) or as a highly motivated self-refashioning to ensure that "William Scofield" adequately cover over the atheism and radicalism of "William Godwin."[45] But that would be to ignore even the full title, *Bible Stories: Memorable Acts of the Ancient Patriarchs, Judges, and Kings: extracted from their Original Historians. For the Use of Children,* and certainly the principles motivating Godwin's compilation, which he articulated in a preface that, some twenty-six years later, he asked to have reprinted in his collected works, a "privilege he did not seek for any of his lesser writings" and that is now fulfilled through its inclusion in the seven-volume *Political and Philosophical Works of Godwin.*[46] Three principles underlie this compilation (and, indeed, all his subsequent histories) "for the use of children":

1. Interest their imaginations by avoiding dry abstractions;
2. Instill a perception of the cultural relativism of history and thus the ongoing relevance of both fabular and factual, ancient and modern histories;
3. Infuse these stories into the very fiber of children's beings so that they will desire to emulate illustrious or world-changing personages. In the process work to revise what constitutes change, world, or progress.

No wonder Trimmer deemed the book "an engine of mischief," despite the pseudonym.[47] Though Godwin's authorship was never discovered in his lifetime, "new philosophy" was readily discernible in and at the book's very foundations.

Of the three principles, the one stressing the centrality of imagination is most familiar to scholars of children's literature and least familiar to scholars of Godwin. Yet the preface to *Bible Stories* begins with an uncharacteristically blunt assertion that the "most essential branch of human nature" is the "imagination," the very faculty that children's authors have totally "left out of their system" over the "past twenty years" (313). Indeed, Godwin's method as well as content rivals the beginning of Percy Shelley's *Defence of Poetry* in defining imagination as "the ground-plot upon which the edifice of a sound morality must be erected," the "characteristic of man," as contrasted to the "dexterities of logic or of mathematical deduction" that compose "a well-regulated machine" and that produce youth who "can explain the process in manufacturing a carpet" or "from what part of the globe you receive every article of your furniture" but know nothing about the essential things of life, which "open the heart," "insensibly initiate the learner in the relations and generous offices of society, and enable him to put himself in imagination into the place of his neighbour, to feel his feelings, and to wish his wishes" (313, 314, 313).[48] A corollary of this distinction stresses the proximity of (what Godwin considers true) history to romance. Whereas the good "old books describ[e] the real tempers and passions of human beings" often set in "supernatural and impossible" scenes, "modern books" abound in "real scenes, but impossible personages," persons "so sober, so demure, and so rational, that no genuine interest can be felt for their adventures" (313). Like the texts produced by modern historians for an adult readership, modern children's books are "dry," "repulsive," and loaded with "abstract and general propositions" that force the life out of history, the past, and its readers.

This corollary also introduces one aspect of the second principle regarding cultural relativism stipulated in the preface. Godwin's commitment to revising the discipline of history so that it achieves a more perfectible society means viewing the Bible as a specific people's history and fabular history generally as part of the world's historical reality. This becomes clear in his comments justifying his substitution of the "more literal" word *Jehovah* for the English translation *Lord*, which is the only exception he makes to otherwise employing the "exact phraseology which distinguishes our translation of the bible" (315). Using *Jehovah* rather than *Lord* "put[s] it in the power of parents or instructors" to emphasize the historical and relativist status of the Bible, since they can explain it as "the individual designation of the God of the Jews," no different in this regard from "the Gods of the Greeks in Homer, or the Gods of the Latins in Ovid" and, moreover, as the "competitor and adversary of the

Gods of the surrounding nations." This leaves scholars free to understand by Jehovah "nothing more" than "that general idea of invisible agents and superior natures" visible in virtually all cultural belief structures, whereas Christian parents, already worried for their children's "eternal welfare," can "expound the term Jehovah by the purest and most spiritualised definition of a first cause," that has chosen this "awful and incommunicable name" through which to make itself known (316–17). A truly striking reworking of the foundation of British culture, identity, and history, Godwin's first foray into children's literature portrays the God of Judeo-Christian scripture as one among several competing first causes.

The motivation underlying this reworking explains several similarities among the two sets of text authored by Edward Baldwin, one set including the *Fables, Ancient and Modern* (1805) and *The Pantheon; or, History of the Gods of Greece and Rome* (1806), and the other including more conventionally understood histories, *The History of England* (1806), *The History of Rome from the Building of the City to the Rise of the Republic* (1809), and *The History of Greece* (1822).[49] Both sets constitute history in Godwin's understanding of the discipline and, even more importantly, both instruct the "rising generation" in fundamentals of Britain's various prehistories—fabular, scriptural, and classical. The chronology of Godwin's composition bears out this logic, whereby *The History of England* comes after composition of *Bible Stories, Fables, Ancient and Modern*, and *The Pantheon* and depends upon them. The relativism, both cultural and rational, that is fundamental to the truth of Godwin's historical method is emphasized in the preface to *History of England*, where he explains the chief values of the various tables appended to the work (the first three concerning religions, heathen gods, and states, nations, or races of men). One value is to aid the memory, but the second is to "convey to the inexperienced reader a vivid feeling, that there are other countries besides England, and other histories worthy to be read" (vi). Relativism on the score of fact is explained in *Fables, Ancient and Modern*. "It is not always necessary that a story should be true." What is necessary is to eschew deliberate deception (11). Equally necessary is explaining in logical fashion what children need to know first before they can proceed to further understanding. Mindful that this book is "the first, or nearly the first, book offered to the child's attention," Godwin's *Fables* patiently unfolds the initial context or final conclusion of each fable, normally treated too "abruptly" by prior narrators, and forges connections between the world of the fable and the contemporary world.[50]

The former strategy "benefit[s] a child" in acquiring "clear and distinct ideas" of the objects and concepts being presented (iv–v). Making these things "visible to the fancy of the learner" in turn secures knowledge of "the most familiar points of natural history"—for example, how bees build their hives, why foxes are cunning, how to drink with a tongue or a beak, the mechanics of hunting, the worth in British pounds of a golden egg—without the child "being subjected to the discouraging arrangements of a book of science."[51] The second strategy helps to instill a historicist perspective toward the world and its fables. "You have heard of Rome, a fine old city," whose consuls once "governed the world, that is, as much of the world as they knew almost anything about, for America and Botany-Bay had never been heard of" (57). "We are animals of the same class, only with a little difference in our education," says the wolf to the dog, who then replies, "so I understand . . . Dr. Mavor [to] observ[e] in his Natural History" (141–42; also 111, 188). Taken together, the method of this first of books works to ensure that young minds learn how various things in the world work and, equally importantly, learn to enjoy learning. Appealing to a child's fancy through "prattle" and vivid explication, such works cultivate a child's affection and therefore his or her mind.[52]

Underscoring its status as a *History of the Gods of Greece*, *The Pantheon* intensifies these strategies by linking a historicist perspective to the question of first causes. In this regard, it joins *Bible Stories* in valuing ancient stories about a people's gods but without suggesting that the truth of history reveals the Judeo-Christian God to be the one and only true God. The preface equivocates to some degree on the status of Christianity, affirming that the current author does not "fear that his pupil might prefer the religion of Jupiter to the religion of Christ," apparently unlike the author of Tooke's *Pantheon*, who indulges in expressions of "rancour" and "elaborate calumny upon the Gods of the Greeks" and which Godwin/Baldwin's *Pantheon* is trying to supplant (*Pantheon*, v–vi). Indeed, the current author claims that it appears "something like blasphemy" to harbor suspicions on that score. Nonetheless, the "duty" that he performs in favor of the Greeks entails making some striking claims regarding not only the centrality of fancy and imagination to awakening a religious sensibility but also the historical continuity among religion, mythology, and poetry. The arguably secular claim that one of the two chief aims of this *Pantheon* is to present "Mythology as the introduction and handmaid to the study of Poetry" and thus to equip youth with the necessary background to "understand the system of the poets of former times" attains a religious connotation when it characterizes the productions of Homer, Horace, and Virgil as "immortal" immediately after characterizing the "religion of Christ" as one in which "life and immortality are brought to life" (vi). This linkage and implicit chronology are made explicit in *The History of England*, when it draws equivalences among "Bramins, Druids, Greeks, Saracens, Minstrels, Monks," and the "modern revivers of literature." In a manner that we again generally associate with Percy Shelley, Godwin's history books for children establish a genealogy that goes from gods to the Judeo-Christian god to poets.

Essential to understanding the Greek pantheon, Godwin writes, and thus the mode of thought that existed in that period and culture, is allegory and an approach to theogony that is "partly historical" (*Pantheon*, 9, 12). The "beauty" of Greek life and culture resides in its total absence of abstraction, its habit of "personifying" ideas and animating "all existence" such that a person "could not walk in the fields," "sit by his hearth," enter into marriage or death without feeling himself in the presence of animate spirits (3, 8). As a system of religion, the value of the Greek pantheon is the commerce it recognizes between gods and men, not just in the sense that the spirit world suffuses the life of humans but also in that a people's gods are "persons who once were men, and who, being regarded as the benefactors of mankind, were worshipped as Gods after their death" (13). Again, while Godwin/Baldwin concedes that the Greek religion, for precisely these reasons, has "perished and gone away for ever" and been replaced by a religion "of the sublimest wisdom" and "most elevated morality," two assertions suggest that comprehension of the Greek pantheon is of far more than antiquarian interest. First, "men are but children of a larger growth" who "never entirely lose the qualities that distinguish them in early life," chief among which is "this love" of having things, ideas, concepts "actually presented before them" (7). Therefore, although the Christian religion is arguably higher or truer because of its sublimity, unity, and antimateriality, it is less effective at (possibly, incapable of) moving the "passions and feelings" of humans (7). Second, understanding this history acquaints young minds with precisely the features that Godwin considers essential to history-writing and the capacity of historical (and a historicist) understanding to improve the world's material conditions. Whether conceived as religion, mythology, history, or poetry, familiarity with the Greek gods is conducive to the aliveness of a people's mental life, spiritual life, and capacity to perceive everything in the world as vital. In this regard, knowledge of the Greek pantheon not only aids in comprehending the mythological allusions of poetry but also ensures that ordinary people perceive the world through a poet's or a child's eyes—seeing absent things as if they were present and as if for the first time.

Such concerns with shaping early on how a child acquires knowledge, how s/he learns to learn and with what attitude, underlies the third principle articulated in the preface to *Bible Stories*, which is discernible in all Godwin's historical writings for children. The goal is to instill not simply knowledge but also love for knowledge into the child's very fiber of being so that s/he learns to desire ever-new, deeper, and more complex material on which to feed. These texts for children are careful to delineate the age, and thus the presumable mental condition, of the child they are addressing, with *Bible Stories* being for very young children, Baldwin's *Fables* for children ages three to eight, and *Outline of English History* also for children aged three to eight—in other words, texts that the author conceives as some of the very first that a child will encounter and thus fundamental to forming his or her attitude toward the world and toward learning.[53] Of particular interest is Godwin's attention to the unconscious dimensions of knowledge acquisition, his efforts to make inquiry or study a passion as well as a habit. Indeed, the chief aim of his selection of material for children is to have these early stories, images, and even phrases become such a part of a child's experience and memory that they continue to influence his or her development in later years. Attaining this unconscious component is diametrically opposed to the learning by rote that makes a child into a "monkey" or an automaton and against which so many romantic writers railed; rather than have a child parrot back facts that are beyond his com-prehension, Godwin advocates imbibing lively and powerful stories of interest-ing personages told in simple, straightforward language. This is the generic advantage of fables and the chief advantage of his compilation of Bible stories; in "seiz[ing]" the "youthful imagination" by excluding all "those accidental appendages" that are "too minute or too general, too dry or too elevated," the reader, when of an age to enter into more subtle disquisitions regarding the "mysteries of religion" or natural science, will already find himself at home with the basic material: "with the grand incidents and outlines of this story I am already acquainted."[54] For this reason, too, these stories should be re-counted in the "exact phraseology which distinguishes our translation of the bible," so that even the rhythms, cadences, and phrases become part of our unconscious heritage, are capable, upon rehearing, of evoking powerful recol-lections of our former selves, and, in the current age, work to reform or counteract the dryness, abstraction, and deadness that has been "in fashion" in literature for children "for the last hundred years."[55]

Viewed in this light, Godwin's writings for children are a truly impressive revision of the fundamentals of British culture and are deeply interconnected with his adult writings on the reform of history. It is as if he literally worked to remake history in his writings for children by re/forming the materials—the human beings—out of which subsequent history would be made. His advocacy of biblical stories recognizes the process and methods of acculturation—how a person and a people get certain texts into their blood—while at the same time providing an account of Holy Scripture as historically relative and in a textual continuum that encompasses religion, mythology, fable, and modern literature. His approach to educing children's minds stresses the pre-eminence of imagination over rational and rationalist activity in forming perfectible beings. "Without imagination we may have a certain cold and arid circle of principles," but "we can neither ourselves love, nor be fitted to excite the love of others." This pre-eminence has consequences for pedagogical practice, which will necessarily go "amiss" if instructors "assign the first place to that [the intellectual faculty] which is only entitled to the second."[56] One major value of attending to Godwin's writings on childhood education is the way that they reorder the conventional account of Godwin's priorities: at this stage, imagination over reason, ancient over modern, personified over abstract, infancy over progress.[57] Indeed, there is an instructive congruence between *The Pantheon* and the *Essay on Sepulchres,* both of 1809, in the way that each text deifies the illustrious dead. While the Greek system calls these former heroes gods and modern secularism calls them poets, artists, or writers, each is portrayed as the truest animator of life in that culture and the essential source for new or better lives for the living.

Godwin's texts for older youth, essays on education, and letters of advice to young men flesh out the skeletal structure that his texts for children form. These texts convey the content that he deems crucial to a proper understanding of British and European history and culture, specify the books that are essential to informing a thinking individual, and establish the principles of study that ensure that early lovers of reading develop a passion for scholarship.[58] These materials are more familiar to readers of Godwin, because they are often part of more canonical texts (*The Enquirer*), are established aspects of his biography (his mentorship of young men), and are often indistinguishable from texts and advice written for adult readers.[59] Virtually unknown, however, is another pseudonymous book by Godwin that links his authorship and mentorship of the rising generation and embodies the second branch of his rewriting of history: individual history or biography, through the reading of which young people learn to know and are prompted to emulate the illustrious dead. Entitled *The Looking Glass: A True History of the Early Years of an*

Artist, and written by Theophilus Marcliffe in order to "awaken the Emulation of YOUNG PERSONS of both Sexes, in the Pursuit of every laudable Attainment: particularly in the cultivation of the Fine Arts," this text epitomizes Godwin's efforts to ensure perfectibility in a hands-on, from-the-ground-up fashion by providing a virtual how-to manual of becoming an artist.

"The juvenile autobiography of one of our best artists," William Mulready, which narrates his year-by-year development from infant to young man accepted into the Royal Academy, *The Looking Glass* depicts the process through which an unremarkable infant becomes an estimable person and that most estimable type of person, an artist.[60] Employing the same unabridged technique that, according to Godwin, ensures that history comes alive and proves generative to the discerning reader, *The Looking Glass* is Godwin's most basic and comprehensive statement on how to construct a person of value. The main point of contrast with his novels is that this protagonist is exemplary, not aberrational. The main difference from his *Lives* is that, in having live access to his biographical subject, he had rich information on the subject's early childhood and thus on those first impressions that formed his being and character.[61]

In its opening assertion that "there is no sentiment which better deserves to be cultivated in youthful minds, than emulation," the preface to *The Looking Glass* establishes Godwin's chief pedagogical principle. Learning through emulation follows from the strictures Godwin has already laid out regarding the importance of having strong images and clear impressions in a child's acquisition of knowledge. Yet emulation is not without its dangers. In contrast to Wollstonecraft and other rationalist female pedagogues, Godwin's main worry about "man [being] an imitative animal" is not that young persons can find very few worthy models to emulate (though that is often the case) but rather that imitation does not cultivate independence and that emulation "cannot be purchased but at the price of envy, hatred, and malice" (iv, v). Both objections are met through a mode of living that is open to the shaping influence of history. In the case of man's imitative nature, Godwin not only implicitly distinguishes between imitation and emulation but also envisions personal and historical development as a building on top of what has gone before. "Why were Homer and Virgil great poets" or "Alexander and Caesar consummate generals?" "Because other men, inferior to them in the same arts, had already done somewhat, and made a certain progress" (v).[62] In the case of envy, Godwin identifies "one obvious remedy against the alloy attendant upon emulation: we may learn to emulate the excellence of persons we never saw and of the dead" (vii). This safeguard underscores two other principles that are essential to healthy development: First, worthy models of living are often texts. Second, the "main source" of any person's "success" is "very simple": *"lov[e] the employment and the studies to which [one's] efforts [a]re devoted"* (xii; original emphasis).

The Looking Glass is distinguished from Godwin's other texts for children by showing the outcome of what the previous books had attempted to inculcate. In focusing on the very early years of his artist protagonist, he is able to detail precisely how the mind of a person of merit is formed. In his choice of subject, moreover, he means to be as encouraging as possible to both children and parents, for, as he specifies from the start, "our young man derived no advantage from splendour of connection or from wealth and refinement in either of his parents" (3). He received no special schooling, no guided instruction in art, nor were his circumstances fortunate in any tangible way. But this absence of advantage serves to highlight the minimal conditions of talent that are, in this way, presented as within the grasp of most people: propensity toward a particular skill or activity that, even if it is not carefully cultivated by others, is also not thwarted or impeded by them. To parents, even of meager means, *The Looking Glass* reflects an enabling image: "How much, though in a humble situation, [parents] may do for their children, if they are possessed of a sound judgment and activated with a genuine solicitude for their children's welfare" (48–49). The steps are easy. Show interest; encourage, but do not flatter; accept advice from others who have your child's interests at heart; "nourish the hope" that your child will supersede you (63). The bottom line of good parenting, rendered literal in the case of our artist: be a good model.

For children, preparation is more extensive and is divided into two stages. The first stage, un- or semiconscious in the case of the emerging subject, requires laying the proper foundation through receiving the proper impressions. Whether the propensity toward a particular talent be a natural endowment or an accident "can scarcely be satisfactorily decided in any single instance" (3). But, once there, it is fostered through emulation, here presented in a graduated series of image-makings and replications. The "earliest particular" in the boy's development as artist is "hearing the name of one Corny Gorman," a friend of his father, who greatly admired Gorman's "skill in drawing teapots, dogs, and other matters" and whom his father "emulated" at "a modest distance" by himself sketching chalk scenes of a hunt "on the vacant space of wainscot immediately over the chimney." "This sort of pictorial composition, forcibly seized upon the boy's attention," so much so that, by the age of three, he would "repair" his father's images by rechalking the lines that had become erased or blurred over time. From repair, he moved to reproduction when, at age four, the entire scene was "obliterated" and he "replaced it entirely with the efforts of his own hand" (3–6). At five, he drew his own version of flowers and grapes on the floor and, when the family moved to London six months later, he was able to recognize St. Paul's from his having copied a print of it that was hanging on their wall in Dublin. This is where the account of mental development as an ongoing storage of impressions on which to draw merges with this particular boy's progress as a developing artist. For on the voyage from Dublin to London, the "impressions which these [natural] objects made upon him, continued distinct and vivid in his mind. Up to the age of manhood, he could shut his eye, and conjure up the whole scene as it appeared to him in the passage" (13). In other words, on this journey the boy acquired the material for art and demonstrated the primary qualification of the artist: the capacity to make absent things present, to re-create the scenes, emotions, and impressions of life. Equally important, he developed a passion for art that made his "delight" in every little "discovery" or advance equal to "what Harvey experienced when he discovered the circulation of the blood; or Newton when he first detected and fixed the law of gravitation" (24–25).

Once such foundations have been laid, it is safe, and necessary, to enter a second, more conscious, stage of training, which is distinguished by two different efforts. On the one hand, our artist acquires and desires an interdisciplinary education, whereby he becomes "addicted" to reading, excels at translation, and becomes engrossed by theatrical declamation, Shakespeare, and actors. On the other, he begins "disciplined study" of "the grounds," even the "science," of his art by profiting from drawing masters (first, those of his schoolfellows, then his own) and learning anatomy. To the "diligence" and "ardour" that characterize the emerging artist is added a third trait, which works to ensure that "the season of boy's play" turns into "business for a man": an insatiable desire for challenge (41, 67, 88). The "Alps upon Alps of difficulty" that he encountered in his initial perusals of Walker's Anatomy "rous[e]" "his very soul" (99). The fact that "difficulty, instead of deterring him, always ultimately stimulated him to greater exertion" is "the best symptom which can discover itself in a young mind" (99).

By looking into this *Looking Glass*, then, young persons discover how to enter the world of art, the world as art, and learn that the artistry that composes the world is in their grasp if they follow certain simple steps. As the cover description suggests, this mirror helps young people assess and perfect their self-image. "The Looking-Glass. A Mirror in which every Good Little Boy and Girl may see what He or She is; and those who are not yet Quite Good, may find what They ought to be." As moralizing as this title sounds, readers are unprepared for the ensuing focus on how to become a good *artist*, rather than a "good" boy or girl, and for the affectionate, colloquial tone that is remarkably free of the sadism, goodyness, and all-knowingness of a Mrs. Mason or the original *Goody Two Shoes*, which is dedicated to "All Young Gentlemen and Ladies who are good or intend to be good."[63] Through this *Looking Glass*, Godwin highlights the connection between aesthetics and ethics that will become famous in Percy Shelley's definition of imagination, but he does it by stressing the centrality of unideal images to education in both domains. "Though I think his actions worthy of record and of praise, I do not wish to pass him for a saint, or a faultless creature." Indeed, honesty about his faults is key to encouraging emulation of him. For "if I described my person-age without faults, you would scarcely know him for a being of your own species, and you would scarcely have the courage while you are reading, to say, I will try and do as well as he did. Let me give you however one caution; imitate what he did that was best; you will have faults enough of your own" (55–56). No project is more fundamental to Godwin's efforts toward perfect-ibility. A better world depends on having more artists and writers in it, and this depends on artists modeling their art and lives for young people in ways that neither mystify nor overidealize either process. This is a markedly different approach from claiming that "the greatest poets have been men of the most spotless virtue, of the most consummate prudence and, if we could look into the interior of their lives, the most fortunate of men."[64] To be an artist, according to Godwin, is to hazard everything in recomposing the fundamen-tals of learning. Key to this effort is revising childhood, children, and the texts that compose a Juvenile Library.

A comment in the appendix captures still-unresolved worries regarding the risk.[65] "When 'The Looking Glass' was published, no one could foretell that the author's policy, or no policy, with regard to his own children, and those for whom he was more or less responsible, would be eminently unhappy and unfortunate" (*Looking Glass*, 121). The comment implies that the disappoint-ing futures of his own progeny are Godwin's responsibility both as a parent whose role is to foretell his child's future and as an author whose preoccupa-tion with writing for the Juvenile Library caused him to neglect his own children—a view shared by many who feel that Godwin neglected his blood daughter's education and was foiled in his efforts to educe an illustrious son.

The latter worry grows stronger when we realize that the subject of his *Looking Glass*, young William Mulready, was one of Godwin's protégés and the illustrator of many books for children, including several published by Godwin's Juvenile Library, one ("Mounseer Nongtongpaw") long attributed, mistakenly, to daughter Mary.[66] Certainly, *she* might have come to find herself an equally worthy subject for reflection in *The Looking Glass* and, as a she, even worthier of emulation because more epoch-changing; in addition, if he had only been watching and not exiling her as a young girl to Scotland, the author would have had optimal access to information regarding her earliest impressions, accidents of training, and development. Once again, her distinctiveness as child, artist, and worthy being is occluded by "William." Moreover, all children in their household known for silence might have felt cheated by the tone of these texts, which "prattle" to child readers and enjoin authors to "become in part children ourselves."[67]

These are difficult worries to resolve, especially given that the characters of children are being formed before they have an ability to evaluate or resist whatever impressions are being made on them, and particularly when those impressions relate to withdrawal or rejection by those supposedly nearest to them. Godwin's life/writings take seriously this fact of a child's impressionability, but they view their responsibility to it in a nonessentialized way, neither necessarily privileging person over book or art in the capacity to impress a child's mind nor maintaining that biological parents are the best persons to educe their child. His point is more progressive. The first things a child encounters are crucial in setting him or her on the way, so proper educators have a responsibility to ensure that those first things inspire trust in their powers of investigation.

Shelley's Hideous Progeny

> And now, once again, I bid my hideous progeny go forth and prosper. I have an affection for it, for it was the offspring of happy days, when death and grief were but words.
>
> Introduction to Frankenstein, 1831

Raised on these children's books, many written by her birth parents, in a household run by a father and a stepmother increasingly desperate to promote and sell their ideas, young Mary learned at a very early age that her welfare was inextricably tied to the reading and re/production of books and that her growth as a child had been prescripted by them. We know that she learned to read by reading Wollstonecraft's "Lessons" (as well as her tombstone) and that the patient, colloquial style of Godwin's books for children is indebted to rehearsing these stories with his children and receiving their feedback.[68] We also know that in the years before Godwin remarried, he consulted the living Mrs. Mason as the best authority on how to employ the precepts of the textual Mrs. Mason and her once-live embodiment, Wollstonecraft.[69] In very real senses, such intimate commerce with her parents' writings for children got Mary off to a promising start: activating her fancy, learning that ideas are compelling, seeing that reading is relational and tied to the ability to interpret one's parents as well as please them, discovering that the process of becoming an artist or an eminent person may not be all that difficult or mysterious. Wash your hands. Kiss me. Read me. Trace my features, then draw your own. Put my stories into your own words. But in other ways, this commerce inhibited her development, for such a life is never sure when or at what point she begins as a distinct individual or what distinguishes her (or any) life from a story, original or not. Moreover, learning her first four letters on her mother's tombstone granted premature knowledge of the contingencies of living, while reading that mother's life in her father's *Memoirs* in later years showed that a woman can be killed through writing as well as giving birth.

Critics often view *Frankenstein* as expressing teen Mary's anger over her parentage, especially over irresponsible fathers who attempt to create life without a woman and who abandon that life to its own devices once it has been made.[70] But few have read *Frankenstein* as a "logical" extension of her parents' efforts to produce a new species of child in their writings for children or as a serious evaluation of what role such new works play in a young creature's development or in the world's progress. For whatever else one makes of the lessons of *Frankenstein,* the book explores the quite striking extent to which a creature can make its way in the world without parental instruction or supervision. It utters a serious warning, not so much against the inadequacy of books as compared to parents (after all, Victor ascribes his entire fate to his father not having given him a patient explanation of the errors in his favorite childhood books), but of the ways that books not only record but also unleash the evil of humanity. *Frankenstein* is not a children's book, conventionally speaking, but it introduces key issues that underlie a maturer Shelley's writings for children, views on childhood development, and understanding of herself as a child/author. Among them, what kind of future do we bequeath our progeny, especially if they are works of a new species? Whose survival is more assured—a book's or a child's? Which has the greater share in composing a future? Which is more life-sustaining for a woman?

The introduction to the 1831 *Frankenstein* is one of Shelley's few auto-biographical statements regarding her early girlhood and authorship meant for publication. It examines the origins of human life as well as of literary composition by way of dutifully answering the "question, so very frequently asked me—'How I, then a young girl, came to think of, and to dilate upon, so very hideous an idea?' "[71] In other words, answering the question regarding the origin of her hideous progeny entailed delineating her origins as the progeny of "two persons of distinguished literary celebrity" (175). The deeply contra-dictory statements addressing the question of origins suggests how conflicted the mature Shelley remained over her originality, imagination, femininity, and adherence to family. On the one hand, describing herself as the child of literary celebrities, whose only named girlhood pastimes were "scribbling" and "writing stories" and whose young "husband" is portrayed as eager for her to "enroll [her]self on the page of fame," she depicts herself as basically destined to be a writer (a destiny and a roadmap mirrored in more than one household portrait or *Looking Glass* [175, 176]). On the other hand, she depicts the origin of the hideous idea that becomes *Frankenstein* and makes her name as arising out of nowhere (neither consciousness nor sleep), as belonging to no one else (definitely not her husband) but also not exactly to herself.[72] Yet, the emer-gence of this unbidden and unprecedented idea is also presented as familiar, for it occurs in the same way as did her "best compositions" of early girlhood: as "airy imagination" and precisely not as writing, since her writing feels so uninspired and derivative[73] (175–76). Moreover, this depiction of the no-origin of *Frankenstein* contradicts the model of invention espoused in the preface (and elsewhere in her writings), by which creation ex nihilo is deemed impos-sible, since there always exists the "something that went before."

Such deep confusions over claiming originality and progeny are related to a second obstacle to her authorship and personhood, namely, gender. The preface portrays her as silent in the company of more eminent male writers—Percy and Byron, but also the ghost story writers and scientists from whom they drew inspiration—even as it prepares to reissue the progeny that had already made her name famous, certainly far better known than her husband's, and would make the name *Frankenstein* legendary. The question of gender is essential to Shelley's reckoning of herself as author and person because it is so troubling to either identity. As author, the question of gender was bequeathed by her celebrity mother, as person by the life/writings of both of her parents, from whose texts she learned from early on how to improve the hideous status of girls and also that her emergence as a girl was hideous to both of them, conceived as s/he was as "William."[74] This knowledge was not reserved for later years, when she was finally granted access to *Memoirs* or the early love letters of her parents. It was published in the very first book that she read, where she learned her letters and her presumed status as a boy. Lesson X: "See how much taller you [Fanny] are than William." Lesson XI: "I carry William, because he is too weak to walk" ("Lessons," 471, 472). Viewed in this context, we might find less baffling why "William" is the first child to go at the creature's hands, since "Mary" literally displaces "William" (and Mary) as a condition of her existence. More affirmatively, we might also see why, from early on, she assigns known features of her character to male and female protagonists. Changing the designation and destinations of "girl" to something more compatible with "boy" is what Shelley contributes to children's literature.

There are intriguing resemblances between Shelley's two acknowledged texts for youth, *Maurice; or, The Fisher's Cot* and *Proserpine*, besides their roughly contemporaneous composition in 1820. Both texts feature young protagonists who are lost to their parents and whose experiences while wandering in the world confront them with repeated losses or betrayals by adults, and both texts, though consistently melancholy, end "happily," that is, with the young person's accommodation to his or her situation, which involves an explicit reunion with parental origins. We are familiar with the plot of *Proserpine* from legend and discussion of Shelley's version in chapter 5, and that of *Maurice* is easily told. Stolen from his well-to-do parents as a baby by a poor sailor's wife (Dame Smithson) who has no children of her own, Maurice (as Dame Smithson calls him—his original name was Henry) proceeds through a series of surrogate families that we learn about mainly through retroactive narration. Mistreated by his first surrogate father, Smithson, who develops an aversion to the sickly child, Maurice runs away to work for Farmer Jackson, who turns him out when he cannot sustain the hard work, and is eventually taken in by a kindly fisherman, Old Barnet, despondent over the recent death of his wife. The narrative begins with a description of the funeral procession for this kindly fisherman, viewed by a traveler who, struck by the grief-stricken and "beautiful" boy, Maurice, is told "all I know" regarding Maurice by a neighbor of Old Barnet (76, 77). This traveler then leaves on business for a few days, during which the "money-loving" brother of Barnet, who died without a will, claims the cot and its possessions for his own, and

turns Maurice out once again into the world (89). Resourceless but unde-
sponding, Maurice is preparing to leave the cottage when the traveler returns,
invites him to come live with him and his wife, and then narrates his own life
story, which ends with the mutual discovery that Maurice is indeed Henry, this
traveler's lost son, for whom he has been looking two months out of every year
since he was taken eleven years ago.

For obvious reasons, newspaper reviews and critical assessments of this
story, which had been lost until Cristina Dazzi discovered it among family
papers in 1997, read it in the context of loss and grief, both as exploring a
thematics of childhood dispossession and wandering and expressing Shelley's
own grief in 1820 over the recent death of three of her children as well as the
deaths of stepsister Fanny and Percy's first wife, Harriet.[75] Even granting its
happy ending, commentators note the melancholy that suffuses the text, the
final image of the cottage itself "crumbling away" expressing Shelley's "la-
men[t] that this kind of probity will not be seen in modern times again."[76]
Some view its narrative structure (a series of interlocking tales) as reminiscent
of *Frankenstein*, but with none of its "seething originality, moral complexity or
sinister Gothic speculativeness," and they seem to regret that, despite repeated
experiences of poverty and hardship, Maurice remains "naturally good" rather
than being made into a fiend through misery.[77] Deemed "a modest affair" or
"slight piece," virtually every commentator agrees that the story is disappointing and that its chief value lies in the long introduction by Claire Tomalin,
which rehearses the background of this tale that Shelley wrote for the then-
ten-year-old Laurette, the elder daughter of Margaret (former Lady Mountcashell) and George Tighe. As one reviewer notes, "so riveting is the preface to
Shelley's short story, in fact, that a more accurate title might have been *An
Introduction by Claire Tomalin with a Long-Lost Tale by Mary Shelley.*[78] Or,
in a formulation that echoes one of the chief points of departure of this book,
Shelley's "own life, as recounted by Claire Tomalin, was to become the more
gripping story, as had been the lives of her parents and their friends."[79]

But if we read *Maurice* in the broader context of Shelley's contribution to
children's literature and her thoughts on the education of daughters and sons,
this long-lost tale acquires greater resonance and im/personal significance.
The topic of loss and mourning in *Maurice* is explicitly linked to the question
of progeny, which is further related, both in text and context, to exchanges between text and child and the exchange of one for the other. For *Maurice* tells a
tale of surrogacy and substitutability, even with the biological parental reunion
staged at the end. Three unrelated people in the short narrative affirm that

they "love" Maurice "as a son." Maurice himself is seen to serve as an adequate substitute for Dame Barnet after she dies, not only by helping Old Barnet with his nets and feeding him on his return from sea but also by reading aloud to the village children as she once did (in this, she and he filling a maternal role for the neighborhood). Though reunited with his birth parents, Maurice continues to spend two months out of each year at the fisher's cot, inhabited throughout the rest of the year by his surrogate mother, Dame Smithson.

The linkage between child and text, child-rearing and children's reading, is stressed in several ways. Dame Barnet teaches the neighbor children to read from the Bible but also "tells them stories of Goody Two-Shoes, and the Babes in the Wood," stories, the first narrator notes, that "pleased us who were older as well as the children" (79).[80] The legitimacy of the "real" father, before he knows himself to be such, rests in his offering Maurice less a place to live than many books to read, books that "told of what good and wise men had done a great many years ago; how some had died to serve their fellow creatures, and how through the exertions of these men everyone had become better, wiser, and happier"—books that promise to supplement the only stories that Maurice is said at this point to know, those concerning the "distress of Joseph, when he was sold to slavery" and "the sorrow of David, when his son Absalom revolted against him" (97). In other words, the promised texts are key to reforming society through altering narratives of familial betrayal and abandonment. Even more intriguingly, Maurice's history of wandering, not his origin, is initiated by the writing of Dame Smithson, for his existence as hers stemmed from her creation of him in the letters she sent to her husband at sea announcing the birth of a child, and how he "was thriving," so that, upon his return two years later, she had to find a live analogue of "her pretended child" (106–7). More precisely, Maurice's origin and existence *are* the products of writing, for "Maurice" renames the "something that went before," originally called "Henry." In a real sense, one can say that Maurice is live fiction.

In themselves, such details suggest an unusual reworking of conventional tales regarding lost orphans, foundlings, or children separated from their parents. Maurice—that is, Henry—is reunited and lives with his parents but continues to stay for two months every year in the fisher's cot, the home of his dead, but beloved, surrogate father (otherwise inhabited by an unrelated surrogate mother). Not only that, but his natal father joins him in this annual part-time arrangement and, while there, adopts the clothing and manners of the neighboring peasants and calls Henry, Maurice. Reunion with his "true" parents, in other words, does not erase or cause him to reject his surrogate families or make one family renounce the other. Even the woman who stole him is loved as, and for being, a "dear, good mother," who not only cared for his welfare but, in a real sense, created him, too. Provocative in themselves, when read in conjunction with Shelley's other children's text, *Proserpine,* such features cannot be seen as accidental. The major change concerns the gender of the protagonist (to which we will return), but *Proserpine,* too, ends with Proserpine affirming a joint-custody arrangement, whereby she spends half the year with Pluto in the underworld and half the year with her mother, Ceres, on earth. Even more intriguing, both texts portray parents perennially searching for their lost children, while the child gets on with the business at hand.

Taken together, both texts are significant revisions of parent-child relations and of conventional responses to the hazards that can befall that first bond. The wandering of *Maurice* is initiated by the too-little of parental involvement, the wandering of *Proserpine* a means to circumvent the too-much of maternal involvement, although both texts also display how each parent's bond with the other parent leaves the child, if not totally alone, then defenseless (Maurice is stolen from the arms of his dozing nurse when his parents, as is their habit, leave him to go off together on a walk; Proserpine is left to gather flowers with her girlfriends when Ceres leaves her to supervise Jove's table). In both cases, too, the child views separation not as a tragedy, though entailing significant hardship, but as an opening. As we saw, Proserpine views her fate not as "misery" but a "slight change / From our late happy lot," and *Proserpine* reworks the classic story to make it less antagonistic toward patriarchy and more open to and for women. Maurice experiences a series of rejections, the final one by death, but remains hopeful. "I loved old Barnet and liked my life here with him and I cried very much when he died—but if I can get work about a farmyard, I hope in a month or two to sing as cheerfully as I used when I saw his white sail among the other boats which you see out at sea" (93–94). In its way, *Maurice* is no less ambitious in revising the children's books and biblical stories about lost children that it names.

One intriguing difference regarding the characterizations of the mother in these two stories returns us to the context of their composition in 1820. Everyone sees the texts written by Shelley in the period spanning 1818 to 1822 as suffused with mourning, as she deals with the loss of her children, which reactivated the trauma of losing her mother as a ten-day-old child. But beyond the point explored in the last chapter, regarding the intensity of the relation between Shelley's works of literature and works of mourning, is how these experiences of loss affected her decision to compose texts for children that treat the same problematic as the adult texts but begin at an earlier stage of loss and thus of possible recovery. In effect, these stories promise children that if they start from an awareness that children can become lost, abandoned, and be-trayed, they stand a better chance of surviving. Too, if they are less defended against the possibility of loss, they will be less defenseless when encountering it. Critics associate Shelley's writing for children with her acquaintanceship with the former Lady Mountcashell and self-named Mrs. Mason, whom she met for the first time at Pisa on October 2, 1819, both because Mrs. Mason was a famous children's author and because Shelley wrote her children's texts for Mrs. Mason's daughters. But the connection goes deeper. In figuring not only deep maternal grief—Mrs. Mason having effectively lost all seven of her children by Lord Mountcashell through their marital separation—but also fresh starts through authorship and a second set of daughters (Laurette [1809] and Nerina [1815]), Mrs. Mason inspires Shelley to write for children about their capacity to start again.[81]

The connection is, however, even more specific than her composing texts that confront loss by speaking about survival to a creature that signifies a fresh start. The condition under which Shelley first met Mrs. Mason was her at-tempt to ensure the survival of her unborn progeny by moving to Florence in order to have the eventual birth of Percy Florence supervised by Dr. Bell. Moreover, who she can be said to have re/encountered in "Mrs. Mason" is multiple and complex: not only the famous children's author published by the Juvenile Library who adopted the name of the mother-figure in her birth mother's *Original Stories from Real Life;* not only her own mother's first surrogate daughter, Margaret, when she worked as a governess for the Kings-boroughs in Ireland; not only the writer—surrogate daughter of Wollstone-craft, whom Shelley's father consulted frequently on his dead wife's child-rearing wishes but also, in some deep sense, a surrogate mother (Mrs. Mason as substitute "Mrs. Mason" as substitute Wollstonecraft) and a sister (surrogate daughter of "Mrs. Mason" and of Wollstonecraft as governess).[82] The impulse to compose children's texts, then, is inseparable from Shelley's encounter with this convergence of progenitors and progeny whose names and lived reality were taken from fiction and literally dependent on fiction-writing—a revised edition of Godwin's falling in love with one of Wollstonecraft's books. In Mrs. Mason, Shelley reconnected with the spirit and letter of her mother and her mother's first daughter, whose own daughter, Laurette, represented a second-generation of progeny and Shelley's renewed hopes of survival for and through her impending child. In this light, Laurette's inquiry, as conveyed in a letter from Mrs. Mason to Shelley acknowledging receipt of her gift of *Frankenstein*, was prescient: whether "that lady had yet *made her child.*"[83]

Viewed in this context, the characterization of Maurice's relation to his parents, especially to his mothers, has two surprising, and interconnected, features. The concluding joint-custody arrangement involves a noticeable sidelining of the birth mother and a quite accommodating treatment of the surrogate mother. For the birth father lives with Henry/Maurice throughout the entire year in both locales, whereas the birth mother is confined to the natal home, and Dame Smithson apparently moves out of the cottage during the annual two-month period of male bonding and housekeeping.[84] Yet this paternal identification is modified not only by the series of men offering to be a father to this son but also by the foregrounding of the issue of naming in this text. Henry (not the surrogate mother) renames himself Maurice in order to escape detection by "the cruel man whom he thought his father" (111) and, as we have seen, keeps this name whenever he resides in the fisher's cot. But there is also no stabilization of his identity in the patronym, for we never learn Henry/Maurice's "family" name or the surname or given name of his natal father, who is referred to primarily as "the traveller" and then finally as "father." Moreover, the title chosen for this story of this boy's life is *Maurice; or, The Fisher's Cot*, indicating that his identity is best signified through a self-naming fiction, not the family or even one's "Christian" or "given" name, and a place that is not home.

It is tempting to interpret these familial revisions "personally," as expressing a still "excessive & romantic attachment to her father" or a growing accommodation to the second Mrs. Godwin, well known for fabricating the paternity of her children. It is more relevant that the natal home is described primarily as a place of reading and that undespairing children call more than one place home (111). Such changes suggest that a child's survival depends on an ability to resignify his or her reality beyond the normal need for any child to grow into, and apart from, his family and given name. Here the resignifying facilitates a literal new start, in which the child gives himself a new given name and avoids mention or recognition altogether of the family name. Revealing, too, is that the child chooses *Maurice* over *Henry*, Henry being the most common male name in fiction of the late eighteenth century, including Wollstonecraft's.[85] Foregrounding this capacity to resignify one's reality is what Shelley contributes to children's literature, by linking the possibility of a new start to the question of gender.

Part of what is at stake in portraying Maurice as a boy is the male's privileged access to experience and thus to creating a name for himself. Of course, women are compelled to change their family name by marrying, but this change only specifies a different possessor of her fate, not something specific to her identity or some new way to stand on her own—possibilities that Wollstonecraft's texts attempt to open by widening the fields into which women can enter. But *Maurice* is not the only children's story that Shelley composed, and, in this light, it is striking that her first children's text, written only a few months earlier, is *Proserpine*—the first of her mythological dramas, paired with *Midas*. Elsewhere I have argued that this mythic pairing allows Shelley to reflect on parental characteristics (authorship, authority, and avarice), while noting the generational asymmetry in foregrounding the daughter, not the mother, in *Proserpine*.[86] But if we view these texts specifically as written for children, as Miranda Seymour does in asserting that "Mary surely had [Laurette and Nerina] in mind when she wrote two mythological dramas," the first "in late spring of 1820," then *Proserpine* and *Maurice* make an appropriate pairing on the score of gender and generational status (though not genre), and the three together constitute a significant familial triangle (father, daughter, son). The choice to pair Maurice with Proserpine (as protagonists and stories), in my view, suggests one major way that Shelley unites the individual legacies of her progenitors in the field of children's literature, for each parent focuses fairly exclusively on his or her own gender in their writings for, and about, children. It also reflects Shelley's long-term interest in the gender-differentiated aspects of helping any youth acquire an identity, whereby, through writing, one can make and change one's name or change what "boy" or "girl" signifies. "Has that lady made her child yet?"

What *Proserpine* adds to the discussion, besides the wandering and accommodation to loss and change that both protagonists share, is focus on sex as a mode of transport from one stage or state of experience to the next. Neither wholly condemnatory nor wholly celebratory, *Proserpine* treats initiation into sex as something that gets Proserpine out of her mother's clutches. It is extremely difficult to separate censorship from prudishness on this topic and unwise to construe the (offstage) portrayal of forced sex as indicative of Shelley's general approach to sexual experience for maidens. What is construable is the effort in *Proserpine* to facilitate a nonphobic reaction to what can go wrong if girls are granted spaces to stray—that terrifying things can befall them in the blink of an eye but that the best way to prepare for such eventualities is not to attempt to prevent them by confining women to the home or circumscribing girls' access to the world. In other words, *Proserpine* takes as its topic the strongest argument against endorsing freedom for girls in order to argue that denying girls freedom is a still more dangerous practice. It warns *against* the conventional warnings seen as protecting girls, such as to beware of curiosity, premature sex, too much sex, men. The legend confirms a parent's worst nightmare (harm to its child, rape of its daughter) and the reality that parental figures can be a child's worst nightmare (incest), but, even granting these realities, it draws a different conclusion. Fundamental harm comes to daughters from seeing their chief virtue and value as an innocence maintained by ignorance. Erase this equation, start from a less defeatist mentality, and girls stand a better chance of circumventing misery when harm befalls them. *Maurice* sets the nightmares at an earlier stage but draws a similar lesson.

For more than two centuries, people have wondered how a young girl came up with the hideous idea that became *Frankenstein*. To me, selecting Proserpine as the protagonist of the first of her children's stories is equally incredible. This is quite a story to tell young girls, the story of how they get severed from their mothers, girlfriends, and girlhoods by being abducted and raped by a male family member. Even with the Shelleyan modifications, especially the linkage Shelley makes between mothering and storytelling, *Proserpine* portrays a world of dangers through which young girls must find their way. No one, to my knowledge, has discussed the implications of writing *Proserpine* for young girls, and Seymour surely dilutes the purpose of *Maurice* in stating that "Mary cannot have intended her young reader to brood on the harsh laws which separated Laurette's mother from the children of her marriage to Lord Mountcashell."[87] Wouldn't this be picking up the storyline and locale at the end of the uncompleted *Wrongs of Woman; or, Maria* in order to foreground the legal system's inhumane treatment of wives and disseminating the lesson to a younger audience? Wouldn't such early training both prepare girls better to meet such eventualities and also encourage the rising generation to change such laws? *Proserpine* offers similar additions and revisions to familial narratives by (off)/staging a young girl's initiation into sex. Here, too, Shelley builds on her mother's reformulations of female fancy, which encourage heightened realism regarding love, sex, women, and men in order to start the training sooner so that precocious girls do not enter that world uninstructed or regret eternally the consequences of their early acts. They also need to learn that desire is at once natural and never innocent or original before they can know how to take or claim responsibility for their actions. In this, Shelley's children's stories include the same harshness that Constance Walker claims differentiates Shelley's fictional treatments of children's deaths from those of "most of her contemporaries" in providing "a more harrowing, honest, and profound version" of living.[88] This form of truth-telling is not exactly "personal," but it is key to her view of a child's or people's survival.

As with most categories in Shelley's life/writing, the boundary between texts for children and adults is not that firm. Her textual focus in both categories is youth of both sexes, her topic how and whether that young person is able to develop within a family. In this regard, the declared texts for youth are more positive in their depictions of family life than the claustrophobic visions of *Frankenstein* and *Matilda*, in which neither boys nor girls are allowed to flourish or are rewarded for setting out on their own. Proserpine and Maurice face less extreme prospects, in part because their multiple and diversified parental attachments do not let early loss overwhelm them. Learning these lessons apparently makes way for the portrayal of girls in *Lodore* and *Falkner*, wherein they learn to redirect their primary attachment from father to husband. This becomes possible now that the current generation of parents is less infantile.

In their support of the wanderings and adventures of youth, Shelley's writings have imbibed the spirit of her father's most infamous reformulation of family and added a major corrective. Choosing the life of Fénelon over a family member actually preserves the future of the young, because Fénelon is a children's author whose famous *Adventures of Telemachus* shaped a people's future by instructing the future king of France how to navigate the world, especially of erotic temptation. Shelley's writings for youth extend that training and future to women in providing a Mentoria for *wandering* girls—in this, taking a step beyond the prior generation of female children's authors, who were concerned to educe rational, but not highly imaginative, girls. If mothers are not yet ready to facilitate this training—apparently not even this mother, whose parenting of Percy Florence was fairly uninspired—Mentor/ias exist so that children are not left defenseless or permanently in reaction against "parent" in order to affirm their independence or confirm that their success is their own. Such is the tendency of the progeny that this family of writers educes. It is fitting, then, that a pirated edition of *Thoughts on the Education of Daughters* was published in Dublin in a volume that included *Instructions to a Governess*, by Fénelon, and that the Mrs. Mason of *Original Stories of Real Life* became the real-life Mrs. Mason, who applied Wollstonecraft's "Lessons" to daughters taught to recompose "girl" while she went on to give *Advice to Young Mothers* "by a Grandmother" (1823).[89]

On Percy's Case

It shows too that a father is not to be trusted for natural instincts
toward his offspring.

Mary Shelley, "Rousseau," *French Lives*

When I was twenty the one true
Free spirit I had heard of was Shelley . . .
Shelley, who, I learned later . . .

Galway Kinnell, "Shelley"

In the entire history of Western literary biography there is no worse nightmare son-in-law or family relation than Percy Bysshe Shelley.[1] Bad enough
that this promising protégé quickly turned his attentions from his mentor to
all three of the young daughters in the Godwin household and then absconded
to the Continent with two of them in the middle of one July night, impreg-
nated one and kept his intentions toward the other sufficiently unclear for her
never to return for any period to the parental household; and did this while
married to another woman, with whom he had fathered one child and conceived another, whom he also invited to join the threesome on the Continent.
He then went on to become one of only two fathers in the history of Britain in
the first half of the nineteenth century to be refused custody rights to his
biological children by the Court of the Chancery (when his first wife, Harriet
Westbrook, committed suicide).[2] The grounds for this denial was a radicalism
of thought that also estranged his titled wealthy father, financial access to
whom was the primary reason that mentor Godwin had welcomed Shelley
into the household in the first place. Once he was denied custody of the
children, he never saw or even tried to see them again. Nor was his repeat
performance as father or husband of Mary Wollstonecraft Shelley much of an

improvement, for wife Mary later held him responsible for the death of at least one of their children, the birth of at least one who was definitely not hers, found herself constantly enjoined to welcome as bosom-sister a series of young women with whom her husband was infatuated, while also packing and moving the household a dizzying number of times. Nor can we make major claims for him as financial provider, flight from debt being one of the chief impulses behind all this movement.

As a family relation Percy Shelley was a nightmare also because, shortly after his death, he eclipsed the life/writings and reputations of all his surrounding family members, an eclipse that holds to this day. The situation has improved markedly since the late 1980s, with the rise in interest in Mary Shelley, especially the "other Mary Shelley," and renewed attention to the extensive writings of Godwin and Wollstonecraft. Still, the literary record is clear that, by the early Victorian period, Percy Shelley's reputation, never solidified in his lifetime, was on the rise and that part of its ascent involved an intentional and inadvertent demotion of the other three.[3] Mary Shelley initiated the process in her devotion to editing and disseminating his works but also in desiring to be written out of the biographical record and by herself facilitating (not simply by publishing) his defense of poetry over against prose.[4] The priority ascribed to Percy Shelley ever after is largely a reflection of (this creation of) the pre-eminence of poetry, lyricism, and imagination in canonical romanticism—of which Shelley has often been the exemplar or representative case. But this epilogue explores how the priority is also the product of conscious and unconscious attempts to evaluate his life/writings apart from his positions on and embeddedness within this family and their writings, *so that* one has a better chance of granting them pride of place. For to focus on Shelley's writings on family and performance as a family man prompts repeated charges that his life/writings are immoral, libertine, adolescent, perverse. To situate them within this writing family occasions the far less frequent, but more productive, claim that his life/writings are derivative.

Though not its ostensible goal, the process of disconnecting Percy from family is visible in a reception history that is remarkable for intertwining literary history and family values. For starters, the tone and vehement sidestaking of this history are instructive, one critic characterizing the history of his reception as a "shouting match," another noting that a "discouraging amount of the writing on Shelley at all periods has been polemical: violently for or against," as if the Shelley legacy entails a form of partisanship that his life/ writings struggled to preclude.[5] More importantly, the phases that demarcate his reception, from "the legend of Shelley" to "the case of Shelley" to "the case of the case of Shelley," all make their cases for him by extracting him from his texts on family or his context in this family. Though in very different ways, they also all manifest constitutive ironies that attend the process of making family part of a case history—a story to tell *as* a secret to keep.

The legend of Shelley, in its two-stage dimension, initiates the process and the ironies. Immediately after his death by drowning, Mary Shelley and close friends Leigh Hunt, Edward Trelawny, and others worked quickly to defend Percy against charges of immorality in his writings and behavior by prefacing his life/writings with descriptions of his ideality, singularity, and ascension above this-worldly concerns.[6] In other words, they all variously foregrounded his ethereality as a way of distracting attention from the forms his body and embodiment took, even though Mary, especially, had as much to lose as gain by his being disembodied. The legend then reached its zenith in the full-scale sanctification effected by son Percy Florence and daughter-in-law Lady Jane Shelley, who went to staggering lengths to cast a positive light on their father/in-law's performance as family man. These included the installation of "the Sanctum" in the drawing room ("given a blue ceiling studded with gold stars") that housed precious relics of the Poet, into which only "kindred feet" might enter, as well as redesigning Shelley's features, right down to redrawing his nose, in order to ensure that nothing of his remains indicated "a breach of decorum" or "insult to the family."[7] It extended to editorial practices of censorship, destruction of (letters and journals that disappeared) or tampering with evidence (circulating rumors regarding Harriet's sexual relations with other men or the Hoppners' perfidies), and conducting loyalty tests as a precondition to having access to Shelley's remains. Taken together, the two stages of the legend making set the challenges for future scholarship on Percy Shelley and his family. Both versions promoted him at the expense of his role and position within family, and both editorial practices complicated the ability to make a neutral evaluation of his life/writings. But whereas the forms of Mary Shelley's partisanship—idealization and silence on his "personal" life—did not destroy evidence as much as await a time more propitious to its interpretation, Lady Jane's editorial practices meant to keep that time from ever arriving. Her linkage of family loyalty to secrecy, censorship, and repression not only undermined the foundational connections that the life/writings of all four of these writers strove to establish but also made truthful relations about domestic affection a betrayal of human value.

The "case of Shelley," as articulated most famously by Frederick Pottle in

1952 but also as it addresses a history of charges against him, works against the life/writings of other family members primarily on generic grounds.[8] Simon Haines identifies two waves of (remarkably symmetrical) critical detraction— the first from 1819–40, the second from 1919–40—both of which claim to be disturbed less by the immorality of the man or even the family man than by the intentional ineffability of his poetry but which often link the two complaints in revealing ways. In essence, detractors in either century want more anchorage in reality as opposed to the figuralism and insubstantiality of his life/writings and more realism about what these qualities at once occlude and signify: thinness, perversity, "weak grasp on the actual," a "puerile" or "adolescent" mentality.[9] The challenge to Percy Shelley and his poetic personae posed by William Hazlitt through to F. R. Leavis is clear: grow up, get real, face the complexities of living. To counter these charges of immaturity, defenders stress the futurity that his poetry at once strives to create and on which a poem depends for its substantive apprehension. That is, defenders show how detractors misunderstand the figurative ways that his poetry apprehends the world differently, less objectively, more analogically. In so doing, they often elevate his lyrics above his other forms of poetry and deem lyric poems to be poetry's highest, because most intense and condensed, form. This idealization of lyric, which is one standard definition of classic romanticism and the primary grounds for Shelley's representative status within it, obviously effaces the writings of surrounding family members, writings that are remarkable for their generic variety and innovation and, given this, for their thoroughgoing avoidance of lyric poetry.[10] The idealization of poetry also establishes the *generic* grounds for the future defense of Shelley's life as well as writings: he is a poet, not a person, and therefore not to be judged by conventional standards of humanity or intelligibility.

The "case of the Case of Shelley" is James Chandler's recent formulation of how the life/writings and reception history of Percy Shelley literally inform late-twentieth-century practices of literary historicism.[11] Chandler views the "case" and case-making that Pottle both makes for and brings into focus through Shelley as exemplary of a mode of historicism that emerged as an antitranscendent "spirit" of the age in the England of 1819 and that has informed the literary-critical turn toward history since the 1980s. In Chandler's account, Shelley is hardly alone in envisioning this historicist spirit, which appears as well in Adam Smith, Anna Letitia Barbauld, Walter Scott, William Hazlitt, Thomas Moore, and others. Nor does Chandler's argument depend on an elevation of poetry and its ahistorical features, but instead draws on the substantial countertradition attentive to the skeptical, political, material, and feminist implications of his life/writings. Instead, Chandler makes a case out of the case of Shelley because of the poet's peculiar fame as a casuist, the depth of his reformulation of causality, and the "unwillingness" of his historicism, which allows it to become visible to Chandler as the product of a historicist epoch.[12]

But even though unidealized, inclusive of many others, and fully contextualized, Chandler's case of the case of Shelley also minimizes the importance of his family members to Shelley's historical situation—that is, to both his specific situation and its effect on his concept of "situationism."[13] There are legitimate reasons for not deeming the writings of Wollstonecraft, Godwin, and Mary Shelley as evincing the same historicist spirit of this age. The first two writers belong to 1790s political debate, which Chandler sees as structured around threshold distinctions, in comparison to post-Waterloo debate, which involves arguments about historical movements, epochs, and formations, and Mary Shelley has long been seen as avoiding explicit political commentary.[14] Yet their life/writings are indispensable to having made Percy Shelley such a case, in part because Wollstonecraft's and Godwin's writings for and on children literally informed his imagination and the hermeneutics of futurity associated with it. Chandler also admits that his emphasis on "England in 1819" was almost undone by the discovery that Mary Shelley not only assigned the sonnet its title but also initially titled it "England in 1820"—an intriguing change, given the significance of that year over the previous one in the household debates over the duty to mourn and the role of the poet in promoting that duty. But my main corrective concerns the underacknowledged role of Godwin in perceiving the poet as legislator and the writer as casuist, while granting Chandler's acknowledgment that the young Shelley took his cultural model of the intellectual's role in history from Godwin.[15] For, as I hope to suggest, foregrounding Godwin's historicist tendency, especially as enacted in *Life of Chaucer*, arguably Godwin's strongest defense of poetry, revises a crucial component of any case, in showing that the priority ascribed to Percy Shelley is a matter of following precedent. It also reveals that Shelley's causality is intimately linked to thoughts on sexuality and reformulations of heteronormativity.

But beyond his distinguished history as a case, Shelley is a nightmare in a third way, which ultimately allows for a better appreciation of his positions on and within this family. For what makes him such a nightmare is the fidelity he showed to his in-laws' life/writings against family in his ongoing infidelities to persons, causes, boundaries, and texts. From the very start, Percy's entry into this family leveled a major assault on person in the name of text (particularly, an assault on Godwin in the name of *Political Justice)*, under the disarming epistolary salutation, "I thought you were dead." Reinforcement came in Shelley's second letter, which imagines the two of them first meeting "in a spot like that in which Fleetwood [indeed!] met Ruffigny."[16] An ideal reader of Godwin and Wollstonecraft—by far the most promising, enthusiastic, and resourceful of Godwin's many protégés[17]—Shelley quickly (and ever after) established his role within the family as the one who troubles reading. He challenged their convictions regarding the power of writing to change the world, especially through reforming the family, at the same time that he strove to activate that power by being difficult to read or grasp.

The immediate crisis provoked by Percy and Mary's elopement concerns what it means to be faithful not only to a person but also to a text. The depth of Godwin's nightmare stemmed from confronting not so much the circulating "joke" that he had sold his daughters to salvage his children's book business.[18] It stemmed from the difficulty of denying that his writings were directly responsible for their elopement, while being utterly convinced that his writings *had* nothing to do with it, a difficulty exacerbated by the paper trail in *Queen Mab* establishing that Shelley's un/principled conduct toward women was firmly grounded in *Political Justice*. On the other side, Percy and Mary were stunned by the "cold injustice" of having one of the two chief *authorizers* of their conduct disclaim it and them as reprehensible, a reaction they sought to exorcize literally by carting around throughout Europe and England texts by Godwin and Wollstonecraft that they read repeatedly (with Claire) in 1814 and at later stages of crisis.[19] Mary suffered the extremes of Percy's merging of person and text by never knowing who or what he was reading and loving in her ("Mary?" "William?" Godwin? Wollstonecraft? the Claire who was not only born on Wollstonecraft's birthday but was also said to best embody her principles?). Poor Harriet's nightmare was in suddenly finding herself at the wrong end of the book's function in arousing love. Godwin's "if ever there was a book calculated to make a man fall in love with its author" was met by Westbrook's "Mr Shelley has become profligate and sensual, owing entirely to Godwin's *Political Justice*. The very great evil that book has done is not to be told."[20] On the deepest level, what the elopement signified to all affected family members was a betrayal of reading by reading that, with the exception of Harriet, preoccupied each of these writers, and their practices of writing, thereafter. In this regard, the case of Shelley represents not only the activation but also the analysis of the threat posed to humanity (and the humanities) by the signifier.

The immediate betrayal could not be handled through a typical familial tactic, by which crisis was softened through being framed as a generational narrative, where youth is impetuous, literalist, and oppositional and maturity sober, gradual, and nuanced. In this family, reading complied no less well than did life or love with being inserted into a developmental frame, as two un-disputed hallmarks of the life/writings of Percy Shelley make plain. First, Shelley never outgrew the impetuosity and penchant for opposition of his youthful reading practice, itself remarkably precocious, nor, unlike the other family members and for reasons besides longevity, did he outlive his youthful radical enthusiasms. Second, the practice of reading in accordance with the tendency of a work—a practice that grounded Godwin's assurance that his life/writings were opposed to these youngsters' life-choices—underlies the mode of reading, and of reading history, that substantiates the case of the case of Shelley and that has kept Godwin's influence underacknowledged. More-over, emphasis on his figurality made by the case of Shelley occludes the literalism with which his life/writings enact the two chief components of Godwin's revision of family: formulating attachment apart from monogamy, sentiment, or person; and embracing death and the dead as (a) familiar. Focus on his Platonism paradoxically reveals the extent to which Shelley's futurity comes into focus through a defense of all forms of sexual practice.

It is only slightly reductive to view Percy Shelley's entire oeuvre as enacting these twin features of Godwin's critique of the magic of "my." In terms of attachment, Shelley's resistance to the institution of marriage and monogamy was unwavering.[21] It is articulated textually as an explicit position from the famous footnotes comparing marriage to prostitution in *Queen Mab* through the quasi-incestuous and distinctly nonmarital coupling of Laon and Cyntha, to the antisacrificial redefinition of love espoused in *Epipsychidion*. Resistance is implied through a showcasing of the profoundly negative consequences of monogamy, as in *Julian and Maddalo* and *The Cenci*, and it is enacted in his pursuit of a series of women and triangular "couplings." Either textual mode condemns monogamy for producing selfish, self-centering, mind-benumbed, mistrustful, and parsimonious character traits, and both modes deem the negative consequences of it harmful to women as well as men.

Privileged forms of attachment are harder to delineate, owing to Shelley's general habit of describing what "is" by what "is not" or what "is most like" and his specific characterizations of ideal protagonists as radically diffused, multiply affiliated, and yet always so alone, so profoundly unattached. However, *On Love* gives us some guidance by asserting that desirable attachments are not exclusive to persons, applying as well to natural objects and intellectual concepts, whether political (liberty, humanity) or Platonic (beauty, poetry, oneness) and, when pertaining to persons, are neither exclusive nor, in any conventional sense, personal. Instead, they flow from and to a person usually portrayed generically in his poetic texts, one whose physical features are barely visible or visualizable. Often, the person is literally mythic as well as frequently an allegory not only of a role (poet, father, lover, seeker of beauty) but also of a concept or goal (hope, revolution, love, woman, the future). Indeed, the most specific thing we can say about Laon, Cyntha, Julian, Maddalo, Rosalind, or Helen is that they represent a character trait or type, but often we are only supposed to view them as tangibly imprecise means to a better, but often otherwise indeterminate, future.

This mode of characterization is extremely difficult to pull off, comprehend, or emulate, and it constitutes a major charge in the case against Shelley ("weak grasp on the actual"). Yet portraying the desired object and desiring subject as precisely not graspable is essential to perfecting humanity by keeping attachment free of the my-ness that blocks the mobility and expansiveness that Percy Shelley, following Godwin, desired to achieve through human connections. The goal of Shelleyan characterization, we might then say, was to inspire new forms of attachment by modeling them through personae to which contemporary readers do not easily relate. In this regard, Shelley's chief stylistic devices—simile and metaphor—serve a doubly essential purpose. The nonessentialist nature of the trope, which approaches what "is" through what it "is like," serves to characterize the desirable form of person and attachment (mobile, transferential, nonfixated) that Shelley's writing seeks to effect.[22] At the same time, as trope it is at once highly familiar and productive not only of resemblance and concatenation but also of a mode of signifying, even of being, to which humans do and can relate—in effect, a being-as-simile, as "one" who knows itself through resemblance to, rather than identity with, an other.[23] Nor does this mode of in/tangibility on the physical level preclude or mean to circumvent highly erotic attachments, for Shelley's poetry, with its repeated heavings, pantings, and tremulous exchanges, contains some of the sexiest language in the period. It just applies these erotic effects to attempted grasps at the ineffable features of the beloved—to intercourse with the other's ideas, tastes, reading itinerary—much in the manner that Wollstonecraft characterizes shared reading as giving rise to "voluptuous" sensations. Such a union intensifies conventional understandings of sexual intercourse as figuring radical self-dissolution by already desubstantializing the bodies (person, text, reading person) being commingled.

This last feature, of sex as figuring radical self-dissolution, is related to the second component of Godwinian impersonality, embracing death and the dead as one's familiar. It is no exaggeration to say that, from start to finish, Percy Shelley's preoccupation with death is central to his occupation as poet. Benjamin P. Kurtz claims that "no English poet of major importance will be found to have equaled Shelley" in the proportion of his utterances on the topic of death. "Out of some fifty-eight compositions written before *Queen Mab*, only four poems, each very short, and three very brief fragments, fail to mention death; and in a great majority of the remaining fifty-one the subject is stressed emphatically." From there, Kurtz deems it "close to the fact" to assert that in "all his later poems there is scarcely an idea about death, or a mood related to it, that was not present, in embryo, at least, in his mind when he wrote *Queen Mab*," whose first line, "How wonderful is Death," sets the recurring theme.[24] The chief character trait—in the sense of being both predominant and desirable—of his poetic protagonists is a form of living for the future that is not only resigned toward death or on familiar terms with its inevitability, antispirit, and spirits but one that cannot wait to die to start a higher form of living. *Adonais* is the best, and best-known, embodiment of this pursuit. But few have mentioned its union of the twin goals of Godwin's *Essay on Sepulchres*, whereby the duty to mourn entails cultivating a special relation to illustrious writers—in Shelley's case, however, by enjoining the (so-called) living poet to die. No other writer in the history of writing was so fated to die young as was Percy Bysshe Shelley. The ending of *Adonais* utters his living-death sentence, but his own accounts of himself in letters, journal entries, and autobiographical writings predict and repeatedly chronicle his imminent demise. Mary Shelley's fictional writings frequently join in, especially in Mathilda's proposal to Woodville that suicide is the only credible proof of his love. No wonder Percy's actual early death came as such a shock to his family. Intimates had grown so familiar with it that they felt it could never really happen. Too, how does a lover face the embodied consequences of her magical thinking, both in wishing him dead and in wishing he would choose to die as a sign of his undying love for her?

Holding together these two Godwinian features of Shelley's life/writings and im/personality shows his indebtedness to the life/writings of his in-laws in ways that complicate the legend of his pre-eminence within and outside of the family. It also brings into view the ways that Godwin and Plato come and stay together in Shelley's intellectual formation and how this underappreciated connection contributes to various legends of Shelley. Usually posed in narratives of Shelley's poetic "development" as an opposition (necessarian vs. idealist) or a progression (from Godwin to Plato after Shelley's translations of 1818), Godwin and Plato stay together in this poet's thoughts on immortality, thoughts that link pursuit of death with avoidance of heterosexual monogamy.[25] Plato and Godwin both conceive the individual good life as lived for, and in relation to, an afterlife uninflected by either "cras[s]" or Christian notions of "personal" immortality, and both deem achievement of immortality as best gained through a life devoted to the pursuit of truth.[26] (That Shelley always distinguished Jesus Christ from institutionalized Christianity explains why the immortality that his Jesus pursues and bestows is achieved through philosophy, poetry, and politics, but not theism or religion.)

Plato and Godwin both also conceive heterosexual monogamy as impeding attainment of immortality. Often, they (Godwin especially) formulate this as a causal relation, whereby the imperative on monogamy, in restricting one's openness to evidence, impedes the search for truth and therefore the attainment, through intellectual and artistic achievement, of immortality. But at times they also deem the sanctioned aim and fruit of heterosexual monogamy —legitimate progeny—as nullifying the immortality conventionally associated with having children. The Socrates of Shelley's translation of *The Symposium; or, The Banquet translated from Plato* (1818) voices this assertion when he reserves "divine honours" only for those who can count as their "progeny" poetic writings, laws, or other "admirable achievements," which are the "pledges of that love" that subsists between a man and the beautiful, but not for those whose progeny are "children" in "human shape."[27] While Godwin's life/writings blur Socrates's distinction between progeny as "children" or "admirable accomplishments," they do so because Godwinian progeny should be ends in themselves and because the conception of a child as something that is rigorously opposed to book, art, or text in his view weakens the life and afterlife of both parent and child.

This linkage between Plato and Godwin, oddly, becomes apprehensible in *the* text that has been least associated with Godwin because of its whole-scale endorsement of poetry and the clear Platonism of its central features: *A Defence of Poetry*, which promotes imagination over reason and poem over story on the grounds of an underlying opposition between the one and the many, the eternal and the historically particular, unity and multeity. Yet we acquire new insights into the connections between Plato and Godwin as well as the sources and modes of defensiveness in Shelley's *Defence* if we acknowledge that Godwin lies behind two of its most famous formulations, the poet as legislator and the priority of imagination over reason. For the poet as legislator receives its *first* trial run not, as is often asserted (though also often frequently ignored by those who oppose Shelley's Platonism to his political commitments), at the concluding paragraph of the first chapter of Shelley's *Philosophical View of Reform*, where poets are coupled with philosophers, but in Godwin's *Life of Chaucer* (1803), where Godwin, by way of defending Chaucer's decision to forego the practice of law for poetry, characterizes "the poet" as "the legislator of generations and the moral instructor of the world" (1:370). One year earlier, point 3 of Godwin's preface to *Bible Stories* (1802) had castigated "modern improvers" for addressing their pedagogical schemes exclusively to children's intellects and leaving out "of their system that most essential branch of human nature, the imagination," imagination then described as the "characteristic of man," the faculty that "open[s] the heart" and enables a person to "put himself" in the "place of his neighbour, to feel his feelings, and to wish his wishes"—assertions that ground the opening paragraph of *A Defence of Poetry*. Interestingly, too, the subjects of both background texts (*Bible Stories* and *The Life of Chaucer*) are elsewhere acknowledged by Percy Shelley as connecting Godwin to Plato as well as to Jesus and Chaucer—all of them precisely as legislators of the world.[28] (As we saw in chapter 5, Mary Shelley adopts this line of reasoning, too, in comparing Fénelon/Godwin to Socrates.) But given Plato's antipathy to poets in the republic, it is Godwin's treatment of Chaucer—the father of English poetry—that establishes poets and poetic truth as the best means of social legislation.

The connection between Godwin and poetry goes underground in *A Defence of Poetry* because of Godwin's association with "story" and the denigration it receives for confining readers to particular manners, bodies, and times. But this is a gross mischaracterization of the ends of story as Godwin, Wollstonecraft, and Mary Shelley variously employ it, all of whom characterize the generic, if not universal, through the individual in their prose fiction and often use their focus on a historical personage (Caleb Williams, Mandeville, Castruccio, Perkin Warbeck) to address present times as well as the thematized differences between the two periods as the grounds for hope. This particularizing of "story" in the *Defence* inverts the aims of *Life of Chaucer*, and Godwin's historical method generally, by which the unassimiliated constituents of any historical period ("its literature, social institutions, manners, opinions") cohere through a historical character (Chaucer) and in their historical character.[29] Equally important, the poem-story distinction itself is subsequently nullified in the *Defence* through the specification of Poetry as including not only poetic and prose writing but also music, sculpture, dance, architecture, law, religion (in short, the "admirable accomplishments" of Plato). Or, as Chandler argues, the "relation of these two forms of mirroring is itself structured by a mirroring or chiastic trope. The poem and story are mirrors of one another's mirroring activities, and if the poem has beauty on its side, the story has reality to claim for itself."[30] This mode of argumentation, by which a distinction is rigorously asserted (poem vs. story, ideal vs. real) but then also annulled through a broader principle of inclusion (Poetry), is key to *A Defence of Poetry* and to conceptualizing poetry's mode of reforming the world. But it is also key to the case for the defense of Shelley as he initiates it in the *Defence,* which establishes the poet as distinct from person or family man and therefore as someone untouched by conventional standards or particular periods of moral evaluation.

We are familiar with the move by which the sins of past poets are washed in "the blood of the mediator and the redeemer Time" and found to be white as snow under the transcendent logic of poetry. But defensiveness over particular sins committed by this poet against the family colors the *Defence* in curious ways. First, there is a covert relation posed between Shelley's Platonism and the "great secret" of imaginative love—"Greek love," or male-male union—which was opened and publicly dis/avowed just a couple years prior in Shelley's translation of *The Symposium* and its accompanying essay, "A Discourse on the Manners of the Ancient Greeks Relative to the Subject of Love" (1818).[31] The reception history of Percy Shelley has yet to come to grips with the significance of these documents and their influence on the defensiveness of *A Defence of Poetry.*[32] As Richard Holmes points out, both the fact and the manner of Shelley's translation of *The Symposium* was unprecedented in his day, and "A Discourse" is a truly striking document in the history of sexuality, one that only saw print in its entirety in 1949 and, even now, is often reprinted in expurgated form.[33] In it, Shelley not only confronts explicitly the particular manner of Greek love but also presents same-sex union as a highly refined mental practice. Granted, "A Discourse" promulgates its own legends in devaluing the physical components of sex, a tactic that is arguably consistent with Shelley's discussions of heterosexuality, but that admittedly is here carried to extremes in deeming it "impossible that a lover" could "subjec[t] the object of his attachment to so detestable a violation" or engage in "so operose and diabolical a machination as that usually described."[34] Still, his frank discussion of male-male love is virtually unique in the period,[35] as was his attempt to comprehend it through a mode of historicizing that cuts both ways: homophobic in its assessment of the attachment as vile and also compensatory, owing to the subordination and devaluation of women in Greek culture, but also liberating in affirming the culturally relative nature of sexual practices and norms. The potential in this affirmation is part of what Eric O. Clarke underlines in longstanding wrangles over ownership of "Shelley's Heart."[36] Beginning with Mary's dispute with Leigh Hunt over which party had the right to claim it, debates over Percy's sexual orientation are carried on to this day, thanks to his skill at equivocal identifications, the majoritizing "We are all Greeks" of *Hellas* being the unofficial motto of the Western humanities and the official motto of gay periodicals.[37]

This possibility of a gay-positive future, like all the not-yet-realized reforms that Shelley envisions, re-emerges in *Defence of Poetry* only in the generalized description of poetry's mode and time of reform, where what is unrealized in the current age sets the conditions for its apprehension, by being shadowed forth and thus positioning future readers to flesh out pre-existing tendencies. I refer to the famous declaration that "the most unfailing herald, companion, and follower of the awakening of a great people to work a beneficial change in opinion or institution, is Poetry."[38] This formulation repeats the strategy by which Poetry manifests its priority by swallowing up all the competition, this time by covering all the temporal bases. It also retains an underground connection to Greek love because the temporal formulation first appears in "A Discourse," where it occurs by way of condemning the "habitual libertine," defined as "a person who is in the custom of seeking a relief from the impulse of the sexual instinct, divested of those associated sentiments which in a civilized state, precede, accompany, or follow such an act."[39] Reading the formulation back into *Defence*, we see how the Poet, by his association with cultivated sentiments, becomes by definition the antibody in sex, whether heterosexual, libertine, or homosexual, and thus how Poet Shelley is cleared on either count before, during, and after he is charged or fired up. More importantly, we see that concerns over sexuality and a philosophical-historicist view of *its* reform lie at the heart of poetry's political designs. Here, too, the historicism cuts both ways by looking in several temporal directions. In the case of homosexuality, it imagines gay-positive futures within a deeply homophobic contemporary environment by foregrounding a time when homo-sex was the dominant practice.[40] In terms of heterosexuality, it affirms contemporary heteronormativity by contrast with a classical homosexual past only insofar as it fosters the ongoing advancement of women.

Viewed in this light, Shelley's defense of poetry follows the political program of his in-laws, both of whose writings view reform of the family as the first step to social reform, reform that entails coupling love and reading. And viewed in this light, we gain a clearer picture of the distinctiveness of Shelley's response to their and his own skepticism toward progress. His remedy for moving society forward entails rethinking historical causality in ways that complicate, according to the logic of transference, what it means to "precede, accompany, or follow" an act.[41] Owing to their special intimacy with the illustrious dead, writers live in the shades that illuminate their present reality and outline the future that their words are evoking. In other words, as Chandler emphasizes, they are situated at the "graves from which a glorious Phantom may / Burst, to illumine our tempestuous day."[42] In some respects, this radically nonlinear approach to progress marks an advance on Godwin's conviction that the world is, and always will be, in its infancy until persons learn to react in a less phobic fashion to the calamity of death. In other respects, Percy Shelley's desire for death and the calamity associated with his death have kept this advance unrealized. They also have kept his life/writings arrested forever at adolescence—and thus at the stage of sexual and textual latency.[43]

How and where this relation to latent possibility repositions Shelley within family can best be evaluated by returning to the topic of his difficulty, which does distinguish his writings, though not life, from those of his in-laws and wife. All four of these writers can be said to manifest a "weak grasp on the actual," owing to the intensity of their desires as well as their specific proposals for change, but only Percy Shelley manifests a weak grasp through the style of his writings. Stylistically, the other three are realists, their writings characterized by a bluntness that makes their voices, even when histrionic and melodramatic, not that difficult to construe, though not necessarily easy to accept. This bluntness has not served them well on any level, as seen in the relative paucity and uniformity of their reception histories as compared to Shelley's, and it occasions a major source and then mode of *their* defensiveness. Rarely are they forced to defend their writings from charges of stylistic obscurity but instead are compelled to offer repeated vindications, owing to the clarity of discrepancies between the content of their writings and of their lives. Yet, even when pertaining to a particular person (themselves, each other, Chaucer), their vindications do not remain at the personal level. They treat their object and subject generically ("woman," certain classes or types of men, an epoch-forming individual), and they combine fiction and nonfiction in apprehending the truth of character. Often, a fictional text precedes, accompanies, or follows a nonfictional text that delineates the general concepts being advocated (as in the sandwiched *Mary*, *Vindication of the Rights of Woman*, *The Wrongs of Woman; or, Maria*; or the companion set *Enquiry concerning Political Justice, Caleb Williams*), and this is achieved primarily through the portrayal of an individual protagonist (Mary, Maria, Caleb Williams, Mandeville) conceived as a genre or class or a psychoanalytic case study (obsession, psychosis, trauma). What differentiates the life/writings of Percy Shelley on this score, then, is merely the lengths to which his im/personality goes. For, however generalized or generic, Wollstonecraft and Godwin's objects of defense are perceived as recognizable, if deeply isolated and aberrational, persons, whereas Percy Shelley's object (and subject) is a spirit-thing, Poetry, valued and evaluated as no particular respecter of them.

Precisely this lack of respect for "person" is the target of the few strains of twentieth-century criticism resistant to Percy Shelley's life/writings and life/style: New Humanists of the 1920s and liberal feminists since the 1970s.[44] For different reasons, both bodies of criticism object to the lack of substance in Shelley's personae and also perceive within that lack the expression of a profound narcissism that is ethically irresponsible and cavalierly indifferent to the hurt felt by others, especially his nearest and dearest. This critique of Shelley on the grounds of the human, especially by liberal feminists who work to restore life and their afterlives to the chief victims of his narcissism (their literal foremothers), has been salutary in restoring critical attention to the life/writings of Wollstonecraft and Mary Shelley and in evaluating the extent to which Shelley's love is out for itself. But if too easily dismissive, the charge can miss the point of his efforts to reformulate the human and thus bypass the opportunity to see what distinguishes his approach to the reformulation from that of the other three: it does not dampen his characteristic warmth, ardency, or enthusiasm. For whereas all four writers embrace detachment as part of their resistance to the magic of "my," only Percy's manner of detachment keeps him warm—whereas the others are all deemed cold, not only because Shelley's warmth makes and keeps them that way. While warmth is generally a major source of the attractiveness and even popularity of his life/writings, it comes under fire when applied to his style of personal relating. The warmth with which he pursues a changing series of female and male erotic objects and *welcomes* these changes distinguishes his mode of relating and apparently sets the limits to his desirability as a commentator on family. Put the other way, twentieth-century readers rarely condemn the amorous subjectivities of Godwin, Wollstonecraft, and Mary Shelley on this ground, because those three stay so serious in these pursuits and so vocal, especially the women, about the misery that it causes them.

This particular approach to living, which Percy Shelley characterizes as an imaginative and analogical connection to objects, the ongoing and ever-changing pursuit of which is the source and sign of a person's aliveness (without which "man becomes the living sepulchre of himself"), is key to the Shelleyan imagination and to what in his lived practice humanist-feminists tend most to condemn.[45] Its objectionable features are nowhere so evident as in the infamous passages of *Epipsychidion* that, in their justification of pursuing a series of "mistress[es]," rival Godwin's passage on Fénelon in the hostility or incredulity they occasion. Both reactions are strengthened by this poem's linkage—even flaunting—of literary and auto/biographical contexts, which not only highlight a personal literary history of male rescue fantasies but also seek to extend the fantasy to the woman "wronged" by them (similar to inviting Harriet to join the threesome on the Continent in 1814). On such grounds, critics find Percy Shelleyan love delusional; interestingly, though, they rarely extend that critique to its source in Shelley's imagination. But two claims from L. O. Aranye Fradenburg's *Sacrifice Your Love: Psychoanalysis, Historicism, Chaucer* suggest how Shelley's visions of love might create space for designing more ethical—that is, enjoyable—im/personal relations that are not self-serving in either sense of the term. The first is her focus on the intimate connection between "privation and desire in discourses of love," discourses that arose in the courtly love tradition of twelfth-century Europe (a dating that both Godwin and Percy Shelley affirm) and that, to varying degrees, constrain practices and theorizations of love thereafter.[46] The second is that, contrary to most ethical traditions, psychoanalysis views sacrifice, self-discipline, and restraint as activities that pursue, rather than oppose, desire and that are not, therefore, as self-evidently noble as those traditions have an investment in asserting.[47]

The offending lines from *Epipsychidion* make it clear that the speaker's pursuit of a series of beloveds represents a critique of reigning ethical practice:

I never was attached to that great sect,
Whose doctrine is, that each one should select
Out of the crowd a mistress or a friend,

And all the rest, though fair and wise, commend
To cold oblivion, though it is in the code
Of modern morals . . . .

.   .   .   .

True love in this differs from gold and clay,
That to divide is not to take away.
Love is like understanding, that grows bright,
Gazing on many truths; 'tis like thy light,
Imagination!

The passage also makes clear that maintaining multiple relations is central to the growth and value of love and that such a love operates in ways similar to the faculties of understanding and imagination—faculties that are more traditionally associated with the pursuit of truth. But, as many critics assert, Shelley sees love as part of this truth-gaining process, whose whole or final end also is love.[48] *On Love* asserts the same thing, love being "that powerful attraction towards all that we conceive or fear or hope beyond ourselves when we find within our own thoughts the chasm of an insufficient void and seek to awaken in all things that are a community with what we experience within ourselves."[49]

The definition of love in *On Love* is, and has been, easier to accept than the lines in *Epipsychidion* because of its depersonalized context, in the senses of the essay having a nonauto/biographical frame and a nonperson-focused notion of the "all" toward which one is attracted because of the void in one's being. But the implications for lived practice are the same, a recognition that prompts the narrator of each text to acknowledge how radically his views on love paradoxically isolate him from other persons.[50] One implication is that the linkage of "true love" and fidelity to one beloved perverts love, truth, and the validity of fidelity. It does not rule out monogamy when it fosters, rather than impedes, the growth of both partners (Laon and Cyntha, Prometheus and Asia), but it condemns the connection for necessarily limiting possibility and promoting a sacrificial relation to one's object relations. A second implication is that one's attachments to other persons need not be deemed the deepest, most prized, or most humane aspects of his or her lived practice. One can attain truth and more ethical living by pursuing intercourse with books, nature, spirits of other ages, and persons whose beings are infused with these. A third implication is that Percy Shelley's love, despite (and, in one sense, because) of its Platonism, works against oneness, identity, for-all-timeness. It means to promote wider access to the world over and across time through not having its object be all-the-world-to-me.

Multiplicity in itself, as Fradenburg writes, "does nothing to disturb the logic of sacrifice," just as periodic free love movements have never fully liberated subjects deemed specially repressed by dominant powers. "So much depends on whether multiplicity tries to repair lack in the Other or registers the open-endedness of the symbolic order."[51] The life/writings of Percy Shelley are split over precisely this recognition, pitting, on the one hand, the triumph of love against the triumph of life, the one against the many, or locating love in a realm beyond time, but then historicizing the practices and manners of erotic life, literature, and political change, on the other. Chandler's account suggests how the one side facilitates, rather than opposes, the other—how the identification with an idealized self, "stript of all" circumstance, *propels* recognition of one's determination by the "particular historical situation in which [one] appears," how Shelley's "respect for historical transcendence" serves "historical relativity," how Shelley's reformulation of the case radically diffuses and multiplies both "cause" and outcome.[52] It prepares for, by refusing the ability to predict, what befalls.

It *is* painful to imagine Mary Shelley transcribing poems, like *Epipsychidion*, that broadcast the rovings of her husband's imagination, even as she was struggling to promote his poetic reputation and rebuild her life and sense of aliveness after his death. Some of that pain is registered by *Epipsychidion* being the only one of his major poems on which she refused to comment as editor. Nor does Percy Shelley always maintain a clear grasp on the anti-sacrificial imperative in his life or texts. But little is served by throwing out the baby with the bath water—or this family's "progeny" because of all the ill-parented babies that compose it—if we want to facilitate the ethical tendencies of their life-long revisions of family. For one thing, Mary Shelley, as chapter 5 suggests, worked through this pain and came to view it, like the person/poet she was deciphering and disseminating, as a textual, as well as an actual, artifact, engagement with which moved her life/writings in new directions. Put another way, we should not continue to read her poem "The Choice" as the last word on her feelings regarding Percy, especially as an expression of deep remorse over her coldness, but instead recognize that the choice of lyric signals a temporary, but deeply desired, merger with him that is subsequently suspended, as is the thematic choice that is reached in the poem: to express her fidelity to the dead beloved by resolving to "cling" to the "myrtle shaded streams and chesnut [sic] woods" of "my adopted" Italy (shades of Ceres in

Proserpine).[53] The choice to cling encompasses Perdita's fate in *The Last Man*, a fate that, as I argued, is split off from that of the other Mary Shelleyan persona, Lionel, who, as the last man ultimately chooses to write his life story and wander the globe. In an ongoing relay, the choice is then refused for the first time by a female character, Lady Katherine, who justifies a second marriage in *The Fortunes of Perkin Warbeck*, and is then reformulated in the topic that informs *Lodore*—consideration of the meaning of fidelity. Perhaps one reason that readers are far less familiar with Mary Shelley's later life/writings is that they do not want to confront the fact that mourning, too, fades, alters, loosens its grasp.

A second reason not to reject Percy Shelley's love on the grounds of fidelity to person, family, or Mary Shelley is that promoting the connection of love to understanding and imagination *constitutes* the life work of this family of writers. In the broadest sense, they all considered the acquisition of knowledge to be enhanced by passion and view learning as a love-enhancing project. This view animated their own marital relations and was key to re/forming family by perpetuating their love of reading. For Godwin, affective attachment is a matter of understanding—a *forging* of connection that links hearts through shared perspectives. His life/writings tend to reverse the emphasis in stressing a passion for scholarship, but the goal is the same: cultivating an erotics of learning, the double register (sexual and cognitive) that "curiosity" tends to signify.[54] Wollstonecraft's entire oeuvre is devoted to making love a more reasonable process and a more rational desire for women, which involves re-educating persons to perceive the voluptuousness of ideas and producing fiction that redirects their fancies and fantasies. Mary Shelley's life/writings expand the fields into which women and their progeny enter and err, fields that do not fence out the realities of loss, bad parenting, or oppressive writing by mystifying them as tragedy. All of these pursuits are less in the service of enlightenment than of "modes of enjoyment" that do not sacrifice the partialities of truth-telling to Truth. Cultivating this possibility is why Godwin, Wollstonecraft, and Mary Shelley devoted so much attention to revising children's books, childhood education, and the foundations of knowledge. Acquaintance with loss is fundamental to learning, but it also spurs desire. For all of them a child's curiosity is to be cultivated, not repressed, even in sexual matters.[55]

A third reason not to reject Percy Shelley's love is that it highlights what he brought to this family: the gift of death. Derrida describes the gift of death as singularity, the one thing that is "absolutely mine," that can be said properly to belong to one, and for which a person has a fundamental response-ability.[56] Shelley's response includes portraying a strikingly nonsacrificial, even rapturous, approach to the reality of dying, an approach that therefore does not allow consciousness of human mortality to dampen one's warmth for living, which also means maintaining warmth for the dead. In several ways, he took the *Essay on Sepulchres* to heart in linking preparation for dying to cultivation of poetry. This can appear as an effort to bypass or transcend mortality, but it also connects deadness, even more than mourning, to the work of art and thus to the insentience of the "inhuman structures that structure" persons who are formed in the image and desire of the other.[57] More than any other body of romantic works, Shelley's life/writings struggle over the status of signification and our being-as-signifier. They go farther than other texts in analyzing the complicity of language in the symbolic order and thus the obstruction that language itself (not this or that oppressive structure that it is representing) poses to change. At the same time, his life/writings theorize and enact the promise of the signifying chain to set meaning in motion through *différance*—and they require future readers to build from there.[58]

As taken up by this family, Shelley's death did almost kill them, not so much through grief but through Mary Shelley's temporary adoption of literary coping mechanisms to allay it. Her application of his idealizing tendencies to his life/writings threatened to obscure the far greater complexity of both of their understandings of this process before his death. Her devotion to disseminating his writings and fostering his reputation came at the expense of Godwin's life/writings and, for a time, her own, though ultimately it gave her the confidence to assert her genius and collaborate with Godwin until his death. But Percy's death also sharpened her struggle with "my," intensifying her sense of his irreplaceability while also striving to place, and thus replace, him in various ways: by situating his life/writings within a series of *Lives of Eminent Men* of Europe or composing fictions in which fathers are reconciled to murderous sons-in-law. What is radical in Mary Shelley's more resigned phase of writing is her nondefended commitment to a notion of life as remains.

The difficulty, the ungraspability, of the life/writings of Percy Shelley is what remains in his death as a life force. "Personified" through his insertion into this family of writers—by them and the literary tradition—then demonized and idealized as a consequence of this entry, Shelley continues to trouble reading by staging humanity's struggle with the signifier: not merely the slippages of signification but the consequences of "my" desire being the desire of the Other (manifested in the nineteenth-century reception history called "Shelley Love"). Perhaps his chief contribution to this staging concerns his full-scale assault on that privileged signifier "father" (whether embodied in God, Pope, King, Oxford authorities, Sir Timothy, Godwin, P. B. Shelley), an assault conducted in the nonname, the "restlessness," of writing. His mode of parenting had similar features, as is evident in "To William Shelley," one of the few poems written in the autobiographical guise of father, in which he seeks to acquaint this "gentle child" with the many forms of tempest that await the living and to "mould" his "growing spirit in the flame / Of Grecian lore." Such efforts do not constitute Shelley a good father but they make a start by critiquing a "good" that is anchored in the law of the father that, among other repressions, starts from the proposition that "life" is (a) good.[59] "How wonderful is death, Death and his brother sleep."

In this regard, the inscription on Shelley's memorial stone in the Protestant Cemetery in Rome perpetuates the rest/lessness that his life sought to make an active part of living, not in what it says but in how the saying relays the signifier.

> Nothing of him that doth fade,
> But doth suffer a sea-change,
> Into something rich and strange.[60]

Highly susceptible of idealization in its invocation of Shakespeare and the comforts of an organic, eternal process of transformation rather than of degeneration, the lines speak other possibilities. Not only do they submerge "father" more than full fathoms five but they position him with other possibilities for group life awaiting their time at the bottom of the ocean: especially Euthanasia in *Valperga*, whose status as an alternative to male tyranny (Castruccio) *and* female tyranny in love (Beatrice) is opposed to patriarchy (explored at its cruelest through Beatrice in *The Cenci*), herself an avatar of the "euthanasia of government" envisioned in *Political Justice*.[61]

The lack of a headstone for William Shelley opens the way for a different reading practice altogether for that "stranger" about to emerge from Wollstonecraft's "Lessons."

Wollstonecraft

"The Cave of Fancy: A Tale" (written in 1787, published 1798), vol. 1 of *The Works of Mary Wollstonecraft*, ed. Janet Todd and Marilyn Butler. London: William Pickering, 1989. Cited as "Cave."

"Lessons" (fragment) (1798), vol. 4 of Todd and Butler, *The Works of Mary Wollstonecraft*.

Letters Written during a Short Residence in Sweden, Norway, and Denmark (1796), vol. 6 of Todd and Butler, *The Works of Mary Wollstonecraft*. Cited as *Short Residence*.

Mary, a Fiction (1788), vol. 1 of Todd and Butler, *The Works of Mary Wollstonecraft*. Cited as *Mary*.

Original Stories from Real Life: with Conversations Calculated to Regulate the Affections and Form the Mind to Truth and Goodness (1788). 1796 edition used in vol. 4 of Todd and Butler, *The Works of Mary Wollstonecraft*. Cited as *Original Stories*.

Thoughts on the Education of Daughters (1788), vol. 4 of Todd and Butler, *The Works of Mary Wollstonecraft*. Cited as *Daughters*.

A Vindication of the Rights of Woman, with Strictures on Moral and Political Subjects (1792), vol. 5 of Todd and Butler, *The Works of Mary Wollstonecraft*. Cited as *Rights of Woman*.

The Wrongs of Woman; or, Maria (1798), vol. 1 of Todd and Butler, *The Works of Mary Wollstonecraft*. Cited as *Wrongs of Woman*.

Godwin

Cloudesley: A Tale (1830), ed. Maurice Hindle, vol. 7 of *Collected Novels and Memoirs of William Godwin*, 8 vols., gen. ed. Mark Philp. London: William Pickering, 1992. Cited as *Cloudesley*.

Deloraine (1833), ed. Maurice Hindle, vol. 8 of Philp, *Collected Novels and Memoirs of William Godwin*. Cited as *Deloraine*.

The Enquirer: Reflections on Education, Manners, and Literature in a Series of Essays (1797), in *Educational and Literary Writings*, ed. Pamela Clemit, vol. 5 of *Political and Philosophical Writings of William Godwin*, 7 vols., gen. ed. Mark Philp. London: William Pickering, 1993. Cited as *Enquirer*.

An Enquiry concerning Political Justice (1793), ed. Mark Philp, vol. 3 of Philp, *Political and Philosophical Writings of William Godwin.* Cited as *Political Justice.*

An Enquiry concerning Political Justice: Variants, ed. Mark Philp, vol. 4 of Philp, *Political and Philosophical Writings of William Godwin.* Cited as *Political Justice Var.*

"Essay of History and Romance" (1797), in *Educational and Literary Writings,* ed. Pamela Clemit, vol. 5 of Philp, *Political and Philosophical Writings of William Godwin.* Cited as "History."

Essay on Sepulchres (1809), in *Essays,* ed. Mark Philp (with researcher Austin Gee), vol. 6 of Philp, *Political and Philosophical Writings of William Godwin.* Cited as *Sepulchres.*

Fables, Ancient and Modern. London: Juvenile Library, 1805. Cited as *Fables.*

Fleetwood; or, The New Man of Feeling (1805), ed. Pamela Clemit, vol. 5 of Philp, *Collected Novels and Memoirs of William Godwin.* Cited as *Fleetwood.*

Life of Geoffrey Chaucer, the Early English Poet: Including Memoirs of His Near Friend and Kinsman, John of Gaunt, Duke of Lancaster. With Sketches of the Manners, Opinions, Arts, and Literature of England of the Fourteenth Century, 2 vols. London: Richard Phillips, 1803. Cited as *Chaucer.*

The Looking Glass: A True History of the Early Years of an Artist ("Theophilus Marcliffe"). London: Thomas Hodgkins at the Juvenile Library, 1805. Cited as *Looking Glass.*

Memoirs of Mary Wollstonecraft ([sic] 1798), ed. Mark Philp, vol. 1 of Philp, *Collected Novels and Memoirs of William Godwin.* Cited as *Memoirs.*

Pantheon; or, History of the Gods of Greece and Rome (1806), intro. Burton Feldman. New York: Garland, 1984. Cited as *Pantheon.*

Thoughts on Man (1831), in Philp, *Essays,* vol. 6 of *Political and Philosophical Writings of William Godwin.* Cited as *Thoughts.*

Travels of St. Leon (1799), ed. Pamela Clemit, vol. 4 of *Collected Novels and Memoirs of William Godwin.* Cited as *St. Leon.*

Shelley

Falkner, a Novel (1837), ed. Pamela Clemit, vol. 7 of *The Novels and Selected Works of Mary Shelley,* 8 vols., gen ed. Nora Crook. London: William Pickering, 1996. Cited as *Falkner.*

The Fields of Fancy (1819), ed. Pamela Clemit, vol. 2 of Crook, *The Novels and Selected Works of Mary Shelley.* Cited as *Fields.*

The Fortunes of Perkin Warbeck, a Romance (1830), ed. Doucet Devin Fischer, vol. 5 of Crook, *The Novels and Selected Works of Mary Shelley.* Cited as *Perkin Warbeck.*

Frankenstein; or, The Modern Prometheus (1818), ed. Nora Crook, intro. Betty T. Bennett, vol. 1 of Crook, *The Novels and Selected Works of Mary Shelley.* Cited as *Frankenstein.*

The Journals of Mary Wollstonecraft Shelley, ed. Paula R. Feldman and Diana Scott-Kilvert. Baltimore: Johns Hopkins Univ. Press, 1987. Cited as *Journals.* Book 4, *The Journal of Sorrow.* Cited as *Sorrow.*

The Last Man (1826), ed. Jane Blumberg with Nora Crook, vol. 4 of Crook, *The Novels and Selected Works of Mary Shelley.* Cited as *Last Man.*

"Life of William Godwin," ed. Pamela Clemit, vol. 4 of *Mary Shelley's "Literary Lives" and*

Other Writings, 4 vols., gen. ed. Nora Crook. London: Pickering & Chatto, 2002. Cited as "Life of Godwin."

Lives of the Most Eminent Literary and Scientific Men of Italy, Spain, and Portugal (1835–37), 3 vols., in Crook, *Mary Shelley's "Literary Lives" and Other Writings*. When referring to the entire project, cited as *Lives of Eminent Men*. Vol. 1, *Italian Lives*, ed. Tilar J. Mazzeo, cited as *Italian Lives*. Vol. 2, *Spanish and Portuguese Lives*, ed. Lisa Vargo, 1–282, cited as *Spanish Lives*.

Lives of the Most Eminent Literary and Scientific Men of France, 2 vols. (1838–39), in Crook, *Mary Shelley's "Literary Lives" and Other Writings*. Vol. 2, *French Lives* (Montaigne to Rochefoucauld), ed. Clarissa Campbell Orr, 293–376. Vol. 3, *French Lives* (Molière to Madame de Staël), ed. Clarissa Campbell Orr. Cited as *French Lives 1, French Lives 2*.

Lodore (1835), ed. Fiona Stafford, vol. 6 of Crook, *The Novels and Selected Works of Mary Shelley*. Cited as *Lodore*.

Matilda (1819), ed. Pamela Clemit, in *Matilda, Dramas, Reviews and Essays, Prefaces and Notes*, vol. 2 of Crook, *The Novels and Selected Works of Mary Shelley*. Cited as *Matilda*.

Maurice; or, The Fisher's Cot, intro. Claire Tomalin. New York: Alfred Knopf, 1998. Cited as *Maurice*.

Proserpine (1820), 72–91, ed. Clemit, in *Matilda, Dramas, Reviews and Essays, Prefaces and Notes*, vol. 2 of Crook, *The Novels and Selected Works of Mary Shelley*. Cited as *Proserpine*.

Valperga: or, The Life and Adventures of Castruccio, Prince of Lucca (1823), ed. Nora Crook, vol. 3 of Crook, *The Novels and Selected Works of Mary Shelley*. Cited as *Valperga*.

Introduction • Family, Writing, Public

1. This is particularly true of the women in the family. E.g., a recent biography of Mary Wollstonecraft begins with the claim that Wollstonecraft "is at her best and most original when her writing interacts with her life," and that "for most writers, their writings matter most; this is so with her contemporary, Jane Austen. But Wollstonecraft insists we attend to her life" (Janet Todd, *Mary Wollstonecraft: A Revolutionary Life* [New York: Columbia Univ. Press, 2000, ix]). It is a critical truism about Mary Shelley, modified only in the last twenty years.

2. According to Elisabeth Bronfen, both Mary and Percy "seem to have assigned a fetish-like quality to the writings of [her] parents" ("Rewriting the Family: Mary Shelley's *Franken-stein* in Its Biographical/Textual Context," in *"Frankenstein": Creation and Monstrosity*, ed. Stephan Bann [London: Reaktion Books, 1994], 16–38, 17). For a comprehensive record of Mary and Percy's reading of Wollstonecraft, see Charles E. Robinson, "A Mother's Daughter: An Intersection of Mary Shelley's *Frankenstein* and Mary Wollstonecraft's *A Vindication of the Rights of Woman*," in *Mary Wollstonecraft and Mary Shelley: Writing Lives*, ed. Helen M. Buss, D. L. Macdonald, and Anne McWhir (Waterloo, ON: Wilfrid Laurier Univ. Press, 2001), 130–31.

3. His heart and other relics were apparently discovered in her writing desk only after her death (Emily W. Sunstein, *Mary Shelley: Romance and Reality* [Baltimore: Johns Hopkins Univ. Press, 1989], 385).

4. MS to Maria Gisborne, 30 October 1834, *The Letters of Mary Wollstonecraft Shelley*, ed. Betty T. Bennett, 3 vols. (Baltimore: Johns Hopkins Univ. Press, 1980–88), 2:215.

5. Here I follow and extend the practice of a recent collection of essays entitled *Mary Wollstonecraft and Mary Shelley: Writing Lives*. The editors (Buss, Macdonald, and McWhir) state that the volume "examines intersecting lives and intersecting texts" of Wollstonecraft and Shelley, construing "lives" as "both lived experience and literary production" and "works" as including "both the process of production and the finished product, whether authorized, edited, distorted, or adapted." For them, "'life writing' refers to a wide range of discursive practices"—not simply "memoir, biography, autobiography, letters, and personal essays" but also "autobiographical novels," "essays and manifestoes informed by the operation of

rational thought working through the felt inspiration of the writer, and the lyric voice of poetry and poetic prose in which poets construct their self-development in their work" ([see note 2], 5, 4, 6).

6. As the editors of *The Other Mary Shelley: Beyond "Frankenstein"* note, "since the publication of [Emily] Sunstein's biography, it has become redundant to observe how poorly Mary Shelley has been served by some three generations of biographers and historians of Romanticism" (ed. Audrey A. Fisch, Anne K. Mellor, Esther H. Schor [New York: Oxford Univ. Press, 1993], 5).

7. I explore this claim, and the reputation of Percy Shelley, in the Epilogue.

8. On their political theories, see (for Wollstonecraft) Gary Kelly, *Revolutionary Feminism: The Mind and Career of Mary Wollstonecraft* (Basingstoke, UK: Macmillan; New York: St. Martin's Press, 1992), Virginia Sapiro, *A Vindication of Political Virtue: The Political Theory of Mary Wollstonecraft* (Chicago: Univ. of Chicago Press, 1992), and (for Godwin) Mark Philp, *Godwin's Political Justice* (London: Duckworth, 1986).

9. As the volume editors note, "Still, for an author who had been persistently overshadowed by critical and biographical attention to her illustrious parents, . . . the irony of being obscured even by her own renown is especially mordant" (*The Other Mary Shelley* [see note 6], 3).

10. See Pamela Clemit, *The Godwinian Novel: The Rational Fictions of Godwin, Brockden Brown, Mary Shelley* (Oxford: Clarendon Press, 1993).

11. See the essays in *Feminist Interpretations of Mary Wollstonecraft*, esp. Virginia L. Muller's "What Can Liberals Learn from Mary Wollstonecraft?" (ed. Maria J. Falco [University Park: Pennsylvania State Univ. Press, 1996]), 47—60) and *Mary Wollstonecraft and 200 Years of Feminisms*, ed. Eileen Janes Yeo (London: Rivers Oram Press, 1997).

12. For Godwin, see Gary Handwerk, "History, Trauma, and the Limits of the Liberal Imagination: William Godwin's Historical Fiction," in *Romanticism, History, and the Possibilities of Genre*, ed. Tilottama Rajan and Julia M. Wright (Cambridge: Cambridge Univ. Press, 1998), 64—85; for Shelley, see Mary Jacobus, "Guilt That Wants a Name: Mary Shelley's Unreadability," *Psychoanalysis and the Scene of Reading* (Oxford: Oxford Univ. Press, 1999), 165—201.

13. Betty T. Bennett draws attention to Shelley's (both Shelleys') interest in revising classic stories in " 'Not this time, Victor': Mary Shelley's Reversioning of Elizabeth, from *Frankenstein* to *Falkner*," in *Mary Shelley in Her Times*, ed. Betty T. Bennett and Stuart Curran (Baltimore: Johns Hopkins Univ. Press, 2000), 1.

14. See especially Jon Klancher, "Godwin and the Genre Reformers: On Necessity and Contingency in Romantic Narrative Theory," in Rajan and Wright, *Romanticism, History, and the Possibilities of Genre*, 21—38.

15. The term is Avery Gordon's in *Ghostly Matters: Haunting and the Sociological Imagination* (Minneapolis: Univ. of Minnesota Press, 1997), 11, 7—18.

16. In this regard, they precede the bourgeoisifying of the royals, usually associated with the reign of Queen Victoria, and the ongoing conflations of public and private life in evaluating American first families.

17. The fact of, and exhaustion over, this search is legible, I believe, in the 1831 preface to *Frankenstein*, which critics often read as articulating Shelley's conformity and desire for

privacy in her later life. But the various ways that writing, especially in this family, invalidates any notion of privacy—especially at this point in her writing career—complicates taking these assertions at face value.

18. Clemit ascribes the interest in personalizing the authors of fiction to Henry Colburn and Richard Bentley's Standard Novels series, launched in 1831. Godwin addresses this tendency in the advertisement to the 1831 republication of *St. Leon:* "The present race of readers are understood to be desirous to learn something of the peculiarities, the 'life, character, and behaviour' of an author" before they pronounce judgment on his work (*The Godwinian Novel*, 211–12).

19. This statement is ascribed to Robert Southey and cited in Ford K. Brown, *The Life of William Godwin* (London: J. M. Dent & Sons; New York: E. P. Dutton, 1926), 134.

20. Bronfen argues that one of the "unambiguous" messages of *Frankenstein* is that the "urge for artistic creativity is always irrevocably intertwined with the urge to destroy" ("Rewriting the Family," in *"Frankenstein": Creation and Monstrosity* [see note 2], 33).

21. See, e.g., Kate Ferguson Ellis, "Subversive Surfaces: The Limits of Domestic Affection in Mary Shelley's Later Fiction," in *The Other Mary Shelley* (see note 6), 220–34; Anne K. Mellor, *Mary Shelley: Her Life, Her Fiction, Her Monsters* (New York: Routledge, 1988), and Mellor, "Mary Wollstonecraft's *"A Vindication of the Rights of Woman* and the Women Writers of Her Day," in *The Cambridge Companion to Mary Wollstonecraft*, ed. Claudia L. Johnson (Cambridge: Cambridge Univ. Press, 2002), 141–59; Gary Kelly, "Politicizing the Personal: Mary Wollstonecraft, Mary Shelley, and the Coterie Novel" (149–59), and Mitzi Myers, "Mary Wollstonecraft Godwin Shelley: The Female Author between Public and Private Spheres," in *Mary Shelley in Her Times* (see note 13), 160–72; Philp, *Godwin's Political Justice*.

22. On the implications for gender and women of discourse regarding the public sphere in the mid to late eighteenth century, see esp. *Gender in Eighteenth-Century England: Roles, Representations, and Responsibilities*, ed. Hannah Barker and Elaine Chalus (London: Longman, 1997); Elizabeth Eger et al., *Women, Writing, and the Public Sphere 1700–1830* (Cambridge: Cambridge Univ. Press, 2001); Dena Goodman, "Public Sphere and Private Life: Toward a Synthesis of Current Historiographical Approaches to the Old Regime," *History and Theory* 31.3 (1992); Harriet Guest, *Small Change: Women, Learning, Patriotism, 1750–1810* (Chicago: Univ. of Chicago Press, 2000); Joan Landes, *Women and the Public Sphere in the Age of the French Revolution* (Ithaca, NY: Cornell Univ. Press, 1988); Lawrence E. Klein, "Gender and the Public/Private Distinction in the Eighteenth Century: Some Questions about Evidence and Analytic Procedure," *The Public and the Nation, Eighteenth Century Studies* 29.1 (Fall 1995): 97–109; Amanda Vickery, *The Gentleman's Daughter: Women's Lives in Georgian England* (New Haven: Yale Univ. Press, 1998), and Vickery, "Golden Age to Separate Spheres? A Review of the Categories and Chronology of English Women's History," *Historical Journal* 36.2 (1993); Jeff Weintraub, "The Theory and Politics of the Public/Private Distinction," in *Public and Private: Perspectives on a Grand Dichotomy*, ed. Jeff Weintraub and Krishan Kumar (Chicago: Univ. of Chicago Press, 1997), 1–42; Kathleen Wilson, *The Sense of the People: Politics, Culture and Imperialism in England, 1715–1785* (Cambridge: Cambridge Univ. Press, 1998). The phrase "extraordinary expansion" is Vickery's. For revisions of discourse regarding the public sphere in the romantic period, see Jon P. Klancher, *The Making of English Reading Audiences, 1790–1832* (Madison: Univ. of Wisconsin Press, 1987), and Klancher, ed., *Romanti-*

cism and Its Publics: A Forum, Studies in Romanticism 33.4 (1994); Andrew McCann, *Cultural Politics in the 1790s: Literature, Radicalism, and the Public Sphere* (Houndmills, UK: Macmillan, 1999); and Gillian Russell and Clara Tuite, "Introducing Romantic Sociability," in *Romantic Sociability: Social Networks and Literary Culture in Britain, 1770–1840*, ed. Gillian Russell and Clara Tuite (Cambridge: Cambridge Univ. Press, 2002), 1–24, esp. 9–14.

23. On the distinction, see Keith Michael Baker, "Defining the Public Sphere in Eighteenth-Century France: Variations on a Theme by Habermas," in *Habermas and the Public Sphere*, ed. Craig Calhoun (Cambridge, MA: MIT Press, 1992).

24. See, e.g., Johanna Meehan, ed., *Feminists Read Habermas: Gendering the Subject of Discourse* (New York: Routledge, 1995).

25. See "Introduction: The Public as Phantom," in *The Phantom Public Sphere*, ed. Bruce Robbins (Minneapolis: Univ. of Minnesota Press, 1993), vii–xxvi.

26. Anne K. Mellor, *Mothers of the Nation: Women's Political Writing in England, 1780–1830* (Bloomington: Indiana Univ. Press, 2000), 2; see 1–12, 101–2.

27. Guest, *Small Change*, 13, 11, 9. Here Guest is discussing differences in the consequences that Kathleen Wilson, in *The Sense of the People*, draws from Amanda Vickery's attention to the "extraordinary expansion" of women's access to print in *The Gentleman's Daughter*.

28. Guest, *Small Change*, 14, 17.

29. Saba Bahar, *Mary Wollstonecraft's Social and Aesthetic Philosophy: "An Eve to Please Me"* (Houndmills, UK: Palgrave, 2002), 7; see also 36–50.

30. Jürgen Habermas, *The Structural Transformation of the Public Sphere: An Inquiry into a Category of Bourgeois Society*, trans. Thomas Burger (Cambridge, MA: MIT Press, 1991), 55.

31. See John Brewer, "This, That, and the Other: Public, Social, and Private in the Seventeenth and Eighteenth Centuries," in *Shifting the Boundaries: Transformation of the Languages of Public and Private in the Eighteenth Century*, ed. Dario Castiglione and Lesley Sharpe (Exeter, UK: Univ. of Exeter Press, 1995); Harriet Guest observes that the "opposition between a masculine public sphere of political power and a sphere of privacy which is much more difficult to characterize, but which almost always includes or overlaps with the domestic" is "complicated by a third site"—whether that be a form derived from Habermas's own "public-within-the-private," or from "whiggish opposition politics in the 1770s," or the "capacity to imagine oneself as a citizen possessed of a political subjectivity" (*Small Change*, 11–12).

32. Habermas, *The Structural Transformation of the Public Sphere*, 51.

33. For a recent account, see the aptly titled last section, "Keeper of the Shrine," in Miranda Seymour, *Mary Shelley* (New York: Grove Press, 2000), 443–562, and the first Appendix, "An Account of the Burial of Shelley's Heart."

34. Clemit, *The Godwinian Novel* (see note 10), 1–12.

35. See esp. the preface to Godwin's *Life of Chaucer* and the introductory frame to Shelley's *The Last Man*.

36. Janet Todd, "Mary Wollstonecraft's Letters," in *Cambridge Companion to Wollstonecraft* (see note 21), 7–24, 8.

37. See John Barrell, *The Political Theory of Painting from Reynolds to Hazlitt: "The Body of the Public"* (New Haven: Yale Univ. Press, 1986).

38. "From every quarter have I heard exclamations against masculine women; but where are they to be found? If by this appellation men mean to inveigh against their ardour in

hunting, shooting, and gaming, I shall most cordially join in the cry; but if it be against the imitation of manly virtues, or, more properly speaking, the attainment of those talents and virtues, the exercise of which ennobles the human character, and which raise females in the scale of animal being, when they are comprehensively termed mankind;—all those who view them with a philosophic eye must, I should think, wish with me, that they may every day grow more and more masculine" (*Rights of Woman*, 74).

39. I mean prebourgeois also in the Habermasian sense—that is, on the model of the urban nobility's "open 'house,' " before "family life turned in on itself" (Habermas, *Structural Transformation of the Public Sphere*, 44). For anxieties regarding new and old men in the romantic period, see Tim Fulford, *Romantic Masculinities: Gender, Politics and Poetics in the Writings of Burke, Coleridge, Wordsworth, DeQuincey, and Hazlitt* (Houndmills, UK: Macmillan, 1999).

40. According to Rajan, Godwin deployed the novel as a "form of skeptical utopianism in which political desire is exposed, through the 'experiment' of fiction, to its own unconscious" ("Between Romance and History: Possibility and Contingency in Godwin, Leibniz, and Mary Shelley's *Valperga*," in *Mary Shelley in Her Times* [see note 13], 89).

41. Gary Handwerk explores the stagnant quality of Godwin's novels in "William Godwin's Historical Fiction," in *Romanticism, History, and the Possibilities of Genre* (see note 12), 64–86, esp. 80–82.

42. This surge has two main factors, beyond the ongoing popularity of feminist-cultural analyses of romanticism: the appearance of new editions of the political and literary works of Godwin (1992, 1998), Wollstonecraft (1989), and Mary Shelley (1996) published by Pickering & Chatto and observations of the bicentennial of the death of Wollstonecraft and birth of Wollstonecraft Shelley in 1997.

43. See Tilottama Rajan, "Autonarration and Genotext in Mary Hays's *Memoirs of Emma Courtney*," *Studies in Romanticism* 32.2 (1993): 149–76, and Rajan, "Framing the Corpus: Godwin's 'Editing' of Wollstonecraft in 1798," *Studies in Romanticism* 39.4 (Winter 2000): 511–31, 518. She also claims that Mary Shelley "was particularly drawn" to autonarration in "Between Romance and History," in *Mary Shelley in Her Times* (see note 13), 88.

44. Graham Allen, "Beyond Biographism: Mary Shelley's *Matilda*, Intertextuality, and the Wandering Subject," *Romanticism* 3.2 (1997): 170–84, 170.

45. Laura Mandell, "The First Women (Psycho)analysts; or, The Friends of Feminist History," *MLQ* 65.1 (2004): 69–92; Gary Handwerk, "William Godwin's Historical Fiction," in *Romanticism, History, and the Possibilities of Genre* (see note 12); Jacobus, "Mary Shelley's Unreadability" (see note 12), 165–201; Tilottama Rajan, "Wollstonecraft and Godwin: Reading the Secrets of the Political Novel," *Studies in Romanticism* 27.2 (1988): 221–51.

46. On being-as-signifier, see Jacques Lacan, *The Seminar of Jacques Lacan*, bk. 7 of *The Ethics of Psychoanalysis, 1959–60*, ed. Jacques-Alain Miller, trans. Dennis Porter (New York: Norton, 1992). For a trenchant explanation of the role of the signifier in history and artistic production, see L. O. Aranye Fradenburg, *Sacrifice Your Love: Psychoanalysis, Historicism, Chaucer* (Minneapolis: Univ. of Minnesota Press, 2002), 20–32.

47. Sigmund Freud, *On the Interpretation of Dreams, (2d Pt.) and On Dreams*, vol. 5 of *The Standard Edition of the Complete Psychological Works of Sigmund Freud*, 24 vols., ed. and trans. James Strachey (London: Hogarth Press, 1964), 279.

48. Jeffrey N. Cox, "Communal Romanticism," *European Romantic Review* 15.2 (2004): 329–34, and Jack Stillinger, *Multiple Authorship and the Myth of Solitary Genius* (New York: Oxford Univ. Press, 1991).

49. On the Edgeworths, see Marilyn Butler, *Maria Edgeworth: A Literary Biography* (Oxford: Oxford Univ. Press, 1972); on the Wordsworth-Coleridge circle, see Bradford Mudge, *Sara Coleridge, a Victorian Daughter: Her Life and Essays* (New Haven, CT: Yale Univ. Press, 1989).

50. Elizabeth Kowaleski-Wallace, *Their Father's Daughters: Hannah More, Maria Edgeworth, and Patriarchal Complicity* (Oxford: Oxford Univ. Press, 1991).

51. Myers, "Mary Wollstonecraft Godwin Shelley," in *Mary Shelley in Her Times* (see note 13), 160–72.

52. Kelly, "Politicizing the Personal," in ibid., 147–60.

53. My title plays on the emphasis on "case" in his reception history as illustrated by Frederick A. Pottle, "The Case of Shelley," in *English Romantic Poets: Modern Essays in Criticism*, ed. M. H. Abrams (New York: Oxford Univ. Press, 1960), 289–306; James K. Chandler, *England in 1819: The Politics of Literary Culture and the Case of Romantic Historicism* (Chicago: Univ. of Chicago Press, 1998).

54. For a particularly chilling assessment of the situation, see Elaine Brown, *The Condemnation of Little B* (Boston: Beacon Press, 2002). See also *2006 Kids Count Data Book* (Baltimore: Annie E. Casey Foundation, 2006), and *America's Children: Key National Indicators of Well-Being* (Washington, DC: Federal Interagency Forum on Child and Family Statistics, 2005).

55. E.g., Markman Ellis, *The Politics of Sensibility: Race, Gender, and Commerce* (Cambridge: Cambridge Univ. Press, 1996); Jeffrey N. Cox, introduction to *Drama*, vol. 5 of *Slavery, Abolition, and Emancipation: Writings in the British Romantic Period*, 8 vols., ed. Peter J. Kitson and Debbie Lee (London: Pickering & Chatto, 1999), vii–xxvii; Felicity Nussbaum, *The Limits of the Human* (Oxford: Oxford Univ. Press, 2003). On critiques of romantic imagination, see Jerome McGann, *The Romantic Ideology: A Critical Investigation* (Chicago: Univ. of Chicago Press, 1981); Kurt Heinzelman, *The Economics of Imagination* (Amherst: Univ. of Massachusetts Press, 1980); Nigel Leask, *The Politics of Imagination in Coleridge's Critical Thought* (Houndmills, UK: Macmillan, 1988); Forest Pyle, *The Ideology of Imagination: Subject and Society in the Discourse of Romanticism* (Stanford: Stanford Univ. Press, 1995); John Whale, *Imagination Under Pressure, 1789–1832: Aesthetics, Politics, and Utility* (Cambridge: Cambridge Univ. Press, 2000).

56. Their embrace of racial difference receives mixed reviews. See Moira Ferguson, "Mary Wollstonecraft and the Problematic of Slavery," in *Feminist Interpretations of Mary Wollstonecraft* (see note 11), 125–50, Delia Jarrett-Macauley, "It Ain't all Black and White," in *Mary Wollstonecraft and 200 years of Feminisms* (see note 11), 104–17.

57. For a major recent re-evaluation of fancy, see Jeffrey C. Robinson *Unfettering Poetry: Fancy in British Romanticism* (New York: Palgrave Macmillan, 2006).

58. Patricia Fara, "An Attractive Therapy: Animal Magnetism in Eighteenth-Century England," *History of Science* 33.100 (1995): 127–77, and Simon During, *Modern Enchantments: The Cultural Power of Secular Magic* (Cambridge, MA: Harvard Univ. Press, 2002).

59. Jacques Derrida, *Spectres of Marx: The State of the Debt, the Work of Mourning, and the New International,* trans. Peggy Kamuf (New York: Routledge, 1994), xix; 21–30.

60. On the performative dimensions of Godwin, see Angela Esterhammer, "Godwin's Suspicion of Speech Acts," *Studies in Romanticism* 39.4 (2000): 553–78.

61. On the currency of these terms, see Fara, "An Attractive Therapy," 127–35.

62. A recent formulation of this as a general feminist position is Robyn Wiegman, "On Being in Time with Feminism," *MLQ* 65.1 (2004): 161–76.

63. William St. Clair, *The Godwins and the Shelleys: A Biography of a Family* (Baltimore: Johns Hopkins Univ. Press, 1989), 280.

64. Wollstonecraft makes the same point about not censoring the books that girls read in *Original Stories,* 415.

65. Rajan, "Godwin's 'Editing' of Wollstonecraft" (see note 43), 511–14.

66. Ibid., 512.

67. James Chandler gives the most comprehensive account of Percy Shelley's contribution to situated reading (without the transcendentalizing impulse) in *England in 1819.* I deal with the implications of this argument in the epilogue.

68. Chandler, *England in 1819* (see note 53), 510–11.

69. It is revealing for the larger argument that links reading for tendency to Godwin's mourning strategies that the quotation in *Essay on Sepulchres* is previewed in the essay that defines tendency, "Of Choice in Reading" (*Enquirer,* 141).

Chapter One • *Making Public Love*

1. On the reception of Wollstonecraft, see P. Hirsch, "Mary Wollstonecraft: A Problematic Legacy," in *Wollstonecraft's Daughters: Womanhood in England and France, 1780–1920,* ed. C. C. Orr (Manchester: Manchester Univ. Press, 1996); B. Caine, *English Feminism, 1780–1980* (Oxford: Oxford Univ. Press, 1997); Eileen Janes Yeo, introduction to *Mary Wollstonecraft and 200 Years of Feminisms* (London: Rivers Oram Press, 1997), 1–15; Cora Kaplan, "Mary Wollstonecraft's Reception and Legacies," in *The Cambridge Companion to Mary Wollstonecraft,* ed. Claudia L. Johnson (Cambridge: Cambridge Univ. Press, 2002), 246–69. Biographer/ critics who argue that Wollstonecraft's love life compromises her political thinking include Claire Tomalin, *The Life and Death of Mary Wollstonecraft* (New York: Harcourt, Brace, Jovanovich, 1974), and S. Tomaselli, "The Death and Rebirth of Character in the 18th Century," in *Rewriting the Self: Histories from the Renaissance to the Present,* ed. Ray Porter (London: Routledge, 1995).

2. Friends enjoyed making fun of the contradiction. According to Fuseli (not an impartial source), "The assertrix of female rights has given her hand to the *balancier* of political justice" (cited in Janet Todd, *Mary Wollstonecraft: A Revolutionary Life* [New York: Columbia Univ. Press, 2000], 422).

3. Mitzi Myers, "Godwin's *Memoirs* of Wollstonecraft: The Shaping of Self and Subject," *Studies in Romanticism* 20.3 (Fall 1981): 299–316.

4. Anne K. Mellor, *Mothers of the Nation: Women's Political Writing in England, 1780– 1830* (Bloomington: Indiana Univ. Press, 2000).

5. On Wollstonecraft's ambivalence toward female sexuality, see Cora Kaplan, "Wild Nights: Pleasure/Sexuality/Feminism," *Sea Changes: Essays on Culture and Feminism* (London: Verso, 1986); Mary Poovey, *The Proper Lady and the Woman Writer: Ideology as Style in the Works of Mary Wollstonecraft, Mary Shelley, and Jane Austen* (Chicago: Univ. of Chicago Press, 1984); Tom Furniss, "'Nasty Tricks and Tropes': Sexuality and Language in Mary Wollstonecraft's *Rights of Woman*," *Studies in Romanticism* 32.2 (1993): 177–209.

6. William St. Clair, *The Godwins and the Shelleys: A Biography of a Family* (Baltimore: Johns Hopkins Univ. Press, 1989), 141; on public reaction to his marriage, 176–79.

7. On the importance of Coleridge, see ibid., 225–37.

8. Though modern editors abbreviate the title to *Memoirs of Wollstonecraft* or *Memoirs of Mary Wollstonecraft*, I prefer the original title, since it conveys the book's intention of celebrating an author, not a person.

9. This is true of the daily component of their sexual affair. As commentators on their letters make clear, much of the content of the notes passed between households (before and after their marriage) concerns various requests for books, ink, or other implements associated with writing that are also requests for sex. To philosophize or not is also classic code for the evening's activity. See *Godwin and Mary: Letters of William Godwin and Mary Wollstonecraft*, ed. Ralph M. Wardle (Lincoln: Univ. of Nebraska Press, 1977).

10. Claudia L. Johnson, *Equivocal Beings: Politics, Gender, and Sentimentality in the 1790s* (Chicago: Univ. of Chicago Press, 1995), 49.

11. See I. Williams, *Novel and Romance, 1700–1800: A Documentary Record* (London: Routledge & Kegan Paul, 1970).

12. Gavin Edwards, however, shows how discourse regarding "family" prompts discourse regarding "story" in "William Godwin's Foreign Language: Stories and Families in *Caleb Williams* and *Political Justice*," *Studies in Romanticism* 39.4 (2000): 533–52.

13. See Jacqueline Pearson, *Women's Reading in Britain, 1750–1835, A Dangerous Recreation* (Cambridge: Cambridge Univ. Press, 1999), 87–121.

14. Heather Jackson explores the variety of practices and meanings associated with marginalia in the romantic period in a recent talk, "What Was Mr. Bennett Doing in His Library, and What Does It Matter?" paper presented at the North American Society for the Study of Romanticism, New York, 1–5 August 2003.

15. In their epistolary relations, Wollstonecraft protests frequently that "esteem" is a "cold word" and counters with "glowing" accounts of her skin, eyes, and countenance the following morning ("I have seldom seen so much live fire running about my features as this morning when recollections—very dear, called forth the blush of pleasure" [cited in Todd, *Mary Wollstonecraft*, 399, 402]). Godwin, famously, is more reserved in this vocabulary, either resorting to French or a system of dots and dashes in his journal. See Appendix 1 of St. Clair, *The Godwins and the Shelleys*, for a decoding of "Godwin's Sexual Relationship with Mary Wollstonecraft" (497–503). Godwin remained unsure of the value of sexual feelings throughout his career. "What Milton calls 'The rites mysterious of connubial love,' would have little charm in them in reflection, to a mind one degree above the brutes, were it not for the mystery they include, of their tendency to give existence to a new human creature like ourselves" (*Thoughts on Man*, 188).

16. As Claudia Johnson shows, the word has more negative connotations in *Rights of Woman* (*Equivocal Beings*, 32–33, 44–45).

17. The letter to Godwin specifies "rapture" as "sublime tranquility" ("it is not rapture"). Also, "when the heart and reason accord there is no flying from voluptuous sensations, I find, do what a woman can—can a philosopher do more?" (MW to WG, 13 September 1796).

18. Eve Kosofsky Sedgwick, "Jane Austen and the Masturbating Girl," *Critical Inquiry* 17.4 (1991): 818–37; reprinted in *Tendencies* (Durham, NC: Duke Univ. Press, 1993), 109–29.

19. Mary A. Favret, "*Letters Written during a Short Residence in Sweden, Norway, and Denmark:* Traveling with Mary Wollstonecraft," in *Cambridge Companion to Wollstonecraft* (see note 1), 209–27; Mary Jacobus, "In Love with a Cold Climate: Traveling with Wollstonecraft," *First Things: The Maternal Imaginary in Literature, Art, and Psychoanalysis* (New York: Routledge, 1995), 63–82.

20. Julie A. Carlson, "Characters: Mary Wollstonecraft and Germaine de Staël," *Modern Philology* 98.2 (2000): 320–38.

21. "Stern," "rugged," "rigid," and "somewhat amazonian" are Godwin's adjectives for much of the voice of *Rights of Woman* (other parts displaying a "luxuriance of imagination and a trembling delicacy of sentiment"), *Memoirs*, 82.

22. Saba Bahar, *Mary Wollstonecraft's Social and Aesthetic Philosophy: "An Eve to Please Me"* (Houndmills, UK: Palgrave, 2002), 132–53.

23. Mary Jacobus, "Traveling with Wollstonecraft," 63; Mitzi Myers, "Mary Wollstonecraft's Literary Reviews," in *Cambridge Companion to Wollstonecraft* (see note 1), 82–98.

24. *Short Residence*, 280, 289, 296, 299, 302–4, 312, 315, 325, 344.

25. Bahar, *Mary Wollstonecraft's Social and Aesthetic Philosophy*, 145–54.

26. Lauren Berlant, "The Female Complaint," *Social Text* 19/20 (1988): 237–59.

27. Julia Kristeva, "Glory, Grief, and Writing (A Letter to a 'Romantic' concerning Madame de Staël)," in *New Maladies of the Soul*, trans. Ross Guberman (New York, 1995), 163 (emphasis in original). For a less affirmative reading of female melancholy, see Mary Jacobus, " 'The science of herself': Scenes of Female Enlightenment," in *Romanticism, History, and the Possibilities of Genre*, ed. Tilottama Rajan and Julia M. Wright (Cambridge: Cambridge Univ. Press, 1998), 240–69.

28. Bahar, *Mary Wollstonecraft's Social and Aesthetic Philosophy*, 51.

29. Gary Kelly, *English Fiction of the Romantic Period, 1789–1830* (New York: Longman, 1989), 41–44; Johnson, *Equivocal Beings* (see note 10), 66–69; also Laura Mandell in a talk, "Bad Marriages, Bad Novels: Mary Hays' *Emma* and Mary Wollstonecraft's *Mary*," paper presented at the North American Society for the Study of Romanticism, New York, 1–5 August 2003.

30. See Johnson on how *Wrongs* "exposes the concealed logic of sentimentality" (*Equivocal Beings* [see note 10], 61, 60–69).

31. Bahar examines this point in its negative dimensions by construing the Abelard-Rousseauvistic figure as a libertine philosopher who seduces his female student through her desire for instruction (*Mary Wollstonecraft's Social and Aesthetic Philosophy* [see note 22], 51–63).

32. Eliza Fenwick takes up this project in *Secrecy*.

33. It also rejects the mode of *Mary*, whose adulterous desires are not actualized.

34. On Godwin's shaping hand in these conclusions, see Tilottama Rajan, "Framing the Corpus: Godwin's 'Editing' of Wollstonecraft," *Studies in Romanticism* 39.4 (2000), 517–19.

35. Maria's substitution of one for the other has already occurred in chapter 2, when, preoccupied with catching a glimpse of "the stranger," the narrator writes: "She found however that she could think of nothing else: or, if she thought of her daughter, it was to wish that she had a father whom her mother could respect and love" (71).

36. On Wollstonecraft's complicated reception of Rousseau, see Gregory Dart, *Rousseau, Robespierre, and Romanticism* (Cambridge: Cambridge Univ. Press, 1999).

37. Johnson, *Equivocal Beings* (see note 10), 60.

38. Bahar, *Mary Wollstonecraft's Social and Aesthetic Philosophy* (see note 22), 116–18.

39. For discussion of her lack of a receptive reading public, see A. Wilson, "Mary Wollstonecraft and the Search for the Radical Woman," *Genders* 6 (1989): 88–101.

40. Bahar makes a similar point about Wollstonecraft's interest in the "struggles of postlapsarian humanity" in her account of Wollstonecraft's readings of Milton's and Fuseli's Eve. "It is, indeed, not the story of Eve's fall, but rather the account of her '*rough* toils and useful struggles with worldly *cares*' *after* the fall that Wollstonecraft seeks to tell" (23, original emphasis). Emphasizing the very "incertitude" of the outcome of striving for virtue in a fallen world is what she claims that Eve bequeaths on all "the Eves who inhabit the world after the fall of the Bastille" (*Mary Wollstonecraft's Social and Aesthetic Philosophy* [see note 22], 16–24).

41. Ford K. Brown, *The Life of William Godwin* (London: J. M. Dent & Sons; New York: E. P. Dutton, 1926), 134; for the negative reception, see Peter H. Marshall, *William Godwin* (New Haven: Yale Univ. Press, 1984), 193–94; and B. Allen Sprague, "The Reaction against William Godwin," *Modern Philology* 16 (1918): 57–75.

42. Chapter 5 explores this work as part of Godwin's efforts to restore life and England's vitality through biography/history.

43. Rajan, "Godwin's 'Editing' of Wollstonecraft," 512.

44. A. E. Rodway, *Godwin in the Age of Transition* (London: G. G. Harrap, 1952), 39.

45. Burton R. Pollin, *Education and Enlightenment in the Works of William Godwin* (New York: Las Americas, 1962), 246; Mark Philp, *Godwin's Political Justice* (London: Duckworth, 1986), 142–60.

46. Godwin omitted these two sentences from the preface of 1799, when *St. Leon* was reissued in 1831 (11n).

47. See Maggie Kilgour, *The Rise of the Gothic* (London: Routledge, 1995), 109.

48. See Gary Handwerk and A. A. Markley, introduction to *Fleetwood; or, The New Man of Feeling* (Peterborough, ON: Broadview Press, 2001), 30–32.

49. Gary Kelly, *The English Jacobin Novel, 1780–1805* (Oxford: Oxford Univ. Press, 1976).

50. See Steven Bruhm, "William Godwin's *Fleetwood*: The Epistemology of the Tortured Body," *Eighteenth-Century Life* 16 (1992): 25–43.

51. The point is strengthened by comparison with *Wrongs of Woman*, which specifies that the marriage "tie, the fetters rather, ate into [Maria's] vitals" (134).

52. With one exception: "Mistake me not, my dear Fleetwood. I am not idle and thoughtless enough, to promise to sink my being and individuality in yours. I shall have my distinct propensities and preferences. . . . In me you will have a wife, and not a passive machine" (187).

53. According to Pollin, this phrase from *Political Justice* is a "favorite term of Godwin's circle" (*Enlightenment and Education*, 24).

54. Elisabeth Bronfen suggests that we should take the point seriously in "Rewriting the Family: Mary Shelley's *Frankenstein* in Its Biographical/Textual Context," in *"Frankenstein": Creation and Monstrosity*, ed. Stephen Bann (London: Reaktion Books, 1994), 16–38, esp. 26–27.

55. "No system was ever so successful as that of chivalry in assigning to each sex its respective department" (*Life of Chaucer*, 1:396).

56. We might term Godwin's fictional project a Series of Novels on the Passions, a connection to Joanna Baillie that Godwin himself makes in his preface to *Mandeville*.

57. Todd, *Mary Wollstonecraft* (see note 2), 396.

58. "On Poetry (from Posthumous Works)," in vol. 7 of *The Works of Mary Wollstonecraft*, 9 (my emphasis).

Epigraph: New Letters of Robert Southey, ed. Kenneth Curry, 2 vols. (New York: Columbia Univ. Press, 1965).

59. St. Clair, *The Godwins and the Shelleys* (see note 6), 192, 195.

60. Charles Kegan Paul, *William Godwin: His Friends and Contemporaries*, 2 vols. (London: Henry S. King, 1876), 1:358.

61. 29 August 1801 to—?, in ibid., 2: 74.

62. "Thoughts Occasioned by the Perusal of Dr. Parr's Spital Sermon," in *Political Writings II*, 170, 171.

63. Attacks by former friends include a series of lectures by James Mackintosh given in January 1799 on "The Law of Nature and of Nations" and Dr. Parr's Spital Sermon. Other satires include Elizabeth Hamilton, *Letters of a Hindoo Rajah* (1797), W. C. Proby, *Modern Philosophy and Barbarism; or, a Comparison Between the Theory of Mr. Godwin and the Practice of Lycurgus* (1798), *Travels of St. Godwin* (1800), Charles Lucas, *The Infernal Quixote* (1801). Serious disagreements are found in Thomas Green's *Examination of the Leading Principle of the New System of Morals as that Principle is Stated and Applied to Mr. Godwin's Enquiry* and Thomas Malthus, *An Essay on the Principle of Population* (1798). See Sprague, "The Reaction against William Godwin" (see note 41).

64. "Introductory Note," "Thoughts Occasioned by the Perusal," in *Political Writings II* (see note 62), 163.

65. "Godwin/Shelley Correspondence," in vol. 1 of *Collected Novels and Memoirs of William Godwin*, 72.

Chapter Two • Forms of Attachment

1. William St. Clair, *The Godwins and the Shelleys: A Biography of a Family* (Baltimore: Johns Hopkins Univ. Press, 1989), 460–64, 411–13; Miranda Seymour, *Mary Shelley* (New York: Grove Press, 2000), 234–35, 169–70.

2. On the history of surface and depth in relation to drawing character, see Deidre Shauna Lynch, *The Economy of Character: Novels, Market Culture, and the Business of Inner Meaning* (Chicago: Univ. of Chicago Press, 1998). Her claim for the "roundness" characteristic of romantic character is another instance of Godwin's difference from his times (123–63).

3. See the "Bibliography on Sensibility, 1978–1998," in *Passionate Encounters in a Time of Sensibility,* ed. Maximillian E. Novak and Anne K. Mellor (Newark: Univ. of Delaware Press, 2000), 265–68; on sympathy in Smith, see David Marshall, "Adam Smith and the Theatricality of Moral Sentiments," *Critical Inquiry* 10 (1984): 592–613; James K. Chandler, *England in 1819: The Politics of Literary Culture and the Case of Romantic Historicism* (Chicago: Univ. of Chicago Press, 1998), 309–19. On background to romantic notions of imagination, see James Engell, *The Creative Imagination: Enlightenment to Romanticism* (Cambridge, MA: Harvard Univ. Press, 1981); Christine Gallant, ed. *Coleridge's Theory of Imagination Today* (New York: AMS Press, 1989); and Richard Gravil, Lucy Newlyn, and Nicholas Roe, eds., *Coleridge's Imagination: Essays in Memory of Pete Laver* (Cambridge: Cambridge Univ. Press, 1985).

4. Mark Philp, *Godwin's Political Justice* (London: Duckworth, 1986), 164–67.

5. "At present [1999], Godwin occupies a special position among the major writers of the Romantic period, including all of the 'Great Romantics' of this series, in that there is no comprehensive edition of his letters or journals" (Introduction to *Godwin,* ed. Pamela Clemit, vol. 1 of *Lives of the Great Romantics III: Godwin, Wollstonecraft, and Mary Shelley by Their Contemporaries* [London: Pickering & Chatto, 1999], xv). Currently Victoria Myers is editing the diaries for Pickering & Chatto and Pamela Clemit is editing *The Letters of William Godwin,* 6 vols., to be published by Oxford Univ. Press.

6. "Autobiography," in vol. 1 of *The Collected Novels and Memoirs of William Godwin,* 35.

7. "Analysis of own Character," in ibid., 59.

8. For critiques of imagination, see Jerome McGann, *The Romantic Ideology: A Critical Investigation* (Chicago: Univ. of Chicago Press, 1981); Kurt Heinzelman, *The Economics of Imagination* (Amherst: Univ. of Massachusetts Press, 1980); Nigel Leask, *The Politics of Imagination in Coleridge's Critical Thought* (Basingstoke, UK: Macmillan, 1988); Forest Pyle, *The Ideology of Imagination: Subject and Society in the Discourse of Romanticism* (Stanford: Stanford Univ. Press, 1995); John Whale, *Imagination under Pressure, 1789–1832: Aesthetics, Politics, and Utility* (Cambridge: Cambridge Univ. Press, 2000). For critiques of sentiment, see Markman Ellis, *The Politics of Sensibility: Race, Gender, and Commerce* (Cambridge: Cambridge Univ. Press, 1996); Jeffrey N. Cox, introduction to *Drama,* vol. 5 of *Slavery, Abolition, and Emancipation: Writings in the British Romantic Period,* 8 vols., ed. Peter J. Kitson and Debbie Lee (London: Pickering & Chatto, 1999), vii–xxvii; Felicity Nussbaum, *The Limits of the Human* (Oxford: Oxford Univ. Press, 2003).

9. On the overlap in the categories, see Naomi Tadmor, *Family and Friends in Eighteenth-Century England* (Cambridge: Cambridge Univ. Press, 2001), 167–71.

10. Anne K. Mellor credits Wollstonecraft and Hannah More with envisioning the "triumphant 'mother of the nation,'" in *Mothers of the Nation: Women's Political Writing in England, 1780–1830* (Bloomington: Indiana Univ. Press, 2000), 121.

11. Cora Kaplan, "Wild Nights: Pleasure/Sexuality/Feminism," in *Sea Changes: Essays on Culture and Feminism* (London: Verso, 1986); Mary Poovey, *The Proper Lady and the Woman Writer: Ideology as Style in the Works of Mary Wollstonecraft, Mary Shelley, and Jane Austen* (Chicago: Univ. of Chicago Press, 1984).

12. *Memoirs of the Late Thomas Holcroft,* vol. 3 of *The Complete Works of William Hazlitt,* 20 vols., ed. P. P. Howe (London: J. M. Dent & Sons, 1932), 135.

13. As late as his *Thoughts on Man,* Godwin is still asserting this position: "He who ever thinks that his 'charity must begin at home' is in great danger of becoming an indifferent citizen, and of withering those feelings of philanthropy, which in all sound estimation constitute the crowning glory of man" (160; cf. 151).

14. I deal with these topics at greater length in "Hazlitt and the Sociability of Theater," in *Romantic Sociability: Social Networks and Literary Culture in Britain, 1770–1840,* ed. Gillian Russell and Clara Tuite (Cambridge: Cambridge Univ. Press, 2002), 145–65.

15. "Autobiography," in *Collected Novels and Memoirs of William Godwin,* 1:11.

16. Pamela Clemit, *The Godwinian Novel: The Rational Fictions of Godwin, Brockden Brown, Mary Shelley* (Oxford: Clarendon Press, 1993), 48.

17. "It is true, that we cannot act without the impulse of desire or uneasiness; but we do not think of that desire and uneasiness; and it is the thing upon which the mind is fixed that constitutes our motive" (*Thoughts,* 155).

18. "Godwin/Shelley Correspondence," in *Collected Novels and Memoirs of William Godwin,* 1:75.

19. Philp, *Godwin's Political Justice* (see note 4), 89–96. For a helpful account of Hartley's necessity, see Jerome Christensen, *Coleridge's Blessed Machine of Language* (Ithaca, NY: Cornell Univ. Press, 1981), 33–57.

20. Burton R. Pollin, *Education and Enlightenment in the Works of William Godwin* (New York: Las Americas, 1962), 115–45.

21. "We seldom recollect the society of which we are politically members . . . thinking only for the most part of ourselves and our immediate connections and attachments" (*Thoughts,* 152).

22. See the distinction between natural and moral independence in *Political Justice* (448–49).

23. "Man is a godlike being. We launch ourselves in conceit into illimitable space, and take up our rest beyond the fixed stars. We proceed without impediment from country to country, and from century to century, through all the ages of the past, and through the vast creation of the imaginable future" (*Thoughts,* 43).

24. See, e.g., the exchange on 17 August 1796, where Godwin confesses his sexual attraction but resolves to "be your friend, the friend of your mind," to which Wollstonecraft replies, "I like your last—may I call it *love* letter? better than the first" (original emphasis); or 21 September 1796 "Say only that we are friends." "Friends? Why not? If I thought otherwise, I should be miserable."

25. See also *Mandeville,* ed. Clemit, vol. 6 of *The Collected Novels and Memoirs of William Godwin,* 241–42.

26. Clemit, introduction to *Godwin* (see note 5), xxiii; Charles Kegan Paul, *William Godwin: His Friends and Contemporaries,* 2 vols. (London: Henry S. King, 1876), 1:292–98.

27. This view is qualified by Judith Barbour, "Mary Shelley: Writing/Other Women in Godwin's *Life,*" in *Mary Wollstonecraft and Mary Shelley: Writing Lives,* ed. Helen M. Buss, D. L. Macdonald, and Anne McWhir (Waterloo, ON: Wilfrid Laurier Univ. Press, 2001), 139–58.

28. See David Marshall, *The Figure of Theater: Shaftesbury, Defoe, Adam Smith, and George Eliot* (New York: Columbia Univ. Press, 1986), 167–92.

29. This passage would profit from comparison to Joanna Baillie's position on the passions, her tragedy on anger, *De Monfort*, being acknowledged in the preface as an influence on *Mandeville* (8).

30. "The wonder rather is, that man, who has so many things to put him in mind to be humble and despise himself, should ever have been susceptible of pride and disdain" (*Thoughts*, 45).

31. Pollin, *Education and Enlightenment*, 99.

32. *The Enquirer* actually endorses books over conversation on the score of their greater nutritional value. "The intellect that depends upon conversation for nutriment, may be compared to the man who should prefer the precarious existence of a beggar, to the possession of a regular and substantial income" (236).

33. On the importance of sociability to formulations of romanticism, see the introduction and collected essays in *Romantic Sociability* (see note 14).

34. Philp, *Godwin's Political Justice* (see note 4), 34–37, 163–65.

35. Ibid., 175–77.

36. "Godwin/Shelley Correspondence," in *Collected Novels and Memoirs of William Godwin*, 81.

37. Ibid.; also *Enquirer*, 237.

38. "Godwin/Shelley Correspondence," in *Collected Novels and Memoirs of William Godwin*, 80; see also *Thoughts*, 108–9.

39. Preface to the "Standard Novels" Edition of *Fleetwood* (R. Bentley, 1832), reprinted in *Caleb Williams*, ed. Gary Handwerk and A. A. Markley (Peterborough, ON: Broadview Press, 2000), 447. Godwin says the same thing of Wollstonecraft's *Wrongs of Woman* in his preface to the posthumous edition.

40. Tilottama Rajan, "Framing the Corpus: Godwin's 'Editing' of Wollstonecraft in 1798," *Studies in Romanticism* 39.4 (2000): 512.

41. This also constitutes his objection to priesthood, which enjoins daily "study" but abstention from "enquiry" (*Enquirer*, 178).

42. "Considerations on Lord Grenville's and Mr. Pitt's Bills," in *Political Writings II*, vol. 2 of *Political and Philosophical Writings of William Godwin*, 132.

43. See ibid., 133.

44. Ibid., 125.

45. Ibid., 123n.

46. Harriet Guest, *Small Change: Women, Learning, Patriotism, 1750–1810* (Chicago: Univ. of Chicago Press, 2000), 19.

47. Guest sketches out the sentimental blueprint in the chapter entitled "This Sentiment of Home" (176–219).

48. For irritation regarding dress, see letters from 12 December 1796 and 12 January 1797.

49. Janet Todd, *Mary Wollstonecraft: A Revolutionary Life* (New York: Columbia Univ. Press, 2000). Todd cites a bemused Barbauld who comments, "In order to give the connection as little as possible the appearance of such a vulgar and debasing tie as matrimony, the parties have established separate establishments, and the husband only visits his mistress like a lover when each is dressed, rooms in order, &c" (ibid., 424).

50. Mary Wollstonecraft, *A Vindication of the Rights of Woman*, chap. 12, "National

Education." See Alan Richardson, "Mary Wollstonecraft on Education," in *The Cambridge Companion to Mary Wollstonecraft*, ed. Claudia L. Johnson (Cambridge: Cambridge Univ. Press, 2002), 24–41, esp. 32–37.

51. Peter H. Marshall, *William Godwin* (New Haven: Yale Univ. Press, 1984), 191.

52. "The door of 41 Skinner Street was always open. If Godwin was poor in money he was rich in wisdom and he redistributed without stint. . . . With the failure to effect change by political action . . . the only hope of resuming the advance lay in patient discussion among individuals. This was an aspect of his life's work which the philosopher never neglected" (St. Clair, *The Godwins and the Shelleys*, 299; 299–305).

53. Mary Hays, *Appeal to the Men of Great Britain in Behalf of Women* (1798).

54. The phrase is St. Clair's in a chapter heading (*The Godwins and the Shelleys* [see note 1], 238–54; on the bookstore, see 284–95); Ford K. Brown, *The Life of William Godwin* (London: J. M. Dent & Sons; New York: E. P. Dutton, 1926), 221–36.

55. The "dust" that comprises illustrous men is explored in *Essay on Sepulchres* in chapter 5.

56. The preface to the satire *Travels of St. Godwin: A Tale of the 16th, 17th, and 18th Centuries. By Count Reginald De St. Leon* (Dublin, 1800) sends up precisely this sentiment. "A book kindly given to the public in the year 1798 contains a sentence which is not more applicable in this place than it is in the highest degree profound and full of mind. I shall quote it. 'IT IS BETTER THAT A MAN SHOULD BE A LIVING BEING THAN A STOCK OR A STONE.' I recommend the reader to ponder on this sentiment, and weigh it well, before he presumes to contradict it" (xix).

57. *Caleb Williams*, vol. 1 of *The Collected Novels and Memoirs of William Godwin*, 443, 439.

58. "Essay on Scepticism," in *Educational and Literary Writings*, vol. 5 of *Political and Philosophical Writings of William Godwin*, 306.

59. "Analysis of Own Character," in vol. 1 of *The Collected Novels and Memoirs of William Godwin*, 59.

60. See, e.g., this from Hazlitt: "Mr. Godwin has rendered an essential service to moral science, by attempting (in vain) to pass the Arctic Circle and Frozen Regions, where the understanding is no longer warmed by the affections, nor fanned by the breeze of fancy!" (*Godwin*, ed. Clemit [see note 5], 53; see also 69, 143).

61. Godwin's brief reflections on etymology are sanguine in comparison (*Enquirer*, 101–2). Indeed, he sees "the necessity and the use of etymology" as "exaggerated." "However extensive are our researches, we must stop somewhere" (101).

62. "The Original Manuscript Ending of the Novel"; reprinted in *Caleb Williams* (see note 39), 443.

Chapter Three • *Family Relations*

1. See especially Anne K. Mellor, *Mary Shelley: Her Life, Her Fiction, Her Monsters* (New York: Routledge, 1988), and "Family Politics," *Romanticism and Gender* (New York, London: Routledge, 1993), 65–70.

2. This argument is found in many critical introductions to *Frankenstein*.

3. *Frankenstein, Matilda, The Last Man, Lodore,* and *Falkner* all explore incestuous relations and all portray various characters who are more in love with death than life. *Frankenstein* and *The Last Man* also pursue homosocial and homosexual feelings between men.

4. In this view, I join critics like Betty T. Bennett and Kate Ellis, who emphasize the continuities between Shelley's early and late novels in their reformist agendas and resistance to conventional norms. See Betty T. Bennett, " 'Not this time, Victor!': Mary Shelley's Reversioning of Elizabeth, from *Frankenstein* to *Falkner*," in *Mary Shelley in Her Times,* ed. Betty T. Bennett and Stuart Curran (Baltimore: Johns Hopkins Univ. Press, 2000), 1–18, esp. 8; also Bennett, *Mary Shelley: An Introduction* (Baltimore: Johns Hopkins Univ. Press, 1998); Kate Ferguson Ellis, "Subversive Surfaces: The Limits of Domestic Affection in Mary Shelley's Later Fiction," in *The Other Mary Shelley: Beyond "Frankenstein,"* ed. Audrey A. Fisch, Anne K. Mellor, and Esther H. Schor (New York: Oxford Univ. Press, 1993), 220–34.

5. E.g., WG to MW of 5 June 1797, MW to WG of 6 June 1797, in which she confesses that she "begin[s] to love this little creature," referred to in the preceding sentence as "Master William," and so forth on up to Mary's birth.

6. Mary Jean Corbett, "Reading Mary Shelley's *Journals:* Romantic Subjectivity and Feminist Criticism," in *The Other Mary Shelley* (see note 4), 73, 78–81.

7. This is an interesting reworking of an image Godwin likes to cite in various contexts, whereby a tyrant of antiquity chains a living body to a dead one (*Deloraine,* 159; cf. *Mandeville*).

8. A fine essay that combines the two approaches is Anne-Lise François and Daniel Mozes, " 'Don't Say I Love You': Agency, Gender, and Romanticism in Mary Shelley's *Matilda,*" in *Mary Shelley's Fictions: From "Frankenstein" to "Falkner,"* ed. Michael Eberle-Sinatra (Basingstoke, UK: Macmillan, 2000), 57–74.

9. I deal with *The Last Man* in chapter 5.

10. Mary Poovey is usually cited as initiating this critical tradition in *The Proper Lady and the Woman Writer: Ideology as Style in the Works of Mary Wollstonecraft, Mary Shelley, and Jane Austen* (Chicago: Univ. of Chicago Press, 1984), 143–71.

11. See, e.g., Fred Botting, "Author(ity) Doubled," in his *Making Monstrous: "Frankenstein," Criticism, Theory* (Manchester: Manchester Univ. Press, 1991), 4–6, 22–24; Chris Baldick, *In Frankenstein's Shadow: Myth, Monstrosity, and Nineteenth-Century Writing* (Oxford: Clarendon Press, 1987), 30–33.

12. Susan J. Wolfson, "Feminist Inquiry and *Frankenstein,*" in *Approaches to Teaching Shelley's "Frankenstein,"* ed. Stephen C. Behrendt (New York: Modern Language Association, 1990), 50–59; Mellor, *Mary Shelley,* 70–126.

13. The 1831 version stresses the connection by having Walton attribute his enthusiasm for polar exploration to Coleridge's poem.

14. Kate Ferguson Ellis, "Monsters in the Garden: Mary Shelley and the Bourgeois Family," in *The Endurance of "Frankenstein,"* ed. George Levine and U. C. Knoepflmacher (Berkeley: Univ. of California Press, 1979), 123–42.

15. In opposing two crucial Wollstonecraftian tenets—exercising, not influencing, a child's mind and seeing knowledge as essential to the unfolding of a child—the maxim discredits itself.

16. Katherine C. Hill-Miller, *"My Hideous Progeny": Mary Shelley, William Godwin, and the Father-Daughter Relationship* (Newark: Univ. of Delaware Press, 1995), 61–62.

17. Bennett, *Mary Shelley*, 6.

18. Bennett, "Not this time, Victor!," 3; Hill-Miller, *"My Hideous Progeny,"* 62ff.

19. Sandra Gilbert and Susan Gubar, *The Madwoman in the Attic* (New Haven: Yale Univ. Press, 1979).

20. Joyce Carol Oates, "Frankenstein's Fallen Angel," in *Mary Shelley's "Frankenstein,"* ed. Harold Bloom (New York: Chelsea House, 1987), 67–79.

21. U. C. Knoepflmacher, "Thoughts on the Aggression of Daughters," in *The Endurance of "Frankenstein"* (see note 14), 88–123.

22. Peter Brooks, " 'Godlike Science/Unhallowed Arts': Language, Nature, and Monstrosity," in ibid., 205–21.

23. U. C. Knoepflmacher, "Thoughts on the Aggression of Daughters," in ibid., 108–9.

24. Elizabeth Nitchie, introduction to *Mathilda*, Extra Series 3 of *Studies in Philology* (Chapel Hill: Univ. of North Carolina Press, 1959), iv–vi; Ranita Chatterjee, "Mathilda: Mary Shelley, William Godwin, and the Ideologies of Incest," in *Iconoclastic Departures: Mary Shelley after "Frankenstein,"* ed. Syndy M. Conger, Frederick S. Frank, and Gregory O'Dea (Madison, NJ: Fairleigh Dickinson Univ. Press, 1997), 130–49; Terence Harpold, " 'Did you get Mathilda from Papa?': Seduction Fantasy and Circulation of Mary Shelley's *Mathilda," Studies in Romanticism* 28.1 (1989): 49–67; Charles E. Robinson, "Mathilda as Dramatic Actress," in *Mary Shelley in Her Times* (see note 4), 77.

25. Robinson, "Mathilda as Dramatic Actress," in *Mary Shelley in Her Times* (see note 4), 76–87; also Charlene E. Bunnell, *"All the World's a Stage": Dramatic Sensibility in Mary Shelley's Novels* (New York: Routledge, 2002), 61–84.

26. François and Mozes, "Agency, Gender, and Romanticism in Mary Shelley's *Matilda,"* in *Mary Shelley's Fictions* (see note 8), 57, 64, 68–72.

27. Robinson, "Mathilda as Dramatic Actress," in *Mary Shelley in Her Times* (see note 4), 83; see also Judith Barbour, " 'The Meaning of the Tree': The Tale of Mirra in Mary Shelley's *Mathilda,"* in *Iconoclastic Departures* (see note 24), 98–114.

28. Mary Jacobus, "Guilt That Wants a Name: Mary Shelley's Unreadability," *Psychoanalysis and the Scene of Reading* (Oxford: Oxford Univ. Press, 1999), 183.

29. Jacques Derrida, *The Ear of the Other: Otobiography, Transference, Translation*, ed. Christie McDonald (New York, Schocken Books, 1985), 19–24.

30. Jacobus, "Mary Shelley's Unreadability," 182.

31. Ibid., 165–201; Tilottama Rajan, "Mary Shelley's *Mathilda:* Melancholy and the Political Economy of Romanticism," *Studies in the Novel* 26.2 (1994): 43–68.

32. Julie A. Carlson, *In The Theatre of Romanticism: Coleridge, Nationalism, Women* (Cambridge: Cambridge Univ. Press, 1994), 187, 190–98.

33. On the centrality of casuistry for Percy Shelley and romantic historicism, see James K. Chandler, *England in 1819: The Politics of Literary Culture and the Case of Romantic Historicism* (Chicago: Univ. of Chicago Press, 2000).

34. Tilottama Rajan, "Between Romance and History: Possibility and Contingency in Godwin, Leibniz, and Mary Shelley's *Valperga,"* in *Mary Shelley in Her Times* (see note 4), 88–102.

35. Barbara Johnson, "My Monster/My Self," in *Mary Shelley's "Frankenstein"* (see note 20), 55–66.

36. Michael Rossington, "Future Uncertain: The Republican Tradition and Its Destiny in *Valperga*," in *Mary Shelley in Her Times* (see note 4), 103–18.

37. On the importance and novelty of Fanny Derham, see Mellor, *Mary Shelley* (see note 1), 206–10; introduction to *Lodore*, ed. Lisa Vargo (Peterborough, ON: Broadview Press, 1997), 21, 32–38. All other references are from this edition and are cited in the text.

38. Lisa Vargo, "Further Thoughts on the Education of Daughters: *Lodore* as Imagined Conversation with Mary Wollstonecraft," in *Mary Wollstonecraft and Mary Shelley: Writing Lives*, ed. Helen M. Buss, D. L. Macdonald, and Anne McWhir (Waterloo, ON: Wilfrid Laurier Univ. Press, 2001), 177–88; Mellor, *Mary Shelley* (see note 1), 206–7.

39. For features associated with the silver-fork novel, see Michael Wheeler, *English Fiction of the Victorian Period, 1830–1890* (London: Longman, 1994), 16–18; Vargo, introduction to *Lodore*, 17.

40. On different grounds, Julia Sanders makes a similar case for the positive reforms effected in Shelley's last novel. See "Rehabilitating the Family in Mary Shelley's *Falkner*," in *Mary Shelley's Fictions* (see note 8), 211–23.

41. Fiona Stafford describes several of the contemporary social issues, especially regarding economics and the Reform Bill, treated in *Lodore* in "*Lodore:* A Tale of the Present Time?" in ibid., 181–93.

42. In this I modify the tendency of Mellor and Ellis to group together *Matilda, Lodore*, and *Falkner*, and I reverse the causality of Mellor's argument that *Matilda* accentuates what the latter two texts suggest, the need to critique the bourgeois family for its reliance on incestuous father-daughter connections. Instead, I see *Lodore* and *Falkner* as admitting and then redirecting the intensity between fathers and daughters to a third party.

43. Claudia L. Johnson, *Equivocal Beings: Politics, Gender, and Sentimentality in the 1790s* (Chicago: Univ. of Chicago Press, 1995), 66–69.

44. Betty T. Bennett, *Mary Diana Dods: A Gentleman and a Scholar* (New York: Morrow, 1991).

Chapter Four • Fancy's History

1. E.g., Emily W. Sunstein, *Mary Shelley: Romance and Reality* (Baltimore: Johns Hopkins Univ. Press, 1989), 26, 32–36.

2. *The Letters of Mary Wollstonecraft Shelley*, ed. Betty T. Bennett, 3 vols. (Baltimore: Johns Hopkins Univ. Press, 1980–88), 2:3–4.

3. Besides Wordsworth's famous lines in *The Prelude*, Book 9, "Bliss was it in that dawn to be alive, / But to be young was very heaven," Hazlitt describes the period 1789–92 as constituting the "only match that ever took place between philosophy and experience." "A new world was opening to the astonished sight; . . . Nothing was too mighty for this new-begotten hope: and the path that led to human happiness seemed as plain—as the pictures in the Pilgrim's Progress leading to Paradise" (William Hazlitt, *Memoirs of the Late Thomas Holcroft*, vol. 3 of *The Complete Works of William Hazlitt*, 20 vols., ed. P. P. Howe [London: J. M. Dent & Sons, 1932], 155, 156).

4. See James Engell, *The Creative Imagination: Enlightenment to Romanticism* (Cambridge, MA: Harvard Univ. Press, 1981), esp. 172–84.

5. On fancy, see Julie Ellison, "The Politics of Fancy in the Age of Sensibility," in *Revisioning Romanticism: British Women Writers, 1776–1837*, ed. Carol Shiner Wilson and Joel Haefner (Philadelphia: Univ. Of Pennsylvania Press, 1994); Jeffrey C. Robinson, *Unfettering Poetry: Fancy in British Romanticism* (New York: Palgrave Macmillan, 2006). On the Cockney School, Jeffrey N. Cox, *Poetry and Politics in the Cockney School* (Cambridge: Cambridge Univ. Press, 1999); on the Della Cruscans, Jerome McGann, *The Poetics of Sensibility: A Revolution in Literary Style* (Oxford: Oxford Univ. Press, 1996); on feminized Keats, Marjorie Levinson, *Keats's Life of Allegory: The Origins of a Style* (Oxford: Blackwell, 1988).

6. Wollstonecraft especially seems to use the terms interchangeably in the same sentence. E.g., "I loved thee ever since I have been acquainted with thine [heart]; thou art the being my fancy has delighted to form; but which I imagined existed only there!" (*Mary*, 67); "And so warmly has [Rousseau] painted, what he forcibly felt, that, interesting the heart and inflaming the imagination of his readers; in proportion to the strength of their fancy, they imagine that their understanding is convinced when they only sympathize with a poetic writer, who skillfully exhibits the objects of sense, most voluptuously shadowed or gracefully veiled" (*Rights of Woman*, 161); "The understanding, it is true, may keep us from going out of drawing when we group our thoughts, or transcribe from the imagination the warm sketches of fancy" (185); "How I am altered by disappointment. When going to Lisbon, the elasticity of my mind was sufficient to ward off weariness, and my imagination could still dip her brush in the rainbow of fancy and sketch futurity in glowing colours" (*A Short Residence*, 310).

7. Editors often refer to it as her "oriental" tale (e.g., Miriam Brody's introduction to the Penguin edition of *A Vindication of the Rights of Woman* [1992], 8).

8. William St. Clair, *The Godwins and the Shelleys: A Biography of a Family* (Baltimore: Johns Hopkins Univ. Press, 1989), 221–38 (the chapter entitled "The Discovery of Poetry" asserts that it was "Samuel Taylor Coleridge who made the deepest impression" [225]).

9. See *Mary*, 52; *Rights of Woman*, 177.

10. *Mary*, 30; *Wrongs of Woman*, 156; also 176.

11. Barbara Taylor, "For the Love of God: Religion and the Erotic Imagination in Wollstonecraft's Feminism," in *Mary Wollstonecraft and 200 Years of Feminisms*, ed. Eileen Janes Yeo (London: Rivers Oram Press, 1997), 15–35.

12. Ibid., 28.

13. As a measure of this difference, compare the cause (revived passion) of the female spirit's seeming "to find myself again, to find the eccentric warmth that gave me identity of character" with the assertion in *Mary* that "good dispositions, and virtuous propensities, without the light of the Gospel, produce eccentric characters" ("Cave," 204; *Mary*, 61).

14. See also *A Short Residence*: "Without the aid of the imagination, all the pleasures of the senses must sink into grossness" (250).

15. On the one hand, *Mary* affirms that only love of God can fill the soul (since the soul is of God, not man); on the other, it acknowledges a "void" in the heart "that even benevolence and religion could not fill" (16, 73). Arguably, the lack in "man" is also a gender critique, applicable to all men and most women, but not the most forward-looking ones (whose [im]morality is the sign that they are beyond the dictates of the world and therefore of God).

16. Pamela Clemit, *The Godwinian Novel: The Rational Fictions of Godwin, Brockden Brown, Mary Shelley* (Clarendon: Oxford Univ. Press, 1993), 13–34.

17. Don Locke, *A Fantasy of Reason: The Life and Thought of William Godwin* (New York: Routledge, 1980).

18. William Godwin, *Lives of the Necromancers; or, An Account of the Most Eminent Persons in Successive Ages Who Claimed for Themselves, or to Whom Has Been Imputed by Others, the Exercise of Magical Powers* (London: Frederick Mason, 1834), 27.

19. Jon Klancher, "Godwin and the Genre Reformers: On Necessity and Contingency in Romantic Narrative Theory," in *Romanticism, History, and the Possibilities of Genre: Reforming Literature, 1789–1837*, ed. Tilottama Rajan and Julia M. Wright (Cambridge: Cambridge Univ. Press, 1998), 21–38, esp. 32–33.

20. On fancy, romance, and romantic medievalism, see David Duff, *Romance and Revolution: Shelley and the Politics of a Genre* (Cambridge: Cambridge Univ. Press, 1994); and Elizabeth Fay, *Romantic Medievalism: History and the Romantic Literary Ideal* (Houndmills, UK: Palgrave, 2002).

21. The historian's evidence-collecting activities have grown more aggressive since their characterization in "Of History and Romance." There Godwin contrasts "courts of justice" with those of history to the latter's discredit. The historian "can administer no oath, he cannot issue his precept, and summon his witnesses from distant provinces, he cannot arraign his personages and compel them to put in their answer. He must take what they choose to tell, the broken fragments, and the scattered ruins of evidence" (367).

22. Mark Salber Phillips, *Society and Sentiment: Genres of Historical Writing in Britain, 1740–1820* (Princeton: Princeton Univ. Press, 2000), 129–46.

23. Richard Hurd, *Letters on Chivalry and Romance*, ed. Hoyt Trowbridge (Los Angeles: Clark Memorial Library, 1963), 118–19.

24. I am drawing on accounts of literary history by Thomas Percy, *Reliques of Ancient English Poetry* (1765) (London: John Nichols, 1794); Hurd, *Letters on Chivalry and Romance*; John Hippisley, *Chapters on Early English Literature* (London: Edward Moxon, 1837); and Thomas Wharton, *The History of English Poetry*, in 4 vols., 2nd. ed. (London: J. Dodsley, 1775–81). I have explored these topics at greater length in a coauthored unpublished paper (with L. O. Aranye Fradenburg), " 'Like a Country in Romance': Loving the Middle Ages."

25. Hurd, *Letters on Chivalry and Romance*, 120.

26. See St. Clair, *The Godwins and the Shelleys* (see note 8), 201–4 (on Lee), 238–43 (on Clairmont), 260 (on starting *Life of Chaucer*).

27. The strength of Godwin's identification with Chaucer and his *Life* is evident in his remarks to a prospective publisher: "I am now writing a book, of which you are to be the publisher. It is to be 'Godwin's Life of Chaucer,' and no other person's." Also, though differently, in the continuation, "My reputation and my fame are at stake upon it. The moment, therefore, I find you alter a word of that book (and you cannot do it without my finding it) that instant the copy stops and I hold our contract dissolved, though the consequence should be my dying in jail" (to Phillips in Charles Kegan Paul, *Godwin: Friends and Contemporaries* [1876], 71).

28. "Letter of Advice to a Young American: On the Course of Studies It Might Be Most Advantageous for Him to Pursue," in *Educated and Literary Writings*, ed. Clemit, vol. 5 of *Political and Philosophical Writings of William Godwin*, 323.

29. Godwin, *Lives of the Necromancers*, 72.

30. Ibid., 5.

31. For details on the composition history of the rough draft and fair copy, see "Introductory Note" to *Matilda*, in vol. 2 of *The Novels and Selected Works of Mary Shelley*, 1–3; see also Pamela Clemit, "From *The Fields of Fancy* to *Matilda*: Mary Shelley's Changing Conception of Her Novella," in *Mary Shelley in Her Times*, ed. Betty T. Bennett and Stuart Curran (Baltimore: Johns Hopkins Univ. Press, 2000), 64–75.

32. Terence Harpold, " 'Did you get Mathilda from Papa?': Seduction Fantasy and the Circulation of Mary Shelley's *Mathilda*," *Studies in Romanticism* 28.1 (1989): 49–67; Elizabeth Nitchie, introduction to *Mathilda*, Extra Series 3 of *Studies in Philology* (Chapel Hill: Univ. of North Carolina Press, 1959).

33. Clemit, "From *The Fields of Fancy* to *Matilda*," in *Mary Shelley in Her Times* (see note 31), 64, 72, 64.

34. Jacobus, "Guilt That Wants a Name: Mary Shelley's Unreadability," *Psychoanalysis and the Scene of Reading* (Oxford: Oxford Univ. Press, 1999), 174–76.

35. Clemit does note that "The Cave of Fancy" is "a frequently cited source for the title and opening" of *Fields* and states that there are "broad parallels" between the frame and chapter 3 of "Cave," but she then proceeds to explore the major impact of Godwin's writing on the text (66).

36. Charles E. Robinson, "A Mother's Daughter: An Intersection of Mary Shelley's *Frankenstein* and Mary Wollstonecraft's *A Vindication of the Rights of Woman*," in *Mary Wollstonecraft and Mary Shelley: Writing Lives*, ed. Helen M. Buss, D. L. Macdonald, and Anne McWhir (Waterloo, ON: Wilfrid Laurier Univ. Press, 2000), 132.

37. See Clemit, "From *The Fields of Fancy* to *Matilda*," in *Mary Shelley in Her Times* (see note 31), 72; see also Anne-Lise François and Daniel Mozes, " 'Don't Say I Love You': Agency, Gender, and Romanticism in Mary Shelley's *Matilda*," in *Mary Shelley's Fictions: From "Frankenstein" to "Falkner,"* ed. Michael Eberle-Sinatra (Basingstoke, UK: Macmillan, 2000), 61–66.

38. Clemit, "From *The Fields of Fancy* to *Matilda*," in *Mary Shelley in Her Times* (see note 31), 66.

39. Ibid., 64.

40. The frame locale is especially connected to P. Shelley's translation of *The Symposium* in 1818.

41. Cathy Caruth, *Unclaimed Experience: Trauma, Narrative, and History* (Baltimore: Johns Hopkins Univ. Press, 1996); Cathy Caruth, ed., *Trauma: Explorations in Memory* (Baltimore: Johns Hopkins Univ. Press, 1995).

42. Jacobus, "Mary Shelley's Unreadability," 196.

43. Graham Allen, "Beyond Biographism: Mary Shelley's *Matilda*, Intertextuality, and the Wandering Subject," *Romanticism* 3.2 (1997): 170–84.

44. Clemit, "From *The Fields of Fancy* to *Matilda*," in *Mary Shelley in Her Times* (see note 31), 67.

45. I am referring to the title and argument of U. C. Knoepflmacher's "Thoughts on the Aggression of Daughters," which primarily discusses *Frankenstein* but also comments briefly on *Matilda*, raising the relevant question, "How could Mary Shelley have had the temerity to

send the manuscript of Mathilda to Godwin?" (*The Endurance of "Frankenstein": Essays on Mary Shelley's Novel*, ed. George Levine and U. C. Knoepflmacher [Berkeley: Univ. of California Press, 1974], 88–122, esp. 113–15).

Chapter Five • Living Off and On

1. Miranda Seymour writes that, despite various forms of preparation, Shelley was unprepared for his death. *Mary Shelley* (New York: Grove Press, 2000), 440.

2. Mark Salber Phillips's treatment is a notable recent exception that also comments on the "little notice" that it "attracted" in its day (*Society and Sentiment: Genres of Historical Writing in Britain, 1740–1820* [Princeton: Princeton Univ. Press, 2000], 322–41, 323n).

3. *British Critic* 35 (1810): 535; *Monthly Review* 61 (1810): 111.

4. Phillips, *Society and Sentiment*, 324, 331.

5. Ibid., 331, 325.

6. Godwin addresses the apparent impracticality of his proposal at the beginning of *Sepulchres*.

7. Godwin works a powerful revision of the memory evoked by Wordsworthian nature, which explains some of the major differences between *Essay on Sepulchres* and Wordsworth's *Essay on Epitaphs*.

8. The Epilogue addresses their centrality to the life/writings of Percy Shelley.

9. "Of History and Romance" asserts that through study of such individuals, we "insensibly imbibe the same spirit, and burn with kindred fires" (23).

10. Joanna Baillie's tragedy *Orra* goes the farthest in trying to dramatize what it means to live in this reality.

11. Standard introductions to the field include Cathy Caruth, *Unclaimed Experience: Trauma, Narrative, and History* (Baltimore: Johns Hopkins Univ. Press, 1996), and Caruth, ed., *Trauma: Explorations in Memory* (Baltimore: Johns Hopkins Univ. Press, 1995); Shoshana Felman and Dori Laub, *Testimony: Crises of Witnessing in Literature, Psychoanalysis, and History* (New York: Routledge, 1992); and, in the discipline of history, Dominick LaCapra, *Writing History, Writing Trauma* (Baltimore: Johns Hopkins Univ. Press, 2001).

12. Sigmund Freud, *Beyond the Pleasure Principle*, vol. 18 of *The Standard Edition of the Complete Psychological Works of Sigmund Freud*, 24 vols., ed. and trans. James Strachey (London: Hogarth Press, 1955), 27–33.

13. Ruth Leys, *Trauma: A Genealogy* (Chicago: Univ. of Chicago Press, 2000), 4.

14. See Gary Handwerk, "History, Trauma, and the Limits of the Liberal Imagination: William Godwin's Historical Fiction," in *Romanticism, History, and the Possibilities of Genre*, ed. Tilottama Rajan and Julia M. Wright (Cambridge: Cambridge Univ. Press, 1998), 64–86, and Tilottama Rajan, "The Powers of Pathology: Godwin's *Mandeville* and the End(s) of the Historical Novel," plenary paper presented at the North American Society for the Study of Romanticism, Montreal, 13–16 August 2005.

15. In this regard, Godwin is an important precedent for the rationale underlying the Truth and Reconciliation Hearings in South Africa.

16. Leys, *Trauma*, 17. On the importance of debates about Mesmer and mesmerism, see Patricia Fara, "An Attractive Therapy," *History of Science* 33.100 (1995): 127–77; on mes-

merism as an important stage in the development of psychoanalysis, see Joel Faflak, " 'The Clearest Light of Reason': Making Sense of Hogg's Body of Evidence," *Gothic Studies* 5.1 (2003): 94–110.

17. For a recent exploration of this problem, see R. Clifton Spargo, *The Ethics of Mourning: Grief and Responsibility in Elegiac Literature* (Baltimore: Johns Hopkins Univ. Press, 2004), 14–38. On "impossible mourning," see Jacques Derrida, *Mémoires for Paul de Man*, trans. Cecile Lindsay et al. (New York: Columbia Univ. Press, 1986).

Epigraph: Jean Laplanche: Seduction, Translation, and the Drives, ed. John Fletcher and Martin Stanton (London, 1992).

18. Tilottama Rajan, "Mary Shelley's *Mathilda:* Melancholy and the Political Economy of Romanticism," *Studies in the Novel* 26 (1994): 43–68; Mary Jacobus, "Guilt That Wants a Name: Mary Shelley's Unreadability," *Psychoanalysis and the Scene of Reading* (Oxford: Oxford Univ. Press, 1999), 165–201.

19. *The Letters of Mary Wollstonecraft Shelley*, ed. Betty T. Bennett, 3 vols. (Baltimore: Johns Hopkins Univ. Press, 1980–88), 1:100.

20. Jacobus, "Mary Shelley's Unreadability," 183–84.

21. LaCapra, *Writing History, Writing Trauma*, 105.

22. Rajan, "Mary Shelley's *Mathilda*," 44–47; Jacobus, "Mary Shelley's Unreadability," 198.

23. Jacobus, "Mary Shelley's Unreadability," 175.

24. Ibid., 197, 196.

25. Ibid.

26. Ibid., 189–90.

27. "Let me now calculate this boasted friendship, and discover its real worth. He got over his grief for Elinor, and the country became dull to him, so he was glad to find even me for amusement; and when he does not know what else to do he passes his lazy hours here, and calls this friendship" (56).

28. Jacobus,"Mary Shelley's Unreadability," 176.

29. See especially, Alan Richardson, "*Proserpine* and *Midas:* Gender, Genre, and Mythic Revisionism in Mary Shelley's Dramas," in *The Other Mary Shelley: Beyond "Frankenstein*," ed. Audrey A. Fisch, Anne K. Mellor, and Esther H. Schor (Oxford: Oxford Univ. Press, 1993), 124–39; Jeffrey N. Cox, "Staging Hope: Genre, Myth, and Ideology in the Dramas of the Hunt Circle," *Texas Studies in Literature and Language* 38.3/4 (Fall/Winter, 1996).

30. See Elizabeth T. Hayes, *Images of Persephone: Feminist Readings in Western Literature* (Gainesville: Univ. Press of Florida, 1994).

31. Richardson, "*Proserpine* and *Midas*," in *The Other Mary Shelley* (see note 29), 136.

32. Ibid.

33. Susan Gubar, "Mother, Maiden, and the Marriage of Death: Woman Writers and an Ancient Myth," *Women's Studies* 6 (1979): 303.

34. Cox, "Staging Hope," 257.

35. Richardson, "*Proserpine* and *Midas*," in *The Other Mary Shelley* (see note 29), 130.

36. In her chapter on *Matilda*, Hill-Miller devotes a few pages to *Proserpine* as Shelley's tale of female sexual initiation. She too notes Shelley's departures from Ovid but in the opposite direction from my analysis. "Rather than portraying her as a disobedient and unre-

flecting child who strays in search of flowers for herself," Shelley's Proserpine is a "thoughtful and self-possessed adolescent" (Katherine C. Hill-Miller, *"My Hideous Progeny": Mary Shelley, William Godwin, and the Father-Daughter Relationship* [Newark: Univ. of Delaware Press, 1995], 110). Also unconvincing in my view is Syndy McMillen Conger's account of the working relation between mother and daughter: "Mothers and daughters working together— Mary Shelley seems to say in her own mythological allegory of justice—can create a force strong enough to change the world" ("Mary Shelley's Women in Prison," in *Iconoclastic Departures: Mary Shelley after "Frankenstein,"* ed. Syndy M. Conger, Frederick S. Frank, and Gregory O'Dea [Madison, NJ: Fairleigh Dickinson Univ. Press, 1997], 94).

37. On wandering in *Matilda*, see Graham Allen, "Beyond Biographism: Mary Shelley's *Matilda*, Intertextuality, and the Wandering Subject," *Romanticism* 3.2 (1997).

38. This latter-day Ceres is an even farther cry from depictions of Demeter in search of Persephone, in one of which she is restored to laughter when Baubo lifts her dress and exposes her genitals (see Carl Kerenyi, *Eleusis: Archetypal Image of Mother and Daughter,* trans. Ralph Manheim [New York: Pantheon, 1967], 39). Freud describes this myth in "A Mythological Parallel to a Visual Obsession," in *On the History of Psycho-analytic Movement, Papers on Metapsychology, and Other Works,* vol. 14 of *The Standard Edition of the Complete Psychological Works of Sigmund Freud,* 24 vols., ed. and trans. James Strachey (London: Hogarth Press, 1957), 338.

39. "After having repeated this idea [of giving advice respecting the children] to her in a great variety of forms, she at length said, with a significant tone of voice, 'I know what you are thinking of,' but added, that she had nothing to communicate to me upon the subject" (*Memoirs*, 139). Terence Harpold draws attention to these missing thoughts and their effect on Shelley in "'Did you get Mathilda from Papa?': Seduction Fantasy and Circulation of Mary Shelley's *Mathilda*," *Studies in Romanticism* 28.1 (1989): 55. St. Clair states that Godwin kept the *Memoirs* from the girls, possibly for this reason.

40. In her account of female trauma survivors, Janice Haaken stresses how focus on "parental invasions" can also have a defensive side. Such "attributions permit an internal engagement with destructive parental images that are less possible through memories of disengaged, overwhelmed, or neglectful parents" ("The Recovery of Memory, Fantasy, and Desire: Feminist Approaches to Sexual Abuse and Psychic Trauma," *Signs: Journal of Women in Culture and Society* 21.4 [1996]: 1084).

41. Richardson, *"Proserpine and Midas,"* in *The Other Mary Shelley* (see note 29), 126.

42. Words are portrayed as satisfying adult thirst too. Arethusa responds to Ceres's request for water from "thine ice-cold spring" by offering "My words [which] are better than my freshest waves" and that tell of fluid exchanges between lovers (2:57, 59).

43. See Juliet Mitchell, "Trauma, Recognition, and the Place of Language," *Diacritics* 28.4 (1998), esp. 121.

44. LaCapra identifies hybrid genres as characteristic of post-traumatic writing.

45. The latter characterizes the songs that he composed for *Proserpine*.

46. P. B. Shelley, Preface to *Prometheus Unbound,* in *Shelley's Poetry and Prose,* ed. Donald H. Reiman and Neil Freistat (New York: Norton, 2002), 207.

47. Janice Haaken shows how Western traditions deprive women of "grand legends that place them at the center of cosmic dramas." Shelley recovers several female legends (Proser-

pine, Cassandra) but refuses to idealize them. See *Pillar of Salt: Gender, Memory, and the Perils of Looking Back* (New Brunswick, NJ: Rutgers Univ. Press, 1998), 1–3.

48. Anne K. Mellor, *Mary Shelley: Her Life, Her Fiction, and Her Monsters* (New York: Routledge, 1989), 148–57, and "Why Women Don't Like Romanticism: The Views of Jane Austen and Mary Shelley," in *The Romantics and Us: Essays on Literature and Culture*, ed. Gene W. Ruoff (New Brunswick, NJ: Rutgers Univ. Press, 1990), 285; Lee Sterrenburg, "*The Last Man:* Anatomy of Failed Revolutions," *Nineteenth Century Fiction* 33 (1978/79): 324–47; Audrey A. Fisch reviews the nihilistic interpretation to different ends in "Plaguing Politics: AIDS, Deconstruction, and *The Last Man*," in *The Other Mary Shelley* (see note 29), 267–86.

49. Mary Shelley, *The Last Man*, ed. Anne McWhir (Peterborough, ON: Broadview Press, 1996), 160n.

50. Writing extends not only one's "point of sight" to encompass the "inclinations and capacities of all human beings" but also makes all of "posterity" one's "heirs." It also constitutes one a "citizen of the world" and "a candidate for immortal honors" (122).

51. Barbara Johnson, "The Last Man," in *The Other Mary Shelley* (see note 29), 258–66 ("the story of *The Last Man* is in the last analysis the story of modern Western man torn between mourning and deconstruction" [265]); Steven Goldsmith, "Of Gender, Plague, and Apocalypse: Mary Shelley's *Last Man*," *Yale Journal of Criticism* 4.1 (1990): 129–73, esp. 153–55.

52. Samantha Webb, "Reading the End of the World: *The Last Man*, History, and the Agency of Romantic Authorship," in *Mary Shelley in Her Times*, ed. Betty T. Bennett and Stuart Curran (Baltimore: Johns Hopkins Univ. Press, 2000), 124, 128.

53. Ibid., 124.

54. McWhir, introduction to *The Last Man*, xx, xxi, xxvi.

55. Johnson, "The Last Man," 258, 265.

56. Jacques Derrida, *Spectres of Marx: The State of the Debt, the Work of Mourning, and the New International*, trans. Peggy Kamuf (New York: Routledge, 1994).

57. Here Shelley draws on the lines that Coleridge calls the "motto" to his *Remorse* (1813): "Remorse is as the heart in which it grows: / If that be gentle, it drops balmy dews / Of true repentance, but if proud and gloomy, / It is a poison-tree, that pierced to the inmost / Weeps only tears of poison!" (1.1.20–24).

58. E.g., introduction to *The Last Man*, ed. Brian Aldiss (London: Hogarth Press, 1985), 1–10; Mary Poovey, *The Proper Lady and the Woman Writer: Ideology as Style in the Works of Mary Wollstonecraft, Mary Shelley, and Jane Austen* (Chicago: Univ. of Chicago Press, 1989); Mellor, *Mary Shelley.* Quoted line is from McWhir, "Introduction" to *The Last Man*, xxii.

59. "To become worthy of him is to assure the bliss of a reunion" (*Percy Shelley, Essays, Letters from Abroad, Translations, and Fragments*, ed. Mary Shelley, 2 vols. [London: Edward Moxon, 1840], 1:12).

60. Though I disagree with elements of his critiques of other commentators, I agree with his assessment that Mary Shelley worked long and hard to produce editions of Percy Shelley's works that would obtain him a readership (Michael O'Neill, " 'Trying to make it as good as I can': Mary Shelley's Editing of P. B. Shelley's Poetry and Prose," in *Mary Shelley in Her Times* (see note 52), 185–97, 186).

61. The echo of this phrase in Deloraine's description of his now-dead first wife, Emilia, as

the "late incomparable companion of my early days" suggests that Godwin's later reflections on mourning are also influenced by Shelley's life/writings (*Deloraine*, 33).

62. U. C. Knoepflmacher, "Thoughts on the Aggression of Daughters."

63. Mary Favret's claim is even stronger, that Mary Shelley's annotations suggest that Percy Shelley's poetry is indecipherable without her prose and that therefore prose has a stronger purchase on reality ("Mary Shelley's Sympathy and Irony: The Editor and Her Corpus," in *The Other Mary Shelley* [see note 29], 17–39, esp. 19–20, 27–30).

64. Susan Wolfson, "Editorial Privilege: Mary Shelley's and Percy Shelley's Audiences," in ibid., 51; see 48–51.

65. The idealizing is clearest in the preface to *Posthumous Poems* (1824) and grows more complicated (more offset by counter-trends of realism, sympathy, prose) in the preface and notes to *Poetical Works* (1839).

66. She was the eighth most prolific contributor of Lardner's thirty-eight authors, and the only woman ("General Editor's Introduction," *Mary Shelley's "Literary Lives" and Other Writings*, 4 vols., ed. Nora Crook [London: Pickering & Chatto, 2002], 1:xix–xxiii).

67. On the interactions and shifts between biography and history in the eighteenth century, see Mark Salber Phillips, *Society and Sentiment: Genres of Historical Writing in Britain, 1740–1820* (Princeton: Princeton Univ. Press, 2000), 131–46.

68. On her foregrounding "trifles," see also 3:263, 245; 2:77. Nora Crook comments that Godwin would have encouraged Shelley's regard for this aspect of Johnson's biographical method and that he himself had intended to write a continuation of Johnson's *Lives* (*Mary Shelley's "Literary Lives" and Other Writings*, 1:xxviii).

69. Greg Kucich, "Mary Shelley's *Lives* and the Reengendering of History," in *Mary Shelley in Her Times* [see note 52], 198–213).

70. See *Italian Lives*, 116. In fact, she sees writers as particular targets of the current "fashion" to "ransack every hidden corner of a man's life," because that life entails fictional writings that, especially in one's youth, are full of folly (*Spanish Lives*, 179).

71. This characterization in *The Last Man* gives nice support to Susan Wolfson's linkage of Shelley's "editorial labor" to Victor's life-invention in *Frankenstein* ("Editorial Privilege: Mary Shelley and Percy Shelley's Audiences," in *The Other Mary Shelley* [see note 29], 39–72, esp. 48–49).

72. On inconsistencies in her censure of suicide, see *Spanish Lives*, xlix–l.

73. I remain intrigued by the journal entry for 2 October 1822, which heads the list of "all except you, my poor boy," who are now "gone" with "Father" (then "Mother, friend, husband, children" [*Journals*, 432]). To my knowledge, no one has commented on this passage.

74. William St. Clair, *The Godwins and the Shelleys: A Biography of a Family* (Baltimore: Johns Hopkins Univ. Press, 1989), 338.

75. *Spanish Lives*, xxiv; for limits to the fictionalizing of truth, however, see 265.

76. Campbell Orr, "Introduction to *French Lives*," in *Spanish Lives*, xxxix. Shelley began work on the memoirs of Godwin in late 1836 but then stopped them to resume work on *French Lives* in early 1837.

77. Syndy McMillen Conger, "Multivocality in Mary Shelley's Unfinished Memoirs of her Father," *European Romantic Review* 9.3 (1998): 306.

78. Elsewhere in the *Lives of Eminent Men* she is eager to contradict ascriptions of

coldness to *writing* about grief. "Unimaginative people fancy that when a poet laments in song, his heart is cold" (*Spanish Lives,* 274).

Chapter Six • *A Juvenile Library*

1. Mary V. Jackson, *Engines of Instruction, Mischief, and Magic: Children's Literature in England from Its Beginnings to 1839* (Lincoln: Univ. of Nebraska Press, 1989), 1.

2. Ibid., 246. According to Janet Todd, "there was a growing market for children's fiction; indeed a distinct literature was coming into being, especially in Dissenting circles, and his neighbour John Newbery had made a good living from it. Formerly children learnt to read through simplified Bible stories, chapbooks, and fairy tales, but now serious parents wanted books delivering their values of probity, benevolence, and thrift in more realistic settings" (*Mary Wollstonecraft: A Revolutionary Life* [New York: Columbia Univ. Press, 2000], 125).

3. Alan Richardson, *Literature, Education, Romanticism: Reading as Social Practice, 1780–1832* (Cambridge: Cambridge Univ. Press, 1994), 113. According to Jackson, in the early decades (1740s–1770s), "juvenile books were thoroughly controlled by trade or business interests" and thus "sought to supply their patrons with what they wanted," whereas after 1780 "reformist authors" sought to "reshape" the views of their patron-readers (*Engines of Instruction,* 3).

4. Richardson, *Literature, Education, Romanticism,* 133.

5. See Sylvia W. Patterson, *Rousseau's Emile and Early Children's Literature* (Metuchen, NJ: Scarecrow Press, 1971), and Samuel F. Pickering Jr., *John Locke and Children's Books in Eighteenth-Century England* (Knoxville: Univ. of Tennessee Press, 1981).

6. Geoffrey Summerland, *Fantasy and Reason: Children's Literature in the Eighteenth Century* (London: Methuen, 1984), 4, 115–18; also Jackson, *Engines of Instruction,* 43.

7. Summerland's *Fantasy and Reason* is devoted to schematizing and disseminating this view.

8. Jerome McGann, *The Romantic Ideology: A Critical Investigation* (Chicago: Univ. of Chicago Press, 1983).

9. Richardson, *Literature, Education, Romanticism,* 103, 91–101; also 121 on the pacifying impulses underlying fairy tales.

10. Mitzi Myers, "Impeccable Governesses, Rational Dames, and Moral Mothers," in *Children's Literature: Annual of the Modern Language Association Division on Children's Literature and the Children's Literature Association* (New Haven: Yale Univ. Press, 1986), 33–34; Norma Clarke, " 'The Cursed Barbauld Crew': Women Writers and Writing for Children in the Late Eighteenth Century," in *Opening the Nursery Door: Reading, Writing, and Child-hood, 1600–1900,* ed. Mary Hilton, Morag Styles, and Victor Watson (London: Routledge, 1997), 91–103. The "cursed Barbauld crew" comes from a letter by Charles Lamb to S. T. Coleridge (23 October 1802, *Works of Charles and Mary Lamb,* 7 vols., ed. E. V. Lucas [London: Methuen, 1903–5], 4:252–53).

11. On the concept, see James K. Chandler, *Wordsworth's Second Nature: A Study of the Poetry and Politics* (Chicago: Univ. of Chicago Press, 1984), 66–69; for implications on education, see 98–104.

12. Jackson, *Engines of Instruction,* 139.

13. Richardson, *Literature, Education, and Romanticism,* 178.

14. Myers, "Impeccable Governesses," in *Children's Literature* (see note 10), 36, 39–40; Myers, "Reform or Ruin: 'A Revolution in Female Manners,'" in *Studies in Eighteenth Century Culture*, vol. 11 ed. Harry C. Payne (Madison: Univ. of Wisconsin Press, 1982), 203–5.

15. Richardson, *Literature, Education, and Romanticism*, 107–8.

16. See especially the chapter "Toys," by Thomas Beddoes, in Richard and Maria Edgeworth's *Practical Education* (1801), ed. Gina Luria (New York: Garland, 1974). On the pragmatic and fanciful character of ABC books, see Jackson, *Engines of Instruction* (see note 1), 29–38.

17. Barbara Taylor, *Mary Wollstonecraft and the Feminist Imagination* (Cambridge: Cambridge Univ. Press, 2003), 32–43.

18. This is Taylor's view of Mrs. Mason, in ibid., 32–33.

19. Myers reminds us that Wollstonecraft "was meticulously revising the 1788 first edition" of *Original Stories from Real Life* while "*Rights of Woman* was gestating in her head" ("Impeccable Governesses," in *Children's Literature* [see note 10], 40; on negative twentieth century assessments of Mrs. Mason, see 40–41). Claudia Johnson also links the two texts but in a more negative (in the sense of sexually repressive) fashion (*Equivocal Beings*).

20. Her translations focus on young boys—Charles, in *Elements of Morality, For the Use of Children . . . Translated from the German of the Rev. C. G. Salzmann* and *Young Grandison. A Series of Letters from Young Persons to their friends, Translated from the Dutch of Madame De Cambon*, vol. 2 of *The Works of Mary Wollstonecraft*. One of her favorite models is Madame de Genlis's *Adelaide and Theodore; or, Letters on Education* (1782).

21. Myers makes this point by way of arguing how female pedagogical writings are also nascent autobiography and cultural critique in "Pedagogy as Self-Expression in Mary Wollstonecraft: Exorcising the Past, Finding a Voice," in *The Private Self: Theory and Practice of Women's Autobiographical Writings*, ed. Shari Benstock (Chapel Hill: Univ. of North Carolina Press, 1988), 193–94, 196.

22. Taylor, *Mary Wollstonecraft and the Feminist Imagination*, 43. Godwin states that the first three years with Joseph Johnson were "the most active period of her life" (quoted in Todd, *Mary Wollstonecraft* [see note 2], 123).

23. Cora Kaplan, "Mary Wollstonecraft's Reception and Legacies," in *The Cambridge Companion to Mary Wollstonecraft*, ed. Claudia L. Johnson (Cambridge: Cambridge Univ. Press, 2002), 246–70; Sonia Hofkosh, "Wollstonecraft's Ways of Knowing," paper presented at the convention of the Modern Language Association, San Diego, CA, December 2003.

24. Claire Tomalin, introduction to Mary Shelley, *Maurice; or, The Fisher's Cot* (New York: Knopf, 1998), 22; see also Edward C. McAleer, *The Sensitive Plant: A Life of Lady Mount Cashell* (Chapel Hill: Univ. of North Carolina Press, 1958); on Wollstonecraft's relation with Lady King, see Todd, *Mary Wollstonecraft* (see note 2), 115–16.

25. Summerland, *Fantasy and Reason* (see note 6), 229.

26. "Later, when both the first and third daughters fell from respectability, there were mutterings about the influence of the extraordinary governess on impressionable girls. Indeed, the adult and republican Margaret flaunted the brief association and 'glorie[d] in having had so clever an Instructress, who had freed her mind from all superstitions'" (Todd, *Mary Wollstonecraft* [see note 2], 116).

27. *The Female Reader; or, Miscellaneous Pieces in Prose and Verse; Selected from the Best Writers, and Disposed Under Proper Heads; for the Improvement of Young Women* (1789), vol. 4 in *The Works of Mary Wollstonecraft*, 56.

28. *Thoughts on the Education of Daughters* is mixed, though generally optimistic, on this topic: "I am very far from thinking love irresistible, and not to be conquered. . . . A resolute endeavour will almost always overcome difficulties" (29; though 28 suggests the opposite).

29. Myers, "Pedagogy in Mary Wollstonecraft," in *The Private Self* (see note 21), 201–2.

30. See also Wollstonecraft's "Fragment of Letters on the Management of Infants," *Posthumous Works of the Author of "A Vindication of the Rights of Woman"* (1798), ed. William Godwin, 2 vols. (reprint, Clifton, NJ: Augustus M. Kelley, 1972), 57 ("If I can persuade any of the rising generation to exercise their reason on this head, I am content").

31. On the term and its corollaries (*Fairy Spectator; or, The Invisible Monitor, Female Guardian*), see Myers, "Impeccable Governesses," in *Children's Literature* (see note 10), 50–54.

32. Proper they are, especially in the ordering of these heads: 1. Narrative Pieces, 2. Didactic and Moral Pieces, 3. Allegories and Pathetic Pieces, 4. Dialogues, Conversations, and Fables, 5. Descriptive Pieces, 6. Devotional Pieces, and Reflections on Religious Objects.

33. "The generality of people cannot see or feel poetically, they want fancy, and therefore fly from solitude in search of sensible objects; but when an author lends them his eyes they can see as he saw, and be amused by images they could not select, though lying before them" (*Rights of Woman*, 186).

34. See Todd, *Mary Wollstonecraft* (see note 2): "The identity [of author] made her feel a superior being to her sisters: 'When I have more strength I read Philosophy—and write—I hope you have not forgot that I am an Author. . . . I have lately been reading a book which I wish Everina to peruse. It is called Paley's philosophy. The definition of virtue I particularly admire—it is short. "Virtue is the doing good to mankind in obedience to the will of God, and for the sake of everlasting happiness." . . . Paley, a kind of theological utilitarian, put morality within life and supported women's education and independence'" (110).

35. Andrew Elfenbein, "Mary Wollstonecraft and the Sexuality of Genius," in *Cambridge Companion to Mary Wollstonecraft* (see note 23), 236.

36. Godwin hints at this logic in his apologetic explanation for "annexing" "Lessons" to *Wrongs of Woman* on the basis of the "slight association" between "the affectionate and pathetic manner in which Maria Venables addresses her infant" and the "agonizing and painful sentiment with which the author originally bequeathed these papers, as a legacy for the benefit of her child" (*Posthumous Works* [see note 30], 1:173–74).

37. *The Female Reader*, in *The Works of Mary Wollstonecraft*, 59.

38. Hofkosh, "Wollstonecraft's Ways of Knowing."

Epigraph: Cited in Pamela Clemit, "Philosophical Anarchism in the Schoolroom, William Godwin's Juvenile Library, 1805–25," *Biblion* 9.1/2 (2000/2001).

39. The standard work remains Burton R. Pollin, *Education and Enlightenment in the Works of William Godwin* (New York: Las Americas, 1962). Recall that when Godwin left the ministry, his first plan was to open a school, the prospectus for which he published in 1783 (*An Account of the Seminary that will be opened*).

40. Clemit, "Philosophical Anarchism in the Schoolroom: William Godwin's Juvenile Library, 1805–25," *Biblion* 9.1/2 (2000/2001), 44–70, is the only analytic investigation of these writings that I have encountered.

41. Charles Kegan Paul calls the Juvenile Library "his greatest and most disastrous venture" (*William Godwin, His Friends and Contemporaries* [London: H. S. King, 1876], 2:129).

42. William St. Clair, *The Godwins and the Shelleys: A Biography of a Family* (Baltimore: Johns Hopkins Univ. Press, 1989), 282–84.

43. William St. Clair, "William Godwin as Children's Bookseller," in *Children and Their Books: A Celebration of the Work of Iona and Peter Opie,* ed. Gillian Avery and Julia Briggs (Oxford: Clarendon Press, 1989), 168–73.

44. Ibid., 177.

45. On Trimmer's *Guardian of Education* and a sympathetic treatment of her concerns, see Nicholas Tucker, "Fairy Tales and Their Early Opponents: In Defence of Mrs Trimmer," in *Opening the Nursery Door* (see note 10), 104–17.

46. "Preface to *Bible Stories*" (1802), in vol. 5 of *Political and Philosophical Writings of William Godwin*, 312.

47. St. Clair, *The Godwins and the Shelleys,* 283–84.

48. Godwin makes the same assertion regarding the importance of imagination in the preface to his *History of England.*

49. Baldwin also issues a much-condensed *Outlines of English History . . . for the Use of Children from Four to Eight Years of Age* (1814) and the *Outlines of English Grammar* (1810).

50. Announcement of "New Books published by Thomas Hodgkins, at the Juvenile Library" (*Fables*) at the end of *The Looking Glass,* 122.

51. *Fables,* iv, vi. See also "If we would communicate improvement to a child, we must become in part children ourselves. . . . Above all, we must make our narrations pictures, and render the objects we discourse about, visible to the imagination of the learner" (121).

52. Ibid., vi; Announcement in *Looking Glass,* 121.

53. Anna Barbauld's *Lessons for Children* (1778–79) is often credited with initiating this age-graded practice (see Clarke, "The Cursed Barbauld Crew" [see note 10], 94).

54. "Preface to *Bible Stories*" (see note 46), 316.

55. Ibid., 314.

56. Ibid.

57. "Letters of Advice to a Young American" begins its advice with the assertion, "It is my opinion, that the imagination is to be cultivated in education, more than the dry accumulation of science and natural facts" (*Political and Philosophical Works of William Godwin,* 5:320).

58. See especially his letters to Joseph V. Bevan, published as a pamphlet "Letters of Advice to a Young American" (1818) and reprinted in the *Edinburgh Magazine* in Britain and the *Analectic Magazine* in America (in ibid., 5:318–38).

59. The Advertisement to the second edition of *The Enquirer* (1823) asserts that, while he would probably revise everything he had written twenty-five years ago, yet there is no "fundamental" difference between "the thoughts here expressed, and the thoughts I now entertain" (5:339). "During a large part of his life, young men looked on him as a kind of prophet-sage, and he exercised a remarkable influence over all with whom he came in contact" (quoted in appendix to *The Looking Glass,* 119).

60. Appendix to *Looking Glass*, 123; on Mulready, see Frederic G. Stephens, *Memorials of William Mulready, R.A.* (New York: Scribner, 1890), and Marcia Pointon, *William Mulready* (London: Victoria & Albert Museum, 1986).

61. According to the Appendix, Mulready related the early history of his life to Godwin when he was about nineteen years old (126).

62. Interestingly, Mary Shelley makes the same argument in her entry on Condorcet, a dispositional surrogate for Godwin (*French Lives*, vol. 2).

63. St. Clair, *The Godwins and the Shelleys* (see note 43), 285.

64. *A Defence of Poetry*, in *Shelley's Poetry and Prose*, ed. Donald H. Reiman and Neil Freistat (New York: Norton, 2002), 531.

65. The appendix, written by F. G. Stephens, is in the 1885 edition of *The Looking Glass* (London: Bemrose and Sons), 119–27.

66. Seymour states that *The Looking Glass* was written in part to "fire lazy Charles with zeal for his schoolwork" (*Mary Shelley* [New York: Grove Press, 2000], 52); on the false attribution, see 55.

67. Advertisement for *Fables, Ancient and Modern* at end of *The Looking Glass*, 121. Coleridge comments on the catacomb-like silence in the Godwin household in letters written in 1800 (Seymour, *Mary Shelley*, 39–40).

68. Seymour, *Mary Shelley*, 43, 53–54.

69. St. Clair, *The Godwins and the Shelleys* (see note 43), 281.

70. The classic, and best, version of this argument is still U. C. Knoepflmacher, "Thoughts on the Aggression of Daughters," in *The Endurance of "Frankenstein": Essays on Mary Shelley's Novel*, ed. George Levine and U. C. Knoepflmacher (Berkeley: Univ. of California Press, 1979), 88–119.

71. "Mary Shelley's Introduction to the 1831 *Frankenstein*," vol. 1 in *The Novels and Selected Works of Mary Shelley*, 175.

72. "The first edition of *Frankenstein* had outsold all the works of her husband put together. It made more money than all P. B. Shelley's works would fetch in his lifetime" (William St. Clair, "The Impact of *Frankenstein*," in *Mary Shelley in Her Times*, ed. Betty T. Bennett and Stuart Curran [Baltimore: Johns Hopkins Univ. Press, 2000], 43).

73. Moreover, as Seymour notes, Shelley "borrows" this depiction from Coleridge's preface to "Kubla Khan" (*Mary Shelley*, 157–58).

74. 6 May 1797, 6 June, 1797. *Godwin and Mary: Letters of William Godwin and Mary Wollstonecraft*, ed. Ralph M. Wardle (Lincoln: Univ. of Nebraska Press, 1977).

75. L. Adam Mekler goes beyond discussion of grief to explore Shelley's "complex, and frequently estranged, relationship to the Godwin household" in "Placing *Maurice* within the Shelley-Godwin Circle," *College English Association* 14 (2001): 23–33.

76. Marina Warner, "Happily Ever After," *New York Times*, 29 November, 1998.

77. Ibid.; John Bayley, "A Monster Discovery," *Times* (London), 20 August 1998.

78. Alix Wilber, "*Maurice; or, The Fisher Cot*," www.amazon.com.

79. Bayley, "Monster Discovery."

80. Mekler, "Placing *Maurice* within the Shelley-Godwin Circle," 31.

81. Tomalin, introduction to *Maurice*, 29–33. Laurette's adult biography mirrors this lesson, entering into a disastrous first marriage to Adolphe Galloni (against everyone's advice)

but later finding happiness in a lover, then second husband, Placido Tardy, and turning to writing (and to Shelley for advice on it) (52–62).

82. Complicating things further was Mrs. Mason's maternal closeness to Claire (ibid., 46, 50. " 'With her, I am as her child,' [Claire] wrote to Mary" [50]).

83. Ibid., 40, original emphasis.

84. Though the text says that "they" lived in "the pretty cottage" two months every year, the ensuing description of their rustic and benevolent activities only specifies father and son.

85. Tomalin notes J. M. S. Tompkin's claim that "eighty per cent of the heroes are called Henry" in her *The Popular Novel in England, 1770–1800* (*Maurice*, 161n).

86. Julie A. Carlson, "Coming After: Shelley's *Proserpine*," *Texas Studies in Literature and Language* 41.4 (1999): 354–56.

87. Seymour, *Mary Shelley* (see note 66), 247.

88. Constance Walker, "*Kindertotenlieder:* Mary Shelley and the Art of Losing," in *Mary Shelley in Her Times* (see note 72), 134.

89. On the pirated edition, see Vivien Jones, "Mary Wollstonecraft and the Literature of Advice," in *Cambridge Companion to Mary Wollstonecraft* (see note 23), 129; on *Advice to Mothers*, see Tomalin, introduction to *Maurice*, 50.

Epilogue • On Percy's Case

1. This is the basic point of Galway Kinnell's poem "Shelley" (*New Yorker*, July 26, 2004), which reads:

> Shelley, who I learned later, perhaps
> almost too late, remarried Harriet,
> then pregnant with their second child,
> and a few months later ran off with Mary,
> already pregnant herself, bringing
> with them Mary's stepsister Claire,
> who very likely also became his lover

and then goes on to name all the deaths on his conscience (or that should be)—Harriet, Fanny, "Claraka," "Wilmouse," Elena, and Allegra—with the conclusion

> and in those days, before I knew
> any of this, I thought I followed Shelley,
> who thought he was following radiant desire.

William Stroup brought the poem to my attention during his paper, "Percy Shelley and the Dream of the Defiant Family," presented at the North American Society for the Study of Romanticism, Montreal, 13–16 August 2005. I am grateful to a conversation with James Chandler that got me thinking in this direction.

2. Michelle Levy, "Byron, Shelley, and Deviant Fatherhood," paper presented at the North American Society for the Study of Romanticism, Montreal, 13–16 August 2005.

3. On the establishment of Percy Shelley's reputation, see Newman Ivey White, *The*

Unextinguished Hearth, Shelley and His Contemporary Critics (Durham, NC: Duke Univ. Press, 1966); Karsten Engelberg, *The Making of the Shelley Myth: An Annotated Bibliography of Criticism of Percy Bysshe Shelley, 1822, 1860* (London: Mansell, 1988); and Robert Metcalf Smith, *The Shelley Legend* (Port Washington, NY: Kennikat Press, 1945, reprint, 1967).

4. E.g., her curious request to Trelawny, "Could you write my husband's life, without naming me it were something" (*The Letters of Mary Wollstonecraft Shelley*, ed. Betty T. Bennett, 3 vols. [Baltimore: Johns Hopkins Univ. Press, 1980–88], 2:72).

5. "Shouting match" is Simon Haines's phrase in *Shelley's Poetry: The Divided Self* (Houndmills, UK: Macmillan, 1997; New York: St. Martin's Press, 1997), 7. He claims that two opposing critical procedures—distinguishing between "a poem and its ideas, between truth and beauty," and "not distinguishing between the events in or character of a person's life and the events in or character of the work or works which that person has written"—seem to be "undertaken more often with Shelley than with any other major English poet" (8). The second quote is from Frederick A. Pottle, "The Case of Shelley," in *English Romantic Poets: Modern Essays in Criticism*, ed. M. H. Abrams (New York: Oxford Univ. Press, 1960), 594.

6. See Haines, *Shelley's Poetry*, 31–36 (esp. helpful is his summary of the "case against," 6–22); Smith, *The Shelley Legend*, 28–35; and Susan Wolfson, "Editorial Privilege," in *The Other Mary Shelley: Beyond "Frankenstein,"* ed. Audrey A. Fisch, Anne K. Mellor, and Esther H. Schor (New York: Oxford Univ. Press, 1993), 51–56.

7. On the Sanctum, see Miranda Seymour, *Mary Shelley* (New York: Grove Press, 2000), 542–43, and Robert Smith, *The Shelley Legend*, 139–41; on the redesigning of the record (portrait, text, myth), see 143–53.

8. Frederick A. Pottle, "The Case of Shelley," in Abrams, *English Romantic Poets* (see note 5), 289–306. In *Shelley's Poetry*, Haines gives a helpful account of the two waves of detraction (see note 5), 6–31.

9. These charges were famously made in 1936 by F. R. Leavis, whose essay provoked Frederick Pottle to make "The Case of Shelley."

10. On this generic struggle as articulated in Mary Shelley, see Mary Favret, "Mary Shelley's Sympathy and Irony: The Editor and Her Corpus," in *The Other Mary Shelley* (see note 6), esp. 27–32; Steven Goldsmith, "Of Gender, Plague, and Apocalypse: Mary Shelley's *Last Man*," *Yale Journal of Criticism* 4.1 (1990), esp. 155–58; on the process more generally, Jay Clayton, *Romantic Vision and the Novel* (Cambridge: Cambridge Univ. Press, 1987), 5–15, and Dino Franco Felluga, *The Perversity of Poetry: Romantic Ideology and the Popular Male Poet of Genius* (Albany: State Univ. of New York Press, 2005).

11. James K. Chandler, *England in 1819: The Politics of Literary Culture and the Case of Romantic Historicism* (Chicago: Univ. of Chicago Press, 1998).

12. Ibid., 489.

13. Ibid., 39; "Shelley is always engaged both with the social situation, what I am calling the 'historical case,' and indeed, quite directly, with its *concept* as well"(489n).

14. Ibid., 24.

15. Ibid., 539n.

16. Literally he writes "I had felt regret that the glory of your being had passed from this earth of ours. It is not so—you still live." As St. Clair interprets these letters, "Shelley was

evidently already viewing his own relationship with Godwin in pre-set literary terms" (*The Godwins and the Shelleys: A Biography of a Family* [Baltimore: Johns Hopkins Univ. Press, 1989], 316); see 315–27.

17. Ibid., 336.

18. "One for 800£, the other for 700£" (ibid., 363).

19. P. Shelley to M. Godwin, 24 October 1814 (ibid., 373). "One of the duties of the overloaded mule was to carry the books which sustained their illusions" (ibid., 366).

20. Bennett, *The Letters of Mary Wollstonecraft Shelley* (see note 4),1:141.

21. E.g., Teddi Chichester Bonca, *Shelley's Mirrors of Love: Narcissism, Sacrifice, and Sorority* (Albany: State Univ. of New York Press, 1999), Nathaniel Brown, *Sexuality and Feminism in Shelley* (Cambridge: Harvard Univ. Press, 1979), and Horst Höhne, *In Pursuit of Love: The Short and Troublesome Life and Work of Percy Bysshe Shelley* (New York: Peter Lang, 2000).

22. See Jerrold E. Hogle, *Shelley's Process: Radical Transference and the Development of His Major Works* (New York: Oxford Univ. Press, 1988).

23. Stuart Peterfreund, *Shelley among Others: The Play of the Intertext and the Idea of Language* (Baltimore: Johns Hopkins Univ. Press, 2002).

24. Benjamin P. Kurtz, *The Pursuit of Death: A Study of Shelley's Poetry* (New York: Oxford Univ. Press, 1933), xii, 3, xxi.

25. The most comprehensive account of Percy Shelley's Platonism is James A. Notopoulos, *The Platonism of Shelley: A Study of Platonism and the Poetic Mind* (Durham, NC: Duke Univ. Press, 1949). Critics who explore the connections between Godwin and Plato in Shelley's development include Samuel Gladden, *Shelley's Textual Seductions: Plotting Utopia in the Erotic and Political Works* (New York: Routledge, 2002), and Jerrold E. Hogle, *Shelley's Process.*

26. Kurtz, *Pursuit of Death,* 9.

27. *The Symposium,* in *Shelley on Love: An Anthology,* ed. Richard Holmes (Austin, TX: Anvil Press, 1980), 157.

28. Point 3 continues, "Imagination is the characteristic of man. The dexterities of logic or of mathematical deduction belong rather to a well-regulated machine; they do not contain in them the living principle of our nature. It is the heart which most deserves to be cultivated: not the rules which may serve us in the nature of a compass to steer through the difficulties of life; but the pulses which beat with sympathy, and qualify us for the habits of charity, reverence and attachment" (313–14). *Essay on Christianity* connects "the *Republic* of Plato and the *Political Justice* of Godwin" as "probable and practical systems" in comparison with the "doctrines of reform" articulated by "Jesus Christ" (Holmes, *Shelley on Love,* 90).

29. The ways in which Chaucer epitomizes a spirit of his age for Godwin illustrate his influence on Percy Shelley and the ways in which they differ. "The person of Chaucer may in this view be considered as the central figure in a miscellaneous painting, giving unity and individual application to the otherwise disjointed particulars with which the canvas is diversified" (Preface to *Life of Chaucer,* ix). Elsewhere, Godwin describes such an individual as a magnet that makes unassimilated materials cohere ("History," 292).

30. Chandler, *England in 1819* (see note 11), 514.

31. "Greek love" is Louis Crompton's phrase for homosexuality in the Georgian period, and he writes that of all the romantic poets, "Shelley was unique in challenging accepted sex mores in his prose as well as in his verse," *Byron and Greek Love: Homophobia in Nineteenth-Century England* (Berkeley: Univ. of California Press, 1985), 284.

32. Colin Carman is writing an important dissertation on this topic, entitled "Shelley's Closet: Sexuality, History, Romanticism."

33. Holmes, ed., *Shelley on Love*, 98. E.g., the collected prose writings of Percy Shelley ends "A Discourse" before it alludes to the physical components of gay sex.

34. "A Discourse on the Manners of the Ancient Greeks Relative to the Subject of Love," in ibid., 110.

35. Jeremy Bentham's scattered but substantial writings on pederasty, particularly as it pertains to the laws against sodomy, are the only competitor, but they too, according to their contemporary editor, Louis Crompton, were never collected for publication.

36. Eric O. Clarke, *Virtuous Vice: Homoeroticism and the Public Sphere* (Durham, NC: Duke Univ. Press, 2000), 148–68.

37. On "majoritizing," see Eve Kosofsky Sedgwick, *Epistemology of the Closet* (Berkeley: Univ. of California Press, 1990). Clarke comments on this motto on the table of contents of the *Grecian Guild Pictorial*, a "U.S. periodical of thinly veiled male homosexual erotica published during the late 1950s and early 1960s." He also notes that twenty years before the Grecian Guild chose this motto for its masthead, Shelley had been characterized as a sexual invert by Edward Carpenter and George Barnefield (*Virtuous Vice*, 127, 149).

38. P. B. Shelley, *A Defence of Poetry*, in *Shelley's Poetry and Prose*, ed. Donald H. Reiman and Neil Freistat (New York: Norton, 2002), 535.

39. Shelley, "A Discourse," in *Shelley on Love* (see note 27), 108.

40. On the depth of Georgian homophobia, see Crompton, *Byron and Greek Love*, 12–63; on differences between Georgian and Continental homophobia, see Louis Crompton, *Homosexuality and Civilization* (Cambridge, MA: Harvard Univ. Press, 2003), 528–35.

41. In Shelley scholarship, see Hogle, *Shelley's Process* (see note 22); for a general formulation of history and transference, see Dominick LaCapra, *History and Memory after Auschwitz* (Ithaca, NY: Cornell Univ. Press, 1998), and Teresa Brennan, *History after Lacan* (London: Routledge, 2003).

42. Shelley, "England in 1819," see Chandler, *England in 1819* (see note 11), 31.

43. Mary Shelley's preface to *Poetical Works* ventures this defense of his life/writings: "It is seldom that the young know what youth is, till they have got beyond its period; and time was not given him to attain this knowledge. It must be remembered that there is the stamp of such inexperience on all he wrote" (vii). Not surprisingly, the "wise friend" she cites as mentioning Percy's youth (and ignorance thereof) was Godwin.

44. The former include Irving Babbitt, F. R. Leavis; the latter, Anne Mellor, Judith Balbour, Teddi Chichester Bonca.

45. *On Love*, in *Shelley on Love* (see note 27), 73; also *Epipsychidion*, "Narrow / The heart that loves . . . One object, and one form, and builds thereby / A sepulchre for its eternity" (ll. 169–73.)

46. L. O. Aranye Fradenburg, *Sacrifice Your Love: Psychoanalysis, Historicism, Chaucer* (Minneapolis: Univ. of Minnesota Press, 2002), 2.

47. Ibid., 3–8.

48. Betty T. Bennett, *Mary Wollstonecraft Shelley: An Introduction* (Baltimore: Johns Hopkins Univ. Press, 1998), 5–6; Holmes, *Shelley on Love* (see note 27), 12. Stuart Peterfreund explores the implications of Shelley's notions of "poetic apprehension" for his views on love as "metaphoric transference" in *Shelley among Others* (see note 23), 3–27, 48.

49. Percy Shelley, *On Love*, in *Shelley's Poetry and Prose* (see note 38), 504.

50. The Advertisement to *Epipsychidion* concludes with poetic lines addressed to the poem: "My Song, I fear that thou wilt find but few / Who fitly shall conceive thy reasoning, / Of such hard matter dost thou entertain"; see also the second paragraph of *On Love* (see note 38), 393, 503.

51. Fradenburg, *Sacrifice Your Love*, 75.

52. Chandler, *England in 1819* (see note 11), 510–14.

53. "The Choice," *Journals*, 490–94.

54. This is part of the force of the distinction Godwin makes between warm and cold hearts (a discussion triggered by his discussion of the two kinds of fire in Greek mythology, that associated with Vulcan [husband of Venus] and Vesta [emblem of chastity]). "In a word, the sincerest warmth is not wild, but calm; and operates in greater activity in the breast of the stoic than in that of the vulgar enthusiast." It is epitomized in the "genius" of Shakespeare (*Sepulchres*, 21–22n).

55. Wollstonecraft's introduction to her translation of Christian Gotthilf Salzmann's *Moralisches Elementarbuch* 1782 (*Elements of Morality*) asserts her desire to "speak to children of the organs of generation as freely as we speak of the other parts of the body, and explain to them the noble use which they were designed for, and how they may be injured," but she then is "induced to leave [such passages] out," knowing that "my conviction will not have sufficient weight with the public to conquer long-fostered prejudices" (vol. 2 in *The Works of Mary Wollstonecraft*, 9).

56. Jacques Derrida, *The Gift of Death*, trans. David Wills (Chicago: Univ. of Chicago Press, 1995), 43, 42–44.

57. Fradenburg, *Sacrifice Your Love*, 13.

58. On both aspects of this process, see Ronald Tetreault, *The Poetry of Life: Shelley and Literary Form* (Toronto: Univ. of Toronto Press, 1987), 12–16.

59. "Our philosophical traditions privilege sentient life—the more sensitive, the better— as though life were self-evidently a good, *the* Good, a gift for which we should be grateful" (Fradenburg, *Sacrifice Your Love*, 15).

60. *Journals*, 397n. The content of the note enacts the vagaries of the signifier in Percy Shelley desiring to have "We will all suffer a sea-change" as the "motto of his boat."

61. There are striking similarities between Mary Shelley's eulogies for Euthanasia and for Percy. "Earth felt no change when she died; and men forgot her. Yet a lovelier spirit never ceased to breathe, nor was a lovelier form ever destroyed amidst the many it brings forth" (*Valperga*, 322). "He died, and the world showed no outward sign; but his influence over mankind, though slow in growth, is fast augmenting" (*Poetical Works*, viii).

182–84; and literary tradition, 108–13; and
reading, 60, 110–13; and Mary Shelley, 60,
103–4, 107–13, 121, 125, 174–75, 178, 182–
83, 186, 255; and Percy Shelley, 111–12

Jacobin novel, 48
Jacobus, Mary, 13, 30–31, 110, 111, 153, 158,
173–75, 177, 291n27
Jesus, 266, 267
Johnson, Barbara, 190, 191, 307n51
Johnson, Claudia, 26, 39, 126, 310n19
Johnson, Joseph, 221, 222
Juvenile Library, 11, 82, 152, 223, 232, 233,
244, 245, 252

Kaplan, Cora, 223–24
Kelly, Gary, 15, 224
Kilner sisters, 214
Kinnell, Galway, 314n1
Knoepflmacher, U. C., 303n45, 313n70
Kristeva, Julia, 31
Kucich, Greg, 201
Kurtz, Benjamin P., 265

Lacan, Jacques, 13–14, 139–40
LaCapra, Dominick, 174, 306n44
Lamb, Charles, 70, 215, 232
Lamb, Mary, 232
language, instability of, 13–14, 91, 276, 277
Lardner, Dionysius, 10, 200, 201
Leavis, F. R., 260, 317n44
Lee, Harriet, 150
Lee, Sophia, 150
Levinas, Emmanuel, 171
Leys, Ruth, 171, 172
life/writings, 3–4, 6–8, 10, 13, 19–20, 131–34,
283n5. *See also* reading; writing
literary form, 6, 11, 37, 260; and Godwin, 6, 11;
and love, 26, 29–30, 31; lyric poetry, status
of, 259–60; poem-story distinction (Percy
Shelley), 267–68; and rhetoric, 17; and
Mary Shelley, 6, 93–94, 99, 121, 185; and
Percy Shelley, 264; and social change, 67,
94, 122–24, 184–85; and Wollstonecraft, 6,
11, 26, 31, 126–27. *See also* fancy; writing
literary tradition: and gender, 52, 53, 56, 61,
97–98, 119, 124, 143, 186; and Godwin, 53,
56, 58, 60, 81, 131, 169; and incest, 108–12;

and repression, 5–6, 52; and Mary Shelley,
97–98, 100, 108–13, 119, 124–25, 131, 175,
177, 184, 186, 190; and Wollstonecraft, 32–
33, 52, 56, 58–59, 124, 143. *See also* reading
Locke, John, 214
love, 2, 15; and death, 132; and fancy, 37–38,
138–43, 225; and Godwin, 2, 23, 24–26,
27–30, 44–45, 47–49, 132, 150; Greek,
268–69; heterosexual, as normative, 36–37;
homosexual, 268–70; and idealization, 35–
36, 38, 139; and imagination, 275; and im
partiality, 25; and justice, 103; narrative di
mensions of, 36, 122–24; and perfectibility,
as impediment to, 24, 26; and possessive
ness, 42; and reading, 26–29, 33, 38–39,
93, 111, 132, 252, 262, 270, 275; and realism,
122–23; and sacrifice, 272, 273, 274; and
selfhood, 30; and Mary Shelley, 93, 95–97,
103, 111, 115–27, 132, 174, 175, 190, 197–98,
252; and Percy Shelley, 198, 263, 264, 268–
69, 271, 272–76; and social change, 117; and
truth, 273; and Wollstonecraft, 23–30, 31–
40, 41, 132, 138–40, 275; and women, as
limitation for, 24, 118–19; and women's edu
cation, 24–25; and writing, 15, 26, 29–31,
32, 38, 39, 132, 224. *See also* attachment;
family; marriage; sentiment and sensibility;
sex

Macaulay, Catharine, 9, 84
MacGavran, James, 215–16
Mackenzie, Henry, 47
Mandell, Laura, 13
marriage: and cohabitation, 78; and female
happiness, 37, 122, 124–25; and Godwin, 4,
23–24, 27, 44–45, 46–52, 54–56, 59, 60,
61–62, 69, 74, 76, 78, 102, 116, 169–70, 208;
as imprisonment, 32, 34, 49, 52; mystifica
tion of, 124; and Mary Shelley, 97, 102, 106,
116, 119, 120, 121–27, 193, 255, 263; and
Percy Shelley, 263; and Wollstonecraft, 4,
32–38, 69, 116, 223, 224, 225. *See also*
attachment; domesticity; family; love
Mason, Mrs. (Margaret King), 222–23, 227–
28, 246, 249, 252–53, 255, 256
McGann, Jerome, 215
McWhir, Anne, 187, 191
melancholy: and fancy, 144; and Godwin, 144,